STATE OF THE
WORLD
1996

Other Norton/Worldwatch Books

Lester R. Brown et al.

State of the World 1984

State of the World 1985

State of the World 1986

State of the World 1987

State of the World 1988

State of the World 1989

State of the World 1990

State of the World 1991

State of the World 1992

State of the World 1993

State of the World 1994

State of the World 1995

Vital Signs 1992

Vital Signs 1993

Vital Signs 1994

Vital Signs 1995

ENVIRONMENTAL ALERT SERIES

Lester R. Brown et al.

Saving the Planet

Alan Thein Durning

How Much Is Enough?

Sandra Postel

Last Oasis

Lester R. Brown
Hal Kane

Full House

Christopher Flavin
Nicholas Lenssen

Power Surge

Lester R. Brown

Who Will Feed China?

STATE OF THE WORLD
1996

A Worldwatch Institute Report on Progress Toward a Sustainable Society

PROJECT DIRECTOR
Lester R. Brown

ASSOCIATE PROJECT DIRECTOR
Christopher Flavin

EDITOR
Linda Starke

CONTRIBUTING RESEARCHERS
Janet N. Abramovitz
Chris Bright
Lester R. Brown
Christopher Flavin
Gary Gardner
Hal Kane
Anne E. Platt
Sandra Postel
David Malin Roodman
Aaron Sachs

W·W·NORTON & COMPANY

NEW YORK   LONDON

The STATE OF THE WORLD and WORLDWATCH INSTITUTE trademarks are registered in the U.S. Patent and Trademark Office.

The views expressed are those of the authors and do not necessarily represent those of the Worldwatch Institute; of its directors, officers, or staff; or of its funders.

The text of this book is composed in Baskerville, with the display set in Caslon. Composition and manufacturing by the Haddon Craftsmen, Inc.

First Edition

ISBN 0-393-03851-3
ISBN 0-393-313935-5 (pbk)

W. W. Norton & Company, Inc., 500 Fifth Avenue, New York, N.Y. 10110
W. W. Norton & Company Ltd., 10 Coptic Street, London WC1A 1PU

1 2 3 4 5 6 7 8 9 0

This book is printed on recycled paper.

Acknowledgments

Every year we take this opportunity to thank our friends and supporters outside the Institute, along with the staff whose names do not appear on the cover of *State of the World*.

First, again we would like to thank the various foundations that support our work. The United Nations Population Fund provided support specifically for the research and writing of *State of the World*. In addition, the Wallace Genetic Foundation provided funding for the research and writing of Chapters 5 and 10. The foundations or funds that support the Institute's overall work are the Geraldine R. Dodge, Ford, George Gund, W. Alton Jones, John D. and Catherine T. MacArthur, Andrew W. Mellon, Curtis and Edith Munson, Edward John Noble, Surdna, Turner, and Weeden foundations; the Lynn R. and Karl E. Prickett and the Rockefeller Brothers funds; Rockefeller Financial Services; and The Pew Charitable Trusts.

Once the manuscript gets past staff review, it goes to independent editor Linda Starke, who then takes charge. She keeps everything on schedule, nursing each chapter through first and second edits, making sure some 650 endnotes make sense, and then getting the whole manuscript to the publisher in record time. At W.W. Norton & Company, Iva Ashner and Andrew Marasia keep the manuscript on a fast track. And at the end of the production process, in an all-too-brief window of time, Ritch Pope of Dexter, Oregon, prepares the index.

Back at the Institute, chapter authors benefit from the helping hands of a dedicated research staff. This year, Anjali Acharya worked on Chapter 4, Toni Nelson helped with Chapter 1, and Odil Tunali did research for Chapter 2. All researchers are helped enormously by Lori Baldwin, who is in charge of the Worldwatch Library and the overall information-gathering system. Library Assistant Laura Malinowski manages to dig her way out of piles of newspapers and journals received at the Institute, supplying staff with up-to-date clips and articles.

That many of you have heard of this book is due to our top-flight communications team: Director of Communications Jim Perry, Deputy Director Denise Byers Thomma, Marketing Manager Steve Kaufman, and Administrative Assistant Tara Patterson. Even as the Institute staff is caught up in the fall crunch of producing *State of the World*, the magazine staff keeps *World Watch* on schedule. Responsibility for this and for coming up with cutting-edge articles rests with Editor Ed Ayres; Associate Editor Chris Bright, who also found time this year to contribute a chapter to *State of the World*; and Designer Jennifer Seher.

The publication of *State of the World* each January means extra work for our ever busy publications office, which responds to your orders. Indeed, the busy part of the year starts even earlier, as we log in advance orders from university and college bookstores preparing for the spring semester. For handling this on-slaught of orders, and for their work throughout the year, we are grateful to Publication Sales Coordinator Millicent Johnson, Publications Assistant Joseph Gravely, and Receptionist Kelly Schneider.

Administrative responsibilities continue to be carried by our first-rate management team of Vice President and Treasurer Blondeen S. Gravely, Executive Assistant to the President and Computer Systems Administrator Reah Janise Kauffman, Assistant Treasurer Barbara Fallin, and Administrative Assistant to the Vice President for Research Suzanne Clift. In addition to helping on Chapter 1, often on weekends, Reah Janise assisted with the fundraising that makes it all possible.

Outside the Institute, we as usual relied on an eclectic group of researchers and policy analysts for reviews of early drafts of the chapters. Their comments are incorporated right through the last round of changes, although of course responsibility for the content rests with the chapter authors. This year, the authors thank the following for their time and thoughtful comments: Domenick Bertelli, Faith Thompson Campbell, Clifford Cobb, Bruce E. Coblentz, Øystein Dahle, Paul Epstein, Harald Frederiksen, Robert J.P. Gale, Duane Gubler, Robin Marantz Henig, Rob Housman, Barbara Rose Johnston, Michael Kane, Ann Kinzig, Nicholas Lenssen, Stuart Levy, Bennett Lorber, Stephen Mills, Deborah Moore, Stephen Morse, Patti Petesch, Neil Popovic, Jacob Scherr, Thomas Sterner, Melanie L. J. Stiassny, Karey Sutten, Jan Paul van Soest, and Amy Vickers.

As we write this, the United Nations is celebrating its fiftieth anniversary, with heads of state gathered in New York to summarize in a mere five minutes their appreciation of U.N. contributions to date and their hopes for the future. This celebration reminds us how much has been accomplished in the last 50 years, but also how much remains to be done. We hope this report on progress toward a sustainable society can contribute to those efforts to move vigorously in a new direction.

Lester R. Brown and
Christopher Flavin

Contents

Acknowledgments vii

List of Tables and Figures xi

Foreword xv

1 **The Acceleration of History,** *by Lester R. Brown* 3

CROSSING THRESHOLDS
FOOD: THE DEFINING ISSUE
TRENDS TO BUILD ON
REGAINING CONTROL OF OUR DESTINY

2 **Facing Up to the Risks of Climate Change,** *by Christopher Flavin* 21

THE EVIDENCE MOUNTS
A CLIMATE OF EXTREMES
GREENHOUSE GAS ESCALATOR
SHOWDOWN IN BERLIN
BREAKTHROUGH

3 **Forging a Sustainable Water Strategy,** *by Sandra Postel* 40

WATER FOR FOOD
DECLINE OF THE AQUATIC
  ENVIRONMENT
COMPETITION AND CONFLICT
SHARING THE WATERS
STRATEGIES FOR A NEW WATER
  EQUATION

4 **Sustaining Freshwater Ecosystems,** *by Janet N. Abramovitz* 60

THREATS TO FRESHWATER SYSTEMS
DAMMING RIVERS, DAMNING THE
  FUTURE
MISUNDERSTANDING FLOODS

GREAT TROUBLES IN GREAT LAKES
A NEW FOCUS: MAINTAINING HEALTHY
  ECOSYSTEMS

5 **Preserving Agricultural Resources,** *by Gary Gardner* 78

LESS LAND, MORE FOOD
A CRUMBLING FOUNDATION
WATER WOES
MANAGING PESTS
THE ROW TO HOE

6 **Understanding the Threat of Bioinvasions,** *by Chris Bright* 95

THE ECOLOGY OF INVASION
CASCADING EFFECTS
PATHWAYS OF INVASION
INFECTING THE ECONOMY
SLOWING THE RATES OF INVASION

7 **Confronting Infectious Diseases,** *by Anne E. Platt* 114

THE BURDEN OF INFECTIOUS DISEASE
OPPORTUNISTIC MICROBES
BIOLOGICAL MIXING AND SOCIAL
  DISRUPTION
LACK OF CLEAN WATER
DRUG RESISTANCE
WRITING THE PRESCRIPTION

8 **Upholding Human Rights and Environmental Justice,** *by Aaron Sachs* 133

THE CASE FOR COLLABORATION
LOCAL INJUSTICES: INDIVIDUALS AND
  COMMUNITIES
INJUSTICES ACROSS BORDERS

HUMAN RIGHTS AND ENVIRONMENTAL
   JUSTICE

9 **Shifting to Sustainable Industries,**
   by Hal Kane   152

THE SOLAR REVOLUTION
RISE OF THE STEEL MINIMILL
A REVOLUTION IN PAPER RECYCLING
RENAISSANCE OF THE BICYCLE AND
   TRAIN
THE ZERO-EMISSION FACTORY

10 **Harnessing the Market for the
   Environment,** *by David Malin
   Roodman*   168

THE STATE OF THE WORLD'S TAXES
UNDERTAXATION OF ENVIRONMENTAL
   DESTRUCTION
THE RISE OF MARKET MECHANISMS
MAKING THE MOST OF THE MARKET
GOING THE DISTANCE

Notes   189

Index   241

Worldwatch Database Disk

*The data from all graphs and tables contained in this book, as well
as from those in all other Worldwatch publications of the past year,
are available on disk for use with IBM-compatible or Macintosh
computers. This includes data from the* Vital Signs *series of books,*
Worldwatch Papers, World Watch *magazine, and the Environmental Alert series of books. The data are formatted for use with
spreadsheet software compatible with Lotus 1-2-3 version 2, including all Lotus spreadsheets, Quattro Pro, Excel, SuperCalc, and many
others. For IBM-compatibles, a 3 ½-inch (high-density) diskette is
provided. Information on how to order the Worldwatch Database
Disk can be found on the final page of this book.*

List of Tables and Figures

LIST OF TABLES

Chapter 1. The Acceleration of History

1-1 United States: Grain Yield Per Hectare by Decade, 1950–90   10
1-2 Countries That Reached Population Stability by 1995   13

Chapter 2. Facing Up to the Risks of Climate Change

2-1 Weather-Related Disasters With Damages Over $3 Billion, 1989–95   27
2-2 Carbon Emissions from Fossil Fuel Burning, Top 20 Emitters, 1994   30

Chapter 3. Forging a Sustainable Water Strategy

3-1 Groundwater Depletion in Major Regions of the World, Circa 1990   42
3-2 Dependence on Imported Surface Water, Selected Countries   49
3-3 United States: Projected Water Savings from Efficiency Standards, 1995–2025   59

Chapter 4. Sustaining Freshwater Ecosystems

4-1 Freshwater Fish: Status and Threats in Selected Areas   62

Chapter 6. Understanding the Threat of Bioinvasions

6-1 Selected Historical Examples of Bioinvasions   97
6-2 Selected Current Examples of Bioinvasions   98

Chapter 7. Confronting Infectious Diseases

7-1 Populations Affected by Various Infectious Diseases, 1993   116
7-2 Selected Infectious Diseases, Vectors, and Symptoms   117
7-3 Global Incidence of Dengue Hemorrhagic Fever   124

Chapter 8. Upholding Human Rights and Environmental Justice

8-1 Attacks Against Environmental Activists, Selected Examples   138
8-2 Community-Level Environmental Injustices, Selected Examples   141
8-3 Community-Based Conservation and Development Initiatives, Selected Examples   142

Chapter 10. Harnessing the Market for the Environment

10-1 Tax Revenue, Total and by Source, Selected Countries, 1993   171
10-2 Gasoline Tax, Price, and Use, Selected Industrial Countries, 1993   179
10-3 Selected Losers and Winners Under Greenpeace Germany Tax Shift Proposal   186

LIST OF FIGURES

Chapter 1. The Acceleration of History

1-1 World Grain Carryover Stocks as Days of Consumption, 1961–96   8
1-2 World Grain Production, 1950–95   8
1-3 World Fertilizer and Grainland Per Person, 1950–94   10
1-4 Grain Production and Consumption in the European Community, 1960–94   12
1-5 World Automobile and Bicycle Production, 1950–94   16

Chapter 2. Facing Up to the Risks of Climate Change

2-1 Temperature Projections With and Without Sulfates Compared With Observations, 1860–2040   24
2-2 World Carbon Emissions from Fossil Fuel Burning, by Economic Region, 1950–94   29
2-3 Economic Losses from Weather-Related Natural Disasters Worldwide, 1980–95   34

Chapter 3. Forging a Sustainable Water Strategy

3-1 Flow of Colorado River Below All Major Dams and Diversions, 1905–92   45
3-2 River Flow into the Aral Sea, 1940–90   46

Chapter 4. Sustaining Freshwater Ecosystems

4-1 Species Extinct and at Risk in North America, 1995   61
4-2 The Changing Fish Population of Lake Victoria   75

Chapter 5. Preserving Agricultural Resources

5-1 World Grain Production Per Person, 1950–95   79
5-2 World Grain Harvested Area Per Person, 1950–95   80
5-3 Pesticide-Resistant Species Since 1908   89

Chapter 6. Understanding the Threat of Bioinvasions

6-1 Spread of European Mustard into Eastern Canada and United States, 1860–1990   110

Chapter 9. Shifting to Sustainable Industries

9-1   World Photovoltaic Shipments, Cumulative, 1975–94   154
9-2   World Wind Energy Generating Capacity, 1980–94   154
9-3   Recycled Content of U.S. Steel, 1984–94   158

Chapter 10. Harnessing the Market for the Environment

10-1   Unemployment and Poverty Trends, European Union and United States, 1973–94   172
10-2   Industrial Discharges of Selected Heavy Metals into Surface Waters, The Netherlands, 1976–91   176

Foreword

As we complete the thirteenth *State of the World*, it is a dark time for environmental policy in Washington, threatening the U.S. leadership role on environmental issues. Yet in many other countries, and among hundreds of corporations and nongovernmental organizations, environmental problems are being taken more seriously than ever.

Prominent among these developments in 1995 was the forceful entry of the insurance industry into international deliberations on climate change. After suffering billions of dollars of losses from more intense storms and other related disasters in the early nineties, some insurance executives are joining the call to slow climate change. Companies such as Lloyd's of London and Munich Re joined environmental organizations, such as the Worldwatch Institute, in sending observers to the first Conference of the Parties to the Framework Convention on Climate Change in Berlin in early 1995.

At the Institute, we find ourselves working more closely with agriculturally related companies than ever before. With crop-withering heat waves, water scarcity, and other environmental forces altering the world food supply/demand balance, corporations are now actively seeking advice from environmental experts. Along with insurance companies, the agricultural community also has an abiding interest in future climate patterns, since heat waves, floods, and droughts each have the potential to re-duce harvests dramatically. In fact, just as we went to press, the Philippine rice crop was devastated as super-typhoon Angela swept across central Luzon.

Bankers are also showing more interest in our work, and specifically in how environmental trends are affecting their investments. Environmental liabilities have undermined the financial viability of many companies, particularly in the chemical industry, and another wave of bad debt could be created by climate change, as rising sea levels and more intense, more powerful storms devastate coastal real estate.

Scientific interest in environmental issues is rising as well. In 1995, leading scientific journals such as *Nature* and *Science* were filled with new findings on climate change, environmentally induced illnesses, and the declining health of the oceans. Also in 1995, for the first time a Nobel Prize was given for environmentally focused science. Atmospheric chemists Sherwood Rowland, Mario Molina, and Paul Crutzen were awarded the Nobel Prize for chemistry for their discovery in the early seventies that chlorofluorocarbons could deplete the thin layer of stratospheric ozone that protects life on earth from harmful ultraviolet radiation. Their pioneering work set the stage for international agreements in the eighties to phase out the most damaging chemicals by 2000. All of humanity is deeply indebted to them for anticipating the change to the ozone layer in time to save it.

Although the Institute has not won any Nobel prizes, *World Watch* magazine was selected by the Population Institute as the world's Best Periodical for coverage of population issues in 1995, an award that the previous year went to *Time*.

In the past, we have noted the publication of *State of the World* in new languages, but now that this annual volume is published in some 27 languages, including all the major ones, it is becoming more difficult to add to the list. The big growth during the past year has been in the publication of more of our other books in individual languages. In Japan, for example, our publisher Diamond Sha not only publishes *State of the World*, but also *Vital Signs* and the Environmental Alert books. Thanks to the strong personal support of Romanian President Ion Iliescu, all our books are now being published in Romanian by Editura Tehnica, the publishing house he once headed.

The extraordinary efforts by Hamid Taravarty, an Iranian medical doctor who publishes our books in Persian, inspires us all. After practicing medicine during the day, he comes home to dinner and then translates a few pages each night before retiring. He has mobilized enough other resources to publish all our books in a country that is only beginning officially to recognize the extent of its population and environmental problems. In Turkey, our publisher T.E.M.A. (Turkiye Erozyonia Mucadele, Agaclandima) is now moving beyond *State of the World* to publish *Vital Signs*, *Power Surge: Guide to the Coming Energy Revolution*, and *Who Will Feed China? Wake-Up Call for a Small Planet*.

State of the World has been published in China since its launching in 1984. But beginning in 1996, the Chinese Academy of Science in Beijing will be doing a Chinese edition of *Vital Signs*. In Southeast Asia, the translation of Worldwatch books into languages such as Indone-sian, Malay, and Thai is largely the result of the dedicated efforts of Ivan Kats, head of the Obor Foundation in Indonesia. And with the publication of *Vital Signs* in Vietnamese, we have opened another publishing front, thanks to Ivan.

We are indebted to Magnar Norderhaug of Worldwatch Norden in Norway for taking the lead not only in getting *State of the World* published in Norwegian, Swedish, Danish, and Finnish, but also in making sure it gets out quickly. Each of these editions comes off the press within a few weeks of the English edition—no small feat, considering the translation effort that is required.

As of 1996, the Institute has 103 publishing contracts in effect for our various books, the Worldwatch Papers, and *World Watch* magazine. At the center of this global process of selling foreign language rights to our publications and the negotiation of publishing contracts is Curtis Brown, one of the world's leading international literary agencies, with its network of agents around the world.

In the United States, W.W. Norton has published every book we have produced over the last 21 years. Although many author-publisher relationships are often difficult, to say the least, ours has been a delight. We cannot imagine a more congenial and supportive relationship than the one we enjoy with Iva Ashner, who manages our books at Norton.

In addition to our print publications, we now also produce the Worldwatch Database Disk, our first electronic product. Sales of the English version of the disk have continued to expand, exceeding $100,000 in 1995. Beyond this, we are now selling rights to the disk in other languages, with Japanese being the first.

Strong supporters of Worldwatch Institute, such as Ted Turner in the United States and Izaak van Melle in Europe, ensure the distribution of *State of the World* to key decision makers. In the

United States, Turner regularly gets *State of the World* into the hands of the Fortune 500 CEOs, members of Congress, and state governors. In Europe, van Melle distributes *State of the World* to each of the 900 corporate CEOs who gather at the World Economic Forum in Davos each January, shortly after the new edition of *State of the World* is released.

As always, we welcome your suggestions on how to improve *State of the World*. You may send them by mail, fax (202–296-7365), or e-mail (worldwatch-@worldwatch.org).

Lester R. Brown
Christopher Flavin

Worldwatch Institute
1776 Massachusetts Ave., NW
Washington, DC 20036

December 1995

STATE OF THE WORLD
1996

1

The Acceleration of History

Lester R. Brown

The pace of change in our world is speeding up, accelerating to the point where it threatens to overwhelm the management capacity of political leaders. This acceleration of history comes not only from advancing technology, but also from unprecedented world population growth, even faster economic growth, and the increasingly frequent collisions between expanding human demands and the limits of the earth's natural systems.[1]

History is not about the status quo; it is about change. Throughout most of the time since civilization began, the agents of change worked slowly. Until recently, in historical terms, the growth of population was so slow as to be imperceptible during an individual's lifetime. Economic expansion was similarly sluggish. But since mid-century, the pace of change has been breathtaking.

Today, it is difficult to grasp the sheer magnitude of human population growth.

Those of us born before 1950 have seen more population growth during our lifetimes than occurred during the preceding 4 million years since our early ancestors first stood upright.[2]

The world economy is growing even faster. It has expanded from $4 trillion in output in 1950 to more than $20 trillion in 1995. In just the 10 years from 1985 to 1995 it grew by $4 trillion—more than from the beginning of civilization until 1950. Countries industrializing now are doing so much faster than in the past, simply because they can draw on the experiences and technology of those who went first. Economic growth in East Asia, for instance, has averaged some 8 percent annually in recent years. And from 1991 to 1995, the Chinese economy expanded by a staggering 57 percent, raising the income per person of 1.2 billion people by more than half.[3]

Yet the benefits of this rapid global growth have not been evenly distributed. Living conditions for roughly a fifth of humanity have remained at subsistence level, essentially unchanged. As

---

Units of measure throughout this book are metric unless common usage dictates otherwise.

a result, the ratio between income in the richest one fifth of countries and the poorest one fifth has widened from 30 to 1 in 1960 to 61 to 1 in 1991, creating tensions between those on the upper rungs of the global economic ladder and those stuck on the bottom steps.[4]

As population has doubled since mid-century and the global economy has nearly quintupled in size, the demand for natural resources has grown at a phenomenal rate. Since 1950, the need for grain has nearly tripled. Consumption of seafood has increased more than four times. Water use has tripled. Demand for the principal rangeland products, beef and mutton, has also tripled since 1950. Firewood demand has tripled, lumber has more than doubled, and paper has gone up sixfold. The burning of fossil fuels has increased nearly fourfold, and carbon emissions have risen accordingly.[5]

These spiraling human demands for resources are beginning to outgrow the capacity of the earth's natural systems. As this happens, the global economy is damaging the foundation on which it rests. Evidence of the damage to the earth's ecological infrastructure takes the form of collapsing fisheries, falling water tables, shrinking forests, eroding soils, dying lakes, crop-withering heat waves, and disappearing species.

Even as the effects of unprecedented population growth are threatening to overwhelm some governments, the collisions between the expanding demands of the global economy and the earth's natural limits are creating additional burdens. Collisions with the sustainable yield limits of fisheries, aquifers, forests, rangelands, and other natural systems are occurring with increasing frequency. As a result, national political leaders and U.N. agencies are spending more and more time dealing with these collisions and their consequences—fishery conflicts, water scarcity, food shortages, increasingly destructive storms, and swelling flows of environmental refugees.

CROSSING THRESHOLDS

As hunters and gatherers, our effect on the earth was limited indeed. Neither our hunting skills nor our gathering capacity threatened many other species, much less whole ecosystems. Only recently has the scale of human activities reached a point where it affects the habitability of the planet.

When a sustainable yield threshold is crossed, it signals a fundamental change in the relationship between the consumer and that which is being consumed. To use an analogy from economics, the distinction is between consuming interest and spending the capital stock itself. If an organization such as a university is living off an endowment, it can operate indefinitely as long as its needs do not exceed the income from the endowment. But if at some point it begins drawing down the principal, it will soon find itself in trouble, forced to cut back operations. If it cannot lower its annual demands to the sustainable yield of the endowment, eventually it will face bankruptcy.

The demands of our generation now exceed the income, the sustainable yield, of the earth's ecological endowment. Since mid-century the sustainable yield thresholds of natural systems have been crossed in country after country. It is difficult, if not impossible, to find a developing country that is not losing tree cover. Every major food-producing country is suffering heavy topsoil losses from erosion by wind and water. (See Chapter 5.) In every country in Africa, rangeland is being degraded by overgrazing. Forests all over Europe are suffering from air pollution and acid rain.

By 1989, all oceanic fisheries were being fished at or beyond capacity. Of the world's 15 leading oceanic fisheries, 13 are in decline. If, as scientists believe, these fisheries are unlikely to sustain a catch of much more than 100 million tons per year—the level reached in 1989—then the seafood available per person will shrink indefinitely as the catch is divided among nearly 90 million more people each year. Our failure to stabilize population size before reaching the limits of oceanic fisheries means that we are now faced with rising seafood prices as far as we can see into the future.[6]

As long as there were more fish in the sea than anyone could hope to catch, managing fisheries was a simple matter of deciding how much to invest in trawlers to satisfy any given level of seafood demand. Now that the demand for seafood exceeds the sustainable yield of fisheries, those managing this resource must determine what the sustainable yield of a fishery is, negotiate the distribution of that catch among the competing interests, and then enforce adherence to the quotas established. Where fisheries are shared among countries, as is often the case, the process becomes infinitely more complex.

These conflicts are evident in cod wars between Norwegian and Icelandic ships, between Canada and Spain over turbot off Canada's eastern coast, between China and the Marshall Islands in Micronesia, between Argentina and Taiwan over Falkland island fisheries, and between Indonesia and the Philippines in the Celebes. Greenpeace describes "tuna wars in the northeast Atlantic, crab wars in the North Pacific, squid wars in the southwest Atlantic, salmon wars in the North Pacific, and pollock wars in the Sea of Okhotsk." Although these disputes make it into the world news only rarely, they are now an almost daily occurrence. Historians may record more fishery conflicts during one year in the nineties than during the entire nineteenth century.[7]

With water use exceeding the sustainable yield of aquifers in so much of the world, overpumping is now commonplace. Even at current levels of consumption, underground water tables are now falling in the southwestern United States, the U.S. Great Plains, several states in India (including the Punjab, the country's breadbasket), in much of northern China, across northern Africa, in southern Europe, and throughout the Middle East. In some cases, the fall in water tables is measured in centimeters per year. In more extreme cases, it is gauged in meters per year.[8]

Historians may record more fishery conflicts during one year in the nineties than during the entire nineteenth century.

Claims on rivers are also becoming excessive, draining some rivers dry before they reach the sea. (See Chapter 3.) China's Huang He (Yellow River) often runs dry before it gets to the Yellow Sea. At one point in early 1995, it dried up some 620 kilometers from the sea. Similarly, the Colorado River, the major river in the southwestern United States, rarely makes it to the Gulf of California; more often it disappears somewhere in the Arizona desert. And the Amu Dar'ya, which originates in the northern Himalayas and once fed the Aral Sea, is now drained dry by Uzbek and Turkmen cotton farmers along the way.[9]

Conflicts over shared river systems are intensifying as well. Bangladesh is protesting India's excessive use of the Ganges, which leaves all too little for

Bangladesh to irrigate its cropland. Israel and Palestine are spending endless weeks negotiating over the allocation of shared water resources. The United States and Mexico compete for the waters of the Rio Grande. Conflicts among countries in central Asia over the waters of the Amu Dar'ya and Syr Dar'ya are intensifying as population pressures build to the point where demand exceeds the sustainable yield of the rivers.[10]

The demand for firewood, lumber, and paper is overwhelming the sustainable yield of forests in many countries. Anyone travelling in the Third World over the last few decades has seen forests receding from villages in country after country as the demand for firewood climbs apace with population. The wholesale deforestation of Southeast Asia to supply lumber to Europe and Northeast Asia is now spreading into Africa and the Amazon basin.[11]

Soil erosion, now a threat to food security in some regions, is a natural process and not a danger unless it becomes excessive, surpassing the natural rate of soil formation. As the pressure to grow more food has intensified, excessive soil erosion has spread, slowly depriving the land of its inherent fertility. The result, as in a country like Haiti, is deprivation and hunger.

The economic toll of crop-damaging heat waves and storms of increasing intensity is now becoming evident.

With the earth's capacity to fix atmospheric carbon dioxide (CO_2) more or less unchanged, the rise in fossil fuel use and carbon emissions has upset the natural balance, pushing CO_2 levels higher each year. As this happens, average temperatures are also rising, altering the earth's climate. No one knows what the long-term consequences will be, but the economic toll of crop-damaging heat waves and storms of increasing intensity is now becoming evident.

In the late twentieth century, some threshold crossings—such as the sustainable yield of oceanic fisheries or the capacity of the atmosphere to absorb CO_2—are global in scope. Others are local, but in an integrated world economy, they have a global effect.

When a country's demand for water begins to press against the limits of its sustainable supply, for instance, the competition between cities and the countryside intensifies. Cities almost always win in this competition, taking the water from agriculture. As farmers lose irrigation water to nonfarm uses, grain imports rise. When a country imports one ton of grain it is in effect importing 1,000 tons of water. Grain has become the currency with which governments balance their water accounts.[12]

The contrast with earlier times is clear. A decline in grain production in the early civilizations of the Middle East as a result of the waterlogging and salting of the irrigation system affected grain supplies and prices only in the Middle East. Today, as the slack goes out of the food system, the loss of cropland to industrialization in Indonesia drives up food prices everywhere. Aquifer depletion in Texas affects the world grain harvest. Soil erosion in Algeria contributes to worldwide grain shortages.

Threshold crossings often trigger a chain of events that affect the course and pace of history. For example, as the excessive demand for forest products leads to deforestation, the soil is left unprotected. Rainfall runoff increases, leaving less water to percolate downward to recharge aquifers. The increased runoff carries topsoil with it, reducing land fertility and silting rivers and reservoirs. As firewood becomes scarce, villagers turn to cow dung and crop residues for fuel, depriving their fields of organic matter and nutrients. The situation in Ethiopia illustrates this cascading series of events. The country was half covered by forests at the turn of the century, but today trees cover less than 3 percent of the land. The resulting erosion, chronic food shortages, and periodic famine are all part of the same package.[13]

Evolution has prepared us to compete with other species, to survive, and to multiply. But it has not equipped us well to either understand or deal with the threat we pose to ourselves with the uncontrolled growth in our numbers. We are at a loss to grasp the meaning of adding 90 million people annually year after year until we are faced with firewood shortages, water scarcity, and rising seafood prices. We have not yet learned how to stabilize our demands within the sustainable boundaries of the earth's ecosystems.[14]

As the nineties progress, a disturbing pattern is emerging. Virtually all the threshold crossings just described—overfishing, overgrazing, aquifer depletion, deforestation, soil erosion, and rising temperatures—make it more difficult to expand the food supply. The environmentally destructive trends of recent decades are collectively beginning to impair the capacity to boost world food production.

As oceanic fisheries and rangelands, together supplying much of the world's animal protein, reach their sustainable yield limits, the pressures shift to croplands to satisfy all future growth in the demand for food. The new reality is that fishers and ranchers are no longer contributing to the growth in the world's food supply. For the first time since civilization began, farmers must carry the burden alone.

Even as the pressure on cropland is mounting, the cumulative effects of soil erosion and aquifer depletion are making it more difficult to expand grain production. The economic manifestations of emerging food scarcity can be seen in rising seafood prices, falling grain stocks, and, most recently, rising grain prices. These and other trends suggest that the history of the next few decades will be defined by food, specifically by rising prices of both oceanic and land-based food products, by a spreading politics of food scarcity, and by an increasingly intense struggle to achieve a sustainable balance between food and people.

FOOD: THE DEFINING ISSUE

Environmentalists and scientists have long maintained that the population and environmental trends of the last few decades could not continue. Some thought environmental mismanagement would show up in the form of an epidemic of pollution-induced illnesses and wholesale rises in death rates. Others thought it might show up in the collapse of local ecosystems. Indeed, these may happen at the local level. But globally, food scarcity may soon become the principal manifestation of continuing population growth and environmental mismanagement. Rising food prices may be the first global economic indicator to signal serious trouble on the environmental front. For those who think the future may be a simple extrapolation of the past, there may be some surprises ahead.

In 1996, world carryover stocks of grain—the amount in the bin when the new harvest begins—are projected to drop to 245 million tons, down from 294 million tons in 1995. This third consecutive annual decline will reduce stocks to an estimated 49 days of consumption, the lowest level on record. (See Figure 1–1.) When world grain stocks were at the previous low of 55 days of consumption in 1973, grain prices doubled, pushing food prices up everywhere. At 49 days of consumption, these stocks represent little more than pipeline supplies— the amount needed to ensure an uninterrupted supply between farmers and urban consumers who may be on the opposite side of the planet.[15]

Against this backdrop of scarcity, the competition among importing countries for exportable supplies is driving grain prices upward worldwide. China's shift from net grain exporter of 8 million tons in 1994 to net grain importer of 16 million tons in 1995—making it second only to Japan as an importer—contributed to the stock decline and price rise. The across-the-board rise in grain prices in 1995 for wheat, rice, and corn of roughly one third signals rising food prices for bread, pasta, and breakfast cereals, and for those livestock products—meat, milk, and eggs—that are derived from grain.[16]

Ever since agriculture began, the challenge of producing enough to make it to the next harvest has been a perennial one. Despite the dramatic advances in agricultural technology and gains in output in recent generations, the fear that the grain bins will be emptied before the next harvest is reemerging as a concern in many national capitals.

The decline in 1996 carryover stocks is the result of an abrupt loss of momentum in the growth of world grain production. The 1995 world grain harvest of 1.69 billion tons was 5 percent below the 1990 bumper harvest of 1.78 billion tons that launched the decade. (See Figure 1–2.) Even if the modest area of cropland that was set aside under farm commodity programs in the United States and Europe were in use, the 1995 harvest would still have fallen short of consumption. Grain stocks would still have declined.[17]

Even as growth in the grain harvest is slowing, growth in the world fish catch has apparently ended. If the oceans cannot sustain a catch any greater than at present, all future growth in animal protein supplies can come only from land-based sources, principally from feeding more grain. Whether feeding fish in ponds or cattle in feedlots, the pressure on supplies of grain, which dominates

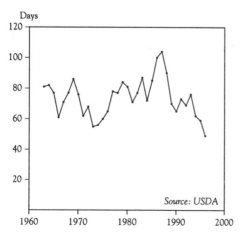

Figure 1-1. World Grain Carryover Stocks as Days of Consumption, 1961-96

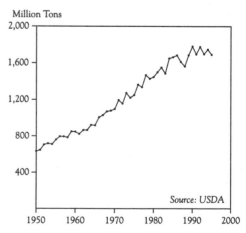

Figure 1-2. World Grain Production, 1950-95

the human diet, will intensify further. In fish farming, it takes about 2 kilograms of grain to produce 1 kilogram of fish. Replacing the historical 2-million-ton annual growth in the seafood catch (the average from 1950 to 1990) with fish from aquaculture would take 4 million tons of additional grain each year, roughly equivalent to the annual consumption in Belgium. If seafood consumers turn instead to poultry, the conversion rate is also roughly 2 kilograms of grain for each kilogram of poultry produced. With pork, it is closer to 4 to 1.[18]

As noted earlier, several longer-term global trends are slowing growth in the world grain harvest, but three stand out: a gradual decline in grainland area since 1981, little or no growth in irrigation water supplies since 1990, and a decline in world fertilizer use since 1989.

After reaching an all-time high of 732 million hectares in 1981, the world's grain harvested area declined to 669 million hectares in 1995. The abandonment of severely eroded land in the former Soviet Union, the loss of cropland to industrialization in Asia, and the conversion of highly erodible cropland back to grassland in the United States account for most of the decline.[19]

From 1950 onward, farmers coped successfully with the steady shrinkage in the cropland area per person, but more recently they have faced a drop in irrigation water per person as well. From 1950 to 1978, the world irrigated area expanded from 94 million hectares to 206 million hectares, or nearly 3 percent a year, raising the irrigated area per person some 28 percent. After 1978, growth slowed to scarcely 1 percent a year, reducing the irrigated area per person some 6 percent by 1990. During the following five years, there appears to have been little or no growth in irrigation water supplies.[20]

Future growth in irrigation will not come easily. The depletion of aquifers cited earlier, rivers running dry, the siltation of reservoirs as a result of deforestation and the associated soil erosion, the loss of irrigated land to waterlogging and salting, and the diversion of irrigation water to nonfarm uses are all combining to reduce irrigated area in many agricultural regions.

For fossil aquifers, such as the Ogallala that underlies the U.S. Great Plains, exhaustion is only a matter of time. Already, irrigated area in Texas has declined by some 11 percent after peaking a decade ago, as the shallow southern end of the Ogallala aquifer is depleted. More recently, irrigated area has begun to drop in neighboring Oklahoma, Kansas, and Colorado, forcing farmers to return to less productive dryland farming.[21]

After land and water, fertilizer is agriculture's most important input. From 1950 to 1989, the world's farmers boosted their use of fertilizer from 14 million to 146 million tons. One of the most predictable trends in the world economy, this tenfold expansion was the engine behind the near tripling of the world grain harvest that occurred from 1950 to 1990.[22]

After increasing almost every year for more than four decades, fertilizer use has actually declined since 1989. In all agriculturally advanced countries, growth in fertilizer use is levelling off. U.S. farmers are using less fertilizer in the mid-nineties than they did in the early eighties. Usage has also stabilized or declined slightly in Western Europe and Japan. Existing crop varieties simply cannot effectively use much more fertilizer than is now being applied.[23]

From 1950 until 1989, as the cropland per person declined, farmers raised productivity by using more fertilizer. During this four-decade span, the world's farmers combined rising fertilizer use and higher yielding varieties with spectacular success, boosting production to ever higher levels. (See Figure 1–3.) But there has been no growth in the world grain harvest since 1990. One year after fertilizer use stopped rising, growth in the grain harvest also came to a halt. The old formula is no longer working. Unfortunately, the inability of agricultural scientists to come up with a new formula to boost output means that production has stalled, posing a threat to economic and political stability that world leaders have not yet grasped.[24]

The challenge to farmers in a land-scarce world is to raise land productivity, but this is becoming progressively more difficult, even in agriculturally advanced countries. In the United States, farmers raised land productivity by more than 40 percent in the fifties and again in the sixties. But the figure fell to 20 percent in the seventies, only 10 percent in the eighties, and it is likely to fall even further during the nineties. (See Table 1–1.)

The difficulty in continuing to substitute fertilizer for land in the effort to feed an ever growing world population presents a formidable challenge to political leaders everywhere. World popula-

Table 1-1. United States: Grain Yield Per Hectare by Decade, 1950–90

Year[1]	Annual Yield Per Hectare	Increase by Decade
	(tons)	(percent)
1950	1.65	
1960	2.40	+ 45
1970	3.43	+ 43
1980	4.13	+ 20
1990	4.56	+ 10

[1]Three-year average used for each year to minimize the effect of weather.
SOURCES: U.S. Department of Agriculture (USDA), Economic Research Service (ERS), "Production, Supply, and Demand View" (electronic database), Washington, D.C., November 1993; production figures for 1950–60 from USDA, ERS, "World Grain Database" (unpublished printout), Washington, D.C., 1992.

tion growth of 90 million a year requires an annual expansion in grain production of 28 million tons of grain, or 78,000 tons a day. If allowance is made for rising affluence, then the annual growth in demand will, of course, be even larger.[25]

Economically, lagging food production is reflected in rising food prices. Prices for seafood have been rising for several years. Those of wheat, rice, and corn climbed by a third between early spring and late fall of 1995. Traditionally, higher food prices meant more investment in productive capacity, but many once promising avenues are now closed. Today, drilling more irrigation wells where water tables are already falling will simply accelerate the depletion of aquifers. Applying more fertilizer in the mid-seventies led to dramatic boosts in yields, but doing so in the late nineties will have limited effect. Twenty years ago, higher food prices led to investment in more fishing trawlers, but today that would simply hasten the collapse of oceanic fisheries.[26]

As food supplies tighten, the potential

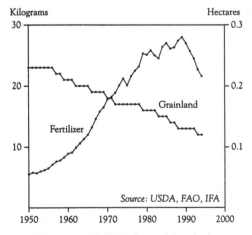

Figure 1-3. World Fertilizer and Grainland Per Person, 1950–94

payoff on investment in agricultural research rises, providing a strong argument for boosting public funding of the international network of 16 agricultural research institutes that make up the Consultative Group on International Agricultural Research. (See Chapter 5.) A new rice prototype under development at the International Rice Research Institute promises to boost average rice yields by 20–25 percent. When it becomes commercially available near the end of this decade, it could add up to 85 million tons of grain, enough to cover world population growth for three years.[27]

Although it may not be realistic to expect plant breeders to come up with new varieties that will lead to a doubling or tripling of yields as the first generation of high-yielding varieties did, there may be still numerous relatively modest opportunities for raising yields that can be profitably exploited. At a time of severe scarcity, any gain in output—however small—becomes disproportionately important.

As grain stocks drop, a politics of scarcity is emerging, similar to the climate that existed in the mid-seventies. The tightening of grain supplies that began in 1995 could mark the conversion of the buyer's market of the last half-century to a seller's market. Competition among exporting countries for markets that never seemed large enough may be replaced by competition among importers for exportable supplies that never seem adequate. Several rounds of trade negotiations under the General Agreement on Tariffs and Trade to reduce trade barriers helped ensure exporting countries' access to agricultural markets, but the issue in a world of food scarcity will be importing countries' access to supplies.

Governments of grain-exporting countries that are facing the prospect of scarcity and inflationary pressures at home are often tempted to impose export embargoes. Within China, for instance, where grain prices rose 55 percent in the first eight months of 1994, some provinces banned grain exports to other provinces. And in early May 1995, Vietnam imposed a temporary embargo on exporting rice. Because prices in neighboring Chinese provinces had risen so far above the world market level, large quantities of rice from Vietnam were crossing the border into China. With rising rice prices in Vietnam making it difficult to control inflation, the government imposed the embargo until the new harvest began. This approach could be repeated time and again: as scarcity spreads, exporting countries may try to control food price rises internally by restricting exports, thus exacerbating scarcity in the rest of the world.[28]

TRENDS TO BUILD ON

In looking at what it will take to build an environmentally sustainable global economy, there are many obstacles and liabilities, but there are also some assets. One is that we know what an environmentally sustainable economy would look like. We know how to build an economic system that will meet our needs without jeopardizing prospects for future generations. And with some trends already headed in the right direction, we have the cornerstones on which to build such an economy.

In a sustainable economy, human births and deaths are in balance, soil erosion does not exceed the natural rate of new soil formation, tree cutting does not exceed tree planting, the fish caught do not exceed the sustainable yield of fisheries, the cattle on a range do not exceed its carrying capacity, and water pumping does not exceed aquifer recharge. It is an economy where carbon emissions and carbon fixation are also again in balance. The number of plant and animal species lost does not exceed the rate at which new species evolve.

With population, the challenge is to complete the demographic transition, to reestablish the balance between births and deaths that characterizes a sustainable society. Since populations are rarely ever precisely stable, for purposes of discussion a stable population is here defined as one with a growth rate below 0.3 percent. Populations are effectively stable if they fluctuate narrowly around zero.

Thirty countries now have stable populations, including most of those in Europe plus Japan. (See Table 1–2.) They provide the solid base for building a world population stabilization effort. Included in the 30 are all the larger industrial countries of Europe—France, Germany, Italy, Russia, and the United Kingdom. Collectively, these 30 countries contain 819 million people or 14 percent of humanity. For this goal, one seventh of humanity is already there.

The challenge is for the countries with the remaining 86 percent of the world's people to reach stability. The two large nations that could make the biggest difference in this effort are China and the United States. In both, population growth is now roughly 1 percent per year. If the global food situation becomes desperate, both could reach stability in a decade or two if they decided it were important to do so.[29]

The world rate of population growth, which peaked around 2 percent in 1970, dropped below 1.6 percent in 1995. Although the rate is declining, the annual addition is still close to 90 million per year. Unless populations can be stabilized with demand below the sustainable yield of local ecosystems, these systems will be destroyed. Slowing growth may delay the eventual collapse of ecosystems, but it will not save them.[30]

The European Union, consisting of some 15 countries and containing 360 million people, provides a model for the rest of the world of an environmentally sustainable food/population balance. At the same time that the region has reached zero population growth, movement up the food chain has come to a halt as diets have become saturated with livestock products. The result is that Europe's grain consumption has been stable for close to two decades at just under 160 million tons—a level that is within the region's carrying capacity. (See Figure 1–4.) Indeed, there is a potential for a small but sustainable export surplus of grain that can help countries where the demand for food has surpassed the carrying capacity of their croplands.[31]

As other countries realize that continuing on their current population trajectory will prevent them from achieving a similar food/population balance, more and more may decide to do what China has done—launch an all-out campaign to

Figure 1-4. Grain Production and Consumption in the European Community, 1960-94

Table 1-2. Countries That Reached Population Stability by 1995

Country	Population Mid-1995	Birth Rate	Death Rate	Annual Rate of Natural Increase Or Decrease[1]
	(million)	(births per thousand population)	(deaths per thousand population)	(percent)
Austria	8	12	10	+ 0.1
Belarus	10	11	13	− 0.2
Belgium	10	12	11	+ 0.1
Bulgaria	8	10	13	− 0.3
Croatia	4	10	11	− 0.1
Czech Republic	10	12	11	0
Denmark	5	13	12	+ 0.1
Estonia	2	9	14	− 0.5
Finland	5	13	10	+ 0.3
France	58	12	9	+ 0.3
Georgia	5	12	10	+ 0.2
Germany	82	10	11	− 0.1
Greece	10	10	9	0
Hungary	10	12	14	0.3
Italy	58	9	10	0
Japan	125	10	7	+ 0.3
Latvia	2	10	15	− 0.5
Lithuania	4	13	12	0
Norway	4	14	11	+ 0.3
Poland	39	12	10	+ 0.2
Portugal	10	12	11	+ 0.1
Romania	23	11	12	− 0.1
Russia	148	9	16	− 0.6
Slovenia	2	10	10	+ 0.1
Spain	39	10	9	+ 0.1
Sweden	9	13	12	+ 0.1
Switzerland	7	12	9	+ 0.3
Ukraine	52	11	14	− 0.4
United Kingdom	59	13	11	+ 0.2
Yugoslavia[2]	11	13	10	+ 0.3

[1]Does not always reflect exactly the difference between birth rates and death rates shown because of rounding.   [2]Reflects the new Yugoslavia, consisting of Serbia plus Montenegro.
SOURCE: Population Reference Bureau, *1995 World Population Data Sheet* (Washington, D.C.: 1995).

stabilize population. Like China, other governments will have to carefully balance the reproductive rights of the current generation with the survival rights of the next generation.

Very few of the group of 30 countries with stable populations had stability as an explicit policy goal. In those that reached population stability first, such as Belgium, Germany, Sweden, and the

United Kingdom, it came with rising living standards and expanding employment opportunities for women. In some of the countries where population has stabilized more recently, such as Russia and other former Soviet republics, the deep economic depression accompanying economic reform has substantially lowered birth rates, much as the Great Depression did in the United States. In addition, with the rising number of infants born with birth defects and deformities since Chernobyl, many women are simply afraid to bear children. The natural decrease of population (excluding migration) in Russia of 0.6 percent a year—leading to an annual population loss of 890,000—is the most rapid on record.[32]

Not all countries are achieving population stability for the right reasons. This is true today and it may well be true in the future. As food deficits in densely populated countries expand, governments may find there is not enough food available to import. Between fiscal year 1993 and 1996, food aid dropped from an all-time high of 15.2 million tons of grain to 7.6 million tons. This cut of exactly half in three years reflects primarily fiscal stringencies in donor countries, but also, to a lesser degree, higher grain prices in fiscal 1996. If governments fail to establish a humane balance between their people and food supplies, hunger and malnutrition may raise death rates, eventually slowing population growth.[33]

Some developing countries are beginning to adopt social policies that will encourage smaller families. Iran, facing both land hunger and water scarcity, now limits public subsidies for housing, health care, and insurance to three children per family. In Peru, President Alberto Fujimori, who was elected overwhelmingly to a second five-year term in a predominantly Catholic country, said in his inaugural address in August 1995 that he wanted to provide better access to family planning services for poor women. "It is only fair," he said, "to disseminate thoroughly the methods of family planning to everyone."[34]

With climate, as with population, there is not universal agreement on the need to stabilize. Evidence that atmospheric CO_2 levels are rising is clear-cut. So too is the greenhouse effect of these gases in the atmosphere. That is a matter of basic physics. What is debatable is the rate at which global temperatures will rise and what the precise local effects will be. Nonetheless, the consensus of the mainstream scientific community is that there is no alternative to reducing carbon emissions. (See Chapter 2.)

As to how to phase out fossil fuels, there is now a highly successful model with chlorofluorocarbons (CFCs). After two British scientists discovered the "hole" in the ozone layer over Antarctica and published their findings in *Nature* in May of 1985, the international community convened a conference in Montreal to draft an international agreement designed to reduce CFC production sharply. Subsequent meetings in London in 1990 and Copenhagen in 1992 further advanced the goals set in Montreal. After peaking in 1988 at 1.26 million tons, the manufacture of CFCs dropped to an estimated 295,000 tons in 1994—a decline of 77 percent in just six years.[35]

As public understanding of the costs associated with global warming increases, and as evidence of the effects of higher temperatures accumulates, support for reducing dependence on fossil fuels is building. At the March 1995 U.N. Climate Convention in Berlin, environmental groups were joined in lobbying for a reduction in carbon emissions by a group of 36 island countries and insurance industry representatives.[36]

The island nations are beginning to realize that rising sea level would, at a minimum, reduce their land area and displace people. For some low-lying island countries, it could actually threaten their survival. And the insurance industry is beginning to realize that increasing storm intensity can threaten the survival of insurance companies as well. When Hurricane Andrew tore through Florida in 1992, it took down not only thousands of buildings, but also eight such firms.[37]

When the U.S. Department of Agriculture released its monthly world crop report in early September 1995, it reported a sharp drop in the estimated world grain harvest because of crop-withering heat waves in the northern tier of industrial countries. Intense late-summer heat had damaged harvests in Canada and the United States, across Europe, and in Russia. If farmers begin to see that the productivity of their land is threatened by global warming, they too may begin to press for a shift to renewable sources of energy.[38]

As with CFCs, there are alternatives to fossil fuels that do not alter climate. Several solar-based energy sources, including wind power, solar cells, and solar thermal power plants, are advancing rapidly in technological sophistication, with a resultant steady fall in cost. The cost of photovoltaic cells has fallen precipitously over the last few decades. In some villages in developing countries where a central grid does not yet exist, it is now cheaper to install an array of photovoltaic cells than to build a centralized power plant plus the grid needed to deliver the power.[39]

Wind power, using the new, highly efficient wind turbines to convert wind into electricity, is poised for explosive growth in the years ahead. In California, wind farms already supply enough electricity to meet the equivalent of San Francisco's residential needs. In terms of new wind-generating capacity installed in 1994, Germany and India surged ahead of the United States and Denmark, the early leaders in the field.[40]

The growth in wind power of 660 megawatts in 1994, pushing the total from 3,050 megawatts to 3,710 megawatts, represents an annual expansion of 22 percent. (See Figure 9–2 in Chapter 9.) Even with few or no government subsidies, wind energy is now growing at an extraordinary rate. The potential is enormous, dwarfing that of hydropower, which provides a fifth of the world's electricity. In the United States, the harnessable wind potential in North Dakota, South Dakota, and Texas could easily meet national electricity needs. In Europe, wind power could theoretically satisfy all the continent's electricity needs. With scores of national governments planning to tap this vast resource, rapid growth in the years ahead appears inevitable.[41]

The consensus of the mainstream scientific community is that there is no alternative to reducing carbon emissions.

Another trend to build on is the growing production of bicycles. Human mobility can be increased by investing in public transportation, bicycles, and automobiles. Of these, the first two are environmentally by far the most promising. Although China has announced plans to move toward an automobile-centered transportation system, and car production in India is expected to double by the end of the decade due to economic reforms and a growing economy, there simply may not be enough land in these countries to support such a system and to meet the food needs of their expanding populations.[42]

Against this backdrop, the creation of bicycle-friendly transportation systems, particularly in cities, shows great promise. Market forces alone have pushed bicycle production to an estimated 111 million in 1994, three times the level of automobile production. (See Figure 1–5.) It is in the interest of societies everywhere to foster the use of bicycles and public transportation—to accelerate the growth in bicycle manufacturing while restricting that of automobiles. Not only will this help save cropland, but this technology can greatly increase human mobility without destabilizing climate. If food becomes increasingly scarce in the years ahead, as now seems likely, the land-saving, climate-stabilizing nature of bicycles will further tip the scales in their favor, and away from automobiles.[43]

The stabilization of population in some 30 countries, the stabilization of the food/people balance in Europe, the reduction in CFC production, the dramatic growth in the world's wind power generating capacity, and the extraordinary growth in bicycle use are all trends for the world to build on. These cornerstones of an environmentally sustainable global economy provide glimpses of a sustainable future.

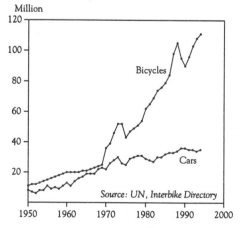

Figure 1-5. World Automobile and Bicycle Production, 1950-94

REGAINING CONTROL OF OUR DESTINY

As the change in the relationship between our growing numbers and the natural systems on which we depend accelerates the pace of history, the realization that we may be facing a shortage of food from both oceanic and land-based sources is a troubling one. Thoughtful people reflecting on these trends are asking, Can we avoid catastrophe? The answer is yes, but not if we keep sleepwalking through history.

Avoiding catastrophe is going to take a far greater effort than is now being contemplated by the world's political leaders. We know what needs to be done, but politically we are unable to do it because of inertia and the investment of powerful interests in the status quo. Securing food supplies for the next generation depends on an all-out effort to stabilize population and climate, but we resist changing our reproductive behavior, and we refrain from converting our climate-destabilizing, fossil-fuel-based economy to a solar/hydrogen–based one.

As we move to the end of this century and beyond, food security may well come to dominate international affairs, national economic policymaking, and, for much of humanity, personal concerns about survival. There is now evidence from enough countries that the old formula of substituting fertilizer for land is no longer working that we need to search urgently for alternative formulas for humanely balancing our numbers with available food supplies.

Unfortunately, most national political leaders do not even seem to be aware of the fundamental shifts occurring in the world food economy, largely because the official projections by the World Bank and the U.N. Food and Agriculture Organization (FAO) are essentially extrapolations of past trends. If we are to understand the challenges facing us, the teams of economists responsible for world food supply and demand projections at these two organizations need to be replaced with an interdisciplinary team of analysts, including, for example, an agronomist, hydrologist, biologist, and meteorologist, along with an economist. Such a team could assess and incorporate into projections such things as the effect of soil erosion on land productivity, the effects of aquifer depletion on future irrigation water supplies, and the effect of increasingly intense heat waves on future harvests.

Existing projections are essentially simple extrapolations. The World Bank team of economists argues that because the past is the only guide we have to the future, this is the only reasonable way to make projections. But the past is also filled with a body of scientific literature on growth in finite environments, which show that biological growth trends typically conform to an S-shaped curve over time.[44]

The risk of relying on these extrapolative projections is that they are essentially "no problem" projections. For example, the most recent Bank projections, which use 1990 as a base and which were published in late 1993, are departing further and further from reality with each passing year. They show the world grain harvest climbing from 1.78 billion tons in 1990 to 1.97 billion tons in the year 2000. But instead of the projected gain of nearly 100 million tons since 1990, world grain production has not grown at all. Indeed, the 1995 harvest, at 1.69 billion tons, is 90 million tons below the 1990 harvest. FAO projections using a similar approach yield similar results. They, too, are fast departing from reality.[45]

One of the most obvious needs today is for a set of country-by-country carrying capacity assessments. Assessments using an interdisciplinary team can help provide information needed to face the new realities and formulate policies to respond to them.

Can we avoid catastrophe? Not if we keep sleepwalking through history.

The growing gap between food demand and food supplies at familiar prices underscores the need for governments to assess their national carrying capacities so that they and the people they serve can understand the difficult choices that lie ahead. Now that the global fish catch has levelled off, we have a good sense of just how much food the oceans can provide sustainably. We now know roughly both how much land will be available for food production in the future, and, based on yields achieved by the most agriculturally advanced countries, what the yield potential of that land is with existing technologies. Barring any new technologies that can lead to quantum jumps in food production, like the discovery of fertilizer or the hybridization of corn, the world is facing unprecedented difficulty on the food front.

On the demand side of the food-population equation, the information needed to calculate future carrying capacity for varying combinations of projected population size and consumption levels is now available. These carrying capacity assessments can help people understand more clearly the difficult choices to be made between family size today and food consumption levels tomorrow. They will help everyone better understand the trade-off between the reproductive rights of the current generation and the survival rights of the next.

The lack of growth of the world grain harvest since 1990 coupled with the con-

tinuing growth in world population and
the increased likelihood of crop-damaging heat waves in the years ahead at least
carries the potential of severe food
shortages. The economic disruption that
is likely to result could dwarf that which
occurred when the Organization of Petroleum Exporting Countries engineered a tripling in the world price of oil
in 1973. People can survive without oil,
but not without food. Oil can be replaced with other energy sources, but
there is no replacement for food.[46]

**Regaining control of our destiny
depends on stabilizing population
as well as climate.**

No other economic indicator is more
politically sensitive than rising food
prices. If the grain scarcity that will now
continue at least until the 1996 harvest
begins should continue indefinitely, millions of low-income breadwinners could
face food price rises that would threaten
the survival of their families. Food prices
spiraling out of control could trigger not
only economic instability but widespread political upheavals. Food scarcity
could call into question the legitimacy of
numerous national governments that
have failed to address the growing imbalance between human reproduction
and food production.

The world today is faced with an enormous need for change in a period of time
that is all too short. Human behavior and
values, and the national priorities that
reflect them, change in response to either new information or new experiences. When Nobel Laureates Sherwood
Rowland and Mario Molina published
their landmark article in 1974 outlining
the threat to the stratospheric ozone
layer from CFCs, they convinced many
thoughtful people of the need to phase

out the use of these chemicals. But it was
not until two British scientists discovered the "hole" in the ozone layer over
Antarctica that the international movement to ban CFCs gained enough
strength to succeed.[47]

The questions now are, What will be
the climate equivalent of the hole in the
ozone layer? What will finally trigger a
meaningful response? Will it be crop-
withering heat waves so intense that they
create food shortfalls so massive that the
resulting food price rises destabilize the
world economy? What will finally con-
vince governments that unless population is stabilized sooner rather than
later, falling food consumption per person will spread, engulfing an ever larger
share of humanity?

The effort now needed to reverse the
environmental degradation of the planet
and ensure a sustainable future for the
next generation will require mobiliza-
tion on a scale comparable to World War
II. As noted earlier, regaining control of
our destiny depends on stabilizing population as well as climate. These are both
key to the achievement of a wide array of
social goals ranging from the restoration
of a rise in food consumption per person
to protection of the diversity of plant
and animal species. And neither will be
easy. The first depends on a revolution
in human reproductive behavior; the
second, on a restructuring of the global
energy system.

Serving as a catalyst for these gargantuan efforts is the knowledge that if we
fail, our future will spiral out of control
as the acceleration of history over-
whelms political institutions. It will almost guarantee a future of starvation,
economic insecurity, and political instability. It will bring political conflict between societies and among ethnic and
religious groups within societies. As
these forces are unleashed, they will
leave social disintegration in their wake.

Offsetting the dimensions of this challenge, including the opposition to change that is coming from vested interests and the momentum of the trends now headed in the wrong direction, are some valuable assets. These include a well-developed global communications network, a growing body of scientific knowledge, and the possibility of using fiscal policy—a potentially powerful instrument for change—to build an environmentally sustainable economy.

Effectively dealing with many of the issues now confronting humanity requires a strong set of global institutions. In today's world, for example, with modern transportation and the continuous flow of people and other disease vectors across national boundaries, societies are faced with entirely new diseases, ones to which people have little resistance and about which the medical community knows too little. (See Chapter 7.)

Among these new maladies are Lyme disease, which was first identified in the mid-seventies in Connecticut and has now spread throughout the continental United States; the AIDS virus, which is now found worldwide though it was unknown to the medical community just 15 years ago; and the Ebola virus found in Zaire. The World Health Organization (WHO) spearheaded the worldwide effort to bring the AIDS epidemic under control. It is WHO that led the successful effort to quarantine the outbreak of the deadly Ebola virus in Zaire in May 1995. If WHO did not exist, it would have to be invented.[48]

Disposing of toxic waste, protecting biological diversity, and managing oceanic fisheries beyond the national 200-mile limits are but a few of the issues that depend on an international approach. Climate stabilization, like protecting the stratospheric ozone layer, cannot be achieved by societies acting unilaterally. Only a cooperative international effort will suffice, as it did on the CFC issue. It was the leadership of the U.N. Environ-ment Programme that led to the Montreal Protocol and subsequent amendments that successfully reduced the manufacture of the ozone-threatening CFCs.[49]

Satisfying the conditions of sustainability—whether it be reversing the deforestation of the planet, converting a throwaway economy into a reuse-recycle one, or stabilizing climate—will require new investment. Probably the single most useful instrument for converting an unsustainable world economy into one that is sustainable is fiscal policy. (See Chapter 10.) At present, governments subsidize many of the very activities that threaten the sustainability of the economy. They support fishing fleets to the extent of some $54 billion a year, for example, even though existing fishing capacity already greatly exceeds the sustainable yield of oceanic fisheries. In Germany, coal production is subsidized even though the country's scientific community has been outspoken in its emphasis on the need to reduce carbon emissions.[50]

With alternative sources of energy such as wind power, photovoltaics, and solar thermal power plants becoming competitive or nearly so, a carbon tax that would reflect the cost to society of burning fossil fuels—the costs, that is, of air pollution, acid rain, and global warming—could quickly tip the scales away from further investment in fossil fuel production to investment in wind and solar energy. Once cheap electricity is available from solar sources, it can be used to electrolyze water, producing hydrogen, a convenient way of storing and transporting solar energy. Today's fossil-fuel-based energy economy can be replaced with a solar/hydrogen energy economy that can meet all the energy needs of a modern industrial society without causing disruptive temperature rises.

Partially replacing income taxes with

environmental taxes is desirable for several reasons. One, income taxes discourage work and savings, which are both positive activities that should be encouraged. At the same time, taxing environmentally destructive activities would help steer the global economy in an environmentally sustainable direction. Among the activities to be taxed are the use of pesticides, the generation of toxic wastes, the use of virgin raw materials, the conversion of cropland to nonfarm uses, and carbon emissions. The time may have come to limit tax deductions for children to two per couple: it may not make sense to subsidize childbearing beyond replacement level when the most pressing need facing humanity is to stabilize population.

The shift from income to environmental taxes would be revenue-neutral, but the elimination of huge subsidies for the use of fossil fuels or water, or for investment in fishing trawlers, to cite just a few examples, would free up a vast sum of capital that could be used to fill the family planning gap, develop an energy- and land-efficient transportation system, reforest the planet, and educate young women in developing countries—a key to accelerating the move to smaller families. In addition to using tax policy to shift private investment to environmentally sustainable activities, once it becomes clear that it is food scarcity rather than military aggression that threatens long-term political stability, public pressure will develop to reorder priorities in the use of public resources as well. Restructuring private investment through fiscal policy shifts and public investment through an ordering of priorities that corresponds with today's needs can easily provide the resources needed to stabilize both population and climate.

The challenge for humanity is a profound one. We have the information, the technology, and the knowledge of what needs to be done. The question is, Can we do it? Can a species that is capable of formulating a theory that explains the birth of the universe now implement a strategy to build an environmentally sustainable economic system?

2

Facing Up to the Risks of Climate Change

Christopher Flavin

When environmental leaders from more than 120 countries gathered in Berlin in March 1995 for the first Conference of the Parties to the Framework Convention on Climate Change, they were greeted by an April snowstorm. The inauspicious spring blizzard seemed a fitting backdrop to a chilly and contentious session, pitting rich nations against poor ones, heavy carbon emitters against less carbon-intensive nations, and small island states against countries that feel less vulnerable.

Yet even as negotiators labored over mind-numbing issues such as "adequacy of commitments" and "joint implementation," the urgency of the climate threat was being heightened by new scientific studies. In a draft assessment released after the meeting, in late summer 1995, the Intergovernmental Panel on Climate Change (IPCC) concluded that "a pattern of climatic response to human activities is identifiable in the climatological record." This U.N. panel of scientists went on to warn of serious economic and human consequences, pointing to the effects on agriculture, forests, and coastal developments. Writing in *Nature*, leading IPCC climatologist Tom Wigley said in August 1995 that recent advances "mark a turning point . . . in our ability to understand past changes and predict the future."[1]

National assessments presented at the Berlin meeting demonstrated that the world is not yet meeting one of the main goals of the climate convention adopted three years earlier at the Earth Summit in Rio de Janeiro: holding industrial-country emissions of greenhouse gases to the 1990 level in the year 2000. By 1994, emissions of carbon dioxide (CO_2), the most important greenhouse gas, were already as much as 5 percent above the 1990 level in some industrial nations. In many developing countries, emissions were up by 10, 20, or even 40 percent. In fact, the climate issue is still being largely ignored by many energy decision makers—in both the public and the private sectors.[2]

Given the magnitude of the problem the world faces, the Berlin conference achieved only modest progress. Despite the pleas of environmental organizations, scientists, and even the insurance industry, which is alarmed by the frequency and severity of weather-related disasters in recent years, negotiators failed to achieve an agreement to reduce emissions of greenhouse gases to levels that scientists have urged. Instead, they opted for a new round of negotiations designed to lead to such commitments by 1997. Meanwhile, this greatest of all unplanned and unregulated experiments with the natural world continues.

THE EVIDENCE MOUNTS

Eight years after climate change was pushed onto the agenda of the world's policymakers and research on the subject accelerated, scientific understanding advanced rapidly in 1995. Government-funded global change research programs launched since 1988 have allowed scientists to detect and model the process of climate change more accurately, leading to a more solid consensus that we are already feeling the early effects of an altered climate.

By 1995, the concentration of carbon dioxide in the atmosphere had reached 360 parts per million (ppm)—higher than at any time in the past 150,000 years, and far above the 280 ppm that existed when fossil fuel burning began. In the eighties, scientists detected increases in other greenhouse gases during the twentieth century—notably chlorofluorocarbons (CFCs) and their substitutes (HCFCs and HFCs), nitrous oxide, and methane—that emanate from many sources, including wetlands, landfills, rice paddies, coal mines, and oil refineries. Each of these chemicals is less abundant in the atmosphere than carbon dioxide is, but they are potent greenhouse gases that together increase the warming effect of CO_2 alone by 50 percent.[3]

Altogether, these gases trap as much heat as would be generated by more than 300,000 nuclear plants. This increase in greenhouse gases coincides with an increase in global average temperatures of 0.6 degrees Celsius over the past century, leading many scientists to surmise that the two trends are linked. In fact, global climate records show that the 10 warmest years in the past century have all occurred since 1980.[4]

Although the heat-trapping effect of greenhouse gases is undisputed, as is their rising concentration, a debate about the seriousness of the climate problem has taken place in the popular press in recent years. Critics such as Patrick Michaels of the University of Virginia and Richard Lindzen of the Massachusetts Institute of Technology have seized on uncertainties inherent in climate projections to argue that computer-generated models are too flimsy to be predictive, that the climate record shows a slower rate of warming than the models suggest, or that "negative feedbacks" will protect us from climate change.[5]

Such arguments are hardly reflected in the scientific literature, and in fact some of the work of these "skeptics" is funded by the coal industry. Moreover, many of their arguments have been undermined by recent scientific advances. The global circulation models used to mimic climate trends using powerful supercomputers have become steadily more sophisticated in recent years. By incorporating the effect of sulfate aerosols, a form of pollution that partly offsets the impact of greenhouse gases, climate modelers have been able to replicate past climate patterns and project future trends far more accurately.[6]

Additional advances have come in the analysis of regional and temporal climate shifts, which have helped both to confirm the overall climate trend and to better anticipate the possible regional effects of climate change in the future. Since climate change is an uneven phenomenon—the poles should warm more rapidly than equatorial regions, and continents more rapidly than areas of deeply circulating ocean—some scientists have identified certain localized "fingerprints" of climate change that should be identifiable quite early in the process.[7]

One fingerprint is the dramatic warming of Antarctica in recent decades, vividly demonstrated just before the Berlin conference when a chunk of Antarctic glacier as big as the state of Rhode Island collapsed into the South Atlantic. Another trend that is consistent with global circulation models is the fact that Siberia is now warmer than at any time since the Middle Ages. Northern Europe, meanwhile, has experienced a string of warm winters and severe winter storms. Related to this is a retreat of Alpine glaciers, exposing ice and rocks that have been buried for thousands of years. And northern interior areas of India have experienced life-threatening heat waves in recent summers.[8]

Additional indications of climate change have emerged at the global level. For example, a new orbiting radar gun has been able to detect an annual rise in sea level of 3 millimeters during the past three years, a trend consistent with the thermal expansion that occurs with warming. The timing of the earth's seasons may also provide a useful barometer of climate change. In early 1995, David J. Thomson, an expert at AT&T's Bell Labs in mathematical analysis of complex trends, published an article in *Science* on the timing of seasonal shifts, incorporating data from as far back as thirteenth-century church records. He found a sizable shift in the timing of seasons that began in 1940, reversing a pattern of stability that had lasted for sev-

eral hundred years. Thomson sees a high probability that this shift is related to the rise in greenhouse gas concentrations.[9]

Such evidence convinced the IPCC to conclude in its landmark 1995 report that recent changes in global climate trends are "unlikely to be entirely due to natural causes." Thomas Karl, senior scientist at the U.S. National Oceanic and Atmospheric Administration, concluded in 1995 that "the data are consistent with the general trends expected from a greenhouse-enhanced atmosphere." And Klaus Hasselmann, director of the Max Planck Institute for Meteorology in Hamburg, Germany, says that there is a 95-percent chance that the rise in temperature over the past century is caused by greenhouse gases.[10]

We are already feeling the early effects of an altered climate.

Scientists are now focusing on the need to better anticipate future climate patterns by using the latest and most complex global circulation models. The 1995 IPCC assessment (which for the first time includes the effects of sulfate aerosols) projects an additional rise of 0.8–3.5 degrees Celsius (1.4–6.3 degrees Fahrenheit) in the global average temperature by 2100. This projected increase covers a wide range, but even at the lower end is faster than any experienced since human civilization began. Indeed, the global average temperature was just 3–5 degrees Celsius cooler during the last ice age than it is today.[11]

Increasingly, climate scientists focus on the rate of warming, reflecting the fact that the faster the pace, the harder it will be for human and natural systems to adapt. In its 1995 report, the IPCC concluded that any rate of change above roughly 0.1 degrees Celsius per decade—about twice the pace experienced over the past century—could cause considerable havoc, yet the upper range of the IPCC projection represents a rate of increase of more than 0.3 degrees per decade.[12]

One factor slowing the pace of climate change is the sulfate aerosols emitted by fossil fuel burning, which have shielded the earth from the full effect of greenhouse gases. Since aerosols last only weeks in the stratosphere once emitted, while carbon dioxide lasts centuries, efforts to reduce the use of oil and coal in coming decades may in the short run actually increase the rate of projected warming. For example, the IPCC estimates that the maximum increase by 2100 could be as high as 4.6 degrees Celsius if sulfate aerosols are removed. (See Figure 2–1.)[13]

Much of the uncertainty about the tempo of climate change is caused by the complexity of the climate system and the many feedback loops involved. Some scientists believe there may be a negative feedback effect that can offset the impact

of rising greenhouse gases. For example, as temperatures rise, so will the amount of water vapor and clouds. Although these have a strong heat-trapping effect, some researchers hypothesize that clouds may also cool the earth by preventing sunshine from reaching the surface. After extensive investigations, scientists now believe that these effects roughly cancel out.[14]

The interactions between the atmosphere, oceans, and biosphere are another critical feedback, since each of these contains a substantial reservoir of carbon. In fact, of the 6 billion tons of carbon released from fossil fuel burning each year, only about 3 billion tons remain in the atmosphere. For the past decade, scientists have searched for the "missing carbon," and have recently determined that the world's oceans and northern hemisphere forests are each absorbing about 1.5 billion tons of carbon a year. The high rate of carbon absorption by forests is a surprise to many scientists, who believe it may result in part from the fertilizing effect of more atmospheric CO_2 and higher temperatures.[15]

This negative feedback appears to be shielding the planet from the full impact of greenhouse gas emissions, but it also suggests future dangers. Carbon contained in forests and soils is not as stable as carbon trapped in the deep oceans. Some scientists believe that as temperatures increase further, the health of forests could decline and their ability to absorb carbon would be reduced. The extensive loss of northern and temperate boreal forests that many scientists believe is possible in the next few decades could release tens of billions of tons of additional carbon into the atmosphere, which would accelerate the rate of warming. The warming of the tundra could also release large quantities of methane, another greenhouse gas. Such

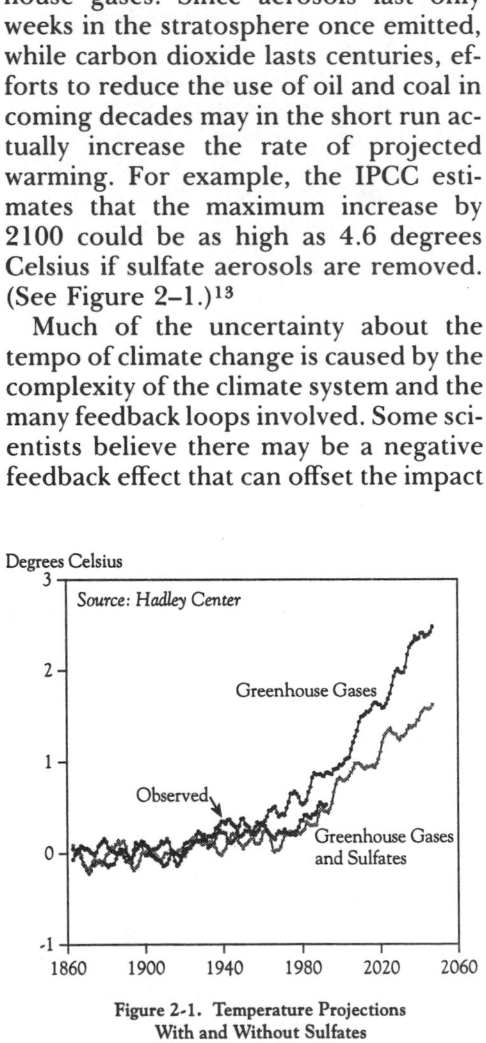

Degrees Celsius

Figure 2-1. Temperature Projections
With and Without Sulfates
Compared With Observations, 1860-2040

effects could cause the rate of climate change to approach or exceed the upper range of the IPCC projections.[16]

The ability of the oceans to absorb carbon may also be at risk. A report in *Nature* in August 1995 suggests that the oceans may be losing fixed nitrogen, an essential fertilizer that allows phytoplankton to grow, absorbing and fixing carbon that is then transferred to the deep ocean. If in fact the oceans are losing nitrogen as they warm, they will tend to absorb less carbon, thus boosting the rate of CO_2 buildup in the atmosphere.[17]

Although such feedbacks are still speculative, the hypotheses do suggest—contrary to the arguments of some skeptics—that uncertainty can cut both ways. The climate system is highly complex and nonlinear, and so it is impossible to predict in detail exactly how it will respond when disturbed. For policymakers, this uncertainty presents a major challenge: how do you respond to a problem whose precise dimensions are unclear? In many other fields, governments and individuals take action in the face of similar or greater uncertainty. Homeowners' investments in insurance and government investments in military armament are obvious examples of taking action to reduce risks despite large uncertainties. If we wait for absolute certainty or for a disaster before slowing greenhouse gas emissions, we will already be committed to several decades of additional climate change before the process can be reversed.

A CLIMATE OF EXTREMES

The chief concern of scientists is not the relatively modest increase in global average temperatures that is projected, but the possible disruption of atmospheric and oceanic systems that regulate weather. Recent studies indicate that a warming world is one in which climate "extremes" will be more common, placing stress on natural systems as well as the human economy. According to the IPCC's 1995 report, "the incidence of floods, droughts, fires and heat outbreaks is expected to increase in some regions" as temperatures rise.[18]

In an age when people live in air-conditioned homes and eat fresh food grown thousands of kilometers away, it is easy to ignore our dependence on the climate. But people still generally live in areas where water is adequate if not abundant, and their nutritional and material needs are met through agricultural, forestry, and fishery systems that require particular temperature, rainfall, and humidity levels. Although societies can cope with an isolated drought, heat wave, or flood by bringing in relief supplies of food or water, simultaneous disruptions in several regions could be unmanageable.

One possible result of a disrupted climate is more frequent droughts. Chronic water shortages already plague 80 countries with 40 percent of the world's population, according to the World Bank, impinging on economic development in many nations. The availability of water is already the main constraint on agricultural production in many areas, and the total area of cropland that is irrigated has begun to level off as rivers and underground aquifers are gradually depleted. At the same time, rapidly growing cities are competing for water in many countries. (See Chapter 3.)[19]

Although a warmer world climate will tend to boost both precipitation and evaporation, atmospheric models suggest that the regional effects would be uneven; some areas that now receive plentiful rainfall might become drier, while others would get more rain. Among the potential beneficiaries are North America and Russia, where grain belts might expand as a result of warmer temperatures and increased precipitation. Even with greater rain, however, increased summer heat would boost evaporation, drying out crop- and forestlands even more and impeding pollination. Other regions, including South and Southeast Asia, tropical Latin America, and sub-Saharan Africa, would probably see a decline in their harvests. Overall, the IPCC concludes that "there may be significant adverse consequences for food security in some regions of the world."[20]

Most forests are adapted to particular regimes of moisture and temperature, and cannot extend their range fast enough to keep up with the pace of climate change now predicted. According to Steven Hamburg, a forest ecologist at Brown University, a staggering one third of the earth's forests could be forced to "move" as a result of the effective doubling of CO_2 concentrations projected by 2100. How this would occur is uncertain, but environmental stresses would likely cause many trees to become infested with insects or disease, which would make them vulnerable to wildfires. Massive and sudden loss of many northern forests is therefore possible, which could spell disaster for the wood-products and tourism industries, as well as for the many species that depend on those forests.[21]

Some biological systems are already changing in ways that suggest a warming trend. Pine trees in northern Finland have taken root in tundra areas in apparent response to warmer temperatures— at a rate of about 40 meters a year according to a scientist at the University of Helsinki. Oceanographers at the Hopkins Institute in Monterey, California, which has been tracking undersea life for 60 years, say that marine snails and other mollusks normally found in warm waters are now expanding their ranges north along the Pacific Coast, while cold water species retreat. In many regions, tropical corals, which are sensitive to water temperature, are dying. And a 130,000-square-kilometer region of the Pacific Ocean has lost 80 percent of its zooplankton as water temperatures have risen.[22]

One aspect of human-induced climate change now being evaluated is whether it will increase the frequency or severity of major storms. A scientific assessment done for a German insurance company, Munich Re, notes: "A warmer atmosphere and warmer seas result in greater exchange of energy and add momentum to the vertical exchange processes so crucial to the development of tropical cyclones, tornadoes, thunderstorms, and hailstorms." Such links have not been definitively confirmed, but a study by the U.S. National Oceanic and Atmospheric Administration indicates a "steady increase in precipitation derived from extreme one-day precipitation events" in the United States in recent decades. In Europe, severe winter storms have become far more frequent in recent years, causing more than $10 billion in damage in 1990 alone.[23]

Tropical hurricanes, cyclones, and typhoons—as they are variously called in different parts of the world—are the most widely destructive and life-threatening of natural disasters. These large, swirling storms have their genesis at a temperature of at least 26 degrees Celsius in warm tropical waters such as the Caribbean, South Pacific, and Indian Oceans. They have destructive winds of 120–320 kilometers per hour, and are accompanied by heavy rain and storm surges that inundate low-lying areas.

Meteorologist Kerry Emanual of the Massachusetts Institute of Technology estimates that the 3–4 degree Celsius rise in sea temperatures projected by atmospheric models could increase the destructive potential of hurricanes by 50 percent and cause sustained storm winds as high as 350 kilometers (220 miles) per hour. Donald Friedman, former director of the Natural Hazards Research Program for the Travelers Insurance Company, calculates that such a warming would lengthen the current hurricane season in North America by two months or more, and allow the storms to move further north before petering out—striking major urban areas such as New York. Other scientists dispute these numbers, however, noting that tropical storms require a complex brew of forces, and that some features of a warmer world could make it more difficult for hurricanes to form.[24]

Still, one fact is undisputed: the past five years have witnessed unprecedented damage from weather-related disasters. (See Table 2-1.) In May 1991, for example, a cyclone with winds of 270 kilometers per hour hit Bangladesh, flooding vast areas of the country's flat coastal plain. An estimated 140,000 people were killed, more than a million homes were damaged or destroyed, and financial losses were put at $3 billion—more than 10 percent of Bangladesh's annual gross national product (GNP). Within the next year, at least five devastating tropical storms caused billion-dollar-plus losses from China to Pakistan and Hawaii. And in August 1994, China was hit by Typhoon Fred, which killed 700 people and caused $1.6 billion in damage.[25]

After two decades of relative calm, the southeastern United States has been struck by a number of serious hurricanes in recent years, including 1995, which had the most active Atlantic hurricane season since the thirties. Although sophisticated warning systems have limited the loss of life, economic damage has been unprecedented because of burgeoning coastal development. South Florida's vulnerability was demonstrated

Table 2-1. Weather-Related Disasters With Damages Over $3 Billion, 1989–95

Disaster	Location	Date	Deaths	Estimated Damages
			(number)	(billion dollars)
Windstorm Daria	Europe	Jan. 1990	n.a.	4.6
Windstorm Vivian	Europe	Feb. 1990	n.a.	3.2
Unnamed Cyclone	Bangladesh	May 1991	140,000	3.0
Flood	China	Summer 1991	3,074	15.0
Typhoon Mireille	Japan	Sept. 1991	62	6.0
Hurricane Andrew	North America	Aug. 1992	74	30.0
Cyclone Iniki	North America	Aug. 1992	4	3.0
Winter Storm	North America	March 1993	246	5.0
Mississippi Floods	North America	July/Aug. 1993	41	12.0
Winter Damage	North America	Jan. 1994	170	4.0
Spring Floods	China	Spring 1994	1,846	7.8
Flood	Italy	Nov. 1994	64	9.3
Winter Floods	North Europe	Jan./Feb. 1995	28	3.5

SOURCE: Gerhard A. Berz, Munich Reinsurance Company, Munich, Germany, private communication, September 1, 1995.

on August 24, 1992, when Hurricane Andrew came ashore with sustained winds of 235 kilometers per hour—the third most powerful hurricane to make landfall in the United States in the twentieth century. Andrew virtually flattened 430 square kilometers of Dade County in Florida, destroying 85,000 homes and leaving almost 300,000 people homeless. Total losses were estimated at $30 billion—equivalent to the combined losses of the three most costly previous U.S. storms. Robert Sheets, then director of the National Hurricane Center, estimated that if Andrew had moved just 30 kilometers further north, it would have caused damages of $100 billion and covered New Orleans in 6 meters of water.[26]

In Bangladesh, millions have no choice but to live and farm in areas vulnerable to flooding.

Although hurricane severity is not definitively linked to climate warming, it is clear that hurricane losses could be multiplied by another feature of a warming world: rising seas. Water expands as it warms, and higher temperatures also tend to melt the glacial ice found near the world's poles. During the past century, sea levels have already risen by 20–40 centimeters, and scientists believe that by 2100 the sea level in local areas will rise between 10 and 120 centimeters above current levels. Such increases would threaten coastal communities, as well as the estuaries and aquifers on which societies depend. According to the IPCC, these increases could flood many deltas, and make portions of some cities uninhabitable. The IPCC's mid-range projections indicate that most of the beaches on the East Coast of the

United States will disappear during the next 25 years.[27]

Sea level rise varies by region, depending on how much local temperatures increase, as well as the degree of localized subsidence caused by freshwater withdrawals and other effects. A study by the Manila-based Asian Development Bank concluded that Bangladesh, India, Malaysia, the Philippines, Sri Lanka, and Vietnam would be particularly hurt. The sea level could rise by 1 meter in Jakarta by 2070, submerging a large portion of the metropolitan area. In Vietnam, rising seas could inundate much of the Red River and Mekong deltas, dramatically reducing production of rice, the country's principal crop.[28]

Developing countries are particularly vulnerable to climatic extremes since many have high population densities and cannot afford to protect farmland or homes, or even evacuate threatened areas expeditiously. In countries such as Bangladesh, where millions have no choice but to live and farm in areas vulnerable to flooding, the results could be devastating. Moreover, people in developing countries generally do not have insurance policies that would compensate them once a disaster is over. A study of the effects of climate change on agriculture found that subsistence crops in developing countries located at tropical latitudes could be hit hard, while industrial countries would be much less affected. The study projects food shortages that could affect hundreds of millions of people—mainly in Africa and Asia. In addition, according to the IPCC, "projected changes in climate are likely to result in a wide range of human health impacts, most of them adverse, and many of which would reduce life expectancy." (See Chapter 7.) The most severe health effects are likely to occur in developing countries.[29]

GREENHOUSE GAS ESCALATOR

Fossil fuel burning is now releasing about 6 billion tons of carbon into the air each year, adding 3 billion tons annually to the 170 billion tons that have accumulated since the Industrial Revolution. To allow the earth's climate to return to equilibrium over the next few centuries, carbon emissions will have to be reduced to the rate at which the oceans and forests can absorb them—1–2 billion tons a year, or as much as 80 percent below today's rate.[30]

If this is the goal, recent developments are discouraging. Global carbon emissions levelled off temporarily in the early nineties, but this was mainly caused by a sharp decline in emissions in central Europe as its centrally planned industries collapsed. The underlying rate of growth in global carbon emissions is still over 2 percent a year. (See Figure 2–2.) Although this represents a slowdown from the pre-oil-crisis days of the sixties, it remains a trend that is moving dangerously in the wrong direction. Most industrial countries have failed to reduce or in some cases even stabilize their emissions. In developing countries, emissions are soaring as economic growth surges in the mid-nineties.[31]

Carbon emission levels vary widely among countries, a disparity that will profoundly affect any climate stabilization strategy and is already causing diplomatic tensions. Per capita emissions range from 5.26 tons in the United States to 2.39 tons in Japan and 0.24 tons in India. (See Table 2–2.) This more than twentyfold range in emission rates reflects many differences, including levels of industrial development and personal incomes. But one striking feature of the world carbon budget is the range of emissions among countries with similar levels of economic development: per capita emissions in China are 75 percent higher than they are in Brazil, for instance, while those in the United States are 120 percent higher than in Japan. Such differences reflect energy efficiency variations in individual countries, as well as the fuels each nation relies on.

Figures on the amount of carbon emitted per million dollars of economic output, a measure of the carbon efficiency of economies, show disparities nearly as great. Among the least carbon-efficient economies are Kazakstan at 1,250 tons of carbon per million dollars of GNP, South Africa at 680 tons, and Russia at 590 tons. The United States, by contrast, emits 210 tons of carbon per million dollars of GNP, while Japan is responsible for only 110 tons. Developing countries show a range varying from 330 tons of carbon per million dollars of GNP in China to 160 tons in India and 70 tons in Brazil. These data reflect several differences, including energy wastefulness in the former Soviet Union, extensive reliance on automobiles in the United States, high levels of energy efficiency in

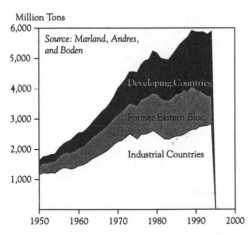

Figure 2-2. World Carbon Emissions from Fossil Fuel Burning, by Economic Region, 1950-94

Table 2-2. Carbon Emissions from Fossil Fuel Burning, Top 20 Emitters, 1994

Country	Total Emissions	Emissions Per Person	Emissions Per Dollar GNP[1]	Emissions Growth 1990–94
	(million tons)	(tons)	(tons per million dollars)	(percent)
United States	1,371	5.26	210	4.4
China	835	0.71	330	13.0
Russia	455	3.08	590	−24.1
Japan	299	2.39	110	0.1
Germany	234	2.89	140	−9.9
India	222	0.24	160	23.5
United Kingdom	153	2.62	150	−0.3
Ukraine	125	2.43	600	−43.5
Canada	116	3.97	200	5.3
Italy	104	1.81	110	0.8
France	90	1.56	80	−3.2
Poland	89	2.31	460	−4.5
South Korea	88	1.98	200	43.7
Mexico	88	0.96	140	7.1
South Africa	85	2.07	680	9.1
Kazakstan[2]	81	4.71	1,250	n.a.
Australia	75	4.19	230	4.2
North Korea[2]	67	2.90	960	n.a.
Iran[2]	62	1.09	270	n.a.
Brazil	60	0.39	70	15.8

[1]GNP data are adjusted for purchasing power parity and are for 1993.   [2]Latest data available are for 1992.

SOURCES: G. Marland, R.J. Andres, and T.A. Boden, "Global, Regional, and National CO_2 Emission Estimates From Fossil Fuel Burning, Cement Production, and Gas Flaring: 1950–1992" (electronic database) (Oak Ridge, Tenn.: Carbon Dioxide Information Analysis Center, Oak Ridge National Laboratory, 1995); Worldwatch estimates based on ibid., and on British Petroleum, *BP Statistical Review of World Energy* (London: Group Media & Publications, 1995); Population Reference Bureau, *1994 World Population Data Sheet* (Washington, D.C.: 1994); World Bank, *The World Bank Atlas 1995* (Washington, D.C.: 1995).

Japan, heavy use of coal in China and South Africa, and extensive use of non-carbon-emitting hydropower and biomass energy in Brazil.[32]

Under the climate convention, industrial countries are urged (though not legally committed) to hold their emissions of greenhouse gases at or below the 1990 level in the year 2000. This goal applies to Eastern Europe and the former Soviet Union, as well as all the members of the Organisation for Economic Co-operation and Development (OECD). Among these 37 nations, compliance with the goal varies widely. Thanks to economic restructuring and a dramatic decline in the most energy-intensive industrial sectors, carbon emissions plummeted 20 percent in Russia, 27 percent in Poland, and 38 percent in Ukraine between 1986 and 1994; as a result, all these countries will easily meet the treaty's goal.[33]

Among western countries, Germany's

emissions are falling the fastest—by 1994, down 10 percent from the 1990 level. This stems largely from industrial restructuring and the declining use of brown coal in the eastern states. In the United Kingdom, emissions are holding roughly steady, and should be below the 1990 level in 2000, thanks to a restructuring of the electric power industry and a resulting decline in the use of coal. And in Japan, emissions remained nearly unchanged in the early nineties, a trend caused mainly by the country's recession, which has kept economic growth below 1 percent per year.[34]

These gains are offset by the rapid increase in emissions in other industrial countries. U.S. emissions are up 4.4 percent since 1990, Canada's are up 5.3 percent, and Australia's, 4.2 percent. All three nations share a pattern of low energy prices, large houses, and heavy use of automobiles. None of these countries is likely to meet the goals of the climate convention. In fact, the increase in U.S. emissions of 157 million tons between 1986 and 1994 is twice the increase in India's emissions during that period, despite the fact that the U.S. population is less than one third as big.[35]

After more than a decade of slow growth provoked by high oil prices and other factors, carbon emissions soared in many developing countries in the early nineties. Between 1990 and 1994, China's emissions went up 13 percent, Brazil's 16 percent, India's 24 percent, and South Korea's 44 percent. These trends are projected to continue, and will likely push global emissions up in the late nineties.[36]

Given the economic boom in Asia and Latin America in recent years, it is surprising that these countries are not experiencing even faster growth in emissions. In China, for example, carbon emissions are growing at only half the rate of the economy at large. One reason is that the fastest economic growth is in light manufacturing and services rather than more energy-intensive sectors. In addition, authorities have made a concerted effort to improve the energy efficiency of Chinese industry. Still, its nineteenth century–style energy system—which is heavily dependent on coal, even for home heating and cooking—makes China the world's second largest emitter of carbon. And it may surpass the United States to become number one within two decades.[37]

Under the terms of the climate convention, all countries must implement a reporting system on greenhouse gas emissions. In addition, industrial countries are supposed to introduce action plans designed to hold greenhouse gas emissions at or below the 1990 level in the year 2000. These plans vary widely in character, and only a handful appear to be having a significant effect on emissions trends.

Germany is the world's fifth-largest carbon emitter and has the most ambitious target. In fact, at the March 1995 Berlin meeting, Chancellor Kohl raised the ante to a 30-percent reduction in carbon emissions from the 1990 level by 2005. Germany's national climate plan includes a number of solid measures to promote energy efficiency in buildings, as well as an "electricity infeed law" that grants generators of renewable electricity the right to sell power to utilities at a generous price of 17 pfennigs (12¢) per kilowatt-hour. As a result, Germany installed more wind turbines in 1994 than any other country. It also has relatively high energy taxes. Its recently increased gasoline tax of about $3 per gallon, for example, is equivalent to $1,200 per ton of carbon.[38]

Yet German climate policy continues to be plagued by contradictions. Coal is the country's traditional energy source, and the industry supports tens of thousands of well-paying jobs in the Ruhr Valley. Since German coal is far too expensive to be competitive on its own, it has been supported by a "kohlepfennig" (coal penny) surcharge of 8.5 percent on the nation's power bills. This serves as a sort of reverse carbon tax (at a rate of roughly $50 per ton), encouraging use of the most carbon-intensive fuel. After German courts declared the surcharge unconstitutional, it was turned into a federal tax in January 1996—budgeted at $5.3 billion for the year. Debate continues over whether to phase it out after 2000. One option being considered is a gradually declining tax on electricity that would be used partly to subsidize coal and partly to favor carbon-free energy sources such as solar power. Germany will easily meet the year 2000 target in the treaty, but is unlikely to meet Chancellor Kohl's more ambitious goal.[39]

The brightest spots for climate policy are Denmark, the Netherlands, and Switzerland.

U.S. climate policy is weaker still. President Clinton's climate action plan, launched at a White House ceremony in 1993, includes 50 measures—mostly voluntary public-private partnerships intended to promote energy efficiency, commercialize renewable energy technologies, and encourage tree planting. Some, such as the "Green Lights" program started by the Bush administration, have committed hundreds of private companies to install efficient lighting and build energy-efficient industrial motors and personal computers. Other helpful initiatives, such as tighter appliance efficiency standards, were included in the Energy Policy Act passed by the U.S. Congress a few months earlier. The plan does not include a significant increase in U.S. gasoline taxes, which remain among the lowest in the world. Nor

does it include automobile fuel economy standards, which were left out due to the opposition of the nation's powerful automakers.[40]

Some two thirds of the emission reductions from the measures outlined in the U.S. plan depend on voluntary programs. According to an evaluation by the Natural Resources Defense Council, the strategy probably could not meet its own target even if aggressively implemented. To make matters worse, in 1994 Congress approved only half the funds called for; the 1995 Congress made even more drastic cuts, and weakened appliance and lighting standards that had been enacted by the 1992 Congress. Recent trends suggest that U.S. carbon emissions will exceed 1990 levels by as much as 10 percent in 2000.[41]

Japan has a similar climate program. It includes a number of voluntary energy efficiency efforts, as well as new efficiency standards for appliances and industrial equipment. But Japanese electric utilities intend to increase coal burning, automobile fuel economy is declining, and renewable energy technologies receive only modest support from the government. Carbon emissions have levelled off in Japan since 1990, but only because the country's economy has stagnated. Emissions may be further restrained in coming years since many Japanese companies are being pushed by the strong yen to move their factories offshore, which will tend to reduce domestic use of fossil fuels. Meeting treaty goals mainly by transferring emissions to poorer neighbors may make it difficult for Japan to lead by example when it hosts the third Conference of the Parties to the Framework Convention on Climate Change in Kyoto in 1997.[42]

The brightest spots for climate policy are three small countries: Denmark, the Netherlands, and Switzerland. Denmark has launched an Energy 2000 plan aimed at reducing carbon emissions to 20 percent below 1988 levels by 2005. Much of the reduction is expected to be achieved through a transport plan that includes a small tax on carbon emissions. In the Netherlands, the National Environmental Policy Plan aims to cut emissions 5 percent by 2000. Here, as in Denmark, the roles of natural gas and renewable energy are to be increased, and the energy efficiency of buildings and appliances improved. Already, gasoline and automobiles are heavily taxed, and 10 percent of the surface transportation budget goes to bicycle facilities. And annual subsidies to public transportation recently were raised to $5.7 billion. Switzerland's plan is also called Energy 2000, and is composed mainly of measures that industry has committed to undertake.[43]

Even these small European countries may fall short of the ambitious goals they have set, but at least they are turning words to action, and demonstrating the potential for emissions reductions in much larger nations. The challenge of reducing carbon emissions is not so much technical or even economic as it is political, led by strong opposition of industries deeply vested in the fossil fuel economy. It is not surprising that the countries with the strongest climate plans lack the large oil and coal industries that have slowed progress in other nations.

SHOWDOWN IN BERLIN

The March 1995 Conference of the Parties to the Framework Convention on Climate Change in Berlin may turn out to have been a turning point in climate politics. In the predawn hours of the final day, a group of exhausted diplomats came perilously close to allowing negotiations over next steps in implementing the convention to collapse, as the world's two leading emitters of carbon—the United States and China—battled over the wording of the final agreement. In a reversal of roles, leaders of the centrally planned and heavily coal-dependent China threatened to walk out if a strong negotiating mandate was not agreed to, while the U.S. administration argued for a weaker agreement.[44]

Shortly after 3:00 A.M., the U.S. government, with a helpful nudge from India, backed down, and the Berlin Mandate was agreed to. Diplomats were charged with developing a protocol to the climate convention aimed for the first time at reducing carbon emissions. Governments also agreed to consider a range of specific measures to reduce emissions, and to launch a series of pilot projects to transfer less carbon-intensive technologies between countries. These new commitments far from guarantee that the global atmosphere will be stabilized, but given the glacial pace of climate negotiations in the three years since Rio, the renewed commitment is encouraging.[45]

The progress in Berlin was the product of a new confluence of political forces. German environmental groups and the public at large put strong pressure on the host government throughout the conference. Their efforts complemented those of hundreds of environmental activists from around the world. Also active in Berlin were scores of local officials, representing 150 cities that are working to reduce their own emissions. At a press conference chaired by the Mayor of Toronto, these officials were critical of the lethargic efforts of national governments.[46]

Another potent force began to assert itself in Berlin: the insurance industry. A climate seminar for insurance executives preceded the conference, and representatives from leading insurers such as Munich Re and Lloyd's of London stayed on to observe the official proceedings. Their involvement reflects the fact that as disaster claims mounted in the early nineties, insurance companies became aware of their vulnerability to global warming. Since then, several have prepared internal reports on the issue. H.R. Kaufmann, the General Manager of Swiss Re, one of Europe's largest insurance companies, says: "There is a significant body of scientific evidence indicating that last year's record insured loss from natural catastrophes was not a random occurrence. . . . Failure to act would leave the [insurance] industry and its policyholders vulnerable to truly disastrous consequences."[47]

Insurance executives are worried that if climatic extremes increase the frequency of weather-related disasters, their companies will be expected to absorb the resulting financial shocks. The dilemma is that companies' rates and coverage policies have always been based on the law of averages. In the case of weather-related coverage, they look to past climate trends and assume that, over time, the frequency of catastrophes will stay the same. But a representative for the U.S.-based Allstate company says: "We purchased our catastrophe protection based on the company's historical loss record before Andrew happened. . . . We're reassessing that protection now."[48]

Since 1990, the worldwide insurance industry has paid out $48 billion for weather-related losses, compared with losses of $14 billion for the entire decade of the eighties. (See Figure 2–3.) Some industry analysts believe that another "bad year" or two, or even a single catastrophic storm, could force major companies out of business. Franklin Nutter, President of the Reinsurance Association of America, sums up his industry's dilemma: "The insurance business is first in line to be affected by climate change . . . it could bankrupt the indus-

try." As a first step, many companies are reducing their exposure in coastal real estate, wildfire-prone regions, and valleys where floods are possible, as well as on Caribbean islands. But if the industry solves its problem by abandoning certain forms of protection, then either governments will have to step in as insurers of last resort or society will lose a vital buffer against the dangers of accelerated climate change.[49]

The entry of the insurance industry into the debate on climate change is a potential watershed. As a business on the front lines of society's most risky activities, the industry has a long tradition of spurring important policy changes to help reduce society's risks. In the United States, for example, the industry's experience with fire-related claims led it to lobby for stricter building codes that reduce the frequency of fires. Similarly, insurers have fought since the early seventies for tougher safety standards for automobiles—often battling directly with auto industry lobbyists. The resulting regulations on crash-resistant bumpers, seat belts, and air bags have saved tens of thousands of lives—and avoided billions of dollars in insurance losses.[50]

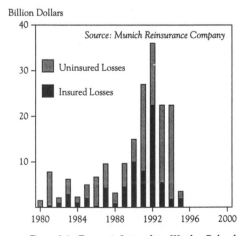

Figure 2-3. Economic Losses from Weather-Related Natural Disasters Worldwide, 1980-95

With this history in mind, industry leaders have begun to argue that insurance companies should take a more direct role in global climate policy. In a follow-up report on the Berlin conference, a representative of Lloyd's of London said: "It is thus probable that the insurance industry is going to have to take some initiatives by itself, or along with the banking industry."[51]

Another voice for action that asserted itself in Berlin was the developing world, led, ironically, by its smallest members. For several years, the Alliance of Small Island States (AOSIS)—some 36 nations that are particularly threatened by rising seas—has been active in climate negotiations. Ieremia Tabai, former president of Kiribati, observes: "If the greenhouse effect raises sea levels by one meter it will virtually do away with Kiribati. . . . In 50 or 60 years, my country will not be here." In Berlin, AOSIS tabled a proposal during the first week that would commit industrial countries to reduce their emissions by 20 percent.[52]

Midway through the conference, the Group of 77 (G77)—led by nations such as Brazil, China, Egypt, India, Malaysia, and the Philippines—broke away from their oil-producing colleagues and endorsed the AOSIS proposal. Their motivation was clear. Senator Heherson Alvarez of the Philippines, who earlier chaired a climate conference of Asian and Pacific leaders, said: "It is the small island states, coastal and archipelagic nations of the Asia Pacific region which are most susceptible [to] climate change."[53]

The resulting G77 proposal, dubbed the Green Paper, reshaped the diplomatic landscape in Berlin. Environmental and clean energy groups applauded it, but governments were deeply split. European officials, including conference chair and German environment minister Angela Merkel, welcomed the Green Paper and supported many of its elements. Kuwait and Saudi Arabia, however, expressed outrage, as did the United States, Australia, and other "carbon club" members who were fighting for a watered-down mandate. Strong behind-the-scenes lobbying by automobile, electric power, and oil companies, and by their conservative allies in the U.S. Congress, seemed to have turned the tide in a U.S. administration that once prided itself for leadership on the climate issue.[54]

Insurance executives are worried that if climatic extremes increase the frequency of disasters, their companies will be expected to absorb the financial shocks.

Unlike the situation in Rio in 1992, when the Europeans gave in to the United States on the question of numerical commitments in the climate convention, this time the Europeans held fast. The final agreement, known as the Berlin Mandate, instructs governments to negotiate a treaty protocol "to elaborate policies and measures, as well as to set quantified limitation and reduction objectives within specified time-frames such as 2005, 2010, and 2020." Likely to be called the Kyoto Protocol, this agreement is to be signed at the third conference of the parties in Japan in 1997.[55]

In Berlin, governments implicitly acknowledged that substantial reductions in emissions are needed, and that most of the climate plans developed so far are inadequate. Still, it remains to be seen how strong and specific a protocol will be agreed to in 1997, since disagreements between the United States and its European allies arose once again at follow-on negotiations in Geneva in August 1995. Approaches vary widely not only on the question of whether to adopt binding post-2000 emission targets, but on whether to begin tackling the policy changes needed to lower emissions: reducing fossil fuel subsidies, raising energy taxes, and lowering market barriers to new energy technologies.[56]

Another issue on which progress was made in Berlin is the role developing countries will play in the effort to lower emissions. With their economies still growing rapidly, most of these nations are reluctant to adopt carbon emissions limits, but some industrial countries argue that the most cost-effective emissions reductions can be achieved in developing nations, whose energy systems are often highly inefficient. Consequently, they have proposed a concept known as joint implementation, which is intended to allow countries to offset their own emissions by investing in clean energy projects or planting trees elsewhere. Developing nations have opposed this concept, arguing that it allows richer nations to avoid responsibility for climate change. The United States and Norway, on the other hand, have supported joint implementation as a way to promote technology exports and take the heat off their own carbon-intensive sectors.[57]

The world is falling well short of the goals outlined in the climate convention.

The compromise reached in Berlin was to establish a pilot phase of joint implementation projects through 1999, during which countries will not be permitted to accumulate credits for the emission reductions achieved. Still, unless and until there are legally binding carbon limits, joint implementation will remain a token means of lowering the 6 billion tons of carbon released into the atmosphere each year. The fact that this divisive North-South issue may now be set aside for a few years is one of the small successes of Berlin.[58]

BREAKTHROUGH

The central goal of the Framework Convention on Climate Change is stated clearly in its second article: "The ultimate objective of this Convention . . . is to achieve . . . stabilization of greenhouse gas concentrations in the atmosphere at a level that would prevent dangerous anthropogenic interference in the climate system. Such a level should be achieved within a time-frame sufficient to allow ecosystems to adapt naturally to climate change, to ensure that food production is not threatened and to enable economic development to proceed in a sustainable manner."[59]

It is clear from the latest scientific assessments and the ongoing increase in greenhouse gas emissions in scores of countries that the world is falling well short of the goals outlined in the climate convention. After more than a dozen official international climate meetings, one global summit, billions of dollars of scientific research, and a host of national climate plans, the impact on global emission trends has been minimal at best. Government policies have been weak to date, as has the commitment of the private sector.

So far, the best that can be said is that the convention may have scared a few investors away from coal projects or that some governments have been encouraged to implement modest programs to accelerate energy efficiency improvements and commercialize carbon-free energy sources. To achieve the roughly 80-percent reduction in greenhouse gas emissions needed during the next half-century to meet the treaty's central goal, the world energy system will have to follow an entirely different trajectory than that now projected by most governments and international agencies. The International Energy Agency, for example, projected in 1995 that without new policy initiatives, world emissions of carbon will exceed the 1990 level by 30–40 percent in 2010.[60]

The controversy over how practical—or expensive—it will be to follow a different energy path has become as heated an element of the international climate debate as the scientific questions. On one side are economists and fossil fuel lobbyists who use econometric models to suggest that holding carbon emissions steady during the next few decades could cost hundreds of billions of dollars and cut economic output by 1.5–2.5 percent. On the other side are scientists, engineers, environmentalists, and energy entrepreneurs who argue that once market barriers are removed, new energy technologies are commercialized, and environmental costs recognized, a low-carbon economy will turn out to be more economical than today's is.[61]

The shape of the practical low-carbon energy economy that could be achieved in the next few decades has been sketched out in recent studies. Its essence would be high levels of energy efficiency throughout the economy, a decentralized system of power generators whose waste heat would be used by homes and industry, and increased reliance on methane gas to replace oil and coal. This is possible with technologies already on the market—such as gas turbines and electronic light bulbs—or that soon will be, such as fuel cells, flywheels, and rooftop solar cells. To illustrate the potential, if a commercial building that gets its heat from a typical natural gas furnace and its electricity from a coal-fired power plant were retrofitted with efficient windows, lighting, electronic controls, and an internal gas-fired heat-and-power system, the carbon emissions associated with meeting its energy needs could be cut by 80–90 percent—all using off-the-shelf technology.[62]

Not all the changes needed to stabilize global atmospheric concentrations of greenhouse gases will be so simple or fast, and most will require sizable up-front investments. But over time, most of these costs can be offset by the lower operating and fuel costs of the new systems, as well as the avoided cost of pollution. During the next 25–30 years, virtually all of today's power plants, refineries, automobiles, appliances, and factories will have to be replaced at least once, providing an opportunity to install much less carbon-intensive technologies. Moreover, the macroeconomic models used in most studies of greenhouse gas abatement have a central flaw: they assume that the current path is economical and unfettered by market barriers, and that technology is static. Moreover, they assume that policymakers will mindlessly focus on carbon taxes alone to bring emissions down, ignoring a range of other reforms.[63]

Some of the biggest gains in slowing carbon emissions can be made using the most obvious of reforms—eliminating the billions of dollars of subsidies to fossil fuel use now in place; getting rid of the rigid monopolies that control the electricity, gas, and oil industries in most nations; and giving consumers a say in the energy marketplace. In states and countries where this has been tried, it has almost always resulted in a combination that would surprise many economists: declining emissions and falling energy bills. California, the Netherlands, and the United Kingdom are good examples.[64]

The next critical step is a system of targeted financial incentives and penalties to spur investment in new technologies. Examples include taxing vehicles based on their emissions profile, and perhaps providing rebates for the cleanest models; allowing purveyors of clean electricity to sell it at a reasonable price, as Germany currently does; and adjusting design and building fees so that architects, engineers, and builders are rewarded for the efficiency of their products. Such programs could be paid for out of the energy savings, or subsidized in part by a tax on carbon emissions that would be raised gradually over time. (See Chapter 10.)

Although national, regional, and local governments have much of the responsibility for lowering greenhouse gas emissions, the Framework Convention on Climate Change could play an important role in shaping those policies. A protocol prescribing reductions in emissions would help motivate such changes, but the Convention could also be used to implement specific measures internationally, such as carbon taxes, appliance and automobile efficiency standards and incentives, and technology transfer programs. Already, technical advisory panels are being formed to consider such options, which could be included in the 1997 Kyoto Protocol.

Despite the prospect that investments in new energy technologies could strengthen many economies, some industries—particularly in the United States—seem to be in a state of denial. The Global Climate Coalition (which represents not just the coal and oil industries, but automakers, electric utilities, and the National Association of Manufacturers) says: "The [climate] issue remains shrouded in controversy, intrigue and misunderstanding. . . . The cost of inaction is very speculative and remote in time." Most of the efforts of this group appear to be aimed at obstructing and delaying the implementation of the treaty.[65]

This late-twentieth-century version of the flat earth society may delay the effort to slow global climate change, but it may also damage the prospects of its corporate members. Scientific evidence suggests that the next couple of decades will see unprecedented rates of climate change that could disrupt regional weather patterns. As individuals and companies begin to suffer the effects of climate disruption, they will demand immediate action, as they have when much milder environmental crises have been identified. Mark Mansley of the Delphi Group, a London-based financial firm, concluded in a 1994 study that "climate change presents major long term risks to the carbon fuel industry. These risks have not yet been adequately discounted by the financial markets. . . . In the worst case [climate change] could seriously affect returns on a number of investments."[66]

One result of the ostrich-like approach of the most carbon-intensive industries is that their political base is already narrowing. A new political coalition that favors strong action on the climate issue is beginning to take shape—ranging from environmental groups to small island states threatened by rising seas and multinational insurance and banking companies. Jeremy Leggett, an environmental scientist with Greenpeace International, has called for "solidarity among the risk community," and is working actively to organize it.[67]

It is easy to imagine how such concerned companies and groups could mobilize in the near future and begin to exercise their substantial economic and political clout. If banks and insurance companies were to dump some of their extensive holdings in oil and coal, or actively invest some of their funds in new, highly energy-efficient and renewable energy technologies—a sort of climate venture fund—they could spur the development of a less carbon-intensive energy system. And if they begin to lobby actively for energy policy change before national parliaments, the climate policy glacier may begin to slip as rapidly as some real ones in Antarctica now are.

Observers in the diplomatic community point out that the ozone issue languished for years until the spring of 1988, when dramatic new scientific evidence emerged at the same time that some of the world's leading chemical companies realized that they could make more money by marketing substitutes for ozone-depleting chemicals. Over a period of just three weeks, they reversed their position on phasing out such chemicals. Soon, world leaders, including British Prime Minister Margaret Thatcher, were calling for swift action, and in 1990 the treaty on the depletion of the ozone layer was revised to call for a complete end to production of the most damaging chemicals by 2000, which has since led to sweeping changes in the chemical industry.[68]

In the past, it has generally required some kind of crisis before the world responded to a major new threat—a pattern that was seen with acid rain in Europe in the early to mid-eighties and with ozone depletion at the global level later that decade. It is unfortunate, but all too common, that humanity seems incapable of taking such steps on the basis of scientific studies. The challenge now is to take advantage of the calm before the storm: readying the policy machinery for action as soon as the political will coalesces.

3

Forging a Sustainable Water Strategy

Sandra Postel

In early May 1995, the government of Mexico submitted a loan request to the United States. Unlike the widely publicized loan following the peso crisis in late 1994, however, this request was not for dollars but for water—some 2.8 million cubic meters from the Rio Grande River. Much of northern Mexico was in the third year of a drought that had already killed crops and cattle. Rising salt levels in the river were killing fish and other aquatic life. Because of inadequate planning, Mexico had used all but about 5 percent of its share of reservoir water set by a 1944 treaty with the United States, so the nation was facing even greater losses if it did not get additional supplies. Although the U.S. government had just a few months earlier promised Mexico $20 billion to shore up its economy, it decided against the water loan. It deferred to the concerns of Texas that a loan to Mexico might leave Texan farm-

ers without enough water for themselves.[1]

Viewed in isolation, the Mexico-Texas water tangle is hardly world-shattering news. But as a foreshadowing of emerging trends, it says a great deal about how water scarcity is likely to shape world affairs in the years ahead. The gap between human demands for water and available supplies is widening persistently in many parts of the world. Water tables are falling, rivers are drying up, and competition for dwindling supplies is increasing. Especially when nature delivers a drought, there is often little cushion left to lean on. And these stresses will inevitably intensify as world population expands by a projected 2.6 billion people over the next 30 years.[2]

As the U.S.–Mexico example shows in microcosm, water scarcity threatens three fundamental aspects of human security—food production, the health of the aquatic environment, and social and political stability. Evidence from many parts of the world suggests that these dangers are real and growing. Yet nei-

Sandra Postel is Director of the Global Water Policy Project in Cambridge, Mass., and a Senior Fellow at Worldwatch Institute.

ther the public nor political leaders appear to comprehend these threats, much less to have taken steps to address them.

An old Inca proverb says, "The frog does not drink up the pond in which it lives." It is a simple wisdom that captures what is rapidly emerging as a critical challenge of modern times—quenching the growing thirst of the human enterprise while protecting water's fundamental ecological support functions. Fortunately, the process of creating a more sustainable water future presents enormous opportunities for improving quality of life and the stability of communities.

WATER FOR FOOD

Without water, life and growth cease—a stark reality that may be taking on ever greater importance: just as the world's food needs are climbing by record amounts, it is becoming increasingly difficult to supply more water to farmers.

Crop production is a highly water-intensive activity. Worldwide, agriculture uses about 65 percent of all the water removed from rivers, lakes, and aquifers for human activities, compared with 25 percent for industries and 10 percent for households and municipalities. It takes about 1,000 tons of water to produce a ton of harvested grain. This figure includes the moisture transpired by crops and evaporated from the surrounding soil, but not the water that is lost because of inefficiencies in irrigation methods. As such, it represents an approximate minimum water requirement for the production of grain, the source of roughly half of human calories.[3]

Crops get the moisture they need from natural rainfall, irrigation, or some combination of these two sources. Because irrigation offers good control over water, it often allows two to three harvests per year from the same parcel of land, making irrigated areas disproportionately important to global food security. Irrigated lands account for only 16 percent of the world's cropland, but they yield some 40 percent of the world's food.[4]

As of 1995, the world as a whole was consuming directly or indirectly (through animal products) an average of just over 300 kilograms of grain per person a year. At this level of consumption, growing enough grain for the 90 million people now added to the planet each year requires an additional 27 billion cubic meters of water annually—roughly 1.3 times the average annual flow of the Colorado River, or about half that of China's Huang He (Yellow River). Grain consumption per person varies widely by country, but assuming the global average remains the same as today, it will take an additional 780 billion cubic meters of water to meet the grain requirement of the projected world population in 2025—more than nine times the annual flow of the Nile River.[5]

Where this water is to come from on a sustainable basis is not obvious. Using more natural rainfall to enhance crop production is constrained by the lack of expansion of cropland area. Grainland area peaked in 1981, so greater use of rainwater has been limited mainly to increasing yields on existing rain-fed lands. Much of the crop production needed to meet future food needs would thus seem to depend on an expansion of irrigation. But serious constraints exist here as well. Falling water tables, depleted river flows, the lack of economical and environmentally sound sites for new supply projects, and rapidly growing urban demands are all placing limits on the availability of water for agriculture.[6]

Groundwater overpumping and aquifer depletion are now occurring in many of the world's most important crop-producing regions. (See Table 3–1.) This not only signals limits to expanding groundwater use, it means that a portion of the world's current food supply is produced by using water unsustainably—and can therefore not be counted as reliable over the long term. A farmer cannot indefinitely pump an aquifer faster than it is being replenished. As water tables drop, the resource becomes either too costly to continue pumping or too salty to irrigate crops as

Table 3-1. Groundwater Depletion in Major Regions of the World, Circa 1990

Region/Aquifer	Estimates of Depletion
High Plains Aquifer System, United States	Net depletion to date of this aquifer that underlies nearly 20 percent of all U.S. irrigated land totals some 325 billion cubic meters, roughly 15 times the average annual flow of the Colorado River. More than two thirds of this occurred in the Texas High Plains, where irrigated area dropped by 26 percent between 1979 and 1989. Current depletion is estimated at 12 billion cubic meters a year.
California, United States	Groundwater overdraft averages 1.6 billion cubic meters per year, amounting to 15 percent of the state's annual net groundwater use. Two thirds of the depletion occurs in the Central Valley, the country's vegetable basket.
Southwestern United States	Water tables have dropped more than 120 meters east of Phoenix, Arizona. Projections for Albuquerque, New Mexico, show that if groundwater withdrawals continue at current levels, water tables will drop an additional 20 meters by 2020.
Mexico City and Valley of Mexico	Pumping exceeds natural recharge by 50–80 percent, which has led to falling water tables, aquifer compaction, land subsidence, and damage to surface structures.
Arabian Peninsula	Groundwater use is nearly three times greater than recharge. Saudi Arabia depends on nonrenewable groundwater for roughly 75 percent of its water, which includes irrigation of 2–4 million tons of wheat per year. At the depletion rates projected for the nineties, exploitable groundwater reserves would be exhausted within about 50 years.
African Sahara	Vast nonrecharging aquifers underlie North Africa. Current depletion is estimated at 10 billion cubic meters a year.
India	Water tables are falling throughout much of Punjab and Haryana states, India's breadbasket. In Gujarat, groundwater levels declined in 90 percent of observation wells monitored during the eighties. Large drops have also occurred in Tamil Nadu.
North China	The water table beneath portions of Beijing has dropped 37 meters over the last four decades. North China now has eight regions of overdraft, covering 1.5 million hectares, much of it productive irrigated farmland.
Southeast Asia	Significant overdraft has occurred in and around Bangkok, Manila, and Jakarta. Overpumping has caused land to subside beneath Bangkok at a rate of 5–10 centimeters a year for the past two decades.

SOURCE: Global Water Policy Project and Worldwatch Institute, based on sources in endnote 7.

it is pulled up from greater depths, or it simply runs out altogether.[7]

Besides depleting supplies, groundwater mining can lead to a variety of other irreversible effects. In coastal areas, overpumping can cause salt water to invade freshwater aquifers, contaminating supplies. This has occurred in the western Indian state of Gujarat, where irrigators have heavily overpumped local aquifers. In Israel, decades of overpumping have caused seawater to invade the nation's coastal aquifer, a key freshwater source. Israeli water officials predict that 20 percent of coastal wells may need to be closed within a few years.[8]

In some cases, groundwater depletion can permanently reduce the earth's natural capacity to store water. The extraction of water may cause an aquifer's geologic materials to compact, eliminating the pores and spaces that held the water. The loss of this storage capacity is irreversible, and it carries a high cost. In California, for example, compaction of overdrafted aquifers in the Central Valley has resulted in a loss of nearly 25 billion cubic meters of storage capacity—equal to more than 40 percent of the combined storage capacity of all human-made surface reservoirs statewide.[9]

As with groundwater, many of the planet's major rivers are suffering from overexploitation. In Asia, where the majority of population growth—and thus food needs—will be centered, many rivers are completely tapped out during the drier part of the year, when irrigation is so essential. According to a 1993 World Bank study, "many examples of basins exist throughout the Asia region where essentially no water is lost to the sea during much of the dry season." These include most rivers in India—among them the Ganges, a principal water source for densely populated and rapidly growing South Asia.[10]

Rising water development costs and the declining number of environmentally sound sites for the construction of dams and river diversions are also contributing to a worldwide slowdown in irrigation expansion. Per capita irrigated area was steady or increasing during most of modern times, but it peaked in 1978 and has declined by more than 5 percent since then.[11]

In addition, much irrigated land is losing productivity or coming out of production altogether as a result of salinization, the steady buildup of salts in the root zone of irrigated soils. Although no firm global estimate of the problem exists, some 25 million hectares—more than 10 percent of world irrigated area—appears to suffer from salt buildup serious enough to lower crop yields. Moreover, salinization is estimated to be spreading at a rate of up to 2 million hectares a year, offsetting a good portion of the gains achieved by irrigation expansion.[12]

More than 10 percent of world irrigated area appears to suffer from salt buildup serious enough to lower crop yields.

And finally, agriculture is losing some of its existing supplies to cities as population growth and urbanization push up urban water demands. Where this water shift results from marginal lands or nonfood crops coming out of production, or from gains in irrigation efficiency, it can be beneficial environmentally and have little impact on food security. But with competition for water increasing in many areas, the ultimate effect on food production and regional economies remains to be seen. In California, for instance, a 1957 state water plan projected that 8 million hectares of irrigated land would ultimately be developed state-wide; yet the state's irrigated area peaked in 1981 at 3.9 million hectares, less than half this amount. Officials in California now project a net decline in irrigated area of nearly 162,000 hectares, with most of the loss due to urbanization as the population expands from 30 million to a projected 49 million by 2020.[13]

Worldwide, the number of urban dwellers will likely double to 5 billion by 2025. With political power and money concentrated in the cities and with insufficient water to meet all demands, governments will face strong pressures to shift water out of agriculture—even as food demands are rising rapidly. In Thailand, for example, water supplies are chronically short in the Chao Phraya basin, which supplies Bangkok. Demand already exceeds supplies, flows for navigation are consistently below optimum, and groundwater levels beneath Bangkok are dropping fast. After a steady climb throughout the seventies, the dry-season crop area in the basin peaked in 1982. Similarly, in China water supplies already are being siphoned away from farmlands surrounding Beijing in order to meet rising urban and industrial demands. With some 300 Chinese cities now short of water, this shift is bound to become more pronounced.[14]

When droughts strike, as they inevitably do, governments also typically favor urban residents over farms when rationing scarce supplies. Many farmers in drought-stricken northern Mexico had their supplies cut off in May 1995, and deliveries had not resumed as of early October. The main irrigation season there is from January through April, so if substantial rains did not arrive during the last quarter of 1995, they are likely facing serious problems in early 1996. There is still the possibility of a minimal water loan from Texas to Mexico, but it

would be for domestic uses, not for agriculture.[15]

Unfortunately, no one has tallied the effect on future food production of the progressive shift of water from agriculture to cities combined with the many forms of unsustainable water use just discussed. Until governments make such assessments, they will have no clear idea how secure their agricultural foundations are, no ability to predict accurately their future food import requirements, and no sense of how or when to prepare for the economic and social disruption that will ensue as farmers run out of water. As Klaus Lampe, general director of the International Rice Research Institute in the Philippines, warns: "Thoughtlessness and ignorance regarding tomorrow's food supply are among the most dangerous of the many factors influencing our political, economic and environmental systems."[16]

DECLINE OF THE AQUATIC ENVIRONMENT

With a deep snowpack in the Colorado Rockies and a spring of heavy rains, 1995 looked to be a year of abundant water in the Colorado River basin. Runoff during the months of April to July was 50 percent greater than normal. Still, the river that carved the Grand Canyon ended up suffering its usual fate: it ran dry before it reached the sea.

Only in years of extremely high precipitation in its watershed does the Colorado run all the way to its final destination, the Sea of Cortez (known north of the border as the Gulf of California). In most years, what remains of its flow after 10 major dams and several large diversions is a paltry trickle that literally disappears into the surrounding desert. (See Figure 3–1.) Much of the river delta's once-abundant wildlife is gone. Fisheries in the Sea of Cortez have declined dramatically. And the delta communities supported by the river are fading with the ecosystem around them.[17]

What has happened to the Colorado is but one example of a disturbing and widespread decline of the aquatic environment. Globally, water use has more than tripled since 1950, and the answer to this rising demand generally has been to build more and bigger water supply projects—especially dams and river diversions. Around the world, the number of large dams (those more than 15 meters high) has climbed from just over 5,000 in 1950 to roughly 38,000 today. More than 85 percent of the large dams now standing have been built during the last 35 years.[18]

This is a massive change in the global aquatic environment in a very short period of time. Many rivers now resemble elaborate plumbing works, with the timing and amount of flow completely controlled, like water from a faucet, so as to maximize the rivers' benefits for humans. But while modern engineering has been remarkably successful at getting water to people and farms when and where they need it, it has failed to protect the fundamental ecological functions of rivers and aquatic systems. The consequences of this failure are just beginning to become clear—from degraded river deltas and species on the brink of extinction to shrinking inland lakes and disappearing wetlands.

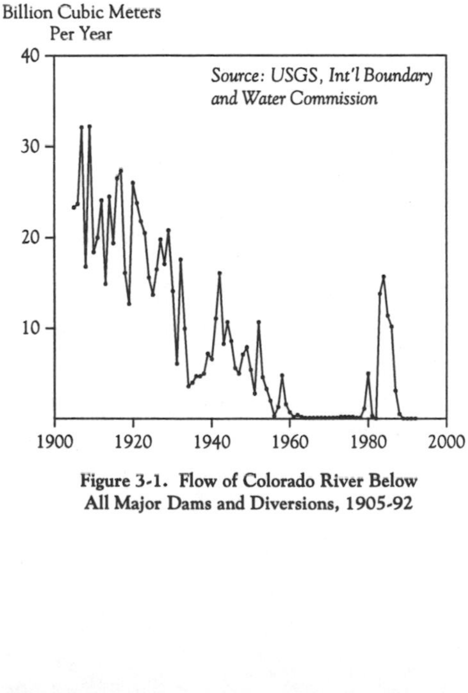

In California, for example, water development has decimated aquatic systems and the life dependent on them. The state has lost 95 percent of its wetlands, and populations of migratory birds and waterfowl, which depend on such areas for food and habitat, have dropped from 60 million around 1950 to just 3 million today. Fish, which are often good indicators of aquatic conditions, have suffered greatly from extensive river damming and destruction of spawning habitat. Overall, California's salmon and steelhead population has fallen by an estimated 80 percent.[19]

Such environmental damage can have a devastating effect on people's livelihoods, particularly in resource-based and subsistence economies. In the region of the Colorado River delta, for instance, the survival of the Cucapá, or "people of the river," is at risk. Just 40–50 families remain south of the border. With little work, many of the younger tribal members have migrated to the cities. Traditionally, the Cucapá ate fish three times a day; now they are lucky to have it once a week. Since the river water has become too salty to grow melons, squash, and other traditional crops, their diets have become less healthy. As one expert on the Cucapá told a *National Geographic* writer several years ago, these people "have been around for a couple thousand years. But

Billion Cubic Meters
  Per Year

Source: USGS, Int'l Boundary and Water Commission

Figure 3-1. Flow of Colorado River Below All Major Dams and Diversions, 1905-92

barring a miracle, you're seeing the last of them."[20]

In South Asia, the mighty Ganges no longer reaches its natural outlet in the Bay of Bengal during the dry season because of India's heavy diversions upstream. The lack of fresh water flowing out to sea has caused the rapid advance of a saline front across the western portion of the river delta in Bangladesh, which is damaging valuable mangrove forests and fish habitat, important resources for the local economy. The Sundarbans, one of the world's largest mangrove forests, is also home to the threatened Bengal tiger. Unless more water is allowed to flow into the delta during the dry season, damage to vegetation and fisheries will continue, spreading disruption to the area's economy.[21]

In the Nile River basin, the High Dam at Aswan was constructed during the sixties to provide virtually complete control over the Nile's waters and a crucial hedge against drought. Lake Nassar is able to store fully two years of the Nile's average annual flow. Not surprisingly, however, the High Dam has greatly altered the river system. Out of 47 commercial fish species in the Nile prior to the dam's construction, only 17 were still harvested a decade after its completion. The annual sardine harvest in the eastern Mediterranean dropped by 83 percent, a likely side effect of the reduction in nutrient-rich silt entering that part of the sea.[22]

One of the most threatening long-term consequences of the disruption of the Nile ecosystem is that the river delta, so essential to Egypt's economy, is slowly falling into the sea: since the completion of the Aswan Dam, and the trapping of virtually all the Nile's silt in Lake Nassar, the delta has been in retreat. Global warming and the anticipated rise

in sea level that higher temperatures will bring greatly increase the threat of inundation. Much of the northern delta lies only 3–4 meters above sea level. Researchers at the Woods Hole Oceanographic Institution in Massachusetts calculate that Egypt could lose up to 19 percent of its habitable land within about 60 years, displacing as much as 16 percent of its population—which by then would likely total well over 120 million—and wiping out some 15 percent of its economic activity.[23]

Some of the most dramatic consequences of river depletion occur where rivers empty into inland lakes or seas. In the Aral Sea basin, what was once the planet's fourth largest lake has lost half its area and three fourths of its volume because of excessive river diversions to grow cotton in the desert. Prior to 1960, the Amu Dar'ya and Syr Dar'ya poured 55 billion cubic meters of water a year into the Aral. Between 1981 and 1990, their combined flow into the sea dropped to an average of 7 billion cubic meters, just 6 percent of their total annual flow. (See Figure 3–2.) Much of the

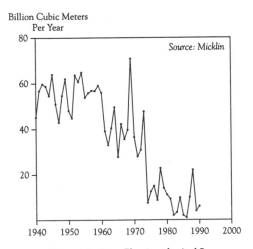

Figure 3-2. River Flow into the Aral Sea, 1940-90

time, these rivers now run virtually dry in their lower reaches.[24]

These heavy diversions have severely degraded both river deltas. According to Philip Micklin of Western Michigan University, a leading U.S. authority on the Aral Sea basin, the tugay forests—willow, tamarisk, and other water-loving trees and shrubs that are vital habitat for the region's animal life—have been decimated. Wetlands have shrunk by 85 percent, which, combined with high levels of agricultural chemical pollution, has greatly reduced waterfowl populations. In the Syr Dar'ya delta, the number of nesting bird species has fallen from an estimated 173 to 38.[25]

The still-unfolding chain of ecological destruction ranks the Aral Sea as one of the planet's greatest environmental tragedies. Some 20 of the 24 fish species there have disappeared, and the fish catch, which totalled 44,000 tons a year in the fifties and supported some 60,000 jobs, has dropped to zero. Abandoned fishing villages dot the sea's former coastline. Each year, winds pick up 40–150 million tons of a toxic dust-salt mixture from the dry sea bed and dump them on the surrounding farmland, harming or killing crops. The low river flows have concentrated salts and toxic chemicals, making water supplies hazardous to drink and contributing to rampant disease. The population of Muynak, a former fishing town, is down from 40,-000 several decades ago to just 12,000 today. The 28,000 people who have fled are "ecological refugees" in the truest sense.[26]

What has happened in the Aral Sea basin shows vividly how damage to economy, community, and human health can follow close on the heels of ecological destruction. It is a linkage poised to repeat as human demands on the earth's water bodies further unravel the workings of the aquatic environment.

COMPETITION AND CONFLICT

A third major threat to human security arises from the heightening competition for water both within and between countries as supplies increasingly fall short of needs. A new politics of scarcity is emerging as farms and cities, states and provinces, and neighboring countries compete for a limited or shrinking pool. Neither governments nor the international community is prepared for the internal social disruption and external conflict that could result as water scarcity deepens and spreads.

Three principal forces conspire to create scarcity and its potential to incite violent conflict: the depletion or degradation of the resource, which shrinks the "resource pie"; population growth, which forces the pie to be divided into smaller slices; and unequal distribution or access, which means that some get larger slices than others. Although all three often play a part, it appears that unequal distribution often has the most important role.[27]

The still-unfolding chain of ecological destruction ranks the Aral Sea as one of the planet's greatest environmental tragedies.

For example, Israel strictly limits Arab access to groundwater in the occupied West Bank, which has fueled tensions. On a per capita basis, Israeli settlers there use four times as much water as neighboring Arabs. Israel has not permitted Arabs to drill new wells for agricultural purposes since 1967, even though more than 30 irrigation wells have been drilled for Israeli settlers. Many Israeli settlements even boast swimming pools. While the links are not clear-cut, it seems likely that inequitable water rights contributed to the anger seen in the Palestinian *intifada* (uprising) on the West Bank. With the agreement reached in late September 1995 that continues transferring authority to the Palestinians, Israel now recognizes Palestinian water rights on the West Bank and has agreed to meet specified future Palestinian water demands, seeming to pave the way for peaceful resolution of this water dispute.[28]

In some cases, dams and other development projects intended to improve conditions for agriculture or the economy can end up fueling tensions if newly created access to the scarce resource worsens existing inequalities, further marginalizes the poor, or creates opportunities for the rich to "capture" the resource. In the Senegal River basin, for example, farming, herding, and fishing traditionally depended on the river's yearly cycle of flooding. In the seventies, concern about chronic food shortages and drought led governments in the region to seek financing for the Manantali Dam in order to expand irrigated agriculture, hydropower production, and river transport. Desiring to capture the benefits that new irrigation water would bring to the land adjacent to the river, the Mauritanian elite—mainly consisting of white Moors—invalidated the rights of black Africans to continue their flood-based activities along the river. Ethnic violence broke out in both Senegal and Mauritania, with the Moors forcing 70,-000 black Mauritanians to move into Senegal.[29]

In the water-short Jodhpur district of Rajasthan, India, village wells tapped by the rural poor are drying up as deeper wells to supply the cities have caused water tables to drop, and as groundwater has increasingly been used on chili peppers and other water-intensive crops grown for commerical sale. As a result of

the poor's loss of access to common water sources, local demand for food and fodder is not being met, villagers take on health-threatening work as low-wage laborers in the quarry mines, and women spend an average of four hours a day collecting water. As researcher Michael Goldman points out: "Peasant families have lost their access to groundwater and have had to watch their herds die, land deteriorate, and their families and communities split up. . . . The privatization of the rural commons is intensifying exploitative social relations and degrading ecological relations."[30]

Although most of the tension and strife over water scarcity to date has occurred within countries, the potential for hostility and conflict between countries is rising as well. Unique among strategic resources, water flows easily across political boundaries. Many countries depend on river water from upstream neighbors for a substantial portion of their surface supplies. (See Table 3–2.) Particularly in the face of population growth and rising water demands, these countries can become highly vulnerable to decisions by upstream countries to siphon off more water for themselves. According to Thomas Homer-Dixon of the University of Toronto, codirector of the Project on Environmental Change and Acute Conflict, the evidence suggests that "the renewable resource most likely to stimulate interstate resource war is river water."[31]

River basins most likely to be hot spots for hostility are those in which the river is shared by at least two countries, water is insufficient to meet all projected demands, and there is no recognized treaty governing the allocation of water among all basin countries. Examples of such potential hot spots include the Ganges, the Nile, the Jordan, the Tigris-Euphrates, and the Amu Dar'ya and Syr Dar'ya in Central Asia.

Outright conflict has the greatest po-

Table 3-2. Dependence on Imported Surface Water, Selected Countries

Country	Share of Total Flow Originating Outside of Border
	(percent)
Turkmenistan	98
Egypt	97
Hungary	95
Mauritania	95
Botswana	94
Bulgaria	91
Uzbekistan	91
Netherlands	89
Gambia	86
Cambodia	82
Syria	79
Sudan	77
Niger	68
Iraq	66
Bangladesh	42
Thailand	39
Jordan	36
Senegal	34
Israel[1]	21

[1]Includes only flows originating outside current borders; a significant additional share of Israel's fresh water originates from occupied, disputed territories.

SOURCES: Turkmenistan and Uzbekistan figures from David R. Smith, "Climate Change, Water Supply, and Conflict in the Aral Sea Basin," presented at the PriAral Workshop 1994, San Diego State University, March 1994; others from Peter H. Gleick, *Water in Crisis: A Guide to the World's Fresh Water Resources* (New York: Oxford University Press, 1993).

tential to emerge when the downstream (most vulnerable) nation is militarily stronger than the upstream (water-controlling) nation and feels that its interests are threatened. Prior to 1967, for example, Israel was in a disadvantageous position with regard to water, felt its interests were at risk, and was relatively more powerful than its immediate neighbors. Syrian attempts to divert the

Banias, one of three sources of the upper Jordan River, contributed to rising tensions and a series of armed confrontations with Israel immediately preceding the Six Day War in 1967. Israel's victory in that conflict included gaining control over two areas of strategic water importance—the West Bank aquifer and the Golan Heights, which feeds the Banias into the Jordan River and also provides access to the site of an intended Jordanian dam on the Yarmouk River.[32]

Egypt is perhaps more vulnerable than any other country to a reduction in water supplies. It depends on Nile water flowing into its territory for 97 percent of its surface supplies. With a population of 60 million climbing by 1 million every nine months, some 2.5 million hectares of cropland totally dependent on irrigation, and a current water demand that is very near the limits of the supply, any cutoff of Nile flow would be highly disruptive, if not disastrous. University of Pennsylvania professor Thomas Naff says: "It is an axiomatic policy of every Egyptian regime that it will go to war, if necessary, to prevent either of its closest upper riparian neighbors, Sudan and Ethiopia, from reducing in any way the flow of the Nile."[33]

Until recently, Egypt was at minimal risk of suffering such reductions, except, of course, from drought. But Ethiopia, which controls 86 percent of the Nile's total flow, now has the political stability and capacity to mobilize resources to store and use water for agricultural and economic advancement. An estimated 3.7 million hectares of Ethiopia's land is potentially irrigable. Using Nile water to irrigate even half this area could reduce downstream flows by some 9 billion cubic meters per year—equal to 16 percent of Egypt's current annual Nile supply—and potentially much more. Moreover, Ethiopia plans to expand hydropower production, with some 80 percent of future hydro schemes located on Nile tributaries. Thus Egypt seems increasingly vulnerable to a loss of Nile water.[34]

A somewhat similar situation exists in the Aral Sea basin. Afghanistan, Iran, and five countries newly independent after the breakup of the Soviet Union—Kazakstan, Kyrgyzstan, Tajikistan, Turkmenistan, and Uzbekistan—form the basin and share the waters of the Amu Dar'ya and Syr Dar'ya. In addition to having to deal with the destruction of the Aral Sea ecosystem and its consequences, these countries face fundamental challenges of water security: there is not enough water in the basin to meet all demands. Disputes have already occurred between Kyrgyz and Uzbeks over water and land in the Fergana area, between Kyrgyz and Tajiks over the allocation of irrigation water, and between Turkmens and Uzbeks over the distribution of irrigation and drainage water in the Amu Dar'ya delta. At the moment, the potential for more-formal conflict seems low, since the five former Soviet countries—which account for the vast majority of the basin's water use—continue to use the water-allocation formula set by Moscow. The status quo, however, is neither equitable nor environmentally sustainable. With the added pressures of population growth and ethnic differences, water scarcity remains a potential source of violence and political instability in the region.[35]

Bangladesh suffers greatly as the last in line to receive water from the Ganges.

When downstream countries are relatively less powerful than water-controlling upstream countries, conflict may be less likely, but social and economic insecurity—which, in turn, can lead to political instability—can be great. For example, as the weaker riparian, Bangladesh will almost certainly not choose to go to war with India. But the nation suffers greatly as the last in line to receive water from the Ganges, which rises in the Himalaya of Nepal and then flows through India and Bangladesh before emptying into the Bay of Bengal.

In the early seventies, India completed the Farakka barrage to divert Ganges water to the port city of Calcutta, which reduced the flow into Bangladesh. The two nations agreed in 1977 to a short-term solution for sharing the dry-season flow, and also guaranteed Bangladesh a minimum amount of water during extremely low-flow periods. That agreement expired in 1982, and was replaced with an informal accord that did not include the guarantee clause for Bangladesh. A follow-up agreement expired in 1988. Since then, the two countries have been deadlocked, leaving Bangladesh with no assurance of minimum flows for its dry-season irrigation needs.[36]

Syria and Iraq are in a similar situation with regard to Turkey, the eastern mountains of which give rise to both the Tigris and the Euphrates Rivers. Turkey is undertaking a huge hydropower and irrigation scheme known as the GAP (after the Turkish acronym), which could reduce the Euphrates flow into Syria by 35 percent in normal years and substantially more in dry ones, besides polluting the river with irrigation drainage. Iraq, third in line for Euphrates water, would see a drop as well, and has the added worry that Syria will also take more Euphrates water.[37]

Turkey and Syria signed a protocol in 1987 that guarantees the latter nation a minimum flow of 500 cubic meters per second, about half of the Euphrates' volume at the border, but Syria wants more—a request Turkey so far has denied. In 1992, Turkish Prime Minister Suleyman Demirel reportedly remarked about Syrian requests for more Euphrates water: "We do not say we should share their oil resources. They cannot say they should share our water resources." Although the government may have a more compromising position than this rhetoric would suggest, bilateral talks have not yet produced a water-sharing agreement.[38]

SHARING THE WATERS

Any river that flows through two or more nations—as at least 214 rivers do—is supported by a watershed that cuts across political bounds. Cooperation is thus essential not only to avert conflict but to protect the aquatic environment that underpins regional economies. This is especially critical now that much of the world has entered a zero-sum game in which increasing the water available to one user means taking some away from another. Whether in the marketplace or in international politics, allowing competition alone to sort out winners and losers is a no-win proposition for all; in today's interdependent world, the spoils of victory would soon be offset by the costs of regional instability and ecological decline. As the basis of life, water requires an ethic of sharing—both with nature and with each other.[39]

Nongovernmental organizations (NGOs), independent research centers, the United Nations, and institutions such as the World Bank and the newly forming World Water Council all have a role to play in defining principles and practices of water sharing. At the moment, international law offers little concrete help in resolving water conflicts since no legal framework governs the allocation and use of international waters. Nor does it recognize beneficial use of water for ecosystems. Upstream countries, given their natural advantage, have been reluctant to accept the notion that international waters should be managed cooperatively and shared equitably. Indeed, some still hold the view that nations have "absolute sovereignty" over water within their borders and have little obligation to their neighbors.

Yet an international code of conduct for shared watercourses has steadily been evolving, primarily through the work of the private International Law Association, which in 1966 laid down the Helsinki Rules (since revised), and the United Nations International Law Commission, which in 1991 issued its draft recommendations. Both put forth a number of important principles, including four obligations: to inform and consult with water-sharing neighbors before taking actions that may affect them, to exchange hydrologic data regularly, to avoid causing substantial harm to other water users, and to allocate water from a shared river basin reasonably and equitably.[40]

Few could quarrel with these principles on paper, but they offer insufficient practical guidance for the real world. In particular, what constitutes "reasonable and equitable"—the crux of any water-sharing agreement—is open to widely differing interpretations. For instance, Egypt's view of such an allocation of the Nile would undoubtedly give great weight to population size and historical water use. Ethiopia, on the other hand, would place relatively greater weight on each nation's contribution to total runoff in the basin and on future irrigation potential. Similarly, during the Israeli-Palestinian peace talks, both sides have invoked the Helsinki rules to support their respective positions on the allocation of West Bank water. But Israelis have given greatest emphasis to the criterion of "prior use" while the Palestinians have viewed this as only one of several criteria that apply.[41]

A catalyzing role might be played by an independent panel of water specialists charged with developing recommendations for distributing water resources equitably in specific river basins. The panel would set criteria and a standard of fair allocation against which any individual country's position or negotiating demands could be evaluated. By developing scenarios that lead to win-win arrangements, the panel could also demonstrate the benefits of cooperation—and thus encourage it. Although governments would have no obligation to accept the conclusions or recommendations, they might at least feel public pressure to moderate extreme views, consider the benefits of cooperation, and entertain the notion of a water-sharing ethic. The American Society of Civil Engineers has established a task force to develop principles and guidelines for international water sharing. It may be, however, that the authority of an interdisciplinary, international panel will be required for widespread acceptance.[42]

In none of today's potential hot spots of water dispute do treaties exist that include all countries within the river basin.

Without a formal body of enforceable law, water sharing and the prevention of conflict depend on treaties among neighboring countries. Governments have concluded more than 2,000 legal instruments relating to international watercourses, with some dating back 900 years. Most of the treaties that set forth allocations of water quantity or quality reflect the basic principle of equitable use, even if they do not use that language. Yet in none of today's potential hot spots of water dispute do treaties exist that include all countries within the river basin.[43]

A 1959 treaty between Egypt and Sudan, for example, allocates an amount of Nile water between them that adds up to nearly 90 percent of the river's average annual flow—even though 86 percent of that flow originates in Ethiopia. Ethiopia is not party to the treaty and, not surprisingly, feels no obligation to respect it. Fortunately, now that Ethiopia is in a position to begin tapping upper Nile waters for its own use, the nations are showing interest in cooperating. At a February 1995 meeting in Tanzania, the water affairs ministers of most of the Nile basin countries—including Egypt and Ethiopia—agreed to form a panel of experts that would be charged with developing a basinwide framework for water sharing aimed at "equitable allocation of the Nile waters." Especially given Egypt's historic position, this is a striking development, one that may not only avert conflict over water in the Nile basin, but also set the stage for more sustainable water management and use.[44]

By contrast, little progress is apparent in the Ganges basin, where a water-sharing agreement between Nepal, India, and Bangladesh becomes more urgent each year. With Nepal holding most of the additional water storage and hydropower potential, India controlling the vast majority of Ganges runoff, and Bangladesh repeatedly capturing international attention with its debilitating floods and droughts, this basin is ripe for creative initiatives. Initial steps might be for an independent panel to develop "reasonable and equitable" arrangements that secure Bangladesh's minimum water needs for food production as well as the minimum water needed to safeguard the Ganges delta. With increasing numbers of Bangladeshi refugees crossing the border into eastern India to escape poverty at least partially induced by lack of water, India may soon see reason to bargain where it saw little before.[45]

In the Aral Sea basin, the presidents of the five newly independent countries met in early 1994 and approved an action plan for improving the tragic situation there. The plan includes the crafting of a regional water management strategy within the context of broader economic and social development. A near-term goal will be to improve health and environmental conditions in the "disaster zone" surrounding the sea. Carrying out the broad water, agriculture, economic, and social reforms that will be needed will be difficult to say the least: the economy of each of the five countries has contracted each year since their independence in 1991, and per capita incomes have declined between 15 and 56 percent.[46]

The inevitability of droughts and the prospect of climate change must also figure into water-sharing agreements. It may no longer make sense for treaties to specify the absolute quantity of water each nation, state, or province receives, since in many years there may not be enough water to meet all treaty requirements. A more sensible approach is for agreements to specify each party's respective share of river runoff, with the absolute amount each gets tied to how much is available in a particular year. To protect a river's ecological functions, treaties would need to specify an absolute quantity and quality of water that is reserved for the environment, and this minimum flow would need to be provided in dry years or wet.

The Murray-Darling River basin in Australia is now managed under such an approach. During the last decade, as water use in the basin approached the sustainable yield of available water resources, pressure increased to better define ownership of water supplies among the three basin states—New South Wales, Victoria, and South Australia— and to share them more equitably, particularly during droughts. In 1989, following 15 years of negotiations, a revised method of water sharing was adopted that includes continuous accounting of water use, sharing of the water actually available in reservoirs, and water trading among the states for added flexibility. The new approach also requires that a specified volume be reserved to protect the integrity of the entire water system. According to Don Blackmore, Chief Executive of the Murray-Darling River Basin Commission, the system provides "a sound basis for future management of the shared water resources of the Basin, and has removed a major impediment to cooperative action."[47]

STRATEGIES FOR A NEW WATER EQUATION

For all its impressive engineering, modern water development has been governed by a fairly simple calculus: estimate the demand for water and then build a new supply to meet it. It is an equation that ignores the complexities of the natural world, questions of human equity, concerns about other species, and the welfare of future generations. In a world of resource abundance, it may have served humanity adequately. But in a world of scarcity, it is a recipe for trouble.

At a number of international gatherings in recent years, government officials and water specialists have recognized the need for a new approach. A statement of principles emerged from a January 1992 conference in Dublin, Ireland, that served as the foundation for the water chapter of Agenda 21, the global action plan developed at the 1992 Earth Summit in Rio. In 1993, after much internal and external debate, the World Bank published a water resources policy paper that establishes a framework for water management that is generally consistent with the Dublin and Rio outcomes. These various documents call for recognition of the links between economic development and protection of natural ecosystems, for water to be treated more as an economic good, and for water planning to involve fuller public participation.[48]

Although helpful as guiding principles, these documents lack concreteness. What is needed is a vision of a more sustainable water future, clear criteria and targets for measuring progress toward it, and a package of policy tools and practical steps to guide water management toward desired and realistic ends. At the core of such a strategy are the basic goals of sustainability—ecological integrity, efficiency, equity, and participatory decision-making.

The setting of ecological criteria that ensure protection of aquatic systems is a critical first step. Unless water is specifically reserved for the aquatic environment, cities, industries, and farms will overexploit and damage it. A sustainability criterion for renewable groundwater is fairly straightforward: net extractions should not exceed recharge. What constitutes sustainable use of rivers, however, is much more complex. Exactly how much water needs to be left in a river will vary with the time of year, the habitat requirements of riverine life, the system's sediment and salt balances, the value local residents place on fisheries and recreation, and other factors specific to each river basin. (See also Chapter 4.) But setting even preliminary "minimum flows" for both average and low-flow periods would provide a needed degree of insurance for the health of river systems—even as scientists progress toward a better understanding of the rivers' complex ecological workings.

In regions where rivers are already overtapped, as in much of the western United States, meeting such minimum requirements will involve shifting some water away from farms and cities over to the environment. In late 1992, for example, the U.S. Congress passed legislation that dedicated 800,000 acre-feet (987 million cubic meters) of water annually from the Central Valley Project in California, one of the largest federal irrigation projects, to maintaining fish and wildlife habitat and other ecosystem needs. Among other things, it set a goal of restoring the natural production of salmon and other anadromous fish (those that migrate from salt water to fresh water to spawn) to twice their average levels over the past 25 years.[49]

Two years later, California and federal officials signed an agreement to limit the amount of fresh water that can be diverted from the San Francisco Bay delta-estuary, a highly productive aquatic environment that is home to more than 120 species of fish. In years of normal rainfall, 494 million cubic meters must be reserved for the ecosystem. Farmers stand to lose the most water from this reallocation, while cities will likely face cutbacks mainly in dry years. But all Californians should gain in the long run, as economic activity comes into better balance with the water environment that supports it. Moreover, the agreement has a high degree of validity, since representatives of all those with a stake in the region's water allocation—including farmers, urbanites, environmentalists, and state and federal officials—were involved in the decision-making process.[50]

Reserving water for the environment may be far more difficult in developing countries, where demands for food and drinking water are rising apace with population. But in these countries as well, ensuring minimum water flows to satisfy ecological needs is critical to protecting fisheries, delta economies, and the health of local people. In the Aral Sea basin, efforts are being made to restore at least some of the region's ecological function. Through a World Bank–coordinated program, activities are under way to construct wetlands and artificial lakes in the Amu Dar'ya delta in order to restore aquatic vegetation, fisheries, and wildlife. But the Aral Sea ecosystem will need a substantial allocation of water just to stop the spiral of decline, much less reverse it. Stabilizing the sea even at its present level would require an annual inflow of some 35 billion cubic meters— five times greater than the average annual inflow registered during the eighties. Shifting this much water back to the environment would take major irrigation efficiency improvements, a reduction in the area planted to cotton and rice, and the removal of marginal lands from irrigation.[51]

An even bigger challenge in this region may be securing the public's participation in decision-making, a prerequisite to ensuring that any "solution" is socially acceptable. The World Bank has taken initial steps to involve NGOs in its program. But it remains to be seen whether government resistance, decades of top-down decision-making, and other barriers to citizen participation can be overcome.

Meeting ecological criteria in water-short areas will require stronger incen- tives to use water more efficiently and to reallocate it more rationally and equitably. Because water development has tended to privatize profits while socializing costs, most water users have had little encouragement to conserve. By heavily subsidizing water, governments give out the false message that it is abundant and can afford to be wasted—even as rivers are drying up, fisheries are collapsing, and species are going extinct.

By heavily subsidizing water, governments give out the false message that it is abundant and can afford to be wasted.

In the western United States, for example, a careful analysis of the Bureau of Reclamation irrigation program from its inception in 1902 up to 1986 showed a total construction cost subsidy of about $20 billion—an average of just under $5,000 per hectare—which represented 86 percent of total construction costs. Western cities have benefited from these projects too: Los Angeles, for instance, has paid just 25¢ per acre-foot and Las Vegas only 50¢ per acre-foot for bulk water from Bureau of Reclamation projects. Municipal water from other sources can cost $100–200 per acre-foot or more. The government's failure to collect adequate fees has not only shifted wealth from taxpayers to these beneficiaries and contributed to budget deficits, it has encouraged farmers to grow low-value crops and to use water inefficiently even where it is very scarce, has supported the unsustainable growth of western cities, and has caused water users to underinvest in conservation.[52]

Similar situations exist in most countries, rich or poor. In India, A. Vaidyanathan of the Madras Institute of Development Studies estimates that less than 10 percent of the total recurring costs for major- and medium-sized irrigation projects built by the government as of the mid-eighties has been recovered. Thailand's irrigation act says that farmers receiving irrigation benefits shall pay a service fee, but the government has made no real attempt to collect it. Although there may be sound social reasons to subsidize irrigation costs to some degree, collecting fees to at least cover operation and maintenance costs and to send a signal about efficiency is essential to achieving more sustainable patterns of water use. There is a broad spectrum of conservation incentive possibilities that fall between full-cost pricing, which could put too many farmers out of business, and a marginal cost of zero to the farmer, which is a clear invitation to waste water.[53]

Where laws, cultural norms, and infrastructure make it possible, water marketing can offer substantial benefits.

Because agriculture accounts for two thirds of total water use worldwide, even small percentage reductions can free up substantial quantities of water for cities, the environment, or other farmers. Savings of up to 25 percent or more from efficiency improvements are well documented for certain locations. For instance, many farmers in northwest Texas, who have had to cope with falling water tables from mining of the Ogallala aquifer, have reduced their water use by 20–25 percent by adopting new irriga-

tion technologies and methods.[54]

Likewise, results from a variety of countries show that farmers who have switched from furrow or sprinkler irrigation to efficient drip systems have cut their water use by 30–60 percent, often while increasing yields at the same time. Among them are growers of tomatoes in Jordan, coconuts in India, and sugarcane in Hawaii. Drip systems, which were commercialized in Israel and are used extensively there, tend to be too expensive for most poor farmers and for use on low-value row crops, but research is under way to make them more affordable. Colorado-based International Development Enterprises is testing a system in India that costs just $50 per half-acre ($123 per half-hectare), about one tenth the cost of current drip systems there.[55]

Just how much water can become available through efficiency improvements will vary from place to place. Worldwide, irrigation efficiency is estimated to average only about 40 percent, but this does not mean that 60 percent of irrigation water is wasted. Some of the water not used by crops runs off the field or seeps back into groundwater and becomes a neighbor's supply. Reducing these losses may improve water quality, allow more water to be left in rivers for fisheries, and produce other important benefits, but it can also reduce supplies to other users elsewhere, producing no real water savings. Studies of Egypt's Nile Valley, for instance, show that the irrigation efficiencies of individual farms are on the order of 40 percent, but the basinwide efficiency is on the order of 90 percent because of the multiple use of Nile water as it flows from the Aswan Dam to the Mediterranean Sea. In such cases, saving water may depend not only on technologies that reduce evaporation losses, but also on switching to less water-intensive crops.[56]

Opportunities to sell water can create incentives to use it more efficiently and, in some cases, to distribute it more equitably. Water marketing is not appropriate or workable everywhere, since it requires clear property rights to water. In the newly independent countries of the Aral Sea basin, for example, the notion of tradable water rights is foreign to both Islamic culture and communist socio-political traditions. In such settings, a more effective water pricing structure may be more suitable. Moreover, few strategies could be more foolhardy than allowing the unrestrained buying and selling of the basis of life. Unless marketing takes place within a regulatory framework that ensures protection of the aquatic environment and of other water users, it could cause more harm than good.[57]

Nonetheless, where laws, cultural norms, and infrastructure make it possible, marketing can offer substantial benefits. Rather than cities or farmers looking to a new dam or river diversion to get additional water, they can purchase supplies from others. In Chile, for example, where water policy directly encourages marketing, water companies that serve expanding cities now frequently buy small portions of water rights from farmers, most of whom have gained their surpluses through efficiency improvements.[58]

In most developing countries, water trading typically consists of spot sales or one-year lease arrangements, often between neighboring farmers. Weak institutions and difficulties with contract enforcement are frequent barriers to permanent sales of water rights. Although this limits marketing's potential benefits, the practice is still widespread. A 1990 survey of surface canal systems in Pakistan found active water trading in 70 percent of them. In India's western state of Gujarat, informal groundwater markets have emerged spontaneously and provide many farmers with water of high quality when needed, thus enhancing crop production. Since marketing may allow farmers who cannot afford to drill their own wells to purchase water from other irrigators, it can help provide the poor with access to irrigation water they otherwise would not have.[59]

If unregulated or monopolistic, however, water markets can lead to overexploitation of water sources, inequalities in water distribution, and exploitative prices. In India's southern state of Tamil Nadu, well-owners pump groundwater, sometimes with the benefit of subsidized electricity, and sell it to intermediaries who in turn sell it to poor households lacking a piped water supply. The poor thus gain access to water, but may pay as much as 10 times more for it than wealthier households connected to the public water system. Again, a legal and regulatory framework is needed to protect the resource base and prevent one user group from unfairly exploiting another.[60]

Markets also allow private organizations and government agencies to purchase existing water rights and dedicate them to restoring the aquatic environment. For example, The Nature Conservancy, based in Arlington, Virginia, has returned water to rivers and wetlands by outright purchases of private water rights as well as by working with state agencies to transfer existing water rights to instream uses. In Colorado, a coal-mining subsidiary of the Chevron Corporation donated $7.2 million worth of water rights on the Black Canyon of the Gunnison River to The Nature Conservancy, which then turned the rights over to the state Conservation Board for conversion to an instream water right. As a result, additional water will remain in this portion of the river to benefit three endangered fish species and a trout fishery.[61]

Depletion taxes are yet another policy tool that can promote more efficient, equitable, and ecologically sound water use. One of many so-called green taxes, which raise government revenues while discouraging pollution and resource consumption (see Chapter 10), a water depletion tax might be particularly applicable to the overpumping of groundwater or to extractions from fossil aquifers. Ideally, the revenues from such a tax would be earmarked for the development of sustainable ways to meet a region's water needs.

In the High Plains of western Texas, where depletion of the Ogallala aquifer continues, water managers have decided to use carrots rather than sticks to encourage conservation. The High Plains Water District, which covers 2.7 million hectares, offers irrigators low-interest loans for the purchase of equipment to improve irrigation efficiency, such as Low Energy Precision Application systems, surge valves, drip systems, and underground pipelines. As of October 1995, cumulative water savings from the program totalled nearly 192 million cubic meters, enough to supply a city of roughly 700,000 people for a year.[62]

Efficiency standards round out the package of policy tools to encourage more sustainable water use. A number of governments, including Mexico and the Canadian province of Ontario, have adopted such standards for household plumbing fixtures. In the United States, legislation passed in late 1992 requires manufacturers of toilets, faucets, and showerheads to meet specified standards of efficiency as of January 1994. Today, the average U.S. resident's use of these fixtures takes an estimated 174 liters per day; within 30 years, this figure

is expected to drop by more than half—to 79 liters per day—as the more efficient models replace the existing stock.[63]

U.S. water utilities can thus plan on lower indoor water use, which translates into reduced capital investments for new water supplies and treatment plants, as well as reduced energy and chemical costs for pumping and treating water and wastewater. (See Table 3–3.) The environment benefits as well, since less water needs to be taken from rivers, lakes, and aquifers to meet urban needs, and since lowered energy use means fewer pollutants are emitted into the atmosphere. Although efficiency standards have so far mainly been applied to household fixtures, they offer potential for water savings in agriculture, industry, and other municipal uses as well.[64]

A creative mix of these various strategies will be needed to satisfy human needs while protecting water's life-support functions. Water strategies alone, however, will not be sufficient. Water is finite, and in contrast to most other resources, it has no substitutes. Living within water's limits will require slowing the growth of the scale of the human enterprise overall. Unless wealthier countries reduce consumption levels and all countries move more quickly to create the conditions needed for population stabilization, water scarcity will lead to greater human and political insecurity. At the individual level, the collective impact of billions of choices about diet will greatly influence how much water is needed to meet future food demands.

By 2025—just a generation away—as many as 3 billion people could be living in countries experiencing water stress or chronic water scarcity. Time to prepare and plan for the consequences of this dire predicament is short. Fortunately,

Table 3-3. United States: Projected Water Savings from Efficiency Standards, 1995–2025

Year	Fixture Water Use[1]		Change
	Without EPAct[2] Standards	With EPAct Standards	
	(billion cubic meters per year)		(percent)
1995	25.8	25.2	−2
2000	25.7	24.0	−7
2010	25.2	20.8	−17
2020	24.3	16.9	−30
2025	25.2	16.1	−36

[1]Water use from toilets, faucets, and showerheads.   [2]U.S. Energy Policy Act of 1992; water use declines slightly without the EPAct standards because of less stringent standards already in place.
SOURCE: Amy Vickers, "Technical Issues and Recommendations on the Implementation of the U.S. Energy Policy Act," prepared for the American Water Works Association, Amy Vickers & Associates, Inc., Boston, Mass., September 1995.

there is a pull as well as a push to creating a sustainable water future. Whether restoring salmon populations in California, sharing the waters of the Nile River, protecting scarce groundwater in India, or securing livelihoods in the Aral Sea basin, the challenge offers promise—but only if it is engaged in time.[65]

4

Sustaining Freshwater Ecosystems

Janet N. Abramovitz

In 1880, a decade before the territory of Washington became a part of the United States, 19,500 tons of salmon and steelhead trout were harvested from the region's most important river, the Columbia. One hundred years later, the harvest was just 50 tons. Fourteen million salmon a year once returned to this river basin to spawn in their ancestral streams; in 1992, only 1.1 million made it back, and most of them had been born in a hatchery. In Idaho, one of the region's five Pacific salmon species—the coho—became extinct in 1986. In 1994, only 400 fall chinook salmon and just one sockeye salmon, nicknamed "Lonesome Larry" by Idaho Governor Cecil Andrus, completed the journey from the Pacific Ocean up the Columbia and Snake Rivers to Idaho's Redfish Lake.[1]

To someone who does not live in the Pacific Northwest, this brief history might seem to be one of those disturbing but unusual environmental disaster reports that occasionally comes out of some far-away and uniquely troubled place. In fact, what has happened to the Columbia River basin is happening to freshwater systems all over the planet— from the Mississippi River to the Mekong, from Lake Erie to Lake Baikal, and in thousands of nameless streams and creeks across every continent. The details vary, and the tragedy may not be as well known, but the causes—and the consequences for human economies and the earth's ecological stability—are much the same.

Most people are unaware of the vulnerability that freshwater environments everywhere share. As biological assets, freshwater systems are both disproportionately rich and disproportionately imperilled. First, 12 percent of all animal species—including 41 percent of all recognized fish species—live in the 1 percent of the earth's surface that is fresh water. (Less than one one-hundredth of 1 percent of the total volume of water on earth is fresh.) At the same time, at least one fifth of all freshwater fish species have become extinct, threatened, or endangered in recent years, and entire freshwater faunas have disappeared.[2]

The plight of Pacific salmon is far from unique. Dramatic declines in freshwater species are seen in every part of the world. The Nature Conservancy reports that in North America, the most thoroughly studied continent, 67 percent of mussels, 64 percent of crayfish, 36 percent of fish, and 35 percent of amphibians are either in jeopardy or—in some cases—already gone. (See Figure 4–1.) In contrast is the more widely recognized plight of terrestrial animals, with 17 percent of mammals and 11 percent of birds extinct or in jeopardy. These high levels of extinction and endangerment are not artifacts of earlier perturbations; they are recent and increasing. Ten fish species disappeared in North America during the last decade alone.[3]

Even more profound than the actual numbers of species extinct and endangered is the fact that the rate at which species—both terrestrial and aquatic— are being lost far exceeds any natural extinction rate. New calculations by Dr. Stuart Pimm and colleagues published in the journal *Science* indicate that recent extinction rates are 100–1,000 times higher than before humans existed. Further, if now-threatened species become extinct in the next century, rates will continue accelerating to 1,000–10,000 times prehuman levels. Today, we are running what Smithsonian Institution biologist Jonathan Coddington refers to as a "biodiversity deficit": we are destroying species (and ecosystems) faster than nature can create new ones. Such a course is even less sustainable over the long term than a growing financial deficit—since extinction truly is forever.[4]

THREATS TO FRESHWATER SYSTEMS

Around the globe, the integrity and inhabitants of freshwater systems are threatened by the actions and interactions of many human activities. (See Table 4–1.) These threats take the form of habitat degradation and fragmentation, competition for water, introduction of nonnative species, pollution, commercial exploitation, and climate change.[5]

Most losses of freshwater fauna can be attributed to a variety of factors acting together, with physical habitat alteration implicated in 93 percent of the declines, according to an American Fisheries Society (AFS) study of North America. This is hardly surprising, since in the United States only 2 percent of the country's 5.1 million kilometers of rivers and streams remain free-flowing and undeveloped. More than 85 percent of U.S. inland waters are artificially controlled and at least half of the country's original wetlands (excluding those in Alaska) have been drained. The amount of wetlands lost between the 1780s and the 1980s averaged more than 24 hectares (60 acres) an

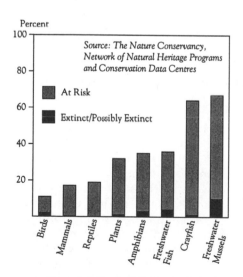

Figure 4-1. Species Extinct and at Risk in North America, 1995

Table 4-1. Freshwater Fish: Status and Threats in Selected Areas

Area	Known Freshwater Fish Species	Share Extinct	Share Imperilled	Principal Threats
	(number)	(percent)		
Global	9,000+[1]	← 20 →		
Amazon River	3,000+[1]	n.a.	n.a.	Habitat degradation
Asia	1,500+[1]	n.a.	n.a.	Habitat degradation
North America	950	4	36	Habitat degradation; introduced species
Mexico (arid lands)	200	8	60	Competition for water; pollution
Europe	193	n.a.	42	Habitat degradation; pollution
South Africa	94	n.a.	63	Habitat degradation; competition for water; pollution
Lake Victoria	350	57	43	Introduced species

[1]Likely to be higher.
SOURCE: See endnote 5.

hour for every hour of those 200 years.[6]

Logging, mining, grazing, agriculture, industrialization, and urbanization alter terrestrial and aquatic habitats in ways that make them less able to support life or provide valuable ecosystem services. Such activities cause erosion and sedimentation, loss of riparian vegetation, and changes in water flow and temperature. These have profound impacts on the reproductive biology and survivorship of aquatic organisms. Aquatic ecosystems must increasingly compete with humans for the very foundation of their existence—water. In fact, so much water is diverted from rivers around the world that many dry up before reaching the sea. (See Chapter 3.)

But physical changes are not the only form of habitat degradation. Industrial and municipal wastes add chemical pollution and sewage. Pesticides and herbicides enter the waterways through runoff from farms and homes. These nonpoint sources of pollution also add excess organic matter and nutrients (such as nitrogen and phosphorus) that

stimulate undesirable plant and algal growth, which robs water of dissolved oxygen needed by aquatic life; silt and sediment that smothers breeding habitat and clogs the gills of fish and mussels; and disease-carrying pathogens such as cryptosporidium that are harmful to humans and aquatic life.

The introduction of nonnative, or exotic, species is the second most common factor in the loss of freshwater species, according to AFS, cited in 68 percent of the cases. Exotics may prey on native fish, compete with them for food and breeding space, and introduce new diseases. The hybridization that often results when an exotic breeds with a native fish can doom the native as a distinct organism. Exotics can also mask ecosystem decline; intentionally introduced exotic sport fish are a kind of fisheries sleight-of-hand. People seeing abundant fish in a stream or lake do not realize these are not native. Many are released regularly from hatcheries or escape from aquaculture operations (see Chapter 6), and some are added to waterways intentionally by recreational fishers who stock local streams or by people who are cleaning out their home aquariums. In North America, for example, more than 400 species of freshwater fish have been introduced into systems outside their natural range; 140 species, including 40 not even native to the continent, have become established. In the east, exotics may constitute 5–10 percent of a state's fish species; on the western side of the continent, they often account for more than half.[7]

The case of the Amazon River illustrates the interaction of a number of these forces and how little is commonly known. The Amazon basin is best known for its vast tropical rain forests and indigenous peoples. But little notice has been given to the river itself and the freshwater ecosystem that supports and nourishes both forests and people. The Amazon, flowing 6,500 kilometers to the Atlantic Ocean, contains one fifth of the world's freshwater discharge into oceans. During half the year, portions of the forest up to 20 kilometers from the river are naturally flooded by several meters of water. These flooded forests constitute at least 150,000 of the 5 million square kilometers of the Amazonian rain forest.[8]

This vast area is far from uniform— the flooded forest has its own unique flora and fauna. For example, some fish feed only during the six-month flood season, surviving the rest of the year on accumulated fat. The Amazon is home to more than 3,000 species of fish alone— more than any other river in the world. Some of the most unique are the more than 200 species that use the flooded forest as a source of fruit and seeds. The forest depends on the fish for seed dispersal, and people depend on both the forest and the fish. Most of the 200,000 tons of fish caught each year in the basin are harvested by small fishers for subsistence and local markets.[9]

A variety of activities threaten the integrity of the Amazon River system. As elsewhere, the primary threat is degradation of the watershed through logging, mining, dam construction, and conversion of the floodplain for agriculture and livestock. In the lower third of the Amazon, only 15–20 percent of the flooded forests remain. Some of the most popular food fish, such as the 30-kilogram tambaqui, are already becoming difficult to find. Biologist Michael Goulding, a specialist in Amazonian ecology, warns that if the rates of deforestation of Brazil's tropical rain forest "are directed to the floodplains, as livestock operations suggest they might be, then the flooded forests will be almost entirely eliminated in the next decade. The destruction of the flooded forests may be the single most significant threat to Amazonian biodiversity. [It] could cause the greatest loss of freshwater fish known in human history, [fish that] have been a primary source of animal protein."[10]

What is happening in other large, modified freshwater systems confirms the often unforeseen and irreversible consequences of degrading watersheds, regulating and engineering rivers, polluting waters, and introducing alien species. Their stories also show that the cumulative impacts of individual actions can exact a high toll. Such changes have far-reaching and long-lasting effects on a region's ecological, cultural, and economic well-being. The status of fish and other aquatic organisms are good indicators of this well-being.

DAMMING RIVERS, DAMNING THE FUTURE

Dams have become a major feature on the natural and political landscape.

Today there are more than 38,000 large dams and countless smaller dams around the world. Over half the large dams are in China, which also leads the world in new dam starts, including the highly controversial Three Gorges Dam project on the Yangtze River. Dams are at once symbols and agents of change. But the problems that they cause can run even deeper than the still waters held in their reservoirs. Many of these problems are surfacing in the Columbia-Snake River basin in North America, a region with a long-standing network of hydro-power dam development.[11]

Because of their unusual life history, salmon are good indicators of the health of this region's rivers and forests. They are among the 1 percent of the world's fish species that are anadromous—living in both fresh and salt water. Salmon hatch in streams and rivers, then make their way to the ocean. After several years, they return to their ancestral streams to mate, and often die. Not only are salmon a symbolic link between the land and the sea, they are also an important nutrient link as their carcasses feed terrestrial and aquatic organisms far inland.[12]

Under the best conditions, the odds are just one in 5,000–10,000 that a salmon egg will be fertilized and survive to a reproducing adult. And because these fish pass through a wide range of habitats and conditions, over distances as long as thousands of kilometers, they are vulnerable to the full range of forces that nature and humankind inflict. The Columbia and its main tributary, the Snake River, had more than 24,000 kilometers (15,000 miles) of rivers and streams that were once salmon habitat. The watershed drains 673,400 square kilometers (260,000 square miles) in seven western states in the United States and portions of the Canadian province of British Columbia. Virtually no part has been untouched by the four forces

implicated in the salmon's decline—hydropower, habitat, hatcheries, and harvest.[13]

Today, the Pacific salmon's biggest obstacles are the 58 hydropower dams and 78 multipurpose dams in the Columbia-Snake River basin. Most were built during the heyday of hydroelectric development 20–50 years ago. Dams alter the temperature and flow regimes of rivers; they are barriers to migrating organisms such as fish, and to the natural movement of sediments, nutrients, and water—all of which feed the surrounding floodplains and ultimately the sea. In the past, a young salmon's journey to the ocean took two weeks; now it takes two months. Habitat modifications—principally dams and reservoirs—take out an estimated 99 percent of the salmon killed by human activity in the region. A large proportion of the survivors must make an extremely unnatural detour: they are hauled around the dams in trucks and barges. Today, only 71 of the river's 1,996 kilometers run free, without the hindrance of dam or reservoir.[14]

There are other significant obstacles to the salmon's journey as well. Logging, grazing, irrigation withdrawals, agricultural runoff, and wetland conversion have all contributed to the extensive degradation of the freshwater habitats of the Pacific Northwest. Nearly 90 percent of its once extensive primary forests has been lost to logging. Throughout the region, even undammed streams have had their salmon populations drop precipitously, because sedimentation and higher water temperatures caused by logging make the streams unfit for salmon for decades after the operations have ceased. The loss of habitat has become so severe that the coho salmon is being listed as threatened throughout most of its range under the U.S. Endangered Species Act. Across the Canadian border, the effects of overfishing, logging, and mining on undammed major rivers, such as the Fraser and the Skeena, have cut salmon populations to less than 20 percent of previously recorded levels.[15]

The serious impact of irrigation withdrawals on freshwater systems is likely to continue, as agriculture's already large share of water use worldwide shows no signs of abating. (See Chapters 3 and 5.) And it is not just migratory species such as salmon that are declining. Many species that spend their entire lives in one locale—"resident species"—are also threatened with extinction.[16]

The loss of aquatic species does not happen simply because the affected species dwindles in number until it disappears. Much of the damage is being done below the species level, by the loss of particular "stocks." Many species, including salmon, are comprised of distinct groups that have evolved unique adaptations to their local environment. These fitness-enhancing characteristics may govern time and place of spawning, migration routes, and so forth. Fisheries biologists see these genetically different stocks as the building blocks of conservation and rehabilitation. Unfortunately, in the Pacific Northwest, the stocks have been sorely depleted. The coho is extinct in 55 percent of its range, declining in 39 percent, and not considered to be declining in just 7 percent. The spring and summer chinook are extinct in 63 percent of their range, and declining in all but 6 percent. An assessment of anadromous fish in the Pacific Northwest by the American Fisheries Society found that 214 native, naturally spawning stocks are in serious trouble. Of approximately 1,000 historic stocks, only 100 are considered somewhat healthy. Almost all of them are threatened by continued habitat degradation. Yet only four populations of salmon have been given official protection under the Endangered Species Act.[17]

In the Pacific Northwest, hatchery-raised salmon have helped bring many native stocks to the brink of extinction while masking the true decline of wild salmon and delaying real remedies. The release of hatchery fish—the standard response to the loss of natural fish populations—has brought in new diseases, additional competition, and fish that are smaller and less fit than wild fish. It has also weakened the genetic base of wild fish through interbreeding. The lower Columbia River is now so dominated by hatchery fish that the National Marine Fisheries Service decided not to list the coho salmon as endangered in Washington state because interbreeding has doomed its chance of rebounding as a distinct organism.[18]

Sedimentation and higher water temperatures caused by logging make streams unfit for salmon for decades after operations have ceased.

Salmon population numbers are subject to some natural variation due to ocean currents and temperatures, amount of rainfall, and so forth, but human-caused declines in numbers and stocks have severely impaired the species' resilience to these natural forces. The decline of salmon is a source of increasing conflict between the fishing and timber industries, between conservation and utility groups, and between the United States and Canada. It has severely affected jobs and revenue throughout the region, and has led to fishing moratoriums on these once abundant species. It has also been a loss to the Native American Indian tribes for whom salmon has been an integral part of culture and treaty rights.[19]

There are some hopeful signs for the

future, however. The Northwest Power Planning Council was established in 1980 to balance regional hydropower demands with the need to protect and enhance wildlife and fisheries resources. A number of detailed analyses have examined possible changes in dam operation, power generation, agriculture, and irrigation that would be economically sound and would benefit salmon recovery. Mitigating the negative impacts of current practices will improve the chances of recovery while fundamental changes needed in land and water management and resource valuation are made. A number of strategies have been put forth for restoring habitat and species integrity and shifting to ecosystem management. Without both the short- and long-term measures, there may be no fish left to recover.[20]

Today the number of wild salmon returning to the Columbia River is less than 6 percent of what it was before the dams were built, despite the assurances of engineers in the thirties that "no possibilities, either biological or engineering, have been overlooked in devising a means to ensure perpetuation of the Columbia River Salmon." In the face of all the cost overruns, as well as the social and environmental costs so long ignored, the successors of those engineers have begun to realize how false such promises were. According to Dan Beard, when he was Commissioner of the U.S. Bureau of Reclamation, the agency responsible for much of the country's water development, "it is a serious mistake for any region in the world to use what we did on the Colorado and Columbia Rivers as examples to be duplicated."[21]

Unfortunately, that is just what has happened. In the forties and fifties, engineers heady from building record-breaking dams in the Columbia basin were ready for another challenge. They drew up plans for controlling the Mekong River, which begins in China and drains Myanmar (formerly Burma), Laos, Cambodia, and portions of Thailand and Vietnam. During the protracted conflict in Southeast Asia, the plans lay idle. Today, there is no shortage of willing investors eager to profit from this populous emerging market rich in natural resources.

If the experience of other tropical dam projects holds in the Mekong, then the longevity and economic returns of hydro projects are being overstated by dam proponents, and the safety problems, the environmental damage, and the economic, health, and social costs are being understated. And just as elsewhere, when dam enthusiasts hold up the promise of taming the Mekong's floods, they generally fail to mention that flooding is a natural part of the river's complex cycle, not a pathological state that needs to be fixed.[22]

Ninety percent of the Mekong's flow comes during the monsoon rains between May and October, when the river swells to 40 times its dry-season volume. During flooding, fish migrate long distances between the river and the surrounding countryside, and then back to the river and estuary as floodwaters recede. It is estimated that 90 percent of the fish in the Mekong basin spawn not in the river but in the submerged forests and fields, where they also forage. The floodwaters enrich agricultural fields as well. Some 52 million people depend on the Mekong for their food and livelihoods. Although the flow and floods of the Mekong may seem out of control to an engineer, the river, the fish, and the people already make up a highly productive system.[23]

The fate of such places (and the people who depend on them) may now be in the hands of a recently resuscitated international body called the Mekong

River Commission. This group has some potential to provide a forum for coordinating sustainable river use and investment by its signatory countries—Thailand, Laos, Cambodia, and Vietnam. But the weakness of its new rules, the uneven balance of power and democracy in the region, and the momentum behind the dam projects raise questions about the cooperation or the sustainable development of the Mekong River promised in a new agreement.[24]

Under the Commission's old rules, member countries could veto diversion or dam projects on the Mekong or its main tributaries. But the new rules ask only that the Commission be "informed" of such plans. The lack of a requirement for consultation could set the stage for serious problems in less powerful downstream countries and in Myanmar and China, which are not signatories. And throughout the region, this approach will ignore the rights and needs of small-scale subsistence resource users, who form the majority of the population.[25]

A driving force in Southeast Asia is Thailand, the region's economic giant. One of its stated priorities is transforming "the Indochinese battlefield into a marketplace." Thailand's demand for electricity is increasing by 10–15 percent a year, but it has less access to the Mekong than most of its neighbors. Power imports from huge hydro developments planned in Laos could give Thailand cheap electricity—and allow it to avoid much of the attendant costs and damage. Imports might also let the government sidestep its growing chorus of critics at home. Relative freedom of speech in Thailand has allowed people to air their concerns about the destruction of forests and fishing grounds, and the social impacts of relocating villages—a common side effect of dam construction.[26]

Thailand's neighbors, on the other hand, have little press freedom. There has been scant public debate in Laos of the government's decision to feed Thailand's energy appetite by building more than 23 dams by the year 2010. Few of the people who will be forced out of their self-sufficient communities—whether by submerging or drying up their land, or by destroying their fish and forest resources—have a hope of influencing these plans.[27]

There has been scant public debate in Laos of the decision to feed Thailand's energy appetite by building more than 23 dams by 2010.

The Pak Mun dam in northeast Thailand may provide a picture of the region's future. Sited on the Mekong's largest tributary in Thailand, the dam was built during the early nineties by the Electricity Generating Authority of Thailand (EGAT) and partly funded by the World Bank on the strength of cursory environmental impact assessments that did not study seasonal fish migrations or the relationship between the river and the local people. Villagers were not asked about their use of the river, nor were they given access to information on the project—they were not even given maps, which would have let them see what was planned. More than 2,000 families were evicted and thousands of others lost their source of food and income. Predictably, since the project was completed in 1994, all 150 fish species have virtually disappeared from the Mun River. In 1995, EGAT admitted this destruction, and conceded to villagers' demands for compensation.[28]

MISUNDERSTANDING FLOODS

In many places, undeveloped rivers and their floodplains, wetlands, and backwaters are seen as wasted and unproductive. This view could not be further from the truth. One of the most common changes made to rivers large and small is the attempt to regulate their free-flowing nature. River systems have a dynamic equilibrium between their biological and physical features. Many systems (including the Mississippi, Nile, Ganges, and Amazon) are adapted to what are often called "pulse" disturbances—events such as naturally occurring seasonal floods. In some places they may last a few weeks; in others, most of the year.[29]

Plants and animals across the gradient of habitats are adapted to this regime. For example, many fish use the floodplain to spawn and as a nursery for their young; some consume and help disburse seeds, while others depend on the temporary abundance of food to sustain them for the entire year. Many plants use the flooded period to germinate and absorb newly available dissolved nutrients, and migratory waterfowl rely on the bounty of the flood period. The flood pulses help maintain the physical and biological interactions between the river and the surrounding floodplain that make them both extremely productive and diverse—much more productive and diverse than either area alone if cut off from the other. As biologist Peter Bayley so aptly describes it, "the flood pulse is not a disturbance; instead, significant departures from the average hydrological regime, such as the prevention of floods, should be regarded as a disturbance."[30]

Most human actions have fallen into the category of "press" disturbances—sustained disruptions that precipitate the breakdown of the physical, chemical, or biological integrity of the system and can cause the entire ecological system to unravel. Human-made press disturbances include building structures such as dams and levees; isolating a river from its floodplain, wetlands, and backwaters; changing the levels, timing, or temperature of water flows; adding chemical substances and excess nutrients from fertilizers and sewage; and creating navigation channels.[31]

In Europe, there are a number of clear indications that the Rhine River is suffering from too much regulation. The Rhine runs 1,320 kilometers from its beginning in the Swiss Alps through Liechtenstein, France, Germany, and the Netherlands out to the North Sea—through the most heavily populated and industrialized part of Europe. Twenty percent of the world's chemicals are produced there. The river and its tributaries provide 20 million people with drinking water. Little wonder that most public attention over the past few decades has focused on reducing water pollution.[32]

Now other signs of more fundamental problems have forced a dramatic change in the way the river is viewed and managed. A major flood in early 1995 caused the evacuation of 250,000 people in the Netherlands and cost 1.5–1.7 billion deutsche marks ($980 million to $1.1 billion) in Germany alone. In fact, flooding over the last 20 years has grown significantly more severe as urbanization, river engineering, and poor floodplain management have increased substantially. At Karlsruhe, for example, a German town on the French border, prior to 1977 the Rhine rose 7.62 meters above flood level only four times this century. Since 1977, it has reached that level 10 times.[33]

In its natural state, the mature Rhine River and its branches meandered through a broad floodplain of fields and forest. In the mid-nineteenth century a German engineer began the process of creating a single, deep, well-defined river highway, 100 kilometers shorter, to speed transportation to the sea and to facilitate growth and industrialization. More recent changes have created a fully engineered river with huge locks, levees, and dams. Ten hydroelectric power plants have been built in the upper Rhine, along with sophisticated locks and levees. Draining marshland and walling off the floodplain from the river with concrete barriers provided land for farming, housing, and industry. It also caused a lowering of groundwater levels.[34]

Today the river is cut off from 90 percent of its original floodplain in the upper Rhine, and flows twice as fast as before. The fast-flowing constricted river is digging an ever deeper channel—up to 8 meters deeper—as it speeds its way to the low countries. Ironically, containing a river in embankments, reservoirs, and other structures does not reduce the volume of floodwater. What it does do is dramatically increase the rate of flow, and thus its force downstream. Some say these structures should not be called flood control but rather "flood threat transfer mechanisms."[35]

The physical and chemical changes in the Rhine River system responsible for the devastating floods have also eliminated most of its fish. The Rhine once supported vibrant fisheries that fed and provided employment for people all along its length. One hundred years ago, 150,000 salmon were caught in just the Netherlands and Germany. By 1920 the catch had fallen below 30,000, and by 1958 it completely disappeared. The 15 salmon—individual fish, not number of species—found in the Rhine recently are believed to have escaped from a Norwegian aquaculture operation. Along with toxic reduction, a major goal of a regional program launched in 1987—the Rhine Action Plan—is a return of salmon by 2000.[36]

Part of the plan is to restore some of the river ecosystem in order to retrieve the benefits of its natural functions, such as providing safe drinking water, recharging groundwater supplies, and absorbing and slowly releasing floodwaters. Germany and France agreed in 1982 to create flood meadows upstream to reduce flooding downstream. So far, only two of the 20 designated areas have been completed. The Netherlands, much of which is below sea and river level and feels the full power of the Rhine's floods and toxic load, is taking steps to rehabilitate some of its floodplain and delta lands. The ultimate goal there is to return 15 percent of the farmland to functioning floodplain. By using some of these nonstructural methods of flood control, the region hopes to reduce the destructive consequences of the regulated Rhine River and restore some of the natural system and the life it supports—and to minimize the threat and cost of future devastating floods.[37]

Along with toxic reduction, a major goal of the Rhine Action Plan is a return of salmon by 2000.

The rising cost, frequency, and severity of floods along the Mississippi River and its tributaries in the United States also shows that massive expenditures on river engineering have actually increased the severity and devastation of floods, and have crippled the river's ability to support native fauna and flora. The construction of 1,576 levees, the creation of deep navigation channels, extensive farming in the floodplain, and the drainage of more than 6.9 million hectares (17 million acres) of wetlands (more than an 85-percent reduction in some states) has cut off the ability of the Mississippi's floodplains to absorb and slowly release rain, floodwater, nutrients, and sediments. Such ecosystem mismanagement comes at great economic cost, as demonstrated by the subsidence of the Mississippi delta, the decline of aquatic species, and the enormous financial toll of the recent flood.[38]

Since 1930, the U.S. Army Corps of Engineers has spent more than $25 billion on flood control and navigation efforts in the Mississippi basin.

The Great Midwest Flood of 1993 is considered the largest and most destructive in U.S. history. Records were set for amounts of precipitation, upland runoff, river levels, flood duration, area of flooding, and economic loss. The floodwaters rendered ineffective more than 1,000 levees spanning 9,650 kilometers (6,000 miles). In hindsight, many now realize that the river was simply—yet forcibly—attempting to reclaim its floodplain.[39]

Today's problems are the result of the cumulative impacts of more than 150 years of actions by public and private interests to expand agriculture, facilitate navigation, and control flooding. Levees, locks, dams, and reservoirs work to keep the river and its tributaries such as the Missouri and Illinois Rivers in a course not of their choosing. Nearly half of the Mississippi River's 3,782 kilometers flows through artificial channels. Paradoxically, these artificial modifications to the Mississippi basin system have actually increased the frequency, severity, and cost of floods. Records show that the 1973, 1982, and 1993 floods were substantially higher than

they would have been before structural flood control began in earnest in 1927. Measured in constant dollars, damages from the 1927 flood were estimated at $236 million, while those from the 1973 flood stood at $425 million. Property damages from the Great Flood of 1993 were estimated between $12 billion and $16 billion.[40]

The management and policy changes begun after the 1927 flood have had a number of profound effects. One was to shift the cost of flood control and relief from the local to the federal level, which in part encouraged people, farms, and businesses to settle in flood-prone areas with the knowledge that they would be bailed out of trouble at taxpayer expense. Since 1930, the U.S. Army Corps of Engineers alone has spent more than $25 billion on flood control and navigation efforts in the Mississippi basin. Billions more have been spent by other federal, state, and private interests.[41]

A National Flood Insurance Program was created in 1968 to provide insurance for those in flood-prone areas that private insurers deemed too risky, and it has encouraged rebuilding in many of those same areas. As with many subsidies that run counter to sound economic and environmental principles, this expensive program benefits relatively few. The General Accounting Office reported that nearly half of the billions of dollars paid out in flood claims went to the repeat flood victims who account for just 2 percent of the policyholders.[42]

The 1993 flooding of the upper Mississippi and Missouri Rivers provided a dramatic and costly lesson on the effects of channelization, and of treating the natural flow of rivers as a pathological condition. As with the Rhine, the human and economic tolls have caused a dramatic rethinking of how large rivers are managed. After the flood, an Interagency Floodplain Management Task Force recommended ending the over-reliance on engineering and structural methods of flood control in favor of floodplain restoration and management. It emphasized managing the river as a whole ecosystem rather than as short segments. These conclusions echoed the findings of an extensive study by a blue-ribbon panel of the independent National Research Council in 1992.[43]

Restoring the floodplains and managing the river basin as an ecosystem would not only help reduce flooding, it would also help restore other ecological services and the river's aquatic life. The separation of fish from their floodplain spawning grounds and upstream reaches virtually eliminated some species and caused many others to decline. Along one stretch of the Missouri River (the Mississippi's largest tributary), for example, the loss of 67 percent of the floodplain area was followed by more than an 80 percent decline in fish catch. After the 1993 flood, record spawning years were reported for flood-adapted species. As writer Ted Williams described it, "1993 wasn't a 'good' year for any life form that had evolved in the Mississippi; it was a *normal* year."[44]

Not only do flood control structures remove the "flood-pulse advantage" for the river's fish (that is, fish are more productive with the flood pulse), they also adversely affect the integrity and productivity of the Mississippi delta and Gulf of Mexico. Because these structures trap sediments rather than allowing them to be carried to replenish the delta, the coastal areas are actually subsiding— inundating wetlands and threatening coastal communities and productive fisheries. Louisiana, for example, has the second highest volume of commercial fish landings in the country, a catch of primarily wetland-dependant species. Yet between the direct loss of wetlands to conversion and the loss due to subsidence, this bounty is imperilled.[45]

The interdependence of species with each other and their environment is also seen in the decline of native mussel species. The Mississippi River basin and the eastern part of North America are home to the world's most diverse freshwater mussel fauna; one third of the world's freshwater mussel species are found there. They have declined in both abundance and diversity. Ten percent of these species have become extinct since 1900. A recent review of the status of the freshwater mussels in the United States and Canada found that 72 percent of the remaining 297 native freshwater mussel taxa (281 species and 16 subspecies) are endangered, threatened, or of special concern. Many may already be extinct. Only 24 percent (70 species) are considered stable. While the Endangered Species Act, which recognizes the importance of intact habitat, has been criticized by conservative politicians as overzealous protection, the fact that only 60 mussel species have received formal designation as threatened or endangered indicates that the government listing actually understates the true extent of the danger.[46]

Freshwater mussels are excellent indicators of habitat and water quality. During their 40–50 year life span, these sedentary creatures remain in the same spot, filtering water and eating microscopic plankton. They serve as food for many species, and they filter and cleanse vast quantities of water every day. Each mussel species has a particular fish species it depends on during a short part of its life cycle. If the fish disappear, the mussels cannot reproduce. If the mussels disappear, the water is not cleansed. The ebony shell mussel and the elephant ear mussel, for example, depend on the skipjack herring for dispersal and development of the young. After a dam on the upper Mississippi blocked the migration of the skipjack herring, the mussels disappeared from the river above the dam. Throughout their range, the single biggest threat to these important and sensitive indicator organisms has been habitat destruction. Unfortunately, the recent spread of nonindigenous organisms such as the zebra mussel may be the fatal blow to the remaining members of the world's most diverse freshwater mussel fauna.[47]

By destroying not only the fauna and flora but the very ecological integrity of the Mississippi River system, we are eliminating valuable current ecological services. We also foreclosing future evolutionary pathways and options for adaptation to climate change. The Mississippi is a geologically old river where species have had a long time to diversify and create complex assemblages. Its richness is reflected in the fact that it is home to almost all the freshwater mussels in the United States and one third of its fish species. It is also home to some of the most ancient lineages of freshwater fish such as gars, sturgeons, and paddlefish. In fact, the entire paddlefish family has only two living species, one in the Mississippi and the other in the troubled Yangtze River in China.[48]

The Mississippi is unique in that its north-south orientation allowed migration to warmer waters during the ice ages. Today it also allows the yearly migration of waterbirds, shorebirds, raptors, and songbirds between northern breeding grounds and winter homes as far as South America. It is this unique north-south orientation that will also play an important role in future evolution and adaptation to climate change.

GREAT TROUBLES IN GREAT LAKES

Large lakes can reflect more than the scenery around them. The picture beneath the surface is a much better reflection of human activities on shore. For many large lakes, the truer image is one of pollution, exotic species, and watershed degradation that destabilize these enclosed ecosystems. Large lakes have been viewed as a bottomless sink for whatever humankind has sought to release in its waters.

The world's largest freshwater ecosystem, the Great Lakes of North America, has already felt the full range of anthropogenic stress. Its 520,590-square-kilometer basin is home to more than 38 million people—and to significant portions of North America's industrial and agricultural activity. Over the last 200 years, the Great Lakes basin has lost two thirds of its once extensive wetlands. Barriers, canals, dams, and channels have eliminated vast fish spawning grounds. The Nature Conservancy has identified 100 species and 31 ecological community types within the Great Lakes system that are at risk on a global basis. And nearly half of these exist nowhere else. Today, less than 3 percent of the lakes' 8,661 kilometers (5,382 miles) of U.S. shoreline is suitable for swimming, for supplying drinking water, or even for supporting any aquatic life.[49]

Pollution is a major cause of the plight of the Great Lakes. More than a century of agricultural runoff, human waste, and household detergents have added excess phosphorus to the water, overstimulating algal growth. The resulting eutrophication causes problems such as dangerously depleted oxygen levels. Large quantities of toxic chemicals also enter the lakes every year, despite improvements brought about by decades of regulation in the United States and Canada. And the toxics from previous years tend to remain in the water and bottom sediments because the basin is a relatively closed system—only 1 percent of its water flows out annually. The large surface area of the Great Lakes makes them vulnerable to deposition of airborne pollutants, which today account for the majority of the most toxic substances entering the system. Some of the pollution blows all the way from farms in Mexico and cement plants in Texas. The Great Lakes' "airshed" is thus even larger than its watershed.[50]

The health of lake fish is a good clue to the health of the whole system. In 1993, two thirds of the nation's 1,279 fish consumption advisories were issued in the Great Lakes region, mostly due to the presence of mercury, PCBs, chlordane, dioxins, and DDT. With more comprehensive data, the picture would likely be much worse; of the 30,000 different chemicals entering the lakes, only 362 are reliably monitored.[51]

The lakes' toxic brew sometimes causes massive fish kills, but the more subtle effects may be just as dangerous. Many chemicals become more concentrated as they pass up through the food web, with top predators—such as humans—receiving the highest doses. The process is known as bioaccumulation and biomagnification. For example, a person would need to drink Great Lakes water for more than 1,000 years to ingest as much PCBs as eating a two-pound trout would provide.[52]

Many of the compounds—such as DDT, PCBs, agricultural chemicals, even some components of detergents and plastics—act as endocrine disrupters. In very minute amounts, they alter a whole spectrum of morphological, physiological, reproductive, and life history traits. Tumors, deformities, reproductive abnormalities, and reduced survivorship are widespread in exposed fish, birds, and mammals. A 50-percent decline in human sperm counts worldwide since 1940 (when these chemicals were created) has been attributed to the ability of many of these widespread chemicals to mimic estrogen, the feminizing hormone. And endocrine disrupters assimilated by one generation can produce

changes in the next generation. The cognitive, motor, and behavioral development problems noted in children of women who eat contaminated fish do not come from what was eaten just during pregnancy, but from what was consumed by the mother throughout her life.[53]

A person would need to drink Great Lakes water for more than 1,000 years to ingest as much PCBs as eating a two-pound trout would provide.

The Great Lakes suffer from a kind of "biological pollution" as well: the spread of exotic species. Two hundred years ago, each of the five Great Lakes had its own thriving aquatic community, with an abundance of members of the salmonid group. In 1900, 82 percent of the commercial catch was still native salmonids; by 1966, natives were only 0.2 percent of the catch. The remaining 99.8 percent were exotic species. And many of the surviving natives are hatchery-bred, not self-sustaining populations.[54]

Some exotics were intentionally introduced, in response to the declines of native fish from overfishing. A hatchery program for sport fish, for instance, supports a $2-billion sport fishery whose value now eclipses the lakes' remnant $41-million commercial fishery. But most of the 130-plus exotics have found their own way into the system by moving through canals or hitchhiking in ships. More than one third of the exotics have entered the system in the 30 years since the inauguration of the St. Lawrence Seaway. The canals are thought to have opened the Great Lakes up to the sea lamprey, an ocean-going parasite that devastated the lake fisheries. In Lakes

Michigan and Huron, the lamprey is credited with driving the annual commercial lake trout catch from 5,000 tons in the early forties to less than 91 tons just 15 years later. The first effective intergovernmental cooperation in the region came about to combat the sea lamprey, and resulted in the Great Lakes Fishery Commission. The lamprey remains in the lakes and its control requires constant vigilance.[55]

Prospects for controlling a more recent invader, the zebra mussel, are far less certain. Inadvertently introduced to the lakes in 1988 from ship ballast water, the zebra mussel has already spread to most major rivers and lakes in the east, and has been found as far away as California. The larvae of this prolific Caspian Sea native attach to hard surfaces, such as rocks, boats, pipes, and other mussels. They form dense colonies on substrate used by spawning fish and native mussels and virtually eliminate plankton needed by native fish and mussels. Workers at Detroit's electric power generating plant have found as many as 750,000 mussels per square meter in the plant's water intake canal. The cost to cities and industries of keeping these tenacious invaders from clogging intake pipes and heat exchanges could reach $5 billion by 2000 in the Great Lakes alone. By that time, the zebra mussel is expected to have colonized virtually all freshwater systems in North America, since an effective method for controlling it has yet to be devised.[56]

Attempts to heal the Great Lakes have been limited largely to episodes of crisis management. Early in the century, when epidemics were traced to the release of sewage, outfall pipes were extended farther into the water. When the native fisheries collapsed, heavily stocked exotics took their place. And most pollution control has focused on end-of-the-pipe management of individual chemicals rather than on comprehensive source re-ductions. Still, some progress has been made, albeit very slowly. Citizen groups in both Canada and the United States have been instrumental in spearheading change. The International Joint Commission, the Great Lakes Fishery Commission, and the Great Lakes Water Quality Agreement (GLWQA) of 1978 have provided forums for bilateral cooperation—on both federal and state levels. Cooperation under the GLWQA has significantly reduced phosphorus levels and eutrophication.[57]

In the United States, regulations by federal and state authorities have substantially reduced inputs of many pollutants, and the agencies have developed flexible guidelines for achieving further reductions. A new five-year strategy developed by federal, state, and nongovernmental agencies and coordinated by the Environmental Protection Agency takes an integrated, ecosystem management approach to problem-solving and decision-making in the region. Although it is too soon to judge its success, the strategy represents an important conceptual leap.[58]

On the other side of the globe, one of Africa's Great Lakes is also suffering from the effects of an introduced species. The Nile perch is conspiring with changing land use, pollution, growing population pressures, and war to rob Lake Victoria of its rich fauna and its people of a valuable source of protein and employment. The three largest lakes in the Rift Valley are not connected to each other, and lie within different river basins. Thus, each one's fauna and ecology are distinct—99 percent of the fish found in each lake are endemic, found only there. Lake Tanganyika is the oldest and deepest, with the most diverse fish fauna of any lake on earth. Bounded by Uganda, Kenya, and Tanzania, the shallower Lake Victoria covers some 62,000 square kilometers. It is the largest of the Rift Valley lakes—and the second largest lake in the world. Individually and together, the lakes, with hundreds of species exhibiting unique behaviors, are a living laboratory for studying trophic radiation and evolutionary processes.[59]

The introduction of the Nile perch to Lake Victoria in 1954—against the prevailing scientific advice of the day—has virtually eliminated the native fish population. (See also Chapter 6.) A 200-kilogram predator more than 2 meters long consumes enormous quantities of little fish: since the perch was introduced, Lake Victoria has lost 200 taxa of endemic cichlids, spectacular species found nowhere else; the remaining 150 or more are listed as endangered. The loss of Lake Victoria's fish is so severe that Boston University biologist Les Kaufman has described it as the "first mass extinction of vertebrates that scientists have had the opportunity to observe."[60]

On shore, there has also been a shift from little fish to big fish. Until recently, the native fish of Lake Victoria were harvested by small-scale fishers and processed and traded by women for local consumption. This kept the nutritional and economic benefits in the lakeside communities. Today, the perch are caught by large, open-water vessels with more destructive gear, then processed and traded by large commercial operations for the export market. Local women are literally left with the scraps—which they must purchase. Deprived of work and unable to afford this higher priced (and less palatable) catch, local people face a serious nutritional predicament. The perch takeover has decimated the primary economic and nutritional resource of 30 million people.[61]

The exact key to its success is uncertain, but the perch is noted for its ability to change its life-style and breeding strategy to suit prevailing conditions. In the late seventies, the lake's water began to lose oxygen through eutrophication,

which is deadly for most aquatic life. At the same time, the perch underwent a massive population explosion, and quickly began consuming and displacing native fish. The results are apparent from fishery statistics. Kenya, for example, reported only 0.5 percent of its commercial catch as perch in 1976 but by 1983 the proportion reached 68 percent. While a small portion of that increase may be attributed to larger fishing vessels and so forth, scientific fish surveys also show the demise of native fish and the takeover by introduced fish species. (See Figure 4–2.)[62]

It is unclear whether eutrophication gave the perch an opening, or whether the perch's voracious consumption of native fish "decoupled" the lake's internal recycling and cleansing loop. Either way, there is clear evidence that the structure of the entire system has changed. Ten years ago, Lake Victoria was oxygenated to its bottom—100 meters down. Now it supports life only in the upper 40 meters or less. Regular mixing events, in which the now suffocating, oxygen-depleted bottom waters rise to the surface, cause frequent

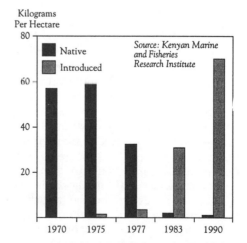

Figure 4-2. The Changing Fish Population of Lake Victoria

fish kills. The perch itself may now be in decline, from overfishing, periodic die-offs, and its own voracious appetite.[63]

There are other pressures on the ecosystem too. Millions of liters of untreated sewage and industrial waste flow into Lake Victoria every day from Kisumu, Kenya's third largest city, and from Mwanza in Tanzania. Watershed degradation and agricultural runoff contribute chemicals, nutrients, and sediment. And from Rwanda came the grisly addition of some 40,000 human corpses—war casualties that floated down the Kagera River in May 1994. Nor is the perch the lake's only alien species problem. Water hyacinth, native to South America, was first found in the lake in 1989. With no predators in Africa, the plant covers waterways quickly, depleting oxygen in the water and clogging intake pipes, irrigation canals, and ports. A single plant can blanket 100 square meters in just a few months. And water hyacinth provides a breeding ground for disease vectors such as bilharzia-carrying snails and malaria mosquitos.[64]

Degraded and simplified, Lake Victoria is no more likely to make a stable "fish ranch" than are the North American Great Lakes. But the institutional challenges of caring for Africa's largest lake are nearly as complex as the ecological ones. A major cooperative effort between all three lakeside countries—Uganda, Kenya, and Tanzania—was recently launched. This Lake Victoria Environmental Management Program will focus on water quality, land use management, restoration of indigenous food fish, control of the Nile perch and water hyacinth, and community-based enforcement. Successful methods developed in pilot zones around the lake during the first few years will then be applied to larger areas. Such cooperation may yet restore Lake Victoria, and could preserve Lakes Malawi and Tanganyika

as well—the other jewels of the Rift Valley.

A NEW FOCUS: MAINTAINING HEALTHY ECOSYSTEMS

Unfortunately, the Columbia, Mekong, Mississippi, and Rhine Rivers and the Great Lakes of North America and East Africa are not isolated cases. Virtually nowhere has been spared the loss of freshwater species and ecosystems. Nor has any place been immune to the cascade of unintended and unanticipated economic and social disruptions that follow the loss of healthy ecosystems. At every level of organization, from genes to species to assemblages to ecosystems, there are indications that the ecological integrity of freshwater systems has been simplified, degraded, and jeopardized. And there is clear evidence that the cumulative and synergistic effects of human actions are responsible for the biodiversity deficit that is severe and deepening.

The disappearing and degraded faunas have much to tell us about what we are doing to these ecosystems and to ourselves—if we choose to listen. Changes in the human condition—health problems, loss of sustenance and livelihoods, creation and exacerbation of conflicts—also provide indicators. So do the severe economic losses that result from ecosystem degradation. Freshwater ecosystems are not just a part of the environment; they are a part of our economies as well. The prospects for human well-being today are bound up in their fate, as are future options for evolution and human use.

When we jeopardize an ecosystem's integrity—its physical, chemical, and biological elements and processes—we compromise its ability to support species and provide the products and services we depend on. The services given include controlling floods, purifying water, recharging aquifers, restoring soil fertility, nurturing fisheries, and supporting recreation. When nature can no longer provide, we must either do without or try to substitute, usually much less effectively and at much higher cost.

To date, our exploitation and management of freshwater resources have tended to focus on only one element at a time—whether navigation, irrigation, power generation, sport or commercial fisheries, or even limited measures of water quality—without regard for the entire system. Even the way we define the systems themselves has not been comprehensive enough. A river does not really stop at the water's edge; a healthy wetland is not simply a place with cattails and ducks.

We need to see these ecosystems in their entirety: rivers and lakes, along with their entire watersheds and all the physical, chemical, and biological elements, are all part of complex, integrated systems. Human inhabitants are also part of those systems. And we need to learn to manage such systems in ways that maintain their integrity. In such a flexible ecosystem-based approach, resources would be managed over large enough areas to allow their species and ecological processes to remain intact while allowing human activity. On a social level, all stakeholders would be involved in defining issues, setting priorities, and implementing solutions.[65]

Most attempts at ecosystem-based management have focused on places already badly degraded—such as the Great Lakes of Africa and North America. Often a first step is rehabilitation efforts such as mitigating pollution, controlling exotics, and improving stream flows and quality. An important part of conservation and restoration is halting further habitat loss and protecting undegraded areas—"strongholds of aquatic biodiversity"—as refuges for healthy populations that can repopulate troubled spots once the pressures of degradation are alleviated. Although the cost of restoration can seem high, it is far less than the price of continued mismanagement. An economic analysis of the slated removal of two aging dams on Washington's Elwha River, for example, found that the $100-million price tag was more than justified by the several billion dollars in nonmarket benefits alone that river and wild salmon restoration would bring. And an extensive study by the National Research Council recommended restoration of aquatic ecosystems to solve water quality, wildlife, and flooding problems at minimal cost and disruption. Restoring 50 percent of the wetlands lost in the United States would affect less than 3 percent of the nation's agricultural, forestry, or urban land.[66]

Restoration and rehabilitation are clearly necessary. But alone they will not be enough. A principal goal now and in the future should be to shift from reactive to preventative management. Places like the Mekong and the Amazon offer chances to avoid the costly mistakes made elsewhere. We already know the heavy price that regulated rivers, water diversion, dam construction, alien species, and habitat degradation and fragmentation can exact from a region. The time has come to act on a corollary principle: over the long term, keeping naturally functioning ecosystems healthy will offer the greatest number of benefits for the greatest number of people.[67]

5

Preserving Agricultural Resources

Gary Gardner

By some measures, global agriculture in the post–World War II era is a clear success. Yields of wheat, corn, and rice—the world's principal crops—have risen steadily, and production has outpaced population growth for most of the period. Real food prices have generally declined as food production soared. Most important, chronic hunger is down: whereas one in three persons faced hunger daily in 1969, fewer than one in five do today. This impressive record is commonly credited to technologies and scientific advances—new seeds, fertilizers, pesticides, and extensive irrigation infrastructure—that boosted production. But copious food production also has a less visible source: unsustainable farming, which overdraws and degrades natural resources to maximize production.[1]

Indeed, if our planet were a bank, disbursing loans of natural resources, agri-

culture would be among its biggest debtors. Each year, agricultural practices erode mountains' worth of topsoil, drain continents of their groundwater reserves, and eliminate plant genetic material in what is essentially colossal resource borrowing from future generations. Because today's farming uses many renewable resources at well beyond their rate of replenishment, and because little effort is made to replace them, agricultural resource debts continue to mount. The borrowing, however, cannot continue indefinitely. As this century draws to a close, clear signs of lender fatigue are evident: five decades of resource overexploitation have drained reserves of natural capital in many regions, and have limited agriculture's opportunities for future growth and resource borrowing.

Today's accelerating resource depletion comes as production—despite its strong showing between 1950 and 1984—is sputtering and food demand is surging. Grain output that easily outpaced population growth for more than

We are grateful to the Wallace Genetic Foundation for their support for this chapter and related work on this topic.

30 years now lags well behind. (See Figure 5–1.) Yields of rice have barely inched up in the nineties, while wheat yields have shown no gain. Carryover stocks of grain, a key indicator of global food security, have shrunk each of the past three years, and now languish at their lowest levels ever. (See Chapter 1.) This sluggish performance comes on the eve of history's largest increase in food demand. Global population, at some 5.7 billion today, is projected to top 8 billion by 2020; nearly all the increase will come in the developing world, where constraints to increased production are especially daunting. The rise in population will be accompanied by an increase in urbanization and incomes, both of which further boost food demand. In all, experts anticipate food demand increases of some 64 percent globally, and almost 100 percent in developing nations, over the next 25 years.[2]

Thus, global agriculture faces twin challenges as we approach the twenty-first century: to meet the growing global demand for food, and to do so without the resource degradation and overconsumption that have accompanied the vast expansion in agricultural output in recent decades. How this will be done is not clear. The leaps in productivity of the sixties and seventies were made under conditions that cannot or should not be repeated: abundant supplies of water, for example, are not as readily available today, while dependence on chemical pesticides poisons farmers and upsets the balance of the agroecosystem. New research in agricultural production—similar to the fruitful research effort of the sixties and seventies, but focused this time on production methods that preserve the resource base—is urgently needed. In the end, however, production increases may not be sufficient to meet the coming food demand. Changes in consumption patterns may be needed to increase food use efficiency and thus food availability.

The good news is that interest in environmentally friendly methods of agriculture is increasingly evident. Measures to build soil health, reduce pesticide use, save water, and conserve genetic diversity have been undertaken by national governments and international institutions, not just a few visionary farmers and scientists. But these initiatives are few and small compared with the effort needed to put food production on a sustainable footing. Only sustainable farming practices will allow agriculture to live within its means today—and to begin to repay the resource debt of decades past.

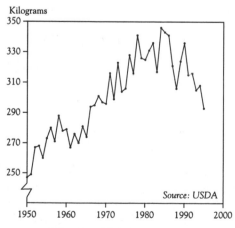

Figure 5-1. World Grain Production Per Person, 1950-95

Source: USDA

LESS LAND, MORE FOOD

One hundred years ago, producing more food required an increase in cultivated land, making land a prime agricultural resource. Since mid-century, the relative importance of land has lessened as agricultural inputs—fertilizer, mechanization, pesticides, irrigation, and improved seeds—contributed significantly to food production increases. Today, land is taking on renewed importance in the face of stagnating yields and a growing need for food. Given the expected 64-percent increase in food demand over the next 25 years, and that expansion onto new lands is impossible in the world's most crowded areas and severely restricted in the rest, cropland is an increasingly precious resource.[3]

In this context, the steady decline in harvested grain area is especially troubling. Grain, which supplies more than half of humanity's daily calories, is a useful barometer of global food security, and land dedicated to grain production is a handy proxy for agricultural land use in general. Average harvested grain area fell 4.7 percent between 1980–84 (the peak years of grainland use) and 1990–94. Today, harvested grain area stands a full 8.5 percent below its 1981 peak, and is equal to the amount of land planted to grain in 1968. The displaced grainland represents lost grain output of approximately 217 million tons annually—roughly 40 percent of the world's average annual rice harvest in the early nineties.[4]

The picture is more compelling when framed in per capita terms. Harvested grainland per person has declined steadily since the fifties, and has fallen a full 25 percent in just the last decade. (See Figure 5–2.) In the past, the loss of grainland was offset by increased yields—the grain produced per hectare. But the anemic yield increases of the last 10 years were well below the rate of loss for harvested area. The result: with continuous increases in demand, grain stocks plummeted, hitting their lowest levels on record in 1995.[5]

Rising demand for food and sluggish growth in yields would seem sufficient motivation to protect remaining cropland, yet farmland around the world continues to be lost to other uses. The

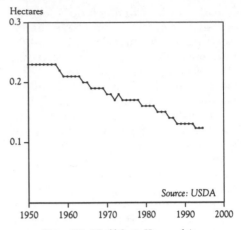

Figure 5-2. World Grain Harvested Area Per Person, 1950-95

growing urbanization of the world's population is pushing cities into the countryside, a trend that is accelerating. With the urban share of global population expected to rise from 43 percent in 1990 to 61 percent in 2025, cities are under increasing pressure to house, employ, transport, and provide recreation for their citizens, all of which requires land. In addition, industrialization—a phenomenon that often, but not always, occurs in cities—is growing rapidly in many developing countries, and requires extensive land area for factories and a range of supporting infrastructure.[6]

In the developing world, Africa and Latin America can absorb urban and industrial expansion without a net loss of agricultural land, but Asia cannot. By one estimate, urban growth in Asia could engulf the equivalent of the continent's remaining uncultivated and croppable land twice over. Competition for land is especially evident in crowded Asian countries whose industrial sectors have boomed. Hong Kong, Singapore, South Korea, and Taiwan saw harvested grain area drop by more than 20 percent between 1980–84 and 1990–94, while East Asia as a whole lost nearly 10 percent of its harvested grain area.[7]

Indeed, increasing urban and industrial claims on agricultural land are the norm throughout much of Asia. China's frenzied industrialization of the past decade spawned more than 200 new cities, and more than 100 million peasants have migrated from rural areas to cities in search of a better life. Much of this growth has come at agriculture's expense. In 1988 and 1989, just prior to the start of China's annual double-digit economic growth, the country lost more than 1 million hectares of cultivated land, 16 percent of which was converted to urban, industrial, or infrastructural uses. (The rest was lost to natural disasters or to "agricultural restructuring": restoration of forests and grasslands, and conversion of cropland to orchards or fish ponds.) If urban and industrial claims on cropland have continued at the same rate in the nineties, China has already paved over 435,000 hectares of cropland in this decade, enough to feed 10 million Chinese. The figure is certainly conservative, however, given the rapid urban and industrial growth of the nineties. Indeed, press reports of land loss this decade indicate a much higher rate than in the late eighties.[8]

Jakarta, Dhaka, and Bangkok also feel pressure to encroach on neighboring agricultural lands. A 1990 World Bank study of Indonesia reported that some 10,000 hectares of agricultural land are needed each year just for house lots. This is consistent with a U.S. Department of Agriculture report that the island of Java loses nearly 20,000 hectares annually to urban growth—enough to grow rice for some 378,000 Indonesians each year. Meanwhile, in Bangladesh, cropland around Dhaka continues to disappear as farmers earn more selling their land for development than they could by farming. And metropoli-

tan Bangkok is projected to expand by 51,000 hectares between 1984 and 2000, an increase of 40 percent. If 80 percent of this expansion engulfs agricultural land in Thailand, the loss will represent rice enough for 344,000 people.[9]

Worse still, urban expansion often claims the best agricultural land. Cities historically were founded near rich agricultural areas; as they grow, some of a country's most fertile land is taken out of production. In the United States, for example, just over 18 percent of all rural land is classified as prime farmland, but within 50 miles of the largest urban areas, 27 percent of farmland is prime. Of the 2.4 million hectares of prime U.S. farmland lost on a net basis between 1982 and 1992, two thirds were converted to rural and urban development.[10]

Java loses nearly 20,000 hectares of cropland annually to urban growth—enough to grow rice for some 378,000 Indonesians each year.

Agricultural lands watered from overdrawn aquifers could also cease production. India, Libya, Saudi Arabia, and the United States rely on overpumping—drawing water from aquifers faster than they are replenished by rainfall—to irrigate extensive tracts of agricultural land. As aquifers are depleted, continued pumping becomes economically or environmentally impractical. Saudi Arabia cut its wheat and barley area by more than a fifth in the past two years, in part for fiscal reasons, but also out of concern for water depletion. Between 1982 and 1992, farmers drawing from the huge Ogallala aquifer in the United States lost three times more irrigated hectares than they gained. In all, five High Plains states and three in the western United States cut irrigated area by nearly 10 percent over this 10-year period as aquifer levels dropped. In a few areas, land taken out of irrigation can continue to be cultivated as rain-fed land, but yields will drop.[11]

Yet another claim to agricultural land will be made if the world experiences a significant increase in temperature. Global warming is expected to raise sea levels by 10–120 centimeters (4–47 inches) by 2100. A World Bank study projects that 9.2 million hectares covering 48 cities would be flooded in China if sea levels rise 50–100 centimeters. This would displace 67 million people, many of whom would undoubtedly relocate on agricultural land. In India, 570,-000 hectares and 7 million people are at risk of inundation. Remedial measures to avoid flooding will be extensive: Vietnam, for instance, may have to build or upgrade some 4,700 kilometers of dikes to protect its coasts.[12]

Sometimes land is so thoroughly damaged that it is essentially lost from production. A 1990 U.N. report on global land degradation, known as the GLASOD study, found that more than 15 percent of agricultural land degraded between 1945 and 1990 was either beyond restoration or so badly damaged that only major engineering works could revive its full productivity. This land is essentially nonproductive. At modest grain yields, the lost land could feed more than 1.5 billion people, more than a quarter of today's global population. Given projected increases in food demand over the next 25 years, the world can little afford continued losses to degradation. Yet various sources estimate that cropland is lost today at least as fast as it was between 1945 and 1990. More worrisome still, nearly two thirds of the most degraded land today is found in Africa and Asia, where demand is rising fastest.[13]

Addressing land degradation can sometimes require that agricultural land be pulled from production. Between 1986 and 1992, for example, the U.S. government paid farmers to not cultivate some 14.6 million hectares (36 million acres)—nearly 10 percent of the nation's cropland—in order to protect marginal lands. But the future of this program is uncertain. Contracts governing two thirds of the protected land are set to expire between October 1995 and the end of 1997; the U.S. Congress will have to decide whether to renew the program. It could be especially useful in protecting vulnerable land in coming years as world demand for U.S. farm products rises, increasing the temptation to bring the marginal land back into production.[14]

Given the pressures on agricultural land today, farmers and policymakers in some areas are searching for new fields to plow. But most potentially cultivable virgin land is already claimed, or clearing it would have calamitous effects on the environment. The U.N. Food and Agriculture Organization (FAO) estimates that cultivating all potential cropland in developing countries (excluding China) would reduce permanent pasture, forests, and woodlands by 47 percent. Forests provide important environmental services, including conservation of water and soils and the preservation of diverse species. They also help regulate global carbon flows. Forests store 20–50 times more carbon than crops and pasture do, so clearing them for agriculture constitutes a huge net release of carbon, a greenhouse gas, into the atmosphere, and likely accelerates global warming. In fact, in the eighties, deforestation—half of which was prompted by agricultural expansion—contributed significantly to global greenhouse gas emissions.[15]

Today, with growth in grain yields trailing growth in food demand and with little room for further expansion, land matters more than ever. In many nations, preservation of agricultural land may even become a national security concern. Unless greater priority is given to preservation of this vital resource, more and more nations will find themselves dependent on imports—if they can find them.

A CRUMBLING FOUNDATION

The U.N.'s 1990 GLASOD study on land degradation included a color-coded map showing the extent and severity of soil degradation around the world. Splotches of pinks, greens, and browns are found in nearly every country. Extensive gray areas, indicating nondegraded expanses, are surprisingly few; they are found only in the sparsely inhabited northern forests of Canada, Scandinavia, and Siberia, and various deserts of the world. The map is a visual expression of the report's findings: that nearly one sixth of the world's vegetated area has suffered some degree of soil degradation since World War II. More than three quarters of this abuse is caused by agriculture and livestock production or by converting forests to cropland. Agricultural mismanagement alone has damaged an area equal to 38 percent of today's cropland. The report was the first global-scale demonstration that soil—the very foundation of agriculture—is under siege around the world.[16]

Abuse of agricultural land ranges from salting and waterlogging, found on poorly managed irrigated lands, to compaction caused by the use of heavy machinery and to pollution from the excessive application of pesticides or manure. But erosion is by far the most common type of land degradation, accounting for 84 percent of affected areas in the U.N.

study. Soil lost to wind and water erosion ranges from 5–10 tons per hectare annually in Africa, Europe, and Australia to 10–20 tons per hectare in North, Central, and South America and nearly 30 tons per hectare in Asia. Because soil is created at roughly 1 ton per hectare a year, current rates of erosion are depleting the nutrient base of agriculture far faster than it is renewed. More than just unsustainable, this loss of topsoil is tragic: in just a few decades, human activity has squandered a natural patrimony that took thousands of years to accumulate.[17]

In just a few decades, human activity has squandered a natural patrimony that took thousands of years to accumulate.

The causes of agriculturally induced erosion range from uninformed farming practices to population growth and social injustice. For generations, moldboard plowing—which overturns soil completely, exposing it to the erosive forces of water and air—was regarded as desirable, and its use became widespread. The plow leaves "clean," black fields, but at a stiff price: scientists estimate that within 50 years of its introduction on the U.S. Great Plains in the nineteenth century, 60 percent of the soil's organic material was washed or blown away. On the other hand, a growing population and unjust land distributions can invite soil degradation, as more farmers are forced to farm marginal lands. In Latin America, for example, the smallest 66 percent of farms cover only 4 percent of farmland. Many children of such farm families face a difficult choice: move to the city, or move to their own farms. Those who choose the latter often end up on hillsides or other low-quality and highly vulnerable land.[18]

The severity of soil degradation globally is best described using the U.N.'s own words. Some 15.6 percent of the world's degraded agricultural land is classified as "strongly" degraded; this is land whose "original biotic functions"— its capacity to convert nutrients into a form usable by plants—"are largely destroyed." Another 51.7 percent is "moderately" degraded, exhibiting "greatly reduced agricultural productivity." The two categories, which essentially describe land that is producing well below its potential, cover two thirds of degraded agricultural land—the equivalent of nearly a quarter of global cropland.[19]

In the nineties, grain yield increases have slowed to scarcely 0.5 percent a year, less than one third the rate of global population growth.

Productivity losses from soil degradation cannot be determined with any precision, but some back-of-the-envelope calculations are possible. Applying researchers' estimates of productivity loss from soil degradation to the categories given in the U.N. study, production on degraded lands was 17 percent lower in 1990, on average, than it would have been without erosion. Continued productivity losses—soil degradation persists unabated in most of the world— represent a serious drag on the effort to meet food demand increases of some 64 percent over the next 25 years.[20]

Degradation-induced loss of soil fertility may have contributed to the marked slowdown in grain yield growth over the past decade. After robust increases averaging 2.3 percent annually between 1950 and 1984, grain yields rose only 1.8 percent a year between 1980–84 and 1990–94, barely faster than population growth. In the nineties, yield increases have slowed still more, to scarcely 0.5 percent a year, less than one third the rate of global population growth. Wheat yields have shown virtually no growth in the first half of this decade. Although the downward slide in grain yield growth rates probably has multiple causes, the continuing deterioration of soil health is undoubtedly a contributing factor.[21]

Soil degradation did not slow yield growth decades earlier largely because farmers applied more fertilizer to compensate for nutrient losses. By recharging soils with nitrogen, phosphorus, and potassium—the principal nutrients that plants need in large quantities—fertilizer quickly and easily replaced soil nutrients lost to erosion or exported from the farm in crops. But today, with increases in fertilizer applications showing smaller and smaller returns, global fertilizer use has plateaued, and may no longer be able to mask increasing soil degradation. And fertilizers are no substitute for true soil health. They cannot supply soil with other essential elements—including organic matter, microorganisms, insects, water, and secondary nutrients—whose interaction creates a supportive environment for plants. As fertilizer applications plateau, the impact of the loss of these other soil elements is likely to become more apparent.[22]

Widespread dependence on fertilizer has created serious shifts in the global cycling of nitrogen and in the supply of phosphorus, two principal plant nutrients. Fertilizer production has increased global levels of fixed nitrogen—nitrogen in a form usable by plants and microorganisms—by some 70 percent over preindustrial levels, and has helped throw the nitrogen cycle out of balance.

Some species use the excess nitrogen more easily than others, leading to differential growth of species and consequent ecosystem disruptions. Moreover, excess nitrogen can change the acidity and organic-matter content of soils, leading to increased leaching of other essential plant nutrients. And water pollution is increased as the excess nitrogen itself is leached from the soil. These and other negative side effects warrant exploration of ways to reduce fertilizer use where possible.[23]

Similarly, fertilizer use contributes to the large-scale transfer of phosphorus from continents to oceans. In 1990, roughly as much phosphorus—33 million tons—was washed into the world's oceans as was applied to cropland. Unlike nitrogen, which cycles between land, seas, and the atmosphere, and which exists in abundance, phosphorus flows only from land to seas, constituting a net nonrecoverable outflow. Because phosphate is the least plentiful of the three principal soil nutrients, chronic outflows will eventually present serious supply difficulties. Phosphate is already in short supply in many regions, especially Africa, and could become difficult and costly to obtain globally if growth in application is strong over the next 100 years. Preservation of soil nutrients on the farm today can minimize their transfer to river and ocean bottoms and avoid a crop nutrient crisis for future generations.[24]

Phosphorus and nitrogen eroded from farmland eventually wind up in rivers, lakes, and oceans, where they cause algal growth and fish deaths. (See also Chapter 4.) In fact, leached and eroded nutrients help make agriculture the largest diffuse source of water pollution in the United States. So extensive is the agricultural pollution of the Mississippi River—the main drainage conduit for the U.S. Corn Belt—that a "dead zone" the size of New Jersey forms each summer in the Gulf of Mexico, the river's terminus. Rich in fertilizer nutrients that feed algae, the zone is devoid of fish and shrimp, which cannot compete with the algae for oxygen. Similar "dead zones," though on smaller scales, are common where agricultural pollutants leach into rivers and lakes.[25]

Growing awareness of the fundamental importance of soil health is prompting soil conservation efforts in some areas. The use of conservation tillage, which reduces erosion by minimizing soil disturbance and by leaving stubble from the previous crop in place, has risen an average of 7 percent annually in the United States since 1989, and it is now used on just over a third of all planted land in the country. Cover crops—plantings that keep soil covered between harvest and the planting of principal crops—also retard erosion and add organic matter to the soil. Measures like these, coupled with programs that retire erosion-prone land, led to a 25-percent reduction in water and wind erosion rates in the United States between 1982 and 1992.[26]

Some regions combat soil degradation through agroforestry, the age-old practice of incorporating trees into cropped fields. Trees surrounding a field can reduce winds and retain soil moisture, both of which help to keep soil in place. Perimeter trees, along with other trees and bushes placed throughout the agroecosystem, provide habitat for pest-eating birds, forage, and fuelwood to villages that need it. Well-placed trees diversify and protect the environment, which in turn increases yields. Although agroforestry is not a panacea, research on 18 crops in 14 countries has shown that its wind protection role alone can increase yields from 6 to 99 percent, depending on the crop and local conditions.[27]

At the global level, however, continued widespread abuse of agricultural soils is the norm. The trend is especially troubling given the ongoing pressure to increase food output and the limited opportunities to expand agricultural area. Reversing soil degradation would not only restore productivity to degraded land, it could also reduce the environmentally harmful effects of overdependence on fertilizer. Only when soils are rehabilitated and conserved will agricultural production be maximized on a sustainable basis.

WATER WOES

Because water is of singular importance to all agriculture, the shortage of clean water is in many areas the greatest resource constraint on agricultural production. Water is indispensable to food production, and has no substitutes. Farming demands prodigious quantities of this resource—some two thirds of the fresh water withdrawn globally from rivers, lakes, and aquifers. Thus when water supplies begin to evaporate or become unfit for agricultural use, the effect on output is immediate. When supplies are available, however, they make all the difference in the world: irrigated cropland, which constitutes only 16 percent of the global total, produces perhaps 40 percent of the world's food.[28]

Regional water shortages are now common, even though global supplies of water are ample. In 26 countries—home to 230 million people—scarce water limits food production, economic development, sanitation, and environmental protection. Ten of these countries actually run a water deficit: they consume more than their annual renewable supply, usually by depleting underground water reserves. As population grows, the ranks of water-scarce nations are expected to swell to 35 by 2020.[29]

In some countries, agriculture survives in part on water borrowed from the future. By pumping groundwater faster than it is renewed by rainfall, China, India, Iran, Libya, Pakistan, Saudi Arabia, and the United States cash in valuable water reserves—essentially insurance water—for short-term economic gain. An estimated 10 percent of China's cultivated area, for example, and 33 percent of Iran's depend on overdrafted groundwater. On the Arabian peninsula, 75 percent of groundwater used on crops is not just overdrafted, it is nonrenewable: trapped underground thousands of years ago, this water is not replenished by rainfall. In the Indian states of Maharashtra, Gujarat, and Haryana, wells are severely overdrawn or flooded with salt water, rendering many unfit for agricultural production. Overconsumption in the southern Great Plains of the United States has pulled thousands of hectares of irrigated land in Texas from active production or converted them to rain-fed farmland. And in the Indus valley of Pakistan, groundwater is pumped at more than 50 percent above the rate that will avoid salinated water.[30]

In each of these cases, regional and national populations have grown dependent on unsustainable agriculture. When groundwater becomes too costly to pump from lower depths or too salty to use on crops, pumping will cease. Without other sources of water, food production in these areas—and the economies and people that depend on it—will simply collapse.

Aquifer overdrafting and other activities related to agriculture shift large quantities of fresh water to the world's oceans. A 1994 study estimated that the world's continents experience a net annual loss of 190 billion cubic meters of water—more than one and a quarter times the water used in South America in 1990—as natural reservoirs on land are drained. The effect over the past several decades has been to raise the global sea level by an estimated 1.1 centimeters. Besides aquifers, other natural reservoirs that now suffer a net outflow of water include tropical forests (where deforestation eliminates water-storing vegetation, causing a loss of 49 billion cubic meters per year), Africa's Sahel (where desertification evaporates 3.4 billion cubic meters of soil moisture each year), and rivers feeding Central Asia's Aral Sea. The study was only a partial documentation of water transfer to oceans, but it gives a sense of how human activities, especially agriculture, can disrupt the global hydrological cycle.[31]

Even where water scarcity is not an issue, other factors may limit the amount of water used in agriculture. FAO estimates that global irrigated area could theoretically increase by 50 percent, but economic and environmental conditions severely limit prospects for irrigation growth. Indeed, irrigated area is expanding at less than 1 percent annually—not even half the rate of growth of the mid-seventies. Because the most easily constructed major irrigation projects are already built, future construction will be far more expensive. This, combined with low food prices and increased citizen opposition to large-scale dams, has dampened interest in expansion of irrigation. As a consequence, irrigation funding has fallen some 25–33 percent since the mid-seventies.[32]

In many regions, as agriculture struggles for water it faces increasing competition from other sectors. Industrial and domestic water demand, which accounts for roughly a third of the total today, is projected to reach 45–50 percent by the year 2025. Urban-rural competition for water will be especially intense in Asia, the most irrigated region in the world. In parts of India, Indonesia, and Malaysia, irrigation water will fall 15–30 percent short of projected demand in coming decades if urban demands are fully met.

In China, where more than 300 cities are short of water today, rapid industrial growth is adding to water stress; China's current urban water shortfall—5.8 billion cubic meters per year—is expected to more than triple by 2000.[33]

In some countries, agriculture survives in part on water borrowed from the future.

To ensure adequate supplies, cities increasingly use their financial clout to buy water rights in rural areas. The practice is becoming common in the southwestern United States. Cities in southern California now pay farmers not to cultivate during drought years, while El Paso, Texas, and other southwestern cities purchase water rights outright from farmers. The cities typically can outbid farmers for the resource: whereas farmers in many parts of the United States pay just a few cents per cubic meter for water, cities commonly pay many times this rate. Reports of cities securing water at well over a dollar per cubic meter are increasingly common.[34]

Today, the environment is increasingly recognized as a legitimate claimant of water. (See also Chapter 3.) Authorities in the Murray-Darling Basin of Australia capped farmers' water withdrawals in 1995 when they learned that only a quarter of the basin's water actually reached the sea. Agricultural use of water otherwise needed by the local environment had led to fish deaths and a rise in river salt levels. Likewise, some federal water projects in the United States now keep river and dam waters at levels high enough to prevent excessive warming of water, which could kill fish. These policy decisions stand in striking contrast to the classic thinking on river flows: that any water reaching the sea is "wasted." It also suggests that the environment's claim on water can be substantial. Indeed, in California, the environment's share of developed water was recently calculated at 45 percent, just ahead of agriculture's 42 percent.[35]

A worrisome wild card in agricultural water supply is the influence of climate change. A warmer climate is expected to increase both rainfall and evaporation; regional effects on agriculture will differ depending on whether increased moisture or warmer temperatures prevail. In addition, rainfall is expected to be more variable and drought more common. (See Chapter 2.) In general, agriculture in developing countries is projected to suffer most from climate change, while countries at higher latitudes—typically industrial nations—could see food production increase. A major study, which used three models of climate change and agricultural scientists in 18 countries to estimate the impact of increased precipitation and temperature on production, concluded that global cereal output could fall slightly.[36]

Despite the increasing stresses on agricultural water, most irrigation systems waste prodigious amounts of this resource. FAO estimates average water loss between source and crops to be some 55 percent: in other words, less than half the water intended for agriculture actually reaches crops. It is not all wasted, however; some of it is used downstream. (See also Chapter 3.) Still, field-level efficiencies can be improved. Highly efficient microirrigation systems—including drip irrigation, which literally drips water at the base of plants—were found on less than 1 percent of irrigated land in 1991. Israel, a leader in the field, now uses drip irrigation on more than half its irrigated land.[37]

But many water-saving solutions require no investment or advanced technology. Irrigating every other furrow in a field can save one third of water with only a slight loss in yields. Intermittent rather than continuous flooding of rice paddies could save 40 percent in water with little loss of output. Cultivating crops suited to the local supply of moisture also helps. A 1995 study of water use in semiarid California showed that shifting agriculture from water-intensive crops such as rice, cotton, and alfalfa would eliminate groundwater overdrafts in the state. In Central Asia, Kazakstan, Uzbekistan, and Kyrgyzstan have reduced the land planted in cotton and rice—in some areas, up to 75 percent—in order to save water.[38]

Reuse of water can also increase water efficiency. Treated wastewater, a largely untapped source of reusable water, is now used for irrigation in parts of California, India, Mexico, and especially the Middle East. More than 70 percent of Israel's treated wastewater is used in irrigation, and Greater Cairo's wastewater potential by 2010 is estimated to be a full 83 percent of its current agricultural water use.[39]

MANAGING PESTS

Modern methods of pest control show clearly that a myopic approach to agricultural problems can degrade farm resources. Farmers stung by losses to pests—which destroy more than a third of the world's crops—often respond with a single-minded vengeance, attacking the weeds, insects, and bacteria that do the damage. But this seeks to eliminate pests rather than control them, and upsets the natural balance necessary for stable functioning of the agroecosystem. Pest overkill is now recognized as often being counterproductive: pests are more prevalent, and crop losses are greater, than ever before.

Kicking the pesticide habit is difficult, however, and pesticide use continues to climb. Global sales of these chemicals reached a record $25 billion in 1994. Industrial countries account for some 80 percent of pesticide use, but sales there have plateaued, and use in developing countries, especially in Asia and Latin America, is projected to grow fastest in the coming years. Brazil, China, and India are major users, and increasingly producers, of pesticides.[40]

Pesticides are frequently marketed as an easy and convenient tool for pest control, but the magic they work is often fleeting. Pests quickly develop resistance to the chemicals, making higher doses and eventually new products necessary to achieve the same level of control. Species resistant to common pesticides now number more than 900, up from 182 in 1965. (See Figure 5-3.) To control these and other pests, more pesticides are applied, but with less effect: between 1945 and 1989 in the United States, insecticide applications increased tenfold, but crop losses to insects nearly doubled—from 7 to 13 percent of the harvest. Although changes in farming practices, such as the adoption of monocropping,

explain part of the higher losses, increased resistance is also an important factor. Today, farmers in some areas of Asia reportedly apply pesticides at up to eight times the dosage level originally recommended, in order to ensure an effective kill.[41]

Pests' nimble capacity to develop resistance has serious economic and social effects as well. Increased applications to counter resistance to the pyrethroid class of pesticides is estimated to cost farmers $2.4 billion annually—just under 10 percent of total pesticide sales in 1994. The cost in human health is also high. In India, in the early sixties, pesticide use reduced the incidence of malaria from several million cases to some 40,000. But as mosquito resistance to pesticides increased, malaria took off, and stands today at some 59 million cases per year in India. (See Chapter 7.) Meanwhile, research and development for new pesticides is increasingly slow and costly; development of a new pesticide requires 10 years, on average, and can cost $20–45 million, compared with $1.2 million in 1956.[42]

Overuse of pesticides can also disrupt the stability of an agroecosystem by eliminating beneficial insects, the pests' natural enemies. Without these other insects, surviving pests are free to dominate a field. At the same time, "secondary" pests—those originally found in small numbers in an ecosystem—often multiply when major pests are decimated. This happened in Indonesia, where the brown rice planthopper proliferated after its natural enemies were routed by pesticides. In a two-year feeding frenzy, this secondary pest ruined some $1.5 billion in rice. The disaster prompted the Indonesian government to withdraw subsidies for pesticide use, in an effort to steer farmers toward alternative methods of pest control.[43]

Farmers, farmworkers, and the public are also adversely affected by pesticide

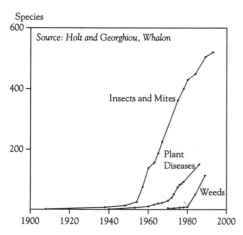

Figure 5-3. Pesticide-Resistant Species Since 1908

use. A 1995 study of the midwestern United States revealed the presence of herbicides in tap water in 28 of 29 cities tested. In more than half of them, herbicide levels exceeded government safety standards. Meanwhile, a 1988 World Health Organization commission estimated that 1 million occupational pesticide poisonings occur annually worldwide. Other estimates range from 3 million to 25 million persons being affected. The problem is especially severe in developing countries, where training in the use of poisons is often lax or nonexistent. Through the mid-eighties, half the pesticide poisonings and more than 80 percent of all pesticide-related deaths occurred in developing countries, which account for only 20 percent of global pesticide use. A 1993 report showed that 21 percent of Indonesian farmers studied exhibited three or more symptoms of pesticide poisoning during the spray period. In China, where many pesticides are unlicensed concoctions, an estimated 10,000 farmers died in 1993 from pesticide poisoning.[44]

Many people are now interested in severely reducing dependence on poisons as a means of pest control.

The dangers to those who handle pesticides are increasing even as the chemicals become less acutely harmful to the environment. Organochlorines such as DDT have given way in many countries to less persistent but more toxic chemicals. Indeed, less than a tenth of a kilo of some of today's pesticides can kill as effectively as 2 kilos of DDT did in 1945.[45]

Part of the tragedy of pesticides' toll on people and ecosystems is that much of the damage is unnecessary. Dramatic

reductions in pesticide use are possible. More accurate placement of the chemical, for example, offers great potential savings. Indeed, many pesticides miss their intended field: only half of the pesticide applied by aircraft actually hits the target area. By contrast, placement rates of 90 percent and better are possible with proper ground application equipment. Training farmers to apply pesticides only when pests are an economic threat, not whenever they appear, and to use spot rather than blanket applications could also sharply reduce pesticide use. And proper timing of applications can be crucial: fungicide use on cereals in U.K. field tests was cut by 50–75 percent simply by applying the chemicals at the right time.[46]

Several countries have recorded significant reductions in the use of these chemicals. Sweden cut pesticide use by half between 1986 and 1991, and is currently pursuing a further 50-percent cut. The Netherlands and Canada have similarly ambitious plans in the works. In Texas, pesticide use on cotton has been reduced by 90 percent since 1966.[47]

Although pesticide use and toxicity continue steadily upward, many people are now interested in severely reducing dependence on poisons as a means of pest control. Integrated pest management (IPM), which emphasizes the use of cultural, biological, and genetic resources to combat pests and views pesticides as a last line of defense, is increasingly being adopted around the world.[48]

Changes in cultural practices can facilitate agroecosystem diversity, which in turn keeps plant-eating pests in check. One example is crop rotations, which alternate host and nonhost crops over a several-year cycle to keep pests from establishing a permanent presence. Abandonment of crop rotations in the United States—the result of a modernizing process that replaced horses with tractors, which did not require a crop of clover as feed—was in part responsible for increased corn losses to pests. Losses to insects stood at 3.5 percent in the forties, when little or no insecticide was applied to corn, but jumped to 12 percent after the introduction of monoculture cropping, even though pesticide use increased one thousandfold. Many farmers have now returned to crop rotations, but monoculture is still the norm for 40 percent of U.S. corn.[49]

Other IPM measures include biological practices, which use natural enemies such as birds, insects, or bacteria to control pests, and manipulation of crop genetics, whether through farmer selection, scientific breeding, or genetic engineering. If cultural, biological, and genetic initiatives fail to control pests, resort to pesticide use may be necessary. But IPM advocates consider pesticides to be a last option—and one that should be used sparingly.

IPM is promoted increasingly around the world as an economical and environmentally sound strategy. FAO has run an IPM program since 1980 in South and Southeast Asia that has logged impressive results. More than 500,000 farmers are now trained in IPM practices; their use of insecticides on rice is down by 50–100 percent. And their yields are up by 10 percent. Successes like these are attracting attention, and the IPM approach to pest control is receiving support at the international level. In 1995 the World Bank, FAO, the U.N. Development Programme, and the U.N. Environment Programme established a facility to promote integrated pest management around the world. Although poorly funded thus far, the initiative is a sign of international interest in reduced dependence on pesticides.[50]

Only when pest control strategies are sensitive to the larger agricultural environment will they achieve a sustainable footing. By working in concert with the agroecosystem, sustainable pest control reduces both agriculture's vulnerability to pests and the pressure on researchers to develop new and more toxic methods of dealing with them.

THE ROW TO HOE

Abuse of agricultural resources cannot continue if the global population of the twenty-first century is to be fed adequately. Measures to protect farmland, conserve soils, save water, and manage pests are needed to preserve the productive base of agriculture. Broadly speaking, three sets of policy initiatives could steer agriculture toward sustainability: removal of mechanisms that encourage unsustainable farming, development of programs that promote sustainable farming, and a deepening of our base of knowledge about sustainable agriculture. Even if these policy thrusts are developed, however, food production may fall short of the levels needed to feed billions more people. Changes in consumption patterns may be needed to increase the efficient use of food, and thereby its supply.

Governments in effect encourage unsustainable farming through the use of subsidies that distort resource use. The members of the Organisation for Economic Co-operation and Development (OECD) alone spend $175 billion a year on subsidies to agricultural producers. These supports take diverse forms, from direct payments for crop production to reduced market prices for water or pesticides. Some subsidies are used to promote sustainable farming, but many have the opposite effect. Where water, pesticides, or fertilizers are priced artificially low—a common occurrence around the world—the result is typically wasteful and often harmful overuse.[51]

The elimination of subsidies that mask the true costs of agricultural inputs or that encourage production on marginal land makes resource abuse more costly and, therefore, less likely. When Indonesia abolished subsidies for pesticides used in rice production, pesticide applications dropped by more than half, from 4.5 to 2.2 per season. The Indonesian treasury also benefited, pocketing $120 million that had previously supported cheap pesticides. Similar results can be expected from the reduction or elimination of subsidies to water and to production, which may encourage overcultivation.[52]

Part of the savings from the elimination of harmful subsidies can be used to promote sustainable farming. Indonesia's end to pesticide subsidies was accompanied by farmer training in IPM techniques, a highly effective investment: those who took the training cut their pesticide applications to less than half the level achieved by elimination of subsidies alone. Initiatives to promote soil conservation, organic methods of increasing soil fertility, and efficient water use are also worthy of support. Efforts like the Conservation Reserve Program in the United States, which paid farmers not to cultivate marginal land, are models of an active approach to ending abuse of agricultural resources.[53]

Investment may also be necessary to protect farmland. Where land is freely bought and sold, farmland has steadily disappeared as developers outbid would-be farmers. If land is dangerously scarce, farmland conversions may need to be outlawed. Combined with compensation to farmers for lost development rights, conversion prohibition is an equitable way to balance the rights of individual farmholders with the national interest in abundant food production. Alternatively, a land tax levied on farmland sold for nonagricultural uses can effectively discourage farmland conver-

sions. In areas with less pressure on farmland, conservation easements, already in use in parts of the United States, may be appropriate. These are voluntary arrangements under which farmers are paid for relinquishing the right to develop their farmland. Government funding of such initiatives could turn them into a serious tool for farmland preservation.[54]

Given the twin challenges posed by anemic yields and rising food demand, a redoubled commitment to agricultural investment is necessary. Yet support for agriculture is dwindling. National investment in agriculture was less in the eighties than in the seventies for about half the world's developing countries. Aid to agriculture in developing countries fell from $12 billion in 1980 to $10 billion in 1990 in constant dollars. And funding for the 16 research centers that make up the Consultative Group on International Agricultural Research fell 22 percent between 1990 and 1994, to $215 million—just a tenth of 1 percent of what the OECD spends each year on agricultural subsidies. The complacency underlying these trends must be overcome if the agricultural challenges of the next decades are to be met.[55]

Not only must support for agriculture increase, its focus must be broadened. The traditional research emphasis—on developing high-yielding crop varieties—must be augmented to include study of production methods that make sustainable use of agricultural resources. Increasing water use efficiency, for example, should be a high priority for study. Adapting super-efficient microirrigation technologies for use on grains—not just fruits and vegetables—and making such technologies affordable to small farmers would encourage their use.

Soil conservation research is another urgent need. A broad approach to this—one that includes work on maintaining levels of organic matter and on cycling nutrients from urban areas back to farms—could have the happy advantage of strengthening soil properties and reducing fertilizer use as it minimizes degradation. Meanwhile, further study of pest management strategies that minimize chemical use and work with the natural resources of the agroecosystem would help reduce health hazards and ecosystem imbalances caused by heavy pesticide use.

Research in each of these areas is most fruitful if undertaken with the full participation of farmers, a widely overlooked and undertapped agricultural resource. By pairing scientific understanding of crops, soils, pests, and water with farmers' knowledge of local ecological and social conditions and their experience with innovation, new agricultural methods that are both sustainable and accepted by local farmers can be developed.

Adopting measures to conserve land, soils, and water and to manage rather than eliminate pests can help put agriculture on a sustainable path. Whether food production under these conditions can keep pace with demand will depend in part on the success of research into sustainable methods of crop production. In the meantime, pressure to make herculean boosts in output with a spartan use of resources can be reduced by ensuring that harvested crops are used efficiently. Much like the energy situation between 1974 and 1994, when energy intensity in industrial countries fell 25–30 percent while economic output expanded by half, efficient use of harvested food could feed more people with the same agricultural output.[56]

One way to improve the use of agricultural produce is to reduce levels of postharvest wastes. More than 20 percent of harvested food never makes it to the dinner table because of spoilage, spillage, and losses to rodents and in-

sects. Cutting these losses would raise food availability without further taxing agricultural resources. Technologies for this include a recently developed tent-sized bag for storing sacks of harvested grain. Virtually airtight, the bag suffocates insects while keeping rodents out. The bag can also increase income: in field tests, Sri Lankan farmers stored their produce in the bags until after the harvest-time glut of food, and saw incomes climb 30 percent.[57]

Farmers are a widely overlooked and undertapped agricultural resource.

Perhaps the greatest way to increase food use efficiency is to reduce the world's consumption of meat. The 38 percent of the world's grain that is fed to animals each year is an inefficient use of cereals. Because a kilogram of feedlot-produced beef represents 7 kilograms of grain, lowering beef consumption could free up grain for direct consumption or as feed to more efficient meat producers (a kilogram of pork represents 4 kilograms of grain, while poultry and fish represent just 2 kilograms). Moving down the food chain would release mountains of grain for consumption by others: if Americans cut their annual grain intake in half, to the level that Italians consume each year, 105 million tons of grain would be saved—enough to feed two thirds of India for a year.[58]

Fortunately for grain stocks, preference for pork and poultry is growing as beef consumption stagnates worldwide. Between 1980 and 1993, world poultry consumption increased 84 percent, 16 times faster than beef. Nevertheless, there is still ample room, especially in industrial nations, to cut meat consumption to levels that are healthier for global grain stocks as well as for individuals. Forty percent of the food energy in the French or American diet, for example, comes from fat, well above the recommended level of 30 percent. One expert notes that cuts in meat consumption that reduced fat intake to the 30-percent level globally would save enough grain to feed the world's population increases for the next five years.[59]

Finally, it is important to note that advances in food use efficiency and in sustainable methods of agriculture mean little unless population growth continues to be dampened. Again, the experience of energy efficiency is instructive. While efficiency improvements since the seventies cut energy per unit of output, the savings were soon devoured by an overall increase in energy consumption. Cars got better mileage, but people increased

their driving; homes became more efficient, but they also got bigger. Similarly, agricultural productivity gains that saved millions from famine in the seventies and eighties have been eaten up by population increases. Unless increased food production and more efficient consumption are accompanied by population stabilization, the world will again be faced with looming food shortages. But by that time, the easy efficiency gains and yield increases will have been exhausted.[60]

Nonetheless, feeding the world in the next century using sustainable methods of food production is an achievable goal. By reaching agreement on the critical importance of a healthy agricultural resource base, half the battle will be won. Then, mobilizing ingenuity and resources to produce food sustainably and abundantly, food security for all in the coming decades can be assured.

6

Understanding the Threat of Bioinvasions

Chris Bright

More than any other place on earth, the Galápagos Islands shaped Charles Darwin's thoughts on evolution. When he visited them in 1835, he found herds of giant tortoises, birds so unused to people they seemed tame, and the iguanas he called "imps of darkness." Darwin and later visitors to the islands have described a host of creatures that live nowhere else: Galápagos mockingbirds and centipedes, hawks, sharks, and penguins—even a Galápagos tomato. This menagerie owes its existence not so much to any special quality of the islands themselves, but to the thousand-kilometer stretch of ocean between them and the coast of Ecuador.[1]

Barriers such as oceans are important instruments of evolution. They help set the terms of life by containing particular assemblages of plants and animals—and by excluding predators, competitors, and diseases that evolved elsewhere. Barriers are not absolute, of course. Mainland creatures arrive on the Galápagos from time to time, but until recently, virtually all of them had come from relatively nearby, and only certain types of creatures could manage the trip. Mainland birds might make it, but large mammals had no way across the water. Even the holes in a barrier work toward stability: any creature from a neighboring region that could get to the islands and survive on them was likely to have discovered them long ago. And so from island to mainland, from one horizon to the next, a subtle matrix of barriers has allowed the communities of life to work out evolutionary answers to a particular spot of land, a stream, or a set of ocean currents.[2]

If Darwin were studying the Galápagos today, he might wonder why so many creatures seem so poorly adapted to each other. On Pinzon Island, black rats kill virtually every hatchling of the local race of giant tortoise; on other islands, feral pigs are eating the eggs of tortoises, iguanas, and the endangered green sea turtle. On some islands, goats have eliminated all the seedlings of several tree species, and feral house cats have eaten most of the lava lizards. On Floreana Island, thickets of the shrub *Lantana camara* are encroaching on the nesting grounds of the darkrumped petrel. The little fire ant has eliminated most of the islands' other ant species. In each of these cases, an "exotic" species is threatening an island creature. An exotic species is an organism that has invaded an ecosystem in which it is not native—one in which it did not evolve. And because they did not evolve with black rats and *Lantana*, the island creatures do not have effective defenses against them.[3]

Bioinvasions like these are hardly unique to the Galápagos. In Lake Victoria, Africa's largest lake, a huge fish from the Nile river was introduced to improve the fishing: it provoked a mass extinction of native fish and destroyed an important food source for 30 million people. In the waterways of eastern North America, a tiny European shellfish was accidentally released: it is radically altering aquatic food chains and doing billions of dollars in industrial damage. In Australia and North America, Eurasian and African grasses are increasing the fire frequency in natural areas, forcing the retreat of forests.[4]

Exotics are at work everywhere on the planet—some intentionally introduced, others simply by-products of the ever-increasing movement of goods and people. Of course, the migration of species into new habitats has always been a part of nature, but human activity has so greatly accelerated the process as to make it, from a global point of view, a new phenomenon in the history of life. The ancient barriers, the molds within which ecosystems formed, are crumbling. The resulting spread of exotic animals is now second only to habitat loss as a category of ecological destruction, according to Harvard biologist Edward Wilson, an authority on biodiversity. Vernon Heywood, a specialist on plant invasions, considers exotic plants among the most serious threats to natural plant communities. And for Bruce Coblentz, an expert on island bioinvasions, exotics have a capacity for self-perpetuation unmatched by most other forms of environmental degradation. A cut-over forest may regrow if given a chance; many pollutants will eventually decay; but if left to themselves, exotics usually just proliferate. Exotics have become, in Wilson's terms, one of the "mindless horsemen of the environmental apocalypse."[5]

THE ECOLOGY OF INVASION

Not all exotics are dangerous. Many—probably most—of the organisms that arrive in a foreign habitat fail to establish themselves, and simply die out. Many that do survive have not proved harmful, and it is occasionally argued that some very successful invaders are "beneficial"—even in a wild context. For instance, a seaweed introduced to Hawaiian coasts for production of the food additive carrageenan may now be a major part of the diet of the endangered green sea turtle. The proportion of exotics that have caused serious trouble varies greatly from one region to the next and is very difficult to estimate. (See Tables 6-1 and 6-2.) But a rough rule of thumb, developed from research during the late eighties by an international organization called the Scientific Committee on Problems in the Environment, is

Table 6-1. Selected Historical Examples of Bioinvasions

Name of Organism	Home Range	Areas Invaded	Some Major Effects
Black and brown rats	East and Southeast Asia	Nearly all land areas except for desert, polar, and some deep forest regions	During 1500s, 30 percent of West European population died from rat-transmitted plague; as predators, rats have driven island bird species into extinction; rats are serious crop pests.
Smallpox	Mediterranean basin	Most inhabited areas (now eradicated)	Perhaps two thirds of New World's native population died of this and other Old World diseases in 1500s; smallpox was killing 2 million people a year as recently as 1958.
Rinderpest virus	India	Africa	Epidemics around 1900 devastated East African cattle and the region's wildlife.
English sparrow	Europe, central and south Asia, parts of North Africa	North, Central, and South America; most islands; southern Africa; Australia; New Zealand	A serious pest of a wide range of crops; as a competitor of other birds, the English sparrow has suppressed many native bird populations.
Wild oats	Eurasia	Virtually all cereal-growing regions	Reduces grain harvests by enough to feed 50 million people.

SOURCE: See endnote 6.

that 10 percent of established exotics have some major ecological effect.[6]

Unfortunately, that 10 percent can cause so much damage that there is little reason to be complacent about the number. For example, direct predation—when an exotic simply eats the natives—is suppressing native prey populations and causing a growing number of extinc-

tions, especially on islands or in island-like ecosystems, such as lakes. In such places, the biota is less likely to have evolved under the full range of pressures that continental organisms must usually contend with. The case of the Nile perch in Lake Victoria has already been mentioned, but there are many others. House cats are thought to be the main

Table 6-2. Selected Current Examples of Bioinvasions

Name of Organism	Home Range	Areas Invaded	Some Major Effects
Zebra mussel	Caspian Sea	Europe, eastern North America	Suppresses many native aquatic species by outcompeting them for plankton; does millions of dollars in damage by encrusting water pipes and boats.
Asian tiger mosquito	Southeast Asia	East Asia, Pacific and Indian Ocean islands, Australia, New Zealand, southern Europe, Nigeria and southern Africa, United States, Brazil	May help spread yellow fever, dengue fever, and encephalitis.
Various grasses	Eurasia, Africa, North America	North America, Pacific islands, Australia, New Zealand	Exotic grasses are increasing the frequency of fires and displacing native vegetation from millions of hectares.
Tilapia fish	Africa	Many lakes and rivers in tropical and warm temperate zones	As competitors or predators, tilapia are suppressing many native fish species.
Sweet pittosporum	Australia	New Zealand, Oceania, Central America, Caribbean and Atlantic islands, South Africa	An efficient colonizer of tropical and subtropical forest in a variety of climates, this shrub shades out native seedlings, preventing the regeneration of the forest.

SOURCE: See endnote 6.

factor in the loss of many of New Zealand's bird populations. Exotic rats—particularly the black rat and the brown rat—have taken a similar toll on many island birds. (Eighty-two percent of the world's major islands now have exotic rat populations.) Perhaps the most spectacular example involves the brown tree snake, which invaded Guam from the Papua New Guinea region around 1950 and has driven 9 of that Pacific island's 18 native birds into extinction, along with several lizards and probably three species of bats.[7]

Herbivores can take a similar toll, as the goats are doing on the Galápagos. Feral goats are to island plants what rats are to island birds—and the goats have plenty of company. The house mouse, for instance, is devouring the seedlings of an ecologically important tree on Gough Island in the South Atlantic. In New Zealand, the brushtail possum, a tiny Australian marsupial, has wiped out entire stands of the 30-meter-tall native Christmas tree. The possum eats the tree's bark, buds, berries, leaves—even its flowers; currently the possum is chewing through New Zealand's vegetation at the rate of 21 tons a night.[8]

Exotic predation, like so many other aspects of bioinvasion, is unpredictable, even when the creature in question is well known and has been intentionally introduced. The American gray squirrel, for example, was released on English estates from the 1870s through the 1920s. It was expected to eat mainly nuts, as it does in its native habitat, but instead it developed a taste for the bark of young deciduous trees, and has become a serious forest pest throughout Britain.[9]

When they do not literally eat the natives, exotics may outcompete them for some essential resource—food, water, or in the case of plants, light. In some Scandinavian lakes, populations of char have been eliminated by introduced whitefish, which are stronger predators for the zooplankton that both depend on. Other forms of competition are less direct. An exotic may, for instance, work some basic change in the "ground rules" of an ecosystem—often to its own benefit, and to the detriment of a native competitor.[10]

One of the most serious forms of this process is the alteration of an area's fire regime by invasive plants. Nearly all natural terrestrial areas have some sort of fire cycle to which the the native vegetation is adapted. But exotic grasses are changing these cycles in natural areas of North America, Hawaii, and Australia. These "fire-adapted" grasses burn more intensely and more frequently than the vegetation native to the areas they are

invading. They also recover from fires more quickly: after each burn, the grasses gain ground and the native plants retreat. In the western United States, fire-adapted Eurasian cheat grass now dominates more than 40 million hectares—an area larger than Germany. The process is less common in ecosystems already adapted to intense fires, but there is precedent for it even there. In South Africa, the invasive neotropical shrub *Chromolaena odorata* has overrun woodland margins, where forest meets savanna. The shrub is highly flammable and regenerates quickly after burning; it brings the savanna fires into the forests, which used to act as firebreaks. The result is a retreat of the forest.[11]

Positive feedback loops like this are not confined to the fire cycle; they occur in the soil as well. In coastal California, for example, the west African iceplant acts as a "magnet" for the salt in the atmospheric moisture. The iceplant accumulates salt in its tissues. This does it no harm, but when the plant dies, the salt is released into the soil, rendering the area unfit for much of the native vegetation. In Hawaiian natural areas, many native plants are adapted to the low organic nitrogen levels typical of new volcanic soil. But a number of exotic invaders are capable of fixing nitrogen—that is, incorporating gaseous nitrogen into organic compounds that can then be used in plant metabolism. Nitrogen fixing boosts soil fertility and that benefits the exotics: they can grow more rapidly than the natives, which are not adapted to taking advantage of the extra nutrient.[12]

Exotics can also pose a kind of internal threat to natives: an exotic that is closely related to a native may interbreed with it, releasing its genes into the native gene pool. Genetic invasions can undermine the distinctiveness or stability of a native population by swamping it in foreign genes. Perhaps the most celebrated instance of this has been caused by the release of hatchery-bred salmon into the rivers of the U.S. Pacific Northwest. The hatchery salmon are homogenizing the wild salmon populations—erasing the variations that were the salmon's way of matching itself to different rivers. (See also Chapter 4.) And the same mechanism is at work elsewhere. The domestic cat, for example, may be undermining the genetic integrity of the African wild cat in southern Africa and the Scottish wild cat in Scotland.[13]

The lakes and rivers of eastern North America are suffering basic changes in the food web with the arrival of the zebra mussel from the Caspian Sea region.

Sometimes interbreeding can produce a new, hybrid species that may be invasive in ways that its forebears were not. Early in the last century, a North American salt-marsh plant called cordgrass (*Spartina alternifolia*) was accidentally introduced into Britain, where it hybridized with a European relative, *S. maritima*, to produce a third species, *S. x townsendii*. A later doubling of chromosomes in that hybrid yielded yet another species, *S. anglica*. American cordgrass is no longer common in Britain, but *S. anglica* has colonized the coastline and estuaries of the British Isles extensively (partly through intentional planting), although in recent years a fungal infection has driven it back. The same process may occur in crop plants, which often have wild relatives with which they interbreed, especially in the tropics, where many crops originated. For example, crosses between domestic and wild potatoes in South America have produced a new weed: the Bolivian weed potato.[14]

Another kind of internal threat is the transmission of diseases. One of the greatest wildlife invasions in history involves a pathogen: the cattle virus called rinderpest, the likely ancestor of the human disease measles. Rinderpest is native to India, where it is a relatively mild cattle infection. But the introduction of infected cattle into the horn of Africa in the 1890s spread the virus to African ungulates, including strains of cattle much more susceptible to the virus and a large number of native species—antelopes, buffalo, the giraffe, and many others. These animals had little immunity, and mortality in some species is thought to have reached 90 percent. Cattle vaccination programs eventually broke the virus's grip, but serious local outbreaks still occur, and according to one authority, past outbreaks may have helped to "sculpt" the present distribution of many wild ungulate populations.[15]

In addition to rinderpest, wildlife populations have recently fallen prey to several other morbilliviruses, as the measles group of viruses is called. During a distemper outbreak among Siberian sled dogs in the late eighties, for instance, people living in southern Siberia dumped dog carcasses into Lake Baikal. Distemper wiped out 70 percent of the lake's seals. Morbilliviruses have also been implicated in a number of marine mammal die-offs in the Atlantic region during the late eighties and early nineties.[16]

Exotics sometimes entangle both people and wildlife in the same cycle of disease. During the mid-eighties, for example, the Asian tiger mosquito invaded the United States from Japan. Among the diseases it can transmit are several forms of encephalitis endemic to North America. (See also Chapter 7.) One of these, La Crosse encephalitis, infects a number of wild animals—especially chipmunks and squirrels. (To date, the vector for human infection has been another, native mosquito.) The Asian tiger mosquito has the broadest host range of any mosquito in the world; it will go after practically anything with a blood-stream—mammals, birds, even turtles and snakes. In the United States, it is already carrying La Crosse encephalitis, so it may transmit the virus to animals that do not now harbor it, such as rats. The result could be a much larger reservoir of disease from which to infect humans.[17]

CASCADING EFFECTS

The effects of an invasion can ripple through an ecosystem, upsetting relationships that would appear to be far removed from the invader itself. Eurasian tamarisk trees, for instance, have altered the basic hydrology of some riparian areas in the western United States. A tamarisk can tap into groundwater as far as 6 meters below the surface, and its rapid transpiration rate can drop water tables quickly, drying up the small pools that sustain so much of dryland life. Native plant communities suffer; native fish populations drop; the lack of water has even caused declines in the native desert bighorn sheep.[18]

Exotics can have a similar effect on the food web—an ecosystem's network of predator-prey relationships. The lakes and rivers of eastern North America are suffering basic changes in the food web with the arrival of the zebra mussel, a small shellfish from the Caspian Sea region. (See also Chapter 4.) The zebra mussel was accidentally introduced into the Great Lakes in the mid-eighties and has spread widely since then, largely by attaching itself to boat hulls. An extraordinarily efficient consumer of plankton,

the mussel has caused plankton populations in invaded waterways to crash. In effect, it is converting pelagic systems, in which the basic food is in the water column, to benthic systems, which are based on bottom sediment—in this case, the material excreted by the mussel.[19]

The likely losers in this process are other plankton-feeding organisms—native mussels, yellow perch, and many other fish species in their larval stages. Bottom-feeding organisms such as crayfish, worms, and bass are likely to profit. Of course, the mussel could confer a huge advantage on any species that finds it attractive prey. Some duck species are reported to be feeding on it, but so are some exotic fish. Two Caspian Sea gobies are living off the mussel in the Great Lakes; they might not have succeeded in establishing themselves there without the mussel.[20]

Food web changes can reach far afield. The opposum shrimp was introduced into the Flathead River in Montana in the United States, to give the river's salmon—an exotic sportfish—additional prey. But the shrimp ate the zooplankton the juvenile salmon depended on. The salmon population crashed, taking with it a substantial amount of terrestrial wildlife that had come to depend on the salmon—eagles, otters, coyotes, and bears. In Madagascar, widespread introduction of a tilapia, a popular tropical food fish, has supported the spread of a bird, the little grebe, which preys on the fish. Although the little grebe is native to the island, its range had not previously overlapped with that of its much rarer relative, the Alaotra grebe. Increasing contact has led to interbreeding, which has apparently doomed the latter bird to extinction as a distinct species.[21]

Of course, exotics are not acting in isolation. Other types of ecological disturbance are helping them spread, or exacerbating the damage they do. Logging a patch of forest may create an opening for invasive weeds; overfishing a lake may reduce the number of predators and competitors an exotic fish might otherwise encounter; building a road through a prairie may alter the roadside soil, allowing exotic plants to get a foothold. It might not be obvious why exotics should do better in disturbed habitat than natives—until the problem is restated from the exotic's point of view. In many cases, it is the ability to thrive in disturbed habitat that makes an organism exotic in the first place. Plants and animals that have evolved to profit from some form of natural flux—for example, the vegetational succession from field to forest—are making the most of human presence.[22]

Exotics often kill the native ecology long before they kill the native species.

A textbook case of this kind of opportunism is the red fire ant, a viciously aggressive stinging ant from Brazil that is now widespread in the southeastern United States. The fire ant thrives in disturbed areas, such as plowed fields. It disburses widely, by mating swarms or by clumping together to form floating mats during floods. Its reproductive abilities are amazing even by insect standards—its colonies may contain hundreds of queens and occur at densities of from 200 to nearly 6,000 mounds per hectare. And fire ants will eat just about anything. In some areas, they have killed off as much as 40 percent of all native insect species. Preference for disturbed habitat, efficient dispersal, rapid population growth, and opportunistic feeding—this complex of "weedy" traits appears to some degree in a huge assortment of other widespread exotics. Cheat grass, rats, and zebra mussels are all weeds.[23]

It would be impossible to draw a comprehensive map of bioinvasion, but the available data show a disease that is already well advanced. Places as disparate as southern Australia, the U.S. West Coast, Chile, and South Africa, which previously had few if any plants in common, now share hundreds of highly invasive weeds, mainly from the Mediterranean region. In Canada, 28 percent of the flora (the total number of plant species growing in a country) is exotic; in New Zealand, the figure is 47 percent. In Hawaii, which like many islands is suffering an epidemic of exotic invasions, as many as 35 new animals and plants arrive every year. Arthropods (insects, arachnids, and their relatives) are invading Hawaii at more than 1 million times the natural rate.[24]

As aggressive "weedy" exotics spread from one community to the next, absorbing more and more of the resources of life, they tend to drain those communities of their distinctive genetic wealth. Native species dwindle, and some eventually die out. According to the U.S. Fish and Wildlife Service, for example, exotics are a factor in about 30 percent of the organisms on the official U.S. Endangered and Threatened List.[25]

But exotics often kill the native ecology long before they kill the native species. A successful invader may overwhelm its new range by sheer biomass, pushing native populations to the point of ecological insignificance. A comb jellyfish from the U.S. East Coast, for instance, now makes up some 95 percent of the Black Sea's wet weight biomass. In Australia, *Mimosa pigra*, a small scrubby tree from the neotropics, has displaced virtually all other vegetation from some 45,000 hectares of wetlands. And although it is occasionally reported that some sort of new stability is achieved, there is little evidence to suggest that such a result is inevitable—or even common. Instead, as ecosystems lose their diversity, they tend to become more brittle, more susceptible to pressures in general. Millions of years worth of intricate local variety yields to an impoverished and homogenized landscape.[26]

PATHWAYS OF INVASION

Bioinvasions are deeply enmeshed in the world's basic economic processes. Trade and travel, for instance, have created hundreds of exotic "pathways"—the means by which organisms spread into new habitats. As trading patterns grow and shift, new pathways spring up and established ones widen, contract, or move their tendrils from place to place—a global capillary network that is continually dissolving and rebuilding itself. The process is far too complex to map, but a look at several major pathways shows how it works.

Container traffic has revolutionized the movement of goods—and may help do the same for exotics. Containers are the large metal boxes that are stacked on ships, then off-loaded onto trucks or trains. From 1980 to 1993, container ships more than tripled their percentage of world shipping tonnage, from 1.6 percent to 4.9 percent, for a total volume of about 100 million 20-foot units a year. The very features that make containers so attractive to shippers also make them ideal for transporting certain types of exotics. Containers can be stacked at port for weeks or even months on end—allowing stowaways plenty of time to board. And they may not be unpacked until they reach their final destination, which means they can carry exotics wherever a road or railroad leads. Containers have broken the old link between shipborne exotic and port infestation: they represent a quantum leap in invasion potential.[27]

Containers are a significant pathway for insects, weed seeds, slugs, and snails. In the United States, they account for at least 15 percent of the latter two types of organisms intercepted by inspectors for the U.S. Department of Agriculture. Container shipments of used tires from Japan brought the Asian tiger mosquito to the United States; apparently the same pathway is responsible for its arrival in South Africa, New Zealand, Australia, and southern Europe. This pathway is effective partly because containers are so difficult to inspect. In the late seventies, for example, a six-month survey of container loads of raw wood coming into Auckland, New Zealand, found that manifests had been improperly completed nearly half the time. Officials suspected the errors were deliberate attempts to avoid quarantine for forest pests.[28]

A shipping pathway that may have even greater potential is ballast water. Ships ballast themselves by pumping water in and out of a set of tanks in proportion to the amount of cargo taken on board. There are 28,000 merchant vessels in the world's major fleets, and some of them use huge quantities of ballast water—a bulk carrier's ballast capacity can approach 50 million gallons. But even an "empty" set of tanks would probably contain several hundred gallons, which is more than enough to be biologically active. This largely hidden form of biotic mixing is working enormous changes in the distribution of all sorts of aquatic species. Ballast intakes suck in fish and shellfish larvae, plankton, algae, and various other inhabitants of the marine water column. Often sediment is sucked in as well, so mud-dwelling organisms such as worms become passengers too. Nor are ballast transfers entirely marine: since ships often move up rivers, freshwater organisms may also enter this pathway.[29]

Ballast water has become an artificial

network of currents that carry legions of creatures all over the world. A study of a single bay in Oregon, for example, recorded 367 types of organisms released from the ballast water of ships arriving from Japan over a four-year period. All the main ecological roles—carnivores, herbivores, scavengers, parasites, and so forth—were represented. Among the more spectacular ballast water invasions are the comb jelly already mentioned (into the Black and Azov Seas) and the zebra mussel (into the Great Lakes). A dinoflagellate "red tide," a type of plankton whose population explodes periodically into poisonous "blooms," was released along the Australian coast from ships arriving from Japan. During the eighties, the red tide devastated Australian fisheries.[30]

Mosquitoes have reportedly survived flights from Africa to Britain in airplane passenger cabins.

Air traffic is another rapidly expanding pathway. Commercial air traffic carried 163 million passengers in 1980; a decade later, the number was 280 million. In 1989, only three airports received more than a million tons of cargo; by 1993, that number had risen to seven. Duane Gubler, director of the Division of Vector-Borne Infectious Diseases at the U.S. Centers for Disease Control and Prevention, calls airplanes an "ideal" means for transporting viruses. (See Chapter 7.) Infected air travelers, he says, "transport viruses all over the world on a regular basis." Mosquitoes have reportedly survived flights from Africa to Britain in airplane passenger cabins. (Even if they do not manage to establish colonies, these mosquitoes could carry disease.) Airplanes carry

larger creatures too. The brown tree snake is occasionally found on the runways of Hawaiian airports, where it has fallen from wheel wells and cargo bays of planes arriving from Guam. These planes get special attention from Hawaiian officials, who fear that the snake could overrun Hawaii, with disasterous consequences for the islands' birds.[31]

Yet this narrow notion of pathways does not begin to capture the full scope of the problem. Bioinvasions are not simply a kind of economic by-product; in some industries, exotics are the means of production. This is most obvious in agriculture, which molds entire landscapes to suit the needs of exotic crops. Many crops are too closely dependent on humans to be dangerous invaders, but there are enough exceptions to make agriculture a serious "biological polluter" in some areas. The olive tree has invaded parts of Australia, and the avocado has gone wild on Santa Cruz island in the Galápagos. The spice cardamom is a problem in lowland moist forests of Sri Lanka and South India, and black pepper has invaded forest edges in Malaysia. The shrub *Chromolaena odorata* is valued by small farmers in Indonesia and many parts of Africa as a fallow crop, but it is a serious pest in at least 13 major tropical crops, such as rubber, oil palm, and coconut—and arguably the single most invasive plant in tropical nature reserves.[32]

Ranching represents agriculture's exotic predicament in perhaps its most extreme form. Cattle can radically alter plant communities by grazing, a process frequently accelerated by the introduction of invasive exotic forage plants better adapted to grazing pressure than natives are. Cattle compete with native wildlife for forage and water. These competitors, and any predators, are often targeted for elimination, as the wolf and the prairie dog have been in the western United States. Cattle introduce exotic diseases—rinderpest in Africa and probably brucellosis in North America. (Brucellosis causes miscarriages in bison and elk, as well as in cattle.) Loss of native species, degradation of rangeland and riparian zones, depletion of water supply, the spread of diseases and pests—small wonder that Reed Noss, editor of the journal *Conservation Biology*, recently noted the widespread opinion among conservationists that "livestock has done more damage to the native biodiversity of western North America than all the chainsaws and bulldozers combined."[33]

Forestry presents a similar predicament. The standard environmental critique of forestry focuses on unsustainable cutting of native, "natural" forests. More extensive use of plantation-grown wood is commonly seen as an important means of relieving the pressure on native forests. But tree farms are often planted with exotic species, and some of these have proved invasive. Plantations of Monterey pine, native to the U.S. West Coast, are scattered all over the world's warm temperate regions, covering a total of 1 million hectares; this species has invaded natural areas in South Africa, Australia, and New Zealand. Fast-growing eucalyptus species from Australia are another common choice for pulp and fuelwood plantations in the tropics and warm temperate regions. These may occasionally be invasive, but the principal danger from eucalyptus has been a kind of "managed invasion." Instead of substituting for native forests, exotic timber like eucalyptus often becomes another reason for logging such areas. In southeastern Brazil, native forest is being cleared to plant eucalyptus, which is grown to fire steel mills. Eucalyptus plantations for fuelwood, pulp, and timber are also apparently among the reasons for logging native forest in Africa and in Brazil's Atlantic forest, one

of the world's rarest and most diverse forest types.[34]

Once the wood is cut and shipped, a second round of invasions may begin if any pests are riding on the lumber. In North America, wood imports in various forms are a major pathway for forest pests, and increasing demand is liable to broaden that pathway. The prospect of Siberian timber imports, for instance, prompted the U.S. Forest Service to inventory organisms associated with Siberian larch, a major timber species; 175 arthropods, nematodes, and fungi were identified. Elsewhere, a pine wood nematode probably native to the U.S. Southeast is killing stands of black pine in Japan. A woodwasp, native to Eurasia and North Africa, is spreading a fungus that is killing pines in New Zealand, Australia, and southern South America. Yellow jackets, venomous wasplike insects, probably invaded Hawaii in shipments of Christmas trees.[35]

Aquaculture is another exotic industry. Fish farming and the growing of other edible aquatic organisms—shellfish, lobsters, even seaweed—is an expanding component of world food production. The global aquaculture yield, both freshwater and marine, stood at around 12 million tons in 1990, and is expected to reach 22 million tons, or about one quarter of the total aquatic harvest, by 2000. In many developing countries, fish farming is already a major source of protein and is promoted aggressively by governments and international development agencies. Exotics—both exotic species and artificial strains of native species—are an important ingredient in this recipe. And in much of the Third World, fish are often just dumped into natural waters, as there are few containment facilities. Consequently, many standard aquaculture species are already extremely widespread. The Mozambique tilapia, for example, is now established in nearly every tropical and subtropical country. In South and Central America, exotic species now dominate many freshwater fisheries.[36]

Industrial countries face the same problem. (See also Chapter 4.) Inadequate containment devices are still more the rule than the exception. In the United States, for example, African blue tilapia have escaped from fish farms in Florida to colonize the waters in the Everglades National Park, where they are a serious management problem. Nor is containment always attempted. An edible Japanese seaweed is now established off the coast of northern France, thanks to an experimental commercial planting—proving that there is actually no such thing as an "experimental" release of an exotic. And aquaculture shipments can be contaminated by various organisms besides the ones intentionally shipped. One researcher in Hawaii, for example, found 18 species of algae, 7 species of protozoans, along with assorted copepods, rotifers, nematodes, and isopods in water from Californian oyster and clam shipments.[37]

By moving genes between organisms that could not possibly interbreed, biotechnology may have broken the ultimate biological barrier.

Aquaculture is also spreading pathogens. Shrimp farming, for instance, is increasingly popular in Latin America and South Asia, where it is driving the destruction of valuable mangrove stands and other important types of coastal habitat. As the shrimp boom proceeds, serious viral and bacterial outbreaks have decimated shrimp farms in China, India, Latin America, and the United States. Transfers of shrimp stock have distributed at least a half-dozen shrimp viruses all over the world, and some of these are known to be highly contagious. The effect on wild shrimp is as yet unknown, but the possibility of infection worries both scientists and the shrimpers dependent on wild populations.[38]

Biotechnology may open up pathways of an entirely new dimension, as well as giving a boost to some established ones. By moving genes between organisms that could not possibly interbreed, biotechnology may have broken the ultimate biological barrier. Many of these transgenic organisms are already in the field-testing stage—fish, crop plants, and insect viruses among them. Critics of the industry see a number of risks in such developments. For instance, among the nearly 1,300 transgenic crops field-tested thus far in the United States, more than three quarters have been engineered for greater herbicide tolerance or for greater resistance to diseases or pests. Many crops interbreed with wild relatives, and it is possible that these "exotic" genes could escape into wild plant populations—or that the crops themselves could escape. The appearance of herbicide-tolerant or disease-resistant wild plants could obviously lead to major ecological—and agricultural—disruptions.[39]

As a supplement to traditional breeding techniques, biotechnology may also reinforce the tendency to spread exotics in the forestry and aquaculture sectors. For instance, a group of scientists from Canada, the United States, and Singapore has produced a transgenic Pacific salmon that grows on average 11 times heavier during its first year than normal members of its species—a glamor candidate for aquaculture. Similarly, a consortium of European firms and a Japanese company are field-testing a form of eucalyptus that has been engineered for low lignin content, making it easier to process into pulp.[40]

In the United States alone, there have been more than 2,700 field tests of genetically engineered organisms. Thus far, in the United States and Europe, most field-testing has been conducted on a fairly small scale. In China, on the other hand, field-testing is already an enormous enterprise: transgenic crops, engineered primarily for virus resistance, are reportedly being planted on thousands of hectares.[41]

As these and hundreds of other pathways wear away the genetic and ecological barriers of the natural world, they reveal a new form of social dysfunction—a new measure of unsustainability. The global consumer economy is degrading the environment not just through its appetite for resources or by the pollution it produces. The economy is unsustainable for another reason as well: its tendency to contaminate one ecosystem with organisms native to another. And like other environmental problems, exotics too can climb back up the chain of economic consequence, and bite the hand the wields it.

INFECTING THE ECONOMY

As their ecological effects spread, exotics inevitably begin to disrupt the world's economies as well. The process is most advanced in agriculture, where losses to pests, many of which have spread over vast areas of the agricultural landscape, are a major constraint on humanity's struggles to feed itself. According to one recent estimate, croplands are home to about 50,000 plant pathogens, 9,000 insects and mites, and some 8,000 weeds. The proportion of these organisms that is exotic varies greatly from

one region—and one crop—to the next, but it could be anywhere from 20 to 70 percent. Some pests are as widespread as the world's major crops. A couple dozen weeds are found nearly everywhere; so are nearly 40 percent of the world's 155 major crop pathogens. In addition to these pests, a few vertebrates, such as rats (especially the brown rat) and the English sparrow, have become extremely successful cropland invaders.[42]

Less than 5 percent of the creatures that inhabit cropland are serious economic pests. But those that are can inflict heavy losses. A Eurasian grass called wild oats, for example, is a pest of more than 20 crops in 55 countries, from Iceland to tropical highlands. It has been estimated that wild oats reduces annual wheat and barley production by 13 million tons—enough to feed 50 million people at the subsistence level.[43]

Regional invasions are also inflicting a heavy price. In the mid-eighties, a new banana disease called black sigatoka appeared in Central America; in one year alone, Honduras lost $10 million to it. By 1988, just two years after its arrival in the United States, the Russian wheat aphid was causing annual losses in excess of $130 million. Losses to the Mediterranean fruit fly in California have run as high as $897 million a year. (At least 235 exotics are having an economically significant impact on U.S. agriculture; half of U.S. weeds are exotic and so are at least 39 percent of serious insect pests.)[44]

The list could be expanded indefinitely, but the problem is more than the sum of these losses. Agriculture has become a conduit through which thousands of organisms move—from one country to another, from cropland to semiwild areas, and back again. We pursue some of these creatures with pesticides and by changing farming techniques, but the process is like trying to play chess when you know only half the rules. An apparently solid advance may invite a devastating reply. In South America, a boom in nontraditional export crops (flowers and certain fruits and vegetables) seems to be causing an explosive spread of viruses: it was recently estimated that 1 million hectares of the continent's cropland had been abandoned because of virus infestation.[45]

Often the game seems to allow our opponents several moves at once. Widespread crop pests have recently inflicted serious damage on China's cotton crop (boll worms), Pakistan's cotton crop (a whitefly-transmitted virus), and potatoes in the Americas (apparently, a new form of the potato blight). The development of pesticide resistance in crop pests may accelerate the spread of outbreaks like these. Pesticide resistance has been detected in more than 500 insect and mite species, nearly 150 plant pathogens, and more than 270 weeds. (See Chapter 5.)[46]

Forestry, too, is vulnerable to bioinvasions. One of the worst forest pests in eastern North America is the gypsy moth, a Eurasian immigrant whose caterpillars chew up huge quantities of leaves. In 1981, the moth defoliated 5.2 million hectares of the northeastern United States, causing an estimated $764 million in losses. Perhaps the greatest loss the eastern forests have suffered was the death of the American chestnut. Devasted by an exotic disease earlier in the century, the chestnut was a keystone species, both for the ecosystem and for the forest economy. (In U.S. forests, among the most actively studied of the surviving large forest tracts, the U.S. Forest Service has identified more than 300 exotic pests.)[47]

As in agriculture, exotics can create a kind of systemic economic problem. Chile, for instance, has built a $1-billion-a-year timber export industry on plantations of Monterey pine and eucalyptus. The profits—along with government "reforestation" subsidies at 75–90 percent of planting costs—have had the predictable effect of encouraging owners of native forests to log them, then replant with exotics. Large landowners have moved more and more land into the program, displacing small farmers, who crowd into the cities in search of jobs that are hard to come by. Working conditions on the plantations are also reported to be very bad. Here is a bioinvasion with a clear social component: it is not just the local trees that are being displaced, but local people as well.[48]

In fisheries, also, exotics are imposing heavy losses. In May 1995, for instance, an exotic shrimp virus took only a few days to destroy $11 million worth of cultured shrimp in south Texas. The invasion of the comb jellyfish has shut down fisheries in the Azov Sea and was estimated to be costing Black Sea fisheries $250 million a year. The spread of the zebra mussel into the U.S. Midwest recently forced the closing of a clam export business worth $1.4 million. (The mussels colonize the clams' shells, preventing them from opening.)[49]

Here, too, exotics sometimes disrupt the system at a basic level, as the Nile perch has done with the traditional fisheries of Africa's Lake Victoria. (See also Chapter 4.) The perch, a voracious predator that can grow to 2 meters, was released into the lake in the fifties to boost declining native stocks. The lake's original complement of nearly 400 native fish supported a traditional shore fishery in the lakeside countries—Kenya, Uganda, and Tanzania. People fished for their own consumption or for local markets. The perch, a big open-water animal, was not available to this shore-based fishery; catching it requires a large boat and expensive tackle. The fishery that grew up around the perch is consequently a major commercial operation, which requires large-scale profits and, therefore, export markets for its products.[50]

In the early eighties, the perch population exploded and the native fish populations collapsed. Nearly half the native species went extinct, almost certainly as a result of direct predation by the perch. Overfishing had probably already begun to undermine the traditional economy before the collapse; afterwards, the shore fisheries quickly went the way of the native fish. The local people have had to turn to scraps from the perch fishery, which they must purchase, to make up the loss in their diet. And the specter of protein malnutrition may now be stalking the 30 million residents of the lake basin. Here, a local economy based on native species has been displaced by an export-oriented "exotic" industry that has destroyed the resource and largely bypassed the local people. Even the future of the perch has been called into question; it is apparently cannibalizing itself and the size of the specimens taken is dropping.[51]

Exotics that transmit human diseases can have a painful economic impact—in productivity lost to sickness and death, in medical expenses, and in pest control. The Asian tiger mosquito, for example, may have been a factor in the 1986 yellow fever epidemic in Rio de Janeiro. About 1 million people were infected. In 1991, the mosquito was discovered during a yellow fever outbreak in Nigeria. In the United States, Florida was hit by several encephalitis epidemics in the early nineties, and the mosquito was suspected as a vector. The state ordered the destruction of an enormous tire dump, a major mosquito breeding site, at a cost of nearly $1.3 million. In addition to yellow fever and encephalitis, this mosquito is a vector for another disease that is rebounding globally: dengue fever. (See Chapter 7.)[52]

Just as bioinvasions can change an ecosystem's ground rules, they sometimes change the ground rules of an economy as well, by imposing new stresses on some part of the infrastructure—stresses that structures had not been designed to withstand. Water hyacinth, for example, a pantropical aquatic weed originally from South America, is one of the world's fastest-growing plants. In Zimbabwe, it sometimes overgrows bridges, dams, and pipes—and crushes them. In the southeastern United States, the red fire ant is drawn to electric current; it gnaws through cables and infests electrical devices, shorting out circuits and occasionally starting fires.[53]

Bioinvasions sometimes change the ground rules of an economy by imposing new stresses on some part of the infrastructure.

One of the costliest forms of infrastructure damage is the heavy colonization of water pipes, boat hulls, and nearly every other solid surface by the zebra mussel in eastern North America. This "fouling" greatly reduces intake pipe efficiency, blocks valves, and slows boats. One expert estimated that the mussel could force the U.S. power industry to spend $800 million on redesign—plus $60 million annually on maintenance. The cost of retrofitting intake pipes around the city of Chicago had already exceeded $1.7 million by 1992. And the U.S. Fish and Wildlife Service has estimated that fouling by the mussel, along with associated losses from boating and fishing, could cost $5 billion in the Great Lakes alone by 2000.[54]

SLOWING THE RATES OF INVASION

Bioinvasions have so far attracted little attention among the general public or policymakers. Stanley Temple, a wildlife ecologist at the University of Wisconsin, observes that exotics are not a research priority even for conservation biologists: "In spite of all that is known about the negative influence of exotics and the obvious conservation benefits of controlling them, their eradication inspires little enthusiasm among most conservationists, the public or governments." Yet we already know, in broad outline, what we must do to reduce the threat of bioinvasion, and we already have the tools to begin the task. Action is needed on three fronts: controlling or eradicating established exotics, blocking pathways through which exotics are accidentally introduced, and preventing unnecessary intentional introductions.[55]

A solid first step in working out control policies might begin with the question, How quickly can a new invasion be countered? Rapid reaction to an invader generally makes the most sense, both economically and ecologically. Early control is the least expensive response, and it can lead to the best result: total eradication. An invader is most vulnerable when it has just arrived, because its numbers are likely to be low, and community resistance to it may be at its highest. Populations of native competitors, for instance, will not yet have declined.[56]

In 1991, rapid reaction to the arrival of the Asian strain of the gypsy moth in ports along the U.S. and Canadian West Coast probably saved thousands of hectares of forest. The program cost $25 million, but an official estimate of the potential losses to the area from a combined invasion of the Asian gypsy moth and its close relative, the nun moth, ranged from $35 billion to $58 billion between 1990 and 2040. This case illustrates the importance of three basic points of procedure: agencies involved in exotic control must have budgeting flexibility, a requirement to respond to scientific assessments of risk, and protocols for rapid response.[57]

It is tempting to avoid the expense of response when an invading organism seems fairly benign, at least at low population levels. But there is no way of knowing when an exotic's population may explode. A European mustard that invaded North America in the last century, for example, was rarely considered a problem as recently as the mid-eighties. Today it is a serious threat to woodland flora over a wide area of the eastern United States and Canada. (See Figure 6–1.)[58]

Control of an exotic that has had time to establish itself is far less likely to lead to total eradication, but often its population can be suppressed to an ecologically insignificant level. A number of techniques are available for the task, but long-term control programs, as well as extensive eradication campaigns, are likely to have a serious side effect: virtu-

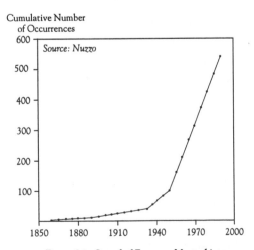

Figure 6-1. Spread of European Mustard into Eastern Canada and United States, 1860-1990

ally all control measures are controversial to some degree. Controlling exotics is therefore a political as well as an ecological task. Shooting and trapping, for instance, may be the only cost-effective way of controlling certain vertebrate pests in reserves, but such programs have tended to offend many people who are strong supporters of conservation in general. The use of pesticides is—rightly—a matter of perennial controversy too. (See Chapter 5.) But sometimes pesticides may be the best or even the only option. The Asian gypsy moth outbreak just mentioned, for instance, was stopped by spraying the biopesticide Bt (the bacterium *Bacillus thuringiensis*). Here too, the people most likely to object form part of the "natural constituency" for conservation.[59]

Another important technique, biological control, has its detractors as well. In its standard form, biocontrol attempts to suppress exotics by releasing predators and diseases to attack them. Modern biocontrol generally uses predators native to the exotic's home range, thereby attempting to reestablish the ecological "balance" the offending exotic presumably had with its natural enemies. Both the target organism and the biocontrol agent would persist in the new habitat, but at very low levels: any increase in the pest population would provoke a corresponding increase in the agent population. That is the ideal, but as biocontrol opponents point out, the technique does not always achieve control, and it has sometimes actually caused additional problems. The moth commonly used for control of prickly pear cactuses, for instance, has invaded Florida from the Caribbean and may now threaten native prickly pears in the United States. Even so, the release of carefully screened agents known to be exclusive predators of the offending organism may be the best option in many cases.[60]

New or unusual control technologies may supplement or supplant some of the more traditional methods. Artificial pheromones (chemicals secreted in some species that act as messengers from one individual to another) are sometimes used to confuse mating reflexes in certain insects, for example, and oral vaccines have been developed that cause infertility in mammals. Additional research may create new methods. But the arsenal of present techniques is so underused, and the need for control so great, that there is no need to wait for further research before acting.[61]

Regardless of the techniques used, an essential component of any program will be convincing the general public of the importance of exotic control. People must come to see that these measures are as important a part of wildlife conservation as saving endangered species—that they are, in fact, saving endangered species. A broad public consensus will greatly ease the burden of dealing with opponents of particular techniques.

The arsenal of present techniques is so underused, and the need for control so great, that there is no need to wait for further research before acting.

Controlling exotics may be futile if we do not also find ways to block the pathways of invasion. Expanding current screening procedures is an obvious place to start. Well-run inspection programs tend to become more efficient in the course of operation, as information on pathways is pooled. In the United States, for instance, when inspectors for the Animal and Plant Health Inspection Service discover a problem in one port, they can issue an "interception alert" on an electronic mail system, to guide inspectors at other ports. Here too, public education has an important role to play. When people understand the threat, and know what they can do to stop it, some important pathways may narrow automatically. There are simple techniques for cleaning boat hulls, for example, that can slow the spread of zebra mussels.[62]

A serious strategy for countering exotics must meet both biological and political challenges.

But the task will require many new techniques as well. These will have to be developed in a largely ad hoc fashion, as need arises and ingenuity permits. Sometimes a relatively simple and inexpensive solution will present itself. In East Asia, for instance, gypsy and nun moths are attracted to lighting on cargo ships; reports indicate that the moths will not seek lights with ultraviolet and blue filters. But far more complex measures will be required for narrowing pathways such as ballast water systems. Canada and the United States have produced voluntary ballast operating guidelines for ships in the Great Lakes. Australia has similar guidelines for its coastal waters in general, and new designs for ballast equipment are also being developed. Yet slowing the rate of ballast water releases will demand a good deal more effort on both the procedural and engineering levels.[63]

Of course, inadvertent introductions are only part of the picture; deliberate introductions often go awry as well. Critical to narrowing these pathways is a clear, science-based review procedure that is insulated as far as possible from the political or commercial interests endorsing the introduction. A "clean list"

approach could be the key to progress here. A clean list is an inventory of organisms that have been shown to be relatively safe: an organism must make it onto the list to qualify for release or importation. The alternative and more common approach is the "dirty list," which bans organisms known to be dangerous, but does nothing to bar unlisted ones. The clean list approach would begin the important process of shifting the burden of proof away from critics of an introduction and onto its proponents. The logical end of that process would be legislation requiring importers of exotics to accept legal liability for any damage their introductions may cause.[64]

Clean lists could also help steer research strategies—not just toward finding "safe" exotics, but toward identifying native species, and preferably native populations, that could replace exotics in particular uses and areas. A substantial amount of research is accumulating on this issue, and it demonstrates the huge potential of such an approach. In the United States, the Illinois Department of Conservation now confines itself almost exclusively to plants native to the state for its planting programs. Recent research on commonly used fuelwood trees in India has shown the native species to be better choices than the exotics. And in Zimbabwe, where eucalyptus has been the mainstay for community-based planting projects, authorities are now also organizing native tree nurseries in response to local interest in natives and local knowledge about them.[65]

A serious strategy for countering exotics must meet both biological and political challenges. Our present ecological understanding is not advanced enough to tell us how far we can ultimately push back the exotic tide, but it tells us clearly that we must begin that effort now. Our political understanding—from work on other aspects of conservation and human well-being—tells us that we can build the constituencies that will be necessary to fight this battle.

People generally accept regulatory shields against chemical pollution, so they can be persuaded of the necessity for blocking the pathways of biological pollution. Industries generally accept legal constraints on what material they can release into the environment, so the industries that use exotics may come to accept constraints on what organisms they can release. And just as health au-thorities have learned to track the spread of dangerous pathogens, biologists can find ways to track other dangerous crea-tures.

It is precisely because exotics present such a formidable threat that they offer such a great deal of common ground for action. For just as bioinvasions are af-fecting life at virtually every level on which it can be examined—genetic, eco-logical, or economic—they are also af-fecting every nation, regardless of its wealth or place in world affairs.

7

Confronting Infectious Diseases

Anne E. Platt

In April 1993, the World Health Organization (WHO) declared a global state of emergency for a disease thought to be well under control as recently as 1985. More than a third of the people in the world are infected with the bacterium that causes tuberculosis (TB), although the infection is inactive in most cases. But in 1994, 8.8 million people contracted active TB—an illness many people associate with sequestered sanatoriums and squalid tenements that were long ago abandoned. During the nineties, 30 million people are expected to die from tuberculosis. The emergence of drug-resistant strains, public health services weakened by cutbacks and layoffs, increased poverty and urbanization, and a focus on other diseases such as cancer have brought about a severe enough epidemic of TB that the world is now experiencing a modern plague.[1]

The new TB epidemic is a classic case of a public health crisis that could be treated inexpensively, for an average of $13 per case in developing countries for an entire course of treatment. The fate of TB—a major killer among the world's infectious diseases—will largely depend on the willingness of government and public health officials to invest in prevention and early intervention. If we ignore the extraordinary opportunity that exists now to fight the epidemic, we will pay a high price in lives and health care costs later.[2]

Today humanity is experiencing an epidemic of epidemics. Tuberculosis is part of a larger pattern that involves many diseases and increasing risks to hundreds of millions of people. Some are transmitted person-to-person—such as TB, HIV (the virus that causes AIDS), measles, and diphtheria—and most directly reflect disrupted social conditions. Other diseases involving two or more species, vectors, or carriers and reservoirs are also affected by ecological and climatic factors. Widespread environmental changes, disrupted ecosystems, and accelerated climate change and variability may have profound and destabilizing impacts on biological control of infectious disease. And although this chapter focuses on human health, the effects of disease outbreaks can ripple through societies and economies.[3]

Disease-causing microorganisms are reappearing all over the world at a time when infectious diseases were thought to be well controlled. Some are newly recognized and unfamiliar, such as Hanta virus and Lassa Fever; some are hardier and more virulent, such as certain drug-resistant strains of bacteria and pneumococcal pneumonia; many are diseases people thought had been beaten, such as TB, malaria, plague, and measles. All are contributing to the growing burden of infectious diseases. Despite improvements in sanitation, personal hygiene, diet, and health education, infectious diseases are still the number one killer worldwide.

THE BURDEN OF INFECTIOUS DISEASE

Worldwide, infectious diseases killed more than 16.5 million people in 1993. By comparison, the death toll from cancer was 6.1 million; from heart disease, 5 million; from cerebrovascular diseases such as stroke, 4 million; and from respiratory diseases such as chronic bronchitis, 3 million. Officially accounting for 32 percent of global mortality, the true figure for infectious diseases is no doubt higher, as some countries lack diagnostic capabilities and some of the infections are put in other categories, such as maternal or perinatal diseases.[4]

The top five infectious killers are acute respiratory infections such as pneumonia (4.1 million deaths), diarrheal diseases (3 million), tuberculosis (2.7 million), malaria (2 million), and measles (1.2 million). (See Table 7–1.) All except measles (which is a virus) and viral types of acute respiratory infections have antibiotic-resistant strains that may mean higher death counts in the future if new treatments are not found and if the spread of the disease is not halted. In addition, AIDS is expected to kill 1.8 million people annually by the end of this decade—more than measles and nearly as many as malaria.[5]

Millions more people become very sick but do not die from infectious diseases. Almost 8.8 million people developed tuberculosis in 1994, as noted earlier, while some 300–500 million people develop new cases of malaria each year. Leishmaniasis, a deadly skin disease transmitted by sandflies primarily in the tropics, infects 13 million people annually, of whom about 500,000 get a full-blown case of the disease. In 1990, 300 million people living in Africa, Asia, and Latin America were infected with tropical diseases such as African trypanosomiasis (sleeping sickness), onchocerciasis (river blindness), and schistosomiasis. In addition, there are more than 100 infectious diseases carried by water, soil, food, or vectors (arthropods or rodents). (See Table 7–2.)[6]

Underreporting and misdiagnosis are serious problems in many areas of the world: some diseases were not identified until recently, diagnostic capabilities do not exist universally, and some infectious diseases and plagues are simply never recorded. The actual incidence could thus be many times higher than what is reported. For example, the Nigerian Health Ministry reported that the 1987 yellow fever epidemic in Oyo State resulted in 883 cases and 477 deaths. Four years later, researchers examined epidemiologic information and

Table 7-1. Populations Affected by Various Infectious Diseases, 1993

Disease	Deaths	Incidence[1]
Acute Respiratory Infections	4.1 million	248 million
Diarrheal Diseases	3.0 million	1.8 billion
Tuberculosis	2.7 million	8.8 million
Malaria	2.0 million	300–500 million (prevalence[2])
Measles	1.2 million	45 million
Hepatitis B	1.0 million	2.2 million
HIV/AIDS	700,000	2–3 million
Whooping Cough (pertussis)	360,000	4.3 million
Bacterial Meningitis	210,000	1.2 million (prevalence[2])
Schistosomiasis	200,000	200 million (prevalence[2])
Leishmaniasis	197,000	7.2 million
Yellow Fever	30,000	200,000
Dengue/DHF	23,000	560,000
Japanese Encephalitis	11,000	40,000
Cholera	6,800	380,000
Polio	5,500	110,000

[1]Number of new cases of a particular disease reported during a certain period of time.   [2]Number of cases of a particular disease reported during a certain period of time.
SOURCES: Report of the Director-General, *The World Health Report 1995: Bridging the Gaps* (Geneva: World Health Organization, 1995); malaria data from "World Malaria Situation in 1992, Part I: Middle South Asia, Eastern Asia and Oceania," *Weekly Epidemiological Record,* October 21, 1994; HIV/AIDS incidence data from Aaron Sachs, "HIV/AIDS Cases Rising Steadily," in Lester R. Brown, Hal Kane, and David Malin Roodman, *Vital Signs 1994* (New York: W. W. Norton & Company, 1994).

put the actual range at 116,000 cases and 24,000 deaths. Based on these data, the 11,000 cases of yellow fever reported for all of Africa between 1986 and 1990 probably represented 1.4 million cases. Similarly, Vietnam confirmed more than 350,000 cases of malaria in 1990, but actual numbers of cases were on the order of 1.5 million.[7]

Deaths from infectious diseases tend to be clustered, depending on weather, climate, susceptibility of the population, and existing health infrastructure. Cases of drug-resistant pneumonia are found primarily in industrial countries, for example, where antibiotics are widely overused. And some 90 percent of malaria deaths occur in sub-Saharan Africa, where tropical conditions lend themselves to *Anopheles* mosquitoes, the malaria parasite's host. Similarly, much of

the suffering from AIDS has been concentrated in Africa and Asia, although Europe and the Americas are hardly immune to this killer. Nearly two thirds of the world's 13–14 million cases of HIV are found among Africans; in 1995, for the first time, more people will contract HIV in Asia than anywhere else.[8]

Despite these grim statistics, considerable progress in the fight against infectious diseases has been made during this century. Smallpox—a highly infectious virus that is spread by respiration or touch and that can disfigure, blind, and even kill its victim—was officially eradicated in 1979. With a concentrated campaign, doctors and health workers vaccinated more than 250 million people against smallpox and rid the planet of this scourge. Measles is nearly gone from the industrialized world. And polio

Table 7-2. Selected Infectious Diseases, Vectors, and Symptoms

Disease	Vector	Symptoms
Viral		
Dengue (breakbone fever)	mosquito	High fever, chills, headaches, vomiting, painful bones and joints, severe exhaustion, hemorrhaging of mucous membrane in skin and abdomen.
Parasitic		
Malaria	mosquito	High fever, chills, sweating, anemia, splenomegaly; can lead to shock, severe diarrhea, vomiting as red blood cells erupt, eventually coma and death.
Visceral leishmaniasis	sandfly	Multiple lesions, inflammation, crusting.
Schistosomiasis (bilharziasis)	snail	Cirrhosis of liver, anemia, swollen internal organs.
Encephalitis	mosquito	Range from mild, flulike symptoms, including high fevers, to fatal inflammation of the brain and central nervous system.
Lyme Disease	tick	Fatigue, headache, stiffness, arthritis.
Bacterial		
Cholera	Feces-contaminated water; also foodborne	Intestinal infection that causes nearly painless watery diarrhea, cramps, gastrointestinal fluid loss, salt depletion, effortless vomiting, and shock.
Escherichia coli	Foodborne, especially hamburger; sometimes waterborne	Bloody diarrhea, kidney failure, urinary tract infections, abscesses, intestinal disease; causes a cholera-like disease.

SOURCES: *Dorland's Illustrated Medical Dictionary*, 27th ed. (Philadelphia: W.B. Saunders Company, 1988); cholera from Council for Agricultural Science and Technology, "Foodborne Pathogens: Risks and Consequences," Task Force Report No. 122, Ames, Iowa, September 1994; *E. coli* from Ruth L. Berkelman et al., "Infectious Disease Surveillance: A Crumbling Foundation," *Science*, April 15, 1994.

is also on the way out; it has already been eliminated in 145 countries. Worldwide, cases of this crippling viral disease dropped 80 percent between 1988 and 1994. China's two-day massive polio vaccination program—which WHO called the world's biggest public health effort—reaches more than 100 million children age five and younger twice a year.[9]

A campaign by UNICEF during the seventies and eighties significantly re-duced many infectious diseases by providing widespread immunization. By 1990, 80 percent of the world's children received immunizations for lethal diseases, including diphtheria, pertussis, tetanus, typhoid, and polio, up from 25 percent in 1980. Vaccines administered in 1992 saved 3 million lives (although another 1.7 million children's deaths could have been prevented with even wider coverage).[10]

Yet many people are still not immunized. Inexpensive treatments are not distributed widely, and basic infrastructure and administrative problems as well as a lack of money, supplies, personnel, and knowledge hamper further improvements. Even though the reduction of deaths from infectious disease has been hailed as the "most significant public health achievement in the 20th century," the burden of infectious diseases weighs constant and heavy among three fourths of the world's population.[11]

Over the last two decades many medical authorities, development agencies, funding organizations, and research scientists turned their attention and funding away from these "old" diseases to "new" ones such as cancer, heart disease, and inherited conditions. Their decisions proved to be premature and optimistic, since "plagues are as certain as death and taxes," as Richard Krause of the National Institutes for Health put it in 1982.[12]

Many of these epidemics are of our own making. Humans play a large role in the spread of diseases through the emergence of drug-resistant strains, poorly planned development projects, and failing public health programs. Even though the method of transmission, the symptoms, and the target population of each disease are different, there are identifiable patterns that upset, aggravate, or amplify the coexistence between microbes and humans and thereby contribute to the spread and resurgence of infectious diseases.

Human-induced environmental changes have increased steadily in the past half-century, creating conditions for unprecedented change in the biological world. (See Chapter 1.) Signs of stress, disruption, and adaptation now appear at all levels of life—from weakened organisms to vulnerable ecosystems. Meanwhile, transmission of infectious diseases through all media—air, water, food, soil, personal contact, and vectors such as insects and other animals—and all populations occurs at accelerated rates because of international travel and migration as well as trade and environmental change. At the same time, the diseases themselves are not sitting still. They are developing hardier and more virulent, sometimes drug-resistant, strains; they are spreading to new areas, crossing species boundaries to infect humans and animals, and reappearing when we thought they were under control.

OPPORTUNISTIC MICROBES

Some microbes—a term that includes bacteria, viruses, and fungi—are necessary for life. Millions of "good" bacteria live in people's intestinal tracts to help the digestive process, for example. And peas and beans host certain bacteria in their roots that convert nitrogen from the atmosphere into a form usable to the plants. Other microbes, however, are harmful and pathogenic—that is, they can cause disease.[13]

Bacteria and viruses cause the majority of human diseases. Bacteria have the ability to copy their own genes (DNA and RNA) and replicate. They can live outside a host, whereas viruses are helpless without a host cell and cannot replicate. High rates of replication and mutation enable microbes to adapt quickly to fluctuating environmental conditions, large-scale physical and biological disruptions, and shifts in human susceptibility to infection. Viruses are a million times more likely to mutate than human cells. An active viral infection can produce 1,000 copies in about 24 hours. Because microbes replicate so fast, they can take advantage of new opportunities and adapt to new ecological niches quickly.[14]

In nature, changes usually favor one life form over another. This common biological pattern applies to all levels, from microbes and algae to mammals and trees. Just as weeds exploit disturbance, infectious microbes take advantage of new opportunities and adapt quickly to changing biological conditions. During ecological disruptions, such as fire, flood, deforestation, earthquake, and land use changes, the balance between people and microbes is skewed in favor of microbes. As we inflict damage on our environment we become more vulnerable to opportunistic species, such as pathogenic microbes. In addition, environmental disturbances harm predators more than opportunistic prey do. (Of course, other risk factors also influence the transmission and virulence of infectious diseases, including diet, social behavior, and heredity, but they are beyond the scope of this chapter.)[15]

Most microbes coexist peacefully with their native host, but this balance can be perturbed in a number of ways. Disruptions—in a person's immunity or the environment at large—can activate a microbe and cause disease to emerge or reemerge. Disruptions allow a microbe to mutate or proliferate within a host or its habitat. Microbes that were once harmless to a host can become active and virulent. An individual can be infected with the tuberculosis bacterium, for instance, but not suffer any ill effects as long as the infection remains latent (inactive). If the person's immune system is compromised by malnutrition, chemotherapy, or HIV, or if the individual undergoes severe stress, the TB infection can be activated and cause a severe pulmonary infection that is contagious.[16]

The outcomes of environmental disruption are complex and unpredictable because ecosystems can be unsettled in so many different ways: through habitat destruction, pollution, climate change, new agricultural practices, population shifts, and migration to cities, for instance. Each of these activities creates chances for microbes, pests, and other opportunistic species to spread and shift their range to colonize new areas and exploit new populations. When several changes occur at once, the effects generally intensify, and the results are even less predictable.

Disruptions in a person's immunity or the environment at large can activate a microbe and cause disease to emerge or reemerge.

Agriculture and economic development projects are frequently identified as causes for the emergence or resurgence of infectious diseases. More than 30,000 people contract Japanese encephalitis while working in the rice paddies across Asia every year, for example. In many areas of Asia the disease is endemic, but when the fields are flooded, mosquitoes that are vectors for Japanese encephalitis breed quickly. The rapidly growing numbers of mosquitoes search out new blood and species to feed on. At the same time, thousands of farmers and field workers in these areas cultivate and harvest the rice. Many of these people were previously unexposed, and are therefore susceptible to infection. After weeks of rain, proliferating swarms of mosquitoes and thousands of susceptible, noninfected people come into contact with each other and trigger annual outbreaks of Japanese encephalitis.[17]

Converting land to agricultural use can increase exposure to new diseases.

For centuries, the fertile temperate pampas area of Argentina supported cattle, weeds, grasses, and wild fauna. Maize production was introduced to the area during the twenties, and by the forties herbicides were being heavily applied to control the native grasses and weeds. Large-scale cultivation of maize altered the ecology of the pampas. Grasses that could withstand the herbicides and grow in the shade under maize stalks began to take over and a once-rare rodent—the field mouse, *Calomys musculinus*—became dominant. This rodent had always been in the pampas, but in small numbers. Feeding on the seeds of this newly dominant grass, the field mouse thrived in maize and alfalfa fields. It is the vector and natural reservoir of Junín virus, which causes Argentine hemorrhagic fever. With growing populations of mice, farmers were exposed to the Junín virus and spread it to their families and others. Since its discovery in 1958, more than 20,000 Argentineans have been infected and nearly one third of these people have died from Junín hemorrhagic fever.[18]

Domesticated animals can also contribute to the spread of infectious diseases. Several human pathogens originally come from cattle, including *Cryptosporidium*, a waterborne protozoan that usually infects cattle but more recently has infected humans through contaminated watersheds. Parasites can sometimes "jump" to and from host species, and sometimes between animals and humans. The classic example is influenza. The world's pandemic strains of influenza originate in China's traditional integrated duck, pig, and chicken farms, a pattern that dates back thousands of years. And every year new strains are tested to produce the annual shots that are distributed worldwide for the flu season.[19]

By displacing wild populations and disrupting habitats, human activities often deprive microbes of their usual hosts and force them to search out and infect new, vulnerable populations. Human activities may even intrude into new areas that pose threats to susceptible populations. Essentially, this is what happened in 1975 with the *Borrelia* bacterium that causes a relapsing fever known as Lyme disease. Early in the seventies many people moved into new suburban developments in Old Lyme, Connecticut, and other previously wooded communities. At the same time, the native deer population increased, since bears and other predators were driven out. As a result, people came into close contact with the ticks—the vectors for the Lyme disease bacterium—that live in the deer's fur. When a tick bites a person or a deer, the bacterium moves from the tick's saliva into the victim's bloodstream. Lyme disease has since spread throughout the United States—due in part to growing numbers of deer and ticks—and is especially rampant in New England, Wisconsin, and Minnesota, where people live and spend time in wooded areas close to deer populations. In 1994, more than 13,000 cases were reported in the United States.[20]

Specialists refer to "manmade malaria" to describe the routine phenomenon of the disease flaring up near irrigation projects, dams, construction sites, standing water, and poorly drained areas where malaria is already present but only during a certain time of the year, when conditions are right for mosquitoes. This is common throughout the tropical areas of Asia, Africa, and the Americas.[21]

After the Indira Gandhi Canal was built in Rajasthan, for instance, to irrigate desertlike areas of India, farmers switched from cultivating traditional crops of jowar and bajra to more commercially profitable wheat and cotton, which require large amounts of water. Many people came to the area in search of work. The main canal—445 kilometers long, from Masitanwali to Ramgarh—turned out to be an ideal breeding site for mosquitoes during the monsoon season. Instead of high crop productivity and prosperity, the heavy rains brought the farmers rapidly spreading cerebral malaria, which if untreated can be quickly fatal as it causes red blood cells to erupt and the brain to hemorrhage. Malaria (and now dengue fever) and waterborne diseases are common during India's monsoon season, but the canals carried the epidemic to a much larger area, exposing workers and farmers who then transmitted the disease to other people. "The ignition wire of construction-related stagnant water, and the gunpowder of immigrant labor, [created] an explosion of malaria," reported a World Bank–commissioned independent review on India's Sardar Sarovar Dam Project.[22]

Climate change will cause disruptions and alterations in the environment; more floods, storms, and droughts are likely, along with changes in rainfall and precipitation. (See Chapter 2.) Although it is difficult to predict the exact effects, this could have serious human health consequences. A number of variables affecting pathogens and their vectors—such as rates of breeding and maturation, location of breeding sites and habitats, time between feeding cycles—are sensitive to temperature, humidity, and rainfall.

Changes in global and local temperatures and rainfall could expand the geographical distribution of parasites and vectors, affect their behavior, and increase the rate of development, thus increasing the risk of transmission of infectious diseases.

Extreme weather conditions, such as heat and heavy flooding, can produce the right environmental conditions for an outbreak. Major upsurges of dengue in some nations, such as Colombia in 1995, follow periods of heavy rains.[23]

Risks are especially great in areas that border current endemic areas or are at higher altitudes within endemic areas, and among people who have no built-in immunity, perhaps through previous exposure. Michael Loevinsohn of the International Development Research Centre in New Dehli linked a 1-degree Celsius increase in average temperature in 1987 in Rwanda to a 337-percent rise in the incidence of malaria over 1984. Higher-altitude mountainous regions of Rwanda, where malaria had previously been "rare or absent," reported a 500-percent increase, compared with 300 percent in lower-lying areas.[24]

Changes in global and local temperatures and rainfall could expand the geographical distribution of parasites and vectors, increasing the risk of infectious disease.

Research on the mosquito *Culex tarsalis*, the primary vector for Western equine encephalitis and St. Louis encephalitis, shows that a rise in average temperatures actually decreases the time it takes the mosquito larvae (and encephalitis viruses) to mature. (The different types of encephalitis vary in severity from mild, flu-like symptoms, including high fevers, to fatal inflammation of the brain and central nervous system.) When it is warmer, mosquitoes breed faster, so the total number of vectors can increase rapidly. Rising temperatures also decrease the time between meals, so the mosquitoes bite humans and animals more frequently, which has the net effect of increasing transmission of the encephalitis parasite. When temperatures are too high, mosquito larvae do not mature. So up to a certain threshold temperature, warmer weather increases the transmission of vectorborne infections.[25]

The Netherlands-based National Institute of Public Health and Environmental Protection reports that a global mean temperature rise of 3 degrees Celsius by 2100 would double the epidemic potential of mosquito populations in tropical regions and would increase it in temperate regions, where malaria is currently rare or nonexistent, more than 10 times. The Institute's model, which examines interactions between climate, mosquitoes, and humans, projects several million more malaria cases per year by 2100. Worldwide, more than a million people could die each year as a result of "the impact of a human-induced climate change on malaria transmission" in the next 60 years. These studies show that high latitudes are projected to have bioclimatic conditions conducive to malaria transmission.[26]

Coordination among policymakers and health officials is important to anticipate future disruptions and to coordinate responses to the health effects of human activities. In the future, along with keeping ecosystems intact and minimizing habitat alterations, communities should require planners to prepare for all the unanticipated consequences of development and to integrate considerations of human health into major human activities, such as canal building and farming. And they would do well to provide ongoing health education for their populations, especially in areas that are particularly vulnerable to environmental disruption or near endemic disease centers.

Still, understanding all the various links between environmental disruption, microbial outbreaks, and health may be nearly impossible. "It's a lottery," according to Paul Ewald, a biologist at Amherst College in Massachusetts, as to whether or not a pathogen will be introduced in the population.[27]

BIOLOGICAL MIXING AND SOCIAL DISRUPTION

In addition to environmental disruptions and changes, the movement of people, plants, animals, and goods—known as biological mixing—can increase exposure to disease. Dr. Stephen Morse, a virologist at Rockefeller University, coined the phrase "viral traffic" to describe the movement of viruses to new species or new individuals, often through human acts. Some human-induced conditions serve as a green light for microbial mixing, while others slow or completely halt the rate of traffic, essentially acting as red lights. As Morse says, "inevitably viral traffic is enhanced by *human* traffic." By understanding the red and green lights, we can better control the traffic.[28]

By transporting microbes and vectors that originate in one geographic location to new places, movement and mixing create the opportunities for microbes to infect new, potentially susceptible populations. Some emerging and reemerging infections are caused by pathogens already present in the environment, but viral traffic and biological mixing bring them out of retirement.[29]

Before Christopher Columbus arrived in the New World at the end of the fifteenth century, an estimated 100 million people lived in the Americas. The European explorers brought more than their religion, language, and cultures with them. They also carried over parasites and pathogens unfamiliar to aboriginal American people. Introducing an infection to a population previously unexposed and unaccustomed to it can have devastating consequences: the population of Mexico dropped from 20 million to 3 million between 1518 and 1568, then declined another 50 percent over the next 50 years. Most of the deaths were from successive epidemics of smallpox, measles, and typhus introduced by consecutive waves of European explorers and conquerors.[30]

Five hundred years later, at the end of the twentieth century, 1 million people per day cross international borders by air. Any person, plant, or animal that moves can potentially carry a microbe or organism that will be foreign at its destination. Today, an infectious pathogen, such as influenza, can easily travel around the world in a matter of hours. Although the likelihood of an isolated case causing a serious medical problem is rather small, rapidly increasing rates of travel boost the chances that such cases will become more frequent and have long-lasting effects on susceptible populations.[31]

In the seventies, for example, the paving of the Kinshasa Highway from Point-Noire, Zaire, to Mombasa, Kenya, gave a fateful boost to the outbreak of AIDS. Although the origin of the AIDS virus, HIV, is not known, the initial spread of AIDS was probably exacerbated by human migration and behavior. Truck drivers along the highway caught HIV from prostitutes, and then transmitted the virus to people in cities, either sexually or by sharing drug needles. Communities along the highway were soon infected with AIDS, and gradually this lethal virus was carried across the planet. By 1994, more than 25 million people worldwide were infected with HIV, and between 5 million and 9 million had developed full-blown AIDS.[32]

The mechanism of biological mixing brings the parasites and vectors to new places, but the conditions must be ripe for long-lasting effects: there must be large enough populations of hosts and victims. And the conditions—biological, social, ecological, and climatological—must be conducive to the spread of disease. For instance, cases of dengue—also known as breakbone fever because of the painful bones, hemorrhaging of the mucous membrane in the skin and abdomen, high fever, chills, headaches, vomiting, diarrhea, and severe exhaustion it causes—have been on the rise in Latin America since the eighties as urbanization and poverty increased. Mosquito spraying programs waned, which led to an increase of mosquitoes and a subsequent rise in cases of dengue fever.[33]

Today, an infectious pathogen such as influenza can easily travel around the world in a matter of hours.

Dengue is carried by the female *Aedes aegypti* mosquito, which thrives in urban areas, living and breeding in small containers of water such as flower pots, tires, birdbaths, gutters, barrels, and even plastic tarps and covers. These hardy urban survivors are found in nearly every major city in the tropics. Each year, up to 100 million people are infected with dengue fever, primarily in cities and tropical urban areas, while 2.5 billion people are at risk of infection. In the past 10 years, cases of dengue have been reported only in isolated outbreaks in several U.S. cities, including Houston, but officials are wary that dengue fever could become established in North America. In 1994, 20,000 people in Puerto Rico were infected with this disease.[34]

At the same time the conditions for *A. aegypti* improved, another successful vector of dengue, *A. albopictus*—better known as the Asian tiger mosquito—established itself in southeastern United States. (See also Chapter 6.) It has extended its range southward into Latin America and northward toward Chicago and Washington, D.C. Originally introduced to Texas in a 1985 shipment of used tires from Asia, the Asian tiger mosquito is a more vicious biter and can survive cold winters better than its tropical cousin.[35]

One of the difficulties of treating dengue is that there are four different types of the fever, and being infected with one does not give a person any immunity to the others. Sequential infections of the different viruses can trigger dengue hemorrhagic fever (DHF), which causes internal bleeding and can lead to shock, or even dengue shock syndrome (DSS), another severe form of dengue fever. But the exact progression from dengue fever to DHF and DSS is not known. DHF first appeared in Manila in 1953 and spread quickly through Southeast Asia in the sixties. In the eighties, DHF appeared in Brazil, Cuba, and Venezuela and is now moving slowly throughout Latin America. Between 1989 and 1994, dengue hemorrhagic fever increased sixtyfold in Latin America. Worldwide, the incidence of DHF has been on the rise because of increasing urbanization, especially in the tropics where dengue is endemic. (See Table 7-3.)[36]

Often, climatic disturbances such as floods, storms, or earthquakes create the right conditions for viral traffic, and then

Table 7-3. Global Incidence of Dengue Hemorrhagic Fever

Years	Cases	Cases Per Year
1956–80	715,283	29,803
1981–85	687,522	137,504
1986–90	1,338,461	267,692

SOURCE: Duane J. Gubler, *Virus Information Exchange Newsletter*, No. 8, 1991, as reprinted in Thomas P. Monath, "The Challenge: Biotechnology Transfer to Public Health. Examples from Arbovirology," in David H. Walker, ed., *Global Infectious Diseases: Prevention, Control, and Eradication* (New York: Springer-Verlag, 1992).

human activity and response in some way magnifies the effects of such disturbances. For example, some experts believe the outbreak of plague in Surat, India, in September 1994 was connected to the flooding of the Tapti River during that summer, and to an earthquake a year earlier. The quake hit the city of Tehri in 1993, leaving the landscape devastated and thousands homeless. Emergency aid and medical supplies were flown in for the survivors, but the outpouring of aid was so successful that there was actually too much food. Excess supplies were stored in warehouses, where rats crawled in and feasted. The rodents reproduced quickly, allowing the plague bacterium—harbored in the fleas that infest the rodents' fur—to extend its range greatly. India experienced an intense heat wave during the summer of 1994, with temperatures reaching 40 degrees Celsius, and fleas swarmed to animals that had collapsed from the heat.[37]

Then a monsoon flooded the Tapti River and inundated the poorest districts of Surat with three meters of water. Again, people were forced to leave their homes. The rodents were also forced to seek shelter on drier land. Rats and people crowded together on the same high ground, increasing people's exposure to the plague bacterium. Although India was medically prepared to deal with waterborne diseases such as gastroenteritis and cholera, and with some vectorborne diseases like malaria and dengue fever, it had no plans for plague. Many doctors who could diagnose and treat plague had already left the area in fear, and the disease had not been seen in several decades.[38]

The combination of weather patterns and environmental damage from the earthquake and flood was exacerbated by social factors: shantytowns, squalid living conditions, excess food in storage, and inadequate health care. Panic was fanned into hysteria by media coverage that focused on the disaster without explaining its causes. What could have been prevented or controlled at an early stage became a financial as well as a social disaster, as international airline flights to and from India were cancelled and trade came temporarily to a halt. India's outbreak of plague was followed by major upsurges of malaria and dengue fever, as mosquitoes proliferated in the monsoon-prone area. The plague faded into obscurity as flea-killing insecticides and DDT were sprayed widely, rat catchers and garbage collectors worked overtime, and isolation wards were set up to treat victims. But the message of the outbreak—that a rapid and effective surveillance system and trained medical workers are vital to protecting the health of a community— remains unheeded in India and elsewhere.[39]

War, civil disorder, and social decay also create conditions ripe for the spread of infectious diseases. The great influenza pandemic of this century, for instance, broke out in 1918 and within four months had spread all over the world, carried home by soldiers. Malnutrition, societal disruption, and underequipped hospitals after the war boosted the chances of this highly contagious infection spreading. Only Iceland and Samoa were spared, and that was before modern air travel. The pandemic killed 20 million people worldwide— more than twice as many as in World War I itself. Today, flu outbreaks cost the United States $5 billion each year in medical expenses. To prevent yearly outbreaks, medical authorities now encourage people to receive shots to vaccinate themselves against recombined strains of influenza.[40]

In present-day Russia, health conditions are worsening because of unstable political conditions, deteriorating infrastructure, high levels of pollution, population movements, and an economy in transition. Nationwide, tuberculosis, measles, and mumps are on the rise, after being successfully controlled with mass vaccinations until the mid-eighties. The incidence of diphtheria, a potentially fatal disease easily prevented by childhood immunization, increased in Russia from 603 cases in 1989 to 39,703 in 1994. On the Pacific coast, the cities of Sovetskaya Gavan and Vadino recorded six times more cases of diphtheria in January 1995 than the entire region had in the previous year. And in 1994, cholera appeared in Moscow, evidently travelling north from the Black Sea coast, where it was detected in the plankton some six months earlier.[41]

But even in the midst of social disruption, there is hope that common sense will prevail. James P. Grant, the late Executive Director of UNICEF, demonstrated throughout his career at that agency that it was possible to provide vaccines to children even in the midst of war. Under his leadership, UNICEF negotiated temporary cease-fires to allow clergy, UNICEF volunteers, nurses, and other medical workers to immunize children and provide minimal supplies of food and medicines to the young victims of war. In El Salvador, for example, UNICEF officials negotiated with President Duarte and guerrilla leaders to hold regularly scheduled "days of tranquility" each year; as a result, children's immunization rates soared from 3 percent in 1984 to 80 percent in 1990 even as a civil war was being waged.[42]

LACK OF CLEAN WATER

Contaminated water is strongly linked to the incidence and spread of infectious diseases. Worldwide, biological waterborne diseases represent more than 99 percent of illnesses related to contaminated water, and hundreds of times more illness than chemical contamination of drinking water does. In developing countries, 25 million people die every year from pathogens and pollution in contaminated drinking water. And diarrhea, which causes severe dehydration and malnutrition, kills nearly 3 million children under age 5 every year and accounts for one fourth of the deaths in this age group. In fact, diarrheal diseases rank second in order of killer infectious diseases, after acute respiratory infections.[43]

Diarrhea kills nearly 3 million children under age 5 every year.

The irony is these diseases are "both preventable and curable," says Dr. Ronald Waldman, former coordinator of WHO's Global Task Force on Cholera Control. Widespread use of oral rehydration therapy (ORT)—an inexpensive mixture of water, sugar, and salt that is administered either as a liquid or as a packet of salts, as soon as a patient can drink—has reduced the number of deaths from most diarrheal diseases. In 1993, ORT saved more than 1 million children's lives and was used for treatment in almost half the developing world. It is much cheaper than intravenous rehydration, which is usually necessary in less than 5 percent of cases of diarrhea. In sub-Saharan Africa, the number of families using ORT nearly doubled between 1988 and 1993. With a rapid and effective response, deaths from diarrhea in connection with cholera and dysentery, for example, can be significantly reduced—by up to 80 percent.[44]

Human pathogens that thrive in aquatic environments can cause hepatitis A, salmonella, and various diarrheal diseases that are linked to *Escherichia coli*, cholera, typhoid, and dysentery. Some pathogens are transmitted by drinking infected water or eating contaminated fish and shellfish; others are spread by swimming, bathing, or wading in infected water; and still others are carried by water-based insects and snails.[45]

The International Drinking Water Supply and Sanitation Decade (1981–90) brought safe drinking water to hundreds of millions of people. Concerted efforts by governments, private groups, and communities during the eighties—including more than $130 billion spent for infrastructure projects and community-based initiatives—made significant progress toward the U.N. goal of providing "safe water and sanitation for all." Access to safe drinking water more than doubled for people in rural areas and increased more than 1.5 times for people in urban areas. But the progress of the decade was undermined by rapid population growth in developing countries. In 1990, for example, more than 1 billion people in developing countries still needed clean drinking water and more than 1.7 billion people—especially in rapidly growing urban developing areas—threw their sewage out untreated.[46]

Even in areas where water supplies are thought to be relatively safe, serious problems remain. Today, cholera, typhoid, and dysentery are rare in industrial countries; illnesses from waterborne microbes fell nearly a thousandfold over the past century in the United States. Yet the U.S. Environmental Protection Agency estimates that waterborne infectious diseases cost the nation about $9.7 billion annually. One study noted that nearly one third of all cases of diarrhea in North America can be associated with consuming inadequately treated drinking water.[47]

Cryptosporidium and *Giardia*, which cause gastrointestinal infections, are the primary waterborne disease-causing agents in U.S. water supplies. More than 400,000 people became ill and 104 died in Milwaukee in 1993 when *Cryptosporidium* contaminated the city's water supply, a disaster that cost the city at least $150 million to control and perhaps more than twice that in medical costs and lost work time. Annually, more than 700,000 Americans contract cryptosporidiosis, which is one of the most serious of all microbial diseases because it can cause infection at a very low dose and may be resistant to levels of disinfection generally applied to drinking water. Nearly 40 percent of treated drinking water supplies in the United States contained either *Cryptosporidium* or *Giardia* in test samples taken by Robert Morris, an assistant professor of epidemiology at the Medical College of Wisconsin.[48]

In Russia, the Volga, the Dvina, and the Ob Rivers are now hazardous to public health. They harbor strains of cholera, typhoid, dysentery, and viral hepatitis that spread through water systems and contaminate drinking supplies. Ukraine's chief epidemiologist, Vitaly Movchanok, stated in 1994 that many Ukrainian rivers were so contaminated by industrial and human waste that virtually all available water filter systems would fail to protect against the cholera bacterium. Improved sewage systems and protected, clean water supplies are needed to control these diseases, along with medical supplies and vaccines.[49]

Even in a well-trained medical community, a seemingly minor event can sometimes trigger an epidemic. In 1991, for example, bilge water from a Chinese freighter was considered responsible for releasing the Asian strain of cholera into Peruvian waters. Once the bacteria were released, they are believed to have spread quickly through plankton in the marine environment and been carried to people through contaminated drinking water, fish, mollusks, and crustaceans. Many people in the region ingested the cholera bacterium directly by eating ceviche (raw fish and lemon juice). Within two years of the initial release, there were more than 500,000 cases of cholera throughout Latin America, with 200,000 in Peru alone. In 1991, Peru lost $750 million in seafood exports because of cholera. The Pan American Health Organization estimated that it will take more than a decade and $200 billion to control the cholera outbreak in Latin America.[50]

Medical providers can curtail outbreaks of waterborne diseases by teaching residents how to diagnose cholera and how to avoid infection—by boiling water for drinking and by washing food thoroughly. Chlorination is used widely in Latin America, for instance, because it is low cost and the results are good. But chlorination does not work on severely polluted water, and it has little or no effect on protozoa such as *Cryptosporidium*, so filtration systems should also be used.[51]

A 1985 community health project sponsored by the Sante Fe de Bogotá Foundation shows that even where it is too expensive to build a sanitation network, individual low-tech systems can be installed and managed by local people. In Bogotá, Colombia, so-called self-built sanitary units—communal septic tanks with soak away trenches and individual sanitary units with drainage to an absorption pit—were installed for 300 families. Wells were also fixed up to further improve water supplies for these families.[52]

In areas with a history of waterborne illness, one way to predict outbreaks of cholera may be to detect and monitor plankton blooms. Cholera emerges seasonally, when the temperature, sunlight, nutrient levels, and acidity are adequate. At other times of year, the bacteria hibernate with their algae hosts. Rita Colwell, a University of Maryland microbiologist, and Dr. Paul Epstein of the Harvard School of Public Health have studied the bacteria that catch a ride with phytoplankton (algae) and zooplankton, and have shown that when there are plankton blooms, there are corresponding outbreaks of diseases in humans, marine mammals, and fish. In Bangladesh, seasonal outbreaks of cholera are associated with heavy rains, El Niño events (warm ocean temperatures), and plankton blooms.[53]

In the late eighties and early nineties, the morbillivirus that caused a series of dolphin die-offs in the Mediterranean Sea was traced to biotoxins that were carried in the mackerel that mammals ate. The dolphins' immune systems may have also been depressed by warmer sea surface temperatures and PCB contamination. Certainly infrastructure solutions, such as sewage systems, are necessary, but maintaining a healthy marine environment is an important part of the solution.[54]

DRUG RESISTANCE

Following Alexander Fleming's discovery of the antibacterial properties of *Penicillium* mold in 1929, the forties and fifties saw enormous progress in controlling the threat and incidence of infectious diseases. With a growing arsenal of therapeutic drugs—including penicillin, tetracycline, and ampicillin—WHO, national governments, and medical authorities initiated campaigns to wipe infectious diseases from the face of the earth. By the sixties, however, naive optimism and expectations of earlier years were tempered by the realization that antibiotics are tools that can control microbes when used effectively—and sparingly.[55]

Drug resistance is as inevitable as evolution. When a drug—such as penicillin—is used, some of the bacteria survive an initial dose of antibiotics; they become immune or resistant to the drugs in the same way that a child can be immunized with a small dose of an infection that will promote resistance to the disease. The bacteria that survive then reproduce; gradually they become the dominant strain of the microbe, and the antibiotics lose their effectiveness. Resistant strains develop particularly fast when doctors overuse antibiotics and try to eliminate the bacteria rather than control them. If you kill 99.9 percent of the bacteria, the survivors are a superstrain.[56]

Almost from the moment Fleming conducted his life-saving experiments, the number of drug-resistant strains grew rapidly. As early as 1955, most countries recognized the problem of overuse and restricted the use of penicillin by requiring prescriptions.[57]

Now, more than a half-century after the discovery of antibiotics, we are at risk of losing these valuable resources. "Almost all disease-causing bacteria are on the pathway to complete resistance," says Robert Naso, vice president of research at Univax Biologics in Rockville, Maryland. Dr. Stuart Levy, the Director of the Center for Adaptation Genetics and Drug Resistance at the Tufts University School of Medicine in Massachusetts, agrees. Today, more and more drug-resistant bacteria are causing infections that no longer respond to antibiotics. And the costs can be staggering: annually, Americans pay more than $4 billion in drug-resistance-related medical costs for bacterial infections, according to the Centers for Disease Control and Prevention (CDC).[58]

One of the most deadly infectious diseases—malaria—has made a recent comeback with the evolution of drug-resistant strains of the parasite *Plasmodium*, which causes malaria. At a penny a dose, chloroquine is prescribed like aspirin in some African countries to treat malaria symptoms. Yet by the late fifties, chloroquine-resistant *Plasmodium falciparum* had evolved in South America and Southeast Asia. By the late seventies, these strains had spread through South Asia, India, the Middle East, and East Africa, sweeping west across sub-Saharan Africa over the next 10 years.[59]

Today, people from Malawi and Zaire report that it is common to suffer from severe (and sometimes cerebral) malaria. In 1995, the direct and indirect costs associated with malaria were expected to reach $1.8 billion in Africa. And in Vietnam, complicated cases of cerebral and hemorrhagic ("blackwater fever") malaria rose by 275 percent between 1987 and 1990 and mortality tripled due to a combination of multi-drug-resistant malaria, migration into forested areas, mining activity, and an inadequate medical care system.[60]

Antibiotic-resistant *Streptococcus pneumoniae*, which causes pneumonia, a leading cause of sickness and even death among young children and the elderly worldwide, was first reported in New Guinea in 1967. Drug-resistant pneumococcal infections became common in South Africa in the seventies, in Europe in the eighties, and in the United States in the nineties. In Europe, penicillin-resistant pneumococci are a growing problem that causes a range of infections including pneumonia and the often fatal blood infection septicemia. In 1979, only 6 percent of pneumococcus strains were penicillin-resistant; by 1989, this number had grown to 44 percent throughout Europe. A case study in Atlanta, Georgia, reported that 41 percent of pneumococcal infections in children under age six were resistant to penicillin.[61]

Drug-resistant infections are not necessarily more dangerous, but they are more difficult to treat. Doctors increasingly have to prescribe longer hospital stays, alternative treatments, and more toxic and expensive drugs as strains of disease resistant to single and multiple drugs become more common. Out of 50 studied types of bacteria, only two—those that cause Lyme disease and syphilis—can be treated with a single antibiotic. To treat the other 48, at least two antibiotics are required.[62]

Some staphylococcal, pneumococcal, and streptococcal infections, which cause high fever, sore throat, earaches, and pneumonia, are resistant to every antibiotic except one: vancomycin. It is just a matter of time until this drug also becomes useless; rare enterococcal infections are already resistant to vancomycin. Enterococci will eventually transfer its vancomycin-resistant plasmid to these other, more common infections.[63]

Out of 50 studied types of bacteria, only those that cause Lyme disease and syphilis can be treated with a single antibiotic.

Strains of multiple-drug-resistant tuberculosis have emerged in U.S. cities and elsewhere, with mortality rates above 50 percent. To treat an active case of non-drug-resistant tuberculosis costs up to $10,000 in the United States, compared with $200,000 to treat an active TB infection that has become drug-resistant. In 1991, almost half the new cases of TB in New York City were resistant to the two main drugs previously used. The costs of hospitalizing New Yorkers with drug-resistant TB skyrocketed, and $40 million in emergency funds were provided that year by CDC and state authorities to compensate for TB control programs discontinued in the eighties. The growth in drug-resistant cases has recently been reversed, with intensive and directly observed treatment of active cases.[64]

More selective and frugal use of antibiotics would go a long way toward winning the battle against drug resistance. In Hungary, for instance, more than half the strains of pneumococcus were resistant to penicillin by 1989. The situation was reversed with a campaign against indiscriminate antibiotic use. By 1992, the number of penicillin-resistant cases of pneumonia dropped to 34 percent. Health clinics and doctors can safeguard the antibiotics that still work by using them sparingly and making sure that patients use them as prescribed. CDC in the United States recommends that hospitals regularly test for vancomycin-resistant enterococci and isolate patients who have this infection.[65]

WRITING THE PRESCRIPTION

To control infectious diseases, we must understand how they are emerging, how they are being transmitted, and how humans increase the possibilities for both. For example, yellow fever was one of the most feared diseases in the western hemisphere until the twentieth century. Not until doctors looked at how the disease was spreading—through the *A. aegpyti* mosquito—could they attack the carrier and reduce transmission. Without this understanding, widespread efforts to control the incidence of yellow fever, using mosquito eradication and vaccines, would have been nearly impossible.[66]

Similarly, more than 60 percent of the rangeland in Kenya is infested with tsetse flies that livestock could not be raised without intensive use of expensive drugs and vaccines; new measures to control tsetse flies, other than widespread insecticide spraying, were needed. The U.N. Food and Agriculture Organization's Animal Health Division and the International Center for Insect Physiology and Ecology developed control measures using muslin traps that smell of cow urine to attract tsetse flies and a small light in a bag that kills the flies by heat stress. The traps cost only about $10 to make and catch about 5,000 flies each day; they are expected to improve the lives of 55 million people and 58 million cattle who are currently threatened by sleeping sickness. Such measures have been helped with the use of Remote Sensing and Geographic Information Systems to better target the habitats and climate conducive to tsetse flies. Assembling topographical, soil, meteorological, and epidemiological data creates a risk map that indicates areas most vulnerable to African trypanosomiasis and other diseases like malaria and Lyme disease.[67]

Ironically, in today's tight financial setting, health workers struggle to maintain a baseline of funding and support for prevention and treatment programs at the same time that governments are spending exorbitant amounts in response to outbreaks. In 1994, for example, one U.S. researcher tried unsuccessfully to raise $200,000 to develop a vaccine for new strains of cholera, while relief agencies spent $140 million in emergency aid for a cholera outbreak in Rwandan refugee camps in Zaire.[68]

Immunization is the best preventive medicine, especially when targeted at the people who need it the most. Health economists estimate that every dollar spent on the vaccine for measles, mumps, and rubella saves $21; for the vaccine for diphtheria, tetanus, and pertussis, the figure is $29; and for the polio vaccine, $6. Based on current projections for the eradication of polio, WHO predicts a global savings of $500 million by 2000. A 13-year program to eradicate smallpox in the United States cost $30 million. Since its successful completion in 1977, the total investment has been returned every 26 days. Infectious diseases can be better controlled by reinvigorating the push during the eighties to vaccinate every child, and by supporting wide distribution of ORT and other basic public health treatments. Preventive strategies, such as mass vaccination campaigns, cost little compared with the lives and money they save.[69]

Beyond money for prevention and treatment programs, another prudent use of scarce funding is for biomedical research and health education, especially by developing countries. The Kenya Medical Research Institute, for instance, is researching tropical diseases with a focus on diagnostic techniques and vaccine development. With qualified staff on location, the difficult questions are more likely to be asked and answered than at present. Then regional and local centers could collaborate closely to provide a network of specialties and to deliver more localized care and protection.[70]

Disease surveillance laboratories to help doctors promptly diagnose diseases and monitor trends are severely lacking in Africa, according to Dr. Oyewale Tomori with the College of Medicine in Ibadan, Nigeria. In the sixties and seventies, labs were staffed and operated by outside agencies and government. In the nineties, well-trained African doctors must use ill-equipped, non-functional labs until outside support is obtained. Meanwhile, disease outbreaks can rage for months unattended.[71]

Epidemiological studies that quantify the link between environmental disruption and the emergence of infectious diseases are also badly needed. Medical anthropologist Carol Jenkins and several staff members of the Papua New Guinea Institute of Medical Research, for instance, have designed an experiment to monitor native people's health before, during, and after a logging operation. By comparing the health of people from four villages—two in the logging region and two in pristine areas—they plan to measure how environmental disruption affects the villagers' health.[72]

Even with the best data available, there is no silver bullet for most infectious diseases. The most cost-effective control measures are a conglomeration of efforts that include improved education, disease prevention and surveillance, closely monitored drug therapy, and alternative treatments such as clean water supplies and mosquito control programs. To this end, the WHO General Assembly passed a resolution in 1995 urging member states to strengthen surveillance, improve rapid diagnosis, communication, and response; conduct routine testing for drug resistance; and increase the number of skilled staff who address infectious diseases.[73]

There is no silver bullet for most infectious diseases.

A call for a worldwide Program for Monitoring Emerging Diseases (ProMED) of humans, animals, and plants was issued in September 1993 by the U.S.–based Federation of American Scientists (FAS). The ProMED electronic conference, an initiative of nongovernmental groups, is chaired by Stephen Morse and represents the communications component of a broader FAS project. ProMED is now an active global on-line network that establishes a direct partnership and communication network among health workers, scientists, and journalists. Since its technical inception in August 1994, the 100 countries and 2,500 individuals represented on the network have taken the initial step in building a global infectious disease network. In May 1995, global health officials and scientists used ProMED to monitor the outbreak of Ebola virus in Kikwit, Zaire. One of the most important roles of ProMED has been to connect with computer users in developing countries, including missionary health workers and researchers in Pakistan, Cameroon, and Uganda.[74]

In a similar move, in 1994 the members of the European Union and European Cooperation in Science and Technology established an on-line network for laboratory-based surveillance of salmonella infections. Known as Salmnet, the network currently shares information among 13 countries, including quality assurance guidelines, standard reporting procedures, and rapid notification of suspected and confirmed cases. An outbreak of *Shigella sonnei* in Sweden that quickly spread to the other Nordic countries and to England and Wales was tracked on Salmnet, which helped medical authorities coordinate their response.[75]

In sum, there are several key measures that governments and the medical community can take in their efforts to deal with new and reemerging infectious diseases. First, recognizing how human-induced changes amplify the spread of microbes and vectors of diseases is crucial

in order to combat the growing fear and inertia that have characterized the world's response to date. Second, seeing people as part of the problem as well as part of the solution will help local citizens, health workers, and policymakers make connections between environment and human health. Third, governments need to realize that outbreaks can often be traced to inadequate infrastructure and distribution rather than lack of knowledge and available medical treatments. Finally, a combination of integrated disease prevention programs, widespread immunization programs, follow-up treatment, public education, up-to-date research and labs, and electronic technology can help ease the burden of future and on-going infectious disease outbreaks.

In the long run, prevention is most important: elevating the role of a healthy environment in controlling—though never eliminating—the emergence and spread of infectious diseases naturally will go a long way toward establishing a healthier world. To be most effective, surveillance for infectious diseases can be integrated with environmental monitoring to better understand the life cycles of diseases and to anticipate the multiple conditions conducive to disease outbreaks. The price of failing to understand these links is clear: rising health care costs and a world in which more than half the people live in fear of plagues that are as certain as death and taxes.

8

Upholding Human Rights and Environmental Justice

Aaron Sachs

The murder of Chico Mendes on December 22, 1988, in a remote section of the Brazilian Amazon, made international headlines largely because of Mendes's connection to the global environmental movement. "Brazilian Who Fought to Protect Amazon is Killed," the *New York Times* reported. Yet Mendes, a lifelong rubber tapper and labor union activist, considered his struggle to be founded not on ecology but on social justice and human rights. He had not even been aware of environmentalism until about three years before his death.[1]

Mendes's principal aim was to protect his fellow rubber tappers' right to earn a livelihood from the forest by extracting latex from rubber trees and gathering nuts in seasons when the rubber was not flowing. Once introduced to the environmental movement, though, he was quick to realize that the international struggle to save the rain forest and his local struggle to empower rain-forest inhabitants amounted to nearly the same thing—and in his felicitous blending of environmentalism and human rights work lay the key to his legacy. Mendes pointed out that an intact forest ecosystem could sustain a substantial population of highly productive rubber tappers, who would have an obvious vested interest in keeping it intact. His advocacy eventually resulted in the creation of the Chico Mendes Extractive Reserve, a tract of nearly 1 million hectares of protected rain forest.[2]

Tragically, by speaking out, by organizing protests, by fighting to ensure that the forests of his home region would be used sustainably and equitably rather than slashed and burned for the benefit of a few rich landowners, Mendes sealed his fate—an angry cattle baron was arrested for the murder. But his example and those of hundreds of other environmental activists around the world whose human rights have been violated serve as powerful reminders of the links between ecology and issues of human rights and

An expanded version of this chapter appeared as Worldwatch Paper 127, *Eco-Justice: Linking Human Rights and the Environment*.

social justice. In living, Mendes proved that the enjoyment of many basic rights depends on protection of the environment. In dying, the victim of frontier lawlessness, he proved that ongoing environmental protection depends on people's secure ability to exercise their basic rights.[3]

Environmental degradation, even in areas that seem remote, usually carries a high human cost. That cost is behind struggles like the one Chico Mendes and his fellow forest dwellers waged—struggles for what has come to be known as environmental justice. While ecologists have long warned of the damage caused by putting the planet's ecosystems under heavy stress, it took social activists like Mendes to point out that the immediate human toll of environmental destruction has usually been borne disproportionately by the people least able to cope with it—people already on the margins of society, who have perhaps been targeted as vulnerable and lacking resources to defend themselves.[4]

The immediate human toll of environmental destruction has usually been borne disproportionately by the people least able to cope with it.

In Chico Mendes's home state of Acre, in 1970, three quarters of the land was publicly owned, unclaimed and undeveloped. By 1980, almost all of it had been bought, and about half of Acre's land was held by only 10 people. By encouraging the fastest possible development of the frontier, the Brazilian government essentially forced the scattered inhabitants of the rain forest to pay the price of deforestation—ranging from air pollution to the spread of disease to flooding and soil erosion—while a few wealthy landowners reaped most of the rewards.[5]

Environmental injustice—meaning the gap between our universally shared dependence on a healthy local environment and our inequitable access to such an environment—arises at all levels of society. Attacks against individual environmental activists often point to much broader injustices and human rights violations, to attacks against entire communities—whether the destruction of the rubber tappers' resource base in the Amazon, or the dumping of hazardous waste in an impoverished, minority town in North Carolina, or the forced relocation of thousands of people in India's Narmada Valley to make way for a gargantuan dam project, or the pollution of black South Africans' drinking water by gold mining operations. At the national level, environmental damage tends to be concentrated in poorer countries, which often overexploit their natural resources in order to feed overconsumption in richer countries. Working toward environmental justice will thus require wide-reaching policy changes in both the ecological and human rights arenas.[6]

Justice of any kind, however, is a fluid concept that depends on constant checks and balances—so one of the most important goals of the environmental justice movement may well be the protection of civil rights. The basic freedoms of civil society, after all—free speech, a free press providing access to information, fair elections, freedom to organize in groups—are the best ways of holding those who wield power accountable. Much environmental destruction occurs in the first place simply because affected communities are powerless to prevent it. Although drastic environmental policy reforms are essential, in other words, guaranteeing the implementation of such reforms will ultimately depend on the full protection of basic human rights—especially the rights of society's most vulnerable people.[7]

THE CASE FOR COLLABORATION

Since Chico Mendes's murder, environmentalists and human rights workers all over the world have staked out common ground much more readily; they are finally beginning to blend their movements. In October 1995, the Sierra Club and Amnesty International issued their first joint letter, on the link between human rights abuses and environmental degradation in Nigeria. The broader the coalition, both groups have realized, the more its policy agendas take on universal relevance and the more political power it attains. As Ashish Kothari, Lecturer in Environmental Studies at the Indian Institute of Public Administration, has noted: "Most mass movements at the grassroots are not just human rights, nor just environmental, but inevitably both. They have to be, if they are conscious of the role of natural resources in their lives, and of the dominant forces exploiting those resources."[8]

This collaboration is still tentative, however. Even though the agendas of the two movements have overlapped for quite a long time, on such issues as environmental health hazards and threats to indigenous peoples' resource bases, the two sets of activists still have a lot to learn from each other. Decades of fostering different approaches to advocacy have led to a certain amount of mutual distrust.[9]

Members of Amnesty International, for instance, famous for their letter-writing campaigns on behalf of individual prisoners of conscience, have tended to feel little sympathy for eco-philosophers trying to make a case for "the rights of nature." They have a hard time understanding why ecologists seem willing to spend so much energy on abstractions, on efforts to prevent some possible future extinction of an obscure species of bird, supposedly for the eventual good of everyone—while human beings are being tortured right here in the present. Similarly, ecologists have tended to grow exasperated with the narrow human-rights focus on single cases of abuse, pointing out that far more people are threatened by such things as desertification and water pollution than by torture.[10]

Some environmentalists have certainly deserved their reputation for neglecting the human element of conservation. Several badly planned ecological preservation projects have come at the expense of local peoples' basic human rights. And such mismanagement, in turn, often jeopardizes the integrity of the supposedly protected areas. This pattern has been especially devastating in the developing world. In many protected areas of India, for instance, local peoples have found themselves suddenly deprived of traditional land rights and access to natural resources because of new conservation regulations. And they have responded, understandably, with increasing hostility. In one case, the creation of the Kutru Tiger and Buffalo Reserve in Madhya Pradesh displaced 52 villages of Maria tribals, many of whom have since joined an insurgent movement that occasionally conducts poaching missions and harasses park guards.[11]

Because of such failures, and because so many developing-world preservation schemes originate with industrial-world environmental organizations, northern environmentalists have had to fend off constant accusations that they care more about the South's trees and birds than about its people. Over the last 5–10 years, though, as they learned to address the social and cultural context of their campaigns, they have been better able to demonstrate the immediate human value of intact ecosystems: the aloof tree-huggers became compassionate defenders of local peoples.[12]

Similarly, human rights activists have recently broadened their appeal by acknowledging the environmental factors behind many of the abuses they work on—but only after decades of dealing with the consequences of ignoring ecology. Sometimes an exclusively rights-based approach to protecting local peoples has opened the door to increased environmental degradation, which in turn tends to erode the peoples' basic rights and well-being.[13]

Along the coasts of Ecuador's Galápagos Islands, for instance, local fishers are currently overharvesting sea cucumbers at a rate likely to wipe out supplies within about four years. By embracing the international economy and selling their bounty to wealthy gourmets in China and Japan, the cucumber fishers, known as *pepineros*, are able to make up to 20 times the profit they could earn from any other locally available species.[14]

The original plan establishing the Galápagos National Park in 1974 pointedly protected indigenous peoples' right to continue their tradition of subsistence fishing. But Ecuadorean officials have failed to distinguish between indigenous peoples and new residents of the islands; many of the *pepineros* moved to the Galápagos region just a few years ago, specifically to collect sea cucumbers. Moreover, Ecuador's government has made no attempt to implement any monitoring mechanisms to ensure that the Galápagueños are keeping their fishing within subsistence levels. As native

Galápagueño ecologist Carlos A. Valle has noted, the *pepineros*, who have gone so far as to take hostages in their fight to keep the fishery open, seem intent on defending their "right to destroy their own future."[15]

Conservationists have been accused of trying to deny the rights of the *pepineros*; yet they could make a strong case that better environmental regulation and monitoring would in the long run strengthen the rights of the fishing community. Indeed, if the *pepinero* community were composed more of indigenous peoples who had a longer-term investment in the local ecosystem, their harvesting strategies might be quite different. In general, when human rights and ecology are given equal weight and local people not only participate in the development decisions that are going to affect them but also have a strong ecological knowledge base, communities end up acting as stewards of the local environment and also flourish socially and culturally—as on the Chico Mendes Extractive Reserve.[16]

An even broader overlap between the human rights and environmental agendas is embedded within the history of the international human rights movement. As early as 1948, just three years after the U.N. Charter entered into force, the General Assembly adopted the Universal Declaration of Human Rights, representing the first international moral consensus about what people should be able to expect from civil society. Besides the personal civil liberties that form the basis of the human rights movement, ranging from free speech to freedom from torture, the Declaration also covered the broader, more communal rights to health, food, shelter, and work—the very rights at the core of the environmental movement. The Universal Declaration itself is not a binding legal document. But in later years, both sets of rights did enter into force as binding international laws in the Covenant on Civil and Political Rights and the broader Covenant on Economic, Social, and Cultural Rights.[17]

Though the distinction between individual civil rights and more communal rights is sometimes perceived as a sticking point between human rights and environmental workers, in the end it reveals the ultimate complementarity of the two movements in working toward environmental justice. Human rights activists, after all, have more and more frequently recognized that some of the worst abuses they deal with originate in environmental damage at the communal or regional level. And environmentalists have realized that upholding basic civil and political rights is one of the best ways of protecting the environment.[18]

In the ecological context, the main difference between the relevant civil and political rights and the relevant economic, social, and cultural rights is that the first are largely procedural and the second are substantive: people exercise their individual rights (such as free speech) in order to protect their environment-related communal rights (the right to an intact ozone layer). The human rights movement and the environmental movement are fighting for both sets of rights. The substantive, communal rights combine moral and scientific perspectives to uphold the protection of life; they serve the crucial purpose of laying out the things all people should be able to expect from the environment, such as clean air and water. They explain just what would constitute an environmental injustice. But it is the procedural rights that perhaps provide the most common ground for the two movements, at the individual, communal, and even national level, because they are the rights that allow people to work toward the prevention of environmental injustice.[19]

LOCAL INJUSTICES: INDIVIDUALS AND COMMUNITIES

Perhaps the most graphic illustrations of the need for human rights workers and environmentalists to join forces are the abuses endured by individual activists—whose only crimes, in general, have been organizing protests and speaking their minds. This is the traditional realm of the human rights movement: by focusing on individual cases, human rights workers have effectively demonstrated that no grassroots campaign can be successful if the basic rights of the individual are not respected, that civil liberties are the most important check on a government's power. They have also found that publicizing the plight of one individual can be a particularly effective way to expose abuses of power and make them tangible to the general public.

When traditional human rights stories—involving the harassment, torture, imprisonment, or murder of activists—actually penetrate the mass media, however, they too often come across as tragic but isolated instances of criminal activities. What environmentalists have added to this realm of advocacy is an awareness of the broader trends driving many of these acts of violence. Certainly, as human rights workers well know, the basic issue is usually one of personal safety and law enforcement. But behind these examples of human brutality are often long-standing struggles over environmental justice.[20]

Tragically, the list of atrocities committed against environmental activists is quite long, and global in scope. (See Table 8–1.) In Honduras, in February 1995, activist Blanca Jeannette Kawas Fernandez was assassinated by an unidentified man who simply walked up to her living room window and shot her. Kawas was the president of PROLAN-

Table 8-1. Attacks Against Environmental Activists, Selected Examples

Activist and Affiliation	Attack
Piotr Kozhevnikov, government water inspector, former Soviet Union	Kozhevnikov was arrested and placed in a psychiatric ward as punishment for trying to publicize illegal government dumping of oil and sludge into the Gulf of Finland in 1986.
Barbara D'Achille, environmental journalist, Peru	D'Achille was murdered on May 31, 1989, by Shining Path guerrillas, who felt threatened by her exposés of the impact of coca cultivation on the rain forest.
Henry Domoldol, Isneg tribal leader, Philippines	Domoldol was murdered on June 26, 1991, by members of a militia with ties to the Philippine Army; Domoldol had publicized military involvement in illegal logging of local tribal lands.
Wangari Maathai, founder of the Green Belt Movement, Kenya	Maathai was beaten unconscious by police in March 1992 while participating in a peaceful protest in Nairobi to condemn the imprisonment of several environmental and political activists.
Guy Pence, Forest Service ranger, United States	Pence was the target of two bomb attacks in 1995 but escaped unharmed; he has been outspoken on the issue of enforcing federal grazing regulations.

SOURCE: Compiled by Worldwatch Institute from sources cited in endnote 21.

SATE, an environmental organization fighting illegal logging and government-backed development in Punta Sal National Park. Other Honduran activists suspect that her murderer is receiving government protection. Similarly, journalist Chan Dara was found dead in Cambodia on December 8, 1994, two days after being warned by the police to stop looking into the military's illegal involvement in the country's timber industry.[21]

In countries like the United States, with a rights-protective regime and an active free press, abuses tend to be less institutional in nature but no less widespread. American environmentalists have been the victims of vandalism, harassment, assaults, and even torture, rape, arson, and murder. Pat Costner, Greenpeace USA's toxics coordinator, watched her house burn to the ground just a few weeks before her report on hazardous waste incinerators was sched-

uled to be published. Investigators later found the fuel can that arsonists had used to express their support of incineration. In Oregon, two local environmental activists were lynched in effigy one day before a conference hosted by Ron Arnold, the founder of the Wise Use movement, which lobbies for expanded logging, ranching, and mining rights and for the abolition of all environmental legislation. The tarred and feathered effigies held a sign that read "Enviros can learn a lot from a couple of dummies."[22]

Institutionalized efforts to recognize and reward the work of individual activists have provided especially useful publicity, since they often furnish the best documentation of the relevant environmental injustices and human rights abuses—which often occur in remote areas under obscured conditions. The San Francisco-based Goldman Foundation, for instance, awards its prestigious

Environmental Prize every spring to one grassroots activist from each of the six continents, and does considerable background research on the winners. Newspaper articles inspired by the award ceremonies and videos produced by the foundation bring the activists' broader environmental justice struggles home to a wide audience and help people understand what is at stake at the most personal level—understand that human rights abuses are not just isolated crimes and that environmentalism is not just about the rights of nature.[23]

Abused environmental activists almost always turn out to be fighting for some group of people—whether an ethnic minority, an indigenous community, a group of marginalized women, or simply those without the resources to secure a home and livelihood—because environmental threats, ranging from air pollution to soil erosion, affect entire areas rather than single individuals. International law guards individual and national sovereignty, but communities and other small groups often find themselves caught in the middle, fighting a mining installation or government-sponsored toxic dump with no official legal protection.[24]

In the industrial world, community-level struggles for environmental justice are often waged against large companies whose public relations people claim that their toxic emissions are unfortunate but necessary by-products of efforts to provide crucial services for customers—or even, in the case of defense contractors, for the sake of national security. One of the first sets of activists to organize itself under the rubric of environmental justice, in the early eighties, documented the link between U.S. communities with high concentrations of minorities and those with high concentrations of pollution.[25]

In the developing world, the issue at hand is almost always one of national development: activists fight projects that seem unduly disruptive on a human level and unsustainable on an ecological level but that are being pushed hard by the government as potential boosts to the country's economy. Sometimes the government, legitimately worried about its external debt, might actually believe that the proposed dam or power plant or tourist resort would benefit most of the country's citizens directly—through jobs or access to water or electricity—as well as provide some foreign exchange. But all too often most of the benefits go to already wealthy elites and most of the costs are borne by already marginalized communities.[26]

The Ogoni people of southern Nigeria are one such community, threatened by the oil-drilling projects of the Shell Petroleum Development Company and fighting not just for environmental justice but for their very survival. Marginal communities become even more vulnerable under rights-repressive regimes like the one currently governing Nigeria. In 1995, a surge of publicity and advocacy surrounded the situation in Ogoniland, thanks largely to the eloquent appeals of Ken Saro-Wiwa, the leader of the Movement for the Survival of the Ogoni People (MOSOP). Saro-Wiwa received the Goldman Environmental Prize in the spring. But on November 10, 1995, he was executed by Nigeria's illegal military regime in retaliation for his activism—and in defiance of international protests. The Ogoni, meanwhile, besides having to absorb this tragic injustice, still face the daunting task of saving their homeland from the local environmental ravages of our global dependence on oil.[27]

Initially, the situation in Ogoniland looked like just one among many instances of systematic human rights abuse perpetrated under the auspices of the Nigerian military dictatorship. Since May 1994, the 1,050-square-kilometer region—home to just 500,000 Ogoni, a minority people who make up about 0.5 percent of Nigeria's population—has also housed an immense military police force with members drawn from the Nigerian Army, Navy, and Air Force. The police force had been installed to "ensure that . . . non-indigenous residents carrying out business ventures . . . within Ogoniland are not molested." The only nonindigenous business people in Ogoniland are employees of Shell, which accounts for 50 percent of Nigeria's crude oil output. Oil profits account for 90 percent of Nigeria's foreign exchange and 80 percent of total government revenue.[28]

MOSOP was founded in 1992 specifically to campaign against what it refers to as Shell's reign of environmental terrorism. The once lush agricultural land of the Niger delta is now covered in oil slicks that stretch for miles; vegetation has died and some rivers run black; gas flares near villages poison the air and cause acid rain; unlined toxic waste pits allow pollution to seep into drinking water supplies. The molestations and disruptions of the peace that allegedly necessitated the military police force have largely consisted of peaceful demonstrations staged by MOSOP, involving mostly peasant farmers and fishers, who have asked that Shell do ecological and social impact studies of their operations and compensate the Ogoni people for damage already caused by oil extraction. Banking on the government's complicity, Shell has never done any environmental assessments before digging wells or laying pipes. Of the total number of spills recorded over the past decade in the 100 or so countries where Shell operates, 40 percent occurred in Nigeria.[29]

The official sacrificing of small communities like those in Ogoniland is, unfortunately, a common phenomenon around the globe—whether under rights-repressive or rights-protective regimes, and whether for the sake of national profits or for "public good" infrastructure projects. (See Table 8–2.) In China, government officials have touted the construction of the Three Gorges Dam, which began in December 1994, as providing better flood control and navigation for downstream communities. But most of the dam's massive electricity-generating capabilities will go to serve the Shanghai metropolitan area, hundreds of kilometers to the east; and several teams of engineers have asserted that building the dam will in fact increase the danger of local flooding and make navigation more difficult.[30]

In addition, scores of international experts have warned that the location of the dam makes it particularly vulnerable to earthquakes and landslides and that silt accumulation in the reservoir will shrink its capacity significantly within just a few years. In the years leading up to the decision to break ground on the project, however, the Chinese government systematically suppressed information and opinions questioning the viability of the dam and arrested the most vocal protesters, including the environmental journalist Dai Qing, who in 1989 edited the first Chinese book criticizing the dam, *Yangtze! Yangtze!*[31]

Without doubt, the construction of the dam will flood 20 towns and 11,000 hectares of farmland, threaten several endangered species such as the Siberian white crane and the White Flag dolphin, and uproot some 1.4 million people—nearly equivalent to the current population of Kuwait. Most of these locals will end up on much higher ground, with colder, poorer soils. A study by the Chinese Academy of Sciences acknowledged that five times as much new land would be necessary to equal crop yields in the fertile valley fields that will soon be below the dam's reservoir.[32]

Table 8-2. Community-Level Environmental Injustices, Selected Examples

Community	Problem
Udege indigenous people, Siberia, Russia	Logging by Russian, Japanese, South Korean, and U.S. firms has destroyed the Udege's resource base and caused severe soil erosion and siltation of river systems.
Mining communities, Wales, United Kingdom	Government encouragement of open-cast coal mining has resulted in water pollution and increased instances of pulmonary disease in local Welsh communities.
Yami indigenous people, Orchid Island, Taiwan	For 13 years, the Taiwanese government has stored nuclear waste on Orchid Island, in metal drums now beginning to rust. In the mid-seventies, the government had told the Yami, who lack formal education, that the storage facility they were building would be a fish cannery.
Amazonian Indians, Oriente region, Ecuador	Oil exploitation has devastated the environments of several indigenous groups, leaving water supplies with 10 to 1,000 times the level of contamination allowable in the United States.
Village fisherfolk, Mdulumanja, Malawi	In 1991, the owner of a hotel on Lake Malawi received government permission to evict an entire community for the sake of tourist development, bulldozing more than 70 homes and offering no relocation plan.

SOURCE: Compiled by Worldwatch Institute from sources cited in endnote 30.

As these examples demonstrate, small communities often come out the losers in rights conflicts with nations and corporations. The larger entities find that they can get away with treating the smaller ones as expendable. That communal vulnerability to injustice is built into most current development policies. Just within the past decade, infrastructure projects involving general urban development as well as road and dam construction have displaced an estimated 80–90 million people globally.[33]

When communal rights receive the respect they deserve, though, communities often turn out to be the best agents of sustainability. Large infrastructure or extraction projects are often inherently destructive to surrounding ecosystems, whereas smaller-scale projects can usually be made to work in harmony with the local landscape. And if the project is small enough that community members themselves can administer it, it is much more likely to be welcomed and accepted. Most communities simply yearn for more control over their fate. And community-based conservation and development schemes are becoming more and more widespread—thanks to local initiatives sponsored both by the communities themselves and by teams of activists who recognize that sustainability must encompass both ecology and social justice as well as economic viability. (See Table 8–3.)[34]

In Costa Rica, for instance, 12 peasant farmers came together in 1988 to form the San Miguel Association for Conservation and Development (ASACODE) in an attempt to keep local forests under the control of local communities. Some 27 percent of Costa Rica's land falls within some sort of preserve, yet the

Table 8-3. Community-Based Conservation and Development Initiatives, Selected Examples

Community/ Organization	Initiative
Sangam project, Deccan Development Society (DDS), Andhra Pradesh, India	DDS helps organize *sangams*, communities of women in South Indian villages, to work toward gender equity, establish credit programs, cultivate and use medicinal herbs, incorporate organic farming techniques and multicropping systems into agricultural practices, and plant trees.
Yanesha Forestry Cooperative (COFYAL), Peruvian Amazon	COFYAL is a sustainable forestry co-op run by the Yanesha Indians, who earn a living exporting forest products to Europe and the United States, while also protecting the rain forest from clear-cutting by ranchers and developers.
Association for the Protection of the Environment (APE), Cairo, Egypt	APE coordinates the efforts of Cairo's trashpickers, who earn a living by recycling paper, using organic wastes as fertilizer, and weaving rugs from discarded scraps of cotton.
InterTribal Sinkyone Wilderness Council (ITSWC), northern California	In early 1995, the 10 tribes of the ITSWC won back some 1,600 hectares of ancestral redwood rain forest from the state of California. Their plan is to create a wilderness park—complete with four traditional villages—that will serve as a model for sustainable land use.
Annapurna Conservation Area Project (ACAP), central Nepal	ACAP has made local participation the cornerstone of its efforts to increase the direct benefits of tourism while decreasing its environmental impact—by improving local lodging services, using kerosene instead of cutting trees for fuelwood, and enforcing a Minimum Impact Code for trekkers.
Kakadu National Park, northern Australia	Kakadu is comanaged by the government's park service and Aborigines who have inhabited the region for more than 50,000 years. Comanagement has fostered effective nature conservation, a tourist industry that provides the Aborigines with a steady income, and the preservation of traditional communities and their cultural legacy.

SOURCE: Compiled by Worldwatch Institute from sources cited in endnote 34.

country has Central America's highest rate of deforestation, because the timber industry, which accounts for 90 percent of forest destruction nationwide, has been systematically buying out small landowners in forested regions like San Miguel. ASACODE provides incentives to local people to hold onto their land by showing them how to harvest and process wood sustainably, without harming the forest. The group has also worked to develop regional markets for artisanal wood products.[35]

More and more locals have been reneging on deals with large timber companies in favor of joining ASA-CODE, because the group's efficient use of wood and targeted marketing have generated immediate profits. Industrial timber operations, which waste up to half of each tree they cut, often insist on paying landowners very low prices for logging rights. Moreover, ASACODE's ecologically sound harvesting techniques leave much more of the forest intact for long-term use. And the association has further encouraged community stability and stewardship by using its profits to start group-managed tree nurseries for native species and to organize study sessions for neighboring villagers.[36]

Communities will be an integral part of any sustainable development schemes that succeed over the long term. Of course, some large infrastructure projects in both the public and private sectors may end up actually fulfilling the goal of working toward the common good. Programs facilitating the transfer of clean energy technologies from northern to southern countries, for instance, have immense potential even if their scope ends up going far beyond community control. Investments in sewage treatment plants or rail lines could also yield high returns. But the majority of environmentally just development projects will probably come out of community-level initiatives that provide local people with relevant ecological information and allow them to take more control of their own destiny. Policymakers could bring us all closer to sustainability by focusing on ways to give local peoples a stake in preserving their local environments.[37]

INJUSTICES ACROSS BORDERS

Despite the significance of communities, some human rights and environmental justice issues inherently go far beyond a local scope. Pollution crosses borders, and so do environmental refugees, as well as certain critical resources like rivers. Many environmental resources are in fact shared globally: oceans, forests, genetic diversity, climate, the ozone layer. No community or even country can singlehandedly protect the oceans to enough of an extent to ensure sustainable yields from saltwater fisheries, or reduce chlorofluorocarbon emissions enough to protect against the increasing skin cancer rates associated with a thinning of the ozone layer, or cut carbon emissions enough to curtail the disruptions in weather caused by global climate change. Such global threats require not just activists from different movements but entire countries to work together.[38]

The United Nations has considerable potential as a binding force to help mount global conservation campaigns. It was founded on the premise of international interdependence, after all, in the wake of World War II. Yet the founding nations were careful to protect their national sovereignty. What one country happened to do with its natural resources, for instance, was nobody else's business. The U.N.'s most crucial role in the future, however, may be mediating between one country's alleged right to burn down its forests and another's alleged right to burn fossil fuels—and perhaps yet another's alleged right to block both of the other entitlements.[39]

Every person on earth depends on a stable climate, an intact ozone layer, clean air and water, and healthy oceans. Yet the elite wealthy classes, in both industrial and developing worlds, tend to contribute more to most types of environmental degradation than any other group of people. And the poorer classes tend to pay more of the costs of ecological damage.[40]

This divide is especially pronounced between the North and South. People in the industrial world account for only about 21 percent of the global population, and that share is decreasing, given the faster rate of population growth in the developing world. But industrial countries consume about 86 percent of the globe's aluminum, 81 percent of its paper, 80 percent of its iron and steel, 75 percent of its energy, and 61 percent of its meat. So they are responsible for the vast majority of the hazardous wastes created by the mining and smelting of aluminum and iron ores, the clear-cutting of forests done for the sake of paper production, the air pollution and buildup of greenhouse gases caused by fossil fuel burning, and the severe soil erosion found on grazing lands.[41]

Industrial countries are responsible for more than 90 percent of the 400 million tons of hazardous waste produced globally each year.

Many of these degrading activities, however, occur disproportionately in developing countries: just as in colonial times, poor nations end up despoiling their own lands in order to export certain products that feed the richer nations' habit of overconsumption—and also to provide their own elites with steady profits. Although developing nations account for only 18 percent of global copper consumption, for instance, they produce about 47 percent of what the world uses. Moreover, because

extractive technologies in such countries tend to be less advanced, and because there is often little enforcement of legal safeguards against pollution, the environmental toll in copper-producing countries of the South—ranging from massive tailings ponds to the release of heavy metals and chemical contaminants in local soils and water supplies—tends to be even worse than the production statistics might imply.[42]

The international trade in toxic substances provides a particularly good illustration of these environmentally unjust trends. Industrial countries are responsible for more than 90 percent of the 400 million tons of hazardous waste produced globally each year. Inherently unsustainable industrial practices in richer countries are directly responsible for almost all the incinerator ash, dioxin, and PCBs in the world. It is almost impossible to keep track of what happens to these wastes, but experts believe that at least 30 million tons a year cross national borders, with a high percentage going to poorer countries. Over the last five years, there have been at least 299 documented dumpings in Eastern Europe, 239 in Asia, 148 in Latin America, and 30 in Africa.[43]

In many cases, increased shipments out of industrial nations have been an unintended consequence of the tightening of domestic dumping regulations. In the late eighties, largely because of new laws, hazardous waste disposal prices in the United States climbed up to about $250 per ton. In Africa, meanwhile, where environmental regulations and appropriate disposal technologies were virtually nonexistent, the per-ton price was often as low as $2.50. Many African countries were willing to accept the toxic shipments because they were accompanied by much-needed foreign exchange. Of course, in many cases, the incoming foreign exchange did not get beyond the particular government officials or businesspeople who worked out the import deal. But the whole country always ends up paying the costs of disposing of the toxic materials.[44]

Pressure to adopt environmentally destructive practices in the developing world is rampant, and comes not just from the North but also from other southern countries. Three large timber conglomerates from Indonesia and Malaysia, for instance, offered the cash-starved government of Suriname a multimillion-dollar deal for the logging rights to a 2.8-million-hectare tract of rain forest—an area that encompasses more than a quarter of the small South American country. Desperate to sustain their businesses as tree stocks shrink back home, the Asian companies have allegedly gone so far as to bribe several of the parliamentarians who will be voting on the proposal. One firm apparently garnered the support of Surinamese foreign minister Subhaas Mungra by appointing his brother to be head of its local operations.[45]

Despite the undeniable infusion of cash and new jobs the companies would provide by investing in Suriname's economy, the deal is patently unfair, with the firms offering approximately one tenth the per-hectare market value for logging rights and giving out a royalty of less than 7 percent. While the loggers are projected to make about $28 million a year over the next 25 years, Suriname is likely to get just $2 million annually. Moreover, the proposal completely ignores Suriname's long-term prospects from both an economic and an ecological standpoint because it makes no provisions for reforestation or any other environmental easement strategies, or even for monitoring of the damage. And the logging as currently planned would decimate the homelands of three groups of indigenous forest dwellers.[46]

The Surinamese people, just like the Galápagos *pepineros* or any other community, have the right to control their own destiny, and sacrificing part of the country's rain forest may eventually become an economic necessity. But Surinamese decision makers also have a responsibility to the country's indigenous peoples and to the international community. Selling off the forest to outside logging companies who have no incentive to protect the environment or Suriname's long-term prospects would seem to serve the best interests of just a few people: an elite group of government officials in Suriname and an elite group of business executives in Indonesia and Malaysia.

Recognizing the extent to which we all depend on the services that forests provide, the international community has proposed alternative schemes that could both prop up Suriname's economy and preserve its ecological treasures. Early in 1995, Inter-American Development Bank (IDB) President Enrique V. Iglesias sent a letter to Suriname President Ronald Venetiaan promising a significant aid package if the country blocked or at least postponed the logging deal. The IDB money would go toward training forestry professionals and launching an ecotourism industry within the nation's already extensive network of wildlife preserves. Iglesias's offer reinforced the value of a strategy human rights workers have advocated for years: both multilateral and bilateral lenders can use their financial leverage to encourage better governance, perhaps by cutting off aid if a government has become repressive, or, more positively, by earmarking funds for sustainable development projects, especially those directly involving the protection of basic rights.[47]

Foreign diplomats and international environmentalists have also contributed sustainable development plans for Suriname. Besides backing Iglesias's nature-based tourism suggestion, the proposals recommend expanding a fledgling project that brings ethnobotanical researchers together with local medicine men to search for drugs that could eventually result in huge profits, to be shared equitably among the local community members, the country as a whole, and any pharmaceutical company involved.[48]

Cross-border environmental justice issues involving the global commons—and necessitating coordinated international action—are plentiful. Threats to cropland, oceanic fisheries, and the protective ozone layer are all serious. But perhaps the most significant, overarching global problem we now face is the prospect of climate change. Global warming is an environmental justice issue both because the North played a much larger role than the South in spurring it, and because the South will likely have a much harder time than the North in dealing with its consequences.

Currently, industrial countries are responsible for about 70 percent of global emissions of carbon, the main contributor to greenhouse gases. Per capita carbon emissions in the United States are about 20 times higher than in India. (See Table 2-2 in Chapter 2.) Yet the average person in India has just as much of a right to a stable climate as the average American does. And people in India and most developing nations will be especially hard hit by global warming because their climate is already quite hot, making them highly susceptible to drought and desertification. Small island states, meanwhile, and the developing world's coastal nations, will have to face a significant rise in the level of the oceans with hardly any dependable infrastructure in place to deal with flooding. For developing nations in particular, the greenhouse effect could mean a crippling loss of cropland, the creation of millions of environmental refugees, and an expansion in the range of tropical diseases.[49]

In attempting to address such problems, which have such a broad scope, the human rights approach—with its roots firmly planted in local activism—might seem out of place. Slowing global warming, for instance, will require action on the most wide-ranging international level, and will entail the reform of the energy industry in richer countries, the transfer of clean technologies to poorer countries, and the reforestation of areas all around the world. Yet a key to reaching even these broadest of goals is without doubt the protection of basic human rights.

Especially because global warming is a justice issue—because some countries are more vulnerable and have more at stake than others—firm measures need to be in place to hold entire nations and industries accountable for their actions, to ensure that all parties are contributing their fair share to what has to be a universal effort. Scientists, government officials, representatives of nongovernmental organizations (NGOs), and private citizen activists—whether from the United States or India—need to have a voice in determining how to cope with climate change, to have full access to information about a country's or a company's carbon emissions, and to be able to spread information in the international media and demand compliance with international standards.

Any U.N. treaty or other international agreement can have an impact beyond the level of abstraction only if each country makes monitoring and enforcement its highest priority. This in turn requires a rights-protective regime and a flourishing civil society, with citizens who recognize their civic duty and are both willing and able to take an active role in their community. Moreover, the best way to spur the adoption of meaningful treaties in the first place is through the active exercising of civil liberties by well-informed, outspoken advocates.

The Montreal Protocol on Substances that Deplete the Ozone Layer, for instance, got signed so quickly and has been so effective largely because of the activist role played by the international scientific community and international environmental organizations, with the support of vocal grassroots activists. In the United States, environmentalists had already convinced policymakers to sign the world's strictest ozone legislation, which in turn had spurred leaders of American industry to become vocal supporters of international regulations that would allow them to compete on a level playing field in the global marketplace.[50]

The free exchange of information and ideas encouraged by the protection of basic rights, then, often leads to the recognition of common ground—sometimes even between environmentalists and industry groups—and subsequently to the building of coalitions that could generate the political will necessary to move toward environmental justice at all levels of society.

HUMAN RIGHTS AND ENVIRONMENTAL JUSTICE

Thanks to more than a decade of documenting problems, protesting, and building coalitions, the environmental justice movement is now in a position to weave its agenda directly into official laws and policies. Taking a cue from the traditional human rights approach, the movement has mounted a significant effort to get the United Nations to set an official standard of environmental justice, to enshrine in international law every person's equal right to a healthy and healthful environment. Such a legal advance would be especially useful in helping victims of environmental injus-

tices to receive compensation. It might also eventually act as a preventive measure: if consistently backed up by swift, compensatory judicial enforcement, an environmental human rights law could potentially force multinational corporations, for instance, to think twice about where and how they drill for oil.[51]

The prevention of injustices will require a drive to integrate basic civil liberties as explicitly as possible into sustainable development policies.

Perhaps even more important than establishing the substantive human rights relating to environmental injustices, however, will be a renewed emphasis on already existing procedural rights. The actual prevention of injustices will require not just strong laws and the threat of punishment from a strong judicial system, but also a drive to integrate basic civil liberties as explicitly as possible into sustainable development policies—locally, nationally, internationally, at corporations, and within institutions such as the World Bank and the International Monetary Fund. If more development projects focused on encouraging environmental organizing, spurring local participation in key decisions, and providing access to environmental information, both the environment and the most vulnerable members of society would benefit substantially.[52]

The campaign to write environmental justice into international law is well under way, spearheaded by environmental lawyers and activists working with the U.N. Sub-Commission on Prevention of Discrimination and Protection of Minorities. In 1989, a coalition of NGOs led by the Sierra Club Legal Defense

Fund convinced the Sub-Commission to appoint a special rapporteur to prepare an international study of the overlap between human rights and environmental issues. Special Rapporteur Fatma Zohra Ksentini issued her final report in August 1994, documenting environmental injustices around the globe and pointing out the potential of combining the ecological and human rights policy agendas. A few months earlier, a group of experts involved in the campaign met in Geneva and issued a Draft Declaration of Principles on Human Rights and the Environment, which proclaimed, among other things, the universal human right to a "secure, healthy, ecologically sound environment." These two documents are now serving as crucial tools in the effort to get the U.N. General Assembly to consider actually writing an official convention safeguarding environmental human rights.[53]

Existing human rights conventions were written too early to reflect an awareness of environmental issues. But it is interesting to note that many accepted rights have implicit environmental components. The Covenant on Civil and Political Rights, for instance, guarantees the basic right to life, and the Covenant on Economic, Social, and Cultural Rights guarantees the right to the highest attainable standard of health— both of which certainly depend on a healthy environment. These and other well-established rights, taken together with accepted ecological principles that have entered international law recently, seem to point to an international moral consensus about each individual's right to freedom from environmental degradation. A few human rights experts have expressed reservations about attempts to add new, hard-to-enforce ecological rights to the international law books, saying they could detract from efforts to enforce the existing civil and political rights that are at the heart of the human

rights movement. But the environmental justice movement is not so much demanding recognition of a new set of substantive rights as ensuring that nations follow through on commitments they have already made.[54]

Follow-through is the key to international law: a U.N. convention protecting environmental human rights can be only as useful as its enforcement capabilities. But one additional reason for couching environmental justice concerns in the language of human rights is that the international human rights system is more accessible than most other international law frameworks, making human rights treaties inherently more enforceable. They have a better chance than most international laws to act as deterrents because under their auspices, individual victims of abuse can often bring a sovereign nation before an internationally recognized tribunal.[55]

The Lubicon Lake Band of Indians in northern Canada, for instance, led by Bernard Ominayak, filed a complaint in 1987 with the Human Rights Committee, the body established to deal with violations of the Covenant on Civil and Political Rights. The petition asserted that state-sponsored oil and gas exploration threatened the Indians' very means of subsistence and thus violated their right to life and to self-determination as a minority. Three years later, the Committee upheld Ominayak's claim and upbraided the Canadian government before the international community. The state responded immediately by proposing to rectify the situation through measures to be deemed appropriate by the Committee. Though the U.N. process certainly labors under undue bureaucracy and general inexpediency, at times it does eventually produce significant results. Of course, national enforcement is still a concern: although the Lubicon Lake decision undeniably provides a powerful legal precedent, its practical significance has so far been minimal, as the Lubicon continue to face pressure from companies eager to capitalize on their resources.[56]

An even better bet for prevention, meanwhile, would be development programs that explicitly foster the free exercising of people's basic civil liberties, the procedural rights whose very purpose is to facilitate the efforts of individuals and communities to safeguard their substantive rights. Perhaps the most important of these procedural rights for officials to focus on is the right of community members to participate fully in decisions that affect their well-being. Participatory projects are concrete, practical ways of applying the concept of self-determination, a right firmly established in the Covenant on Civil and Political Rights and other instruments of international law. And by involving affected communities in the design, implementation, and evaluation processes, such projects have proved over and over again to be excellent tools in the effort to achieve environmental justice. On the central plateau of Burkina Faso, for instance, a participatory program surveyed farmers from 240 marginal villages to find out what sort of development schemes they would support. As a result of the small-scale dryland agriculture projects the farmers then designed and implemented, the average family's food deficit of 645 kilograms per year turned into a 150-kilogram surplus.[57]

It is a fundamental principle of moral philosophy, after all, that bridging the gap between decisions and the consequences of those decisions increases the likelihood that the decisions will be moral. When people who will be directly affected by pollution or development projects are sitting at the same decision-making table as industry representatives and government officials, development is much more likely to proceed in an ecologically sensitive manner: developers have a much harder time treating the local landscape or community as expendable.

Of course, community members cannot be full participants in development schemes unless their right to information is respected. And they cannot make good decisions about their future unless they have access to the full body of scientific literature relating to any environmental threats they might encounter—unless they know all their options and the likely consequences of each one. From a policy standpoint, guaranteeing this particular set of procedural rights will involve both spurring governments and corporations to make full disclosures of their activities and empowering citizens to educate themselves about their local environment and conduct their own audits and investigations.

Community members cannot be full participants in development schemes unless their right to information is respected.

One promising means of increasing institutional transparency is community right-to-know legislation, pioneered by the United States in the 1986 Emergency Planning and Community Right-to-Know Act and several related laws. Under this type of legislation, in the United States and a few other countries, the government must furnish a wide array of environmental data, must make proposed environmental laws available for public comment, must publish information regarding failure to comply with environmental laws, and must provide details of environmental enforcement procedures. In Mexico City, for instance, under the provisions of the North American Free Trade Agreement, the Mexican government's National Institute of Ecology each day monitors and reports local air pollution levels.[58]

Getting national governments to pass and comply with such laws, however, especially in countries governed by rights-repressive regimes, will take considerable international pressure both from other countries and from watchdog organizations. And getting corporations to comply with environmental laws and live up to the same standards of transparency applied to governments in right-to-know legislation will be another formidable task. Official policies can certainly help make companies accountable for their environmental records, though. The World Bank, for instance, now requires developers to do an environmental impact statement before beginning work on most Bank-funded projects.[59]

Environmental justice is a powerful concept: it brings everyone to the level of shared dependence on an intact, healthy environment.

In the United States, the push for more transparency that led the government to embrace communities' right to information also had a significant impact on the corporate world. One of the most important results of the Emergency Planning and Community Right-to-Know Act was the creation of the Toxics Release Inventory, an annual computerized record of about 300 toxic chemicals released into the environment by more than 24,000 industrial facilities. American manufacturers in addition must now file a Materials Safety Data Sheet, disclosing to employees the substances they might be exposed to and how that exposure could potentially affect their health.[60]

In Manchester, Texas, after a serious accident at the local Rhône-Poulenc chemical plant landed 27 people in the hospital in mid-1992, citizens demanded not only an explanation but also an opportunity to participate in monitoring the plant's hazardous activities. The legally binding agreement they won from Rhône-Poulenc was that the company would pay for a comprehensive environmental audit by an independent outside expert, to be accompanied and overseen by representatives of the community, the plant's work force, and a local environmental organization called Texans United.[61]

Development programs stressing community efforts to gather and process environmental information are often excellent safeguards against abuses of those communities' environmental rights. Land-use mapping projects run by groups as diverse as rubber tappers on the Chico Mendes Extractive Reserve in Brazil and Nunavik Inuit Indians on land they own in northern Canada have helped prevent illegal incursions by loggers and hunters and have facilitated the development of management plans to ensure equitable, sustainable harvests. In the western United States, the federal government's Bureau of Indian Affairs has initiated a program to train tribal governments to use computerized Geographic Information Systems, which could provide hard data that would drastically improve their ability to defend themselves in ongoing disputes over land and water rights.[62]

Some communities that have used participatory information-gathering strategies to protect themselves have even initiated training programs for other at-risk communities. Early in 1995, with the support of the International Development Research Centre in Canada, a few native technicians from the Split Lake Cree community travelled to Chile and taught bacteriological water-testing skills to two bands of Mapuche Indians.[63]

Projects like this one, linking two small communities in two different hemispheres, suggest both the broad scope of environmental problems and the broad applicability of human rights solutions to those problems. Traditionally, high-minded international treaties and top-down development policies have merely eased consciences or even exacerbated the inequitable distribution of environmental damage. But by targeting community empowerment through participation and access to information, not only local NGOs but also national governments and institutions such as the World Bank could make significant contributions to the struggle for environmental justice.[64]

In the end, environmental justice is such a powerful concept because it brings everyone down to the same level—that of shared dependence on an intact, healthy environment. The potential coalition surrounding environmental justice issues, in other words, is immense. Everyone is willing to fight for something like clean water. And the universal human rights framework is designed to give every individual the power to fight such a battle. If all the vulnerable members of society—the impoverished, indigenous peoples, ethnic minorities, women, children—had access to environmental information and could exercise their right to free speech, if they had a voice in determining their own future access to resources, then potential polluters and profligate consumers would no longer be able to treat them as expendable and would have to seek alternatives to their dirty activities and their overconsumption. The environmental justice movement is not just trying to spread

out the costs of environmental damage more equitably—it is trying to reduce the overall amount of environmental damage.

Currently, contaminated drinking water kills an estimated 25 million people every year in developing countries. (See Chapter 7.) Almost all these deaths are easily preventable. So far, the human rights movement's efforts to give individuals power and the environmental movement's efforts to protect freshwater ecosystems have made only a small dent in this problem. But the combination of moral and scientific credibility that could be gained by a closer marriage of the two movements might carry significant political weight; such a coalition could effectively prove the link between human and environmental stress. Campaigns run by environmentalists, human rights activists, and public health advocates and designed to spur government investment in sanitation, river protection, and pollution prevention could probably eliminate most fatalities from contaminated water.[65]

Environmentalists often talk about prevention, about the importance of reducing pollution at the source and simply avoiding ecological damage rather than dealing with its consequences. It is easier and more efficient to cope with hazardous waste by producing less of it, for example, than by finding more places to dump it. What environmentalists have learned from human rights activists is that confronting the dumpers with the dumped-on is the best preventive measure of all. Protecting the rights of the most vulnerable members of our society, in other words, is perhaps the best way we have of protecting the right of future generations to inherit a planet that is still worth inhabiting.

9

Shifting to Sustainable Industries

Hal Kane

The world's economy is temporarily upsetting the balances that occur in nature.
It is putting carbon into the atmosphere
faster than the flora can remove it.
Under its management, the rate of extinction of species far exceeds the rate of
their evolution. The balances long established in the world's forests, prairies,
and oceans are being undone. This cannot continue indefinitely. Just as the
water in a well can be drawn down faster
than it replenishes itself only for a short
time before the well runs dry, so all these
balances must eventually be restored.[1]

It often becomes clear just how temporary these trends are when they reach
a sudden end. Many such limits have recently appeared, for example, just in the
fisheries sector: The Aral Sea has dried
up, suspending virtually all industry
there. Others, like the Black Sea, are following suit. The world's fishing industry
plunged into recession when the catch
stopped growing at around 100 million
tons. The Chesapeake Bay in the United
States yields few shellfish or crabs today,

though it once produced more food than
the Mediterranean did.[2]

Fortunately, the end of unsustainable
industries often brings new beginnings.
This was the case recently in Oregon,
where many predicted that restrictions
on the logging industry would mean disaster for the state. Instead, its economy
is booming and the state has the lowest
unemployment rate in a generation, just
over 5 percent. Tree farms have replaced primary forest as sources of timber, while the state's growing economy
has added nearly 100,000 jobs—the
exact amount the timber industry said
would be lost with government restrictions—many of them in computer production and other high-tech areas.[3]

The imperative of restoring environmental balance is increasingly going to
shape the evolution of the global economy. We are only at the beginning of this
restructuring. New industries are emerging to reestablish natural balances—
based on technologies that can produce
heat and light without putting carbon

into the atmosphere; on metals made out of the scrap of past buildings and cars; on papers made out of what was once considered wastepaper. Some homes and offices are heated entirely by the sun or from electricity generated by the wind.

Shifting to renewable sources of energy or to recycling does not mean being cold in the winter or sitting in the dark. Solar and wind technologies and efficient light bulbs and heaters can provide the same warmth and light as traditional technologies with much less unwanted pollution. Shifting to recycled paper and steel does not mean accepting lower quality products—new machines make products of equal quality with fewer resources and less energy.

Much of industry will have to mimic nature, reusing and recycling every chemical or material that it uses in cyclical processes.

These technologies and industries have often developed slowly and have gradually replaced more damaging industries. Yet sudden change is in prospect as well. Production of chlorofluorocarbons, which deplete the earth's protective ozone layer, fell 77 percent between 1989 and 1994 in response to determined international efforts to protect the stratosphere, for example. And the wind power industry has sprung up as quickly as the nuclear power industry did in its early years. Virtually overnight, these two parts of the economic system have taken steps toward sustainability.[4]

Other sustainable industries have taken centuries to develop or have adapted old technologies that have long played important roles in a balanced economy. Perhaps foremost among

those are the bicycles that transport billions of people every day—far more people than ride in automobiles—while producing no pollution. Far from being a part of the past, technologies like the bicycle hold the key to the future in many regions, including many highly industrialized countries.[5]

The imbalances in today's economy are so large that industrial flows of nitrogen and sulfur are larger than the natural flows. For metals such as cadmium, zinc, arsenic, mercury, nickel, and vanadium, the industrial flows are as much as twice the natural ones. To avoid ecological disturbances and increasing illness in human beings, the world needs to switch to a form of industrial production that produces fewer of these pollutants and recaptures the rest. Much of industry will have to mimic nature, reusing and recycling every chemical or material that it uses in cyclical processes, rather than discarding them as "waste."[6]

THE SOLAR REVOLUTION

A sustainable economy is one with a stable climate. (See Chapter 2.) Achieving this will mean phasing out fossil fuels, which contribute to the buildup of heat-trapping carbon dioxide (CO_2) and other gases in the atmosphere. A fossil-fuel-based economy can only exist temporarily, because in the long run these fuels disrupt the natural systems on which the economy depends. To slow global warming, coal and oil production will have to decline.

Fortunately, several new technologies are poised to reduce the carbon dependence of today's economy. Various kinds of solar power are chief among them, from the photovoltaic (PV) cells that convert sunlight into electricity to the large windmills that capture energy that stems from the uneven heating of the earth by sunlight. Every year the sales of these technologies rise substantially and their prices fall.[7]

World shipments of small, silicon-based photovoltaic chips that directly produce electricity from sunlight jumped by more than 50 percent between 1990 and 1994, for example. (See Figure 9–1.) Likewise, global wind power generating capacity leapt 22 percent in 1994 alone, boosting installed capacity to more than 3,700 megawatts a year. (See Figure 9–2.)[8]

Today, the energy generated by various kinds of solar power is small in relation to that from fossil fuels. Wind power, for instance, provides less than 0.1 percent of the world's electricity. But the hopeful side of their differences lies in their growth patterns. Oil production has not grown since 1979—indeed, it is now about 170 million tons below the peak it reached that year. No more coal is produced today than in 1988, and far less than the peak reached in 1989. Meanwhile, solar cells and wind turbines register double-digit growth during any typical year.[9]

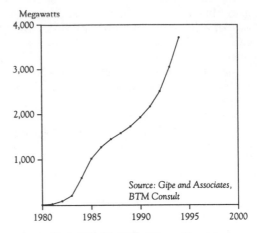

Figure 9-2. World Wind Energy Generating Capacity, 1980-94

The annual worldwide market for wind power is about $1 billion and, including activities such as retail sales and installation, the world PV market consisted of roughly another $1 billion worth of business in 1993. These are dwarfed, of course, by the total annual global market for grid-connected power of about $800 billion. But several factors are at work to change the proportions of energy production.[10]

Modern manufacturing techniques are only now being applied to the production of photovoltaic cells. This means that past prices have been higher than necessary, putting PV cells at a disadvantage in the mass production marketplace. Despite that inhibition, by 1993 the average wholesale price of photovoltaics had dropped to between $3.50 and $4.75 a watt, or roughly 25–40¢ a kilowatt-hour. In 1994, United Solar Systems Corporation announced the development of a triple-junction PV module that can generate power at about $1 per watt or 10–12¢ per kilowatt-hour—less than a third of the average cost of PV electricity in 1993. Manufacturers may be able to bring the cost of solar electricity down to 10¢ a kilowatt-hour by 2000,

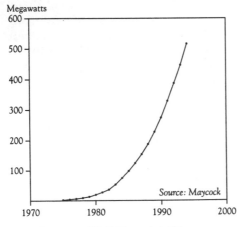

Figure 9-1. World Photovoltaic Shipments, Cumulative, 1975-94

or perhaps 4¢ by 2020. If so, photovoltaics could become one of the world's largest industries.[11]

Wind power is even closer to taking over large shares of electricity generation. In some areas the electricity produced by wind turbines is already cost-competitive with conventional generation. In the early eighties, wind machines typically cost $3,000 per kilowatt and produced electricity for more than 20¢ a kilowatt-hour (1993 dollars). By the late eighties, the machines were larger and more efficient and their capital cost, including installation, had fallen to about $1,000–1,200 per kilowatt. At an average annual wind speed of 5.8 meters per second and a maintenance cost of a penny per kilowatt-hour, this yields an average generating cost of 7¢ per kilowatt-hour for wind turbines installed in the United States in the early nineties, compared with 4–6¢ for new power plants fueled by natural gas or coal. Wind developers using the newest technologies of all have signed contracts to sell wind-generated electricity at less than 5¢ per kilowatt-hour.[12]

Wind and sunlight are abundant in almost all areas of the world, and could grow to replace fossil fuels when the economics improve. And many factors are converging to make the growth of renewable energy possible—indeed, necessary. The first is the growing need to move away from a carbon-based economy. The Framework Convention on Climate Change signed in Rio de Janeiro in 1992 has become increasingly important as scientists have become more convinced that the earth's climate is warming. (See Chapter 2.) The signatories will not be able to meet its requirements while still relying almost entirely on fossil fuels.

Certain industries have a large interest in avoiding the possibility of human-induced climate change. Insurance companies, for example, would have to pay enormous claims that would accompany increasing numbers of hurricanes, droughts, and floods and rising sea levels. Farmers have an interest in maintaining today's rainfall patterns, because the locations of their farms and irrigation systems were chosen in part to suit existing rainfall.

Apart from avoiding the costs of climate change, many investors stand to benefit from the emergence of large-scale solar industries. Solar power is especially well suited to the investment structure of poorer areas, where money is not available for large facilities. Many small producers will gain business opportunities to deliver electricity that previously could only have been supplied by large corporations with massive capital to invest in oil- or coal-fired plants. These people can buy a small wind farm or focus solar panels toward the sky on land they already own, while still raising food or grazing animals. This has the potential to create local businesses in developing countries that otherwise would have imported their power or have brought in foreign power companies.

Solar power is also particularly well suited to rural communities that have dispersed dwellings and buildings, or ones difficult to reach with power cables. Nepal is an example of a country where decentralized power may make more sense than a few large power plants. And with the 1995 cancellation of a massive World Bank–funded hydroelectric project there, the way is cleared for investments in such technologies as localized solar power. In this mountainous country, local solar or wind farms have an advantage over a single, centralized dam.[13]

Similarly, in the past few years, 20,000 Kenyan homes have been electrified using solar cells compared with 17,000 new homes that were hooked up to the central power grid. And in India, a wind boom is under way because the government has opened the power grid to independent developers and given tax incentives for renewable energy. India is already the world's second most active wind market, with a wind potential estimated at 20,000–50,000 megawatts.[14]

Parts of the world that have not yet committed to large-scale centralized sources of power have the opportunity to move directly to solar power. More than half of South Africa's households have no electricity, for example. Now South African companies are building a photovoltaic manufacturing plant near the Alexandra township north of Johannesburg that will electrify 10,000 homes, 600 clinics, and 1,000 schools with solar power. Its first solar panels were delivered in August 1995 to a primary school in Soweto township that had no electricity.[15]

The jobs in industries that create clean supplies of energy will be high-quality ones.

Renewable energy is also appealing to the world's health ministries and fiscal planners. The technologies would produce little of the pollution that causes millions of premature deaths from air pollution annually worldwide, thereby taking a massive burden off of national health care budgets. Some 60,000 deaths are caused by particulates found in air pollution in the United States every year, according to researchers at the Harvard School of Public Health, and that does not include other common pollutants in the air—from sulfur dioxide to lead, ozone, carbon monoxide, and nitrogen oxides. If the costs of caring for these patients or of the productivity lost to sick days or premature death were added to the price of burning coal, oil, or natural gas, then those sources

would be seen as more expensive today than many forms of solar power. (See Chapter 10.)[16]

Many calculations have also found that shifting to renewable energy creates jobs. A 1992 study cosponsored by the American Gas Association, the Solar Energy Industry Association, and the Alliance to Save Energy estimated that emphasizing efficiency, renewables, and natural gas would conservatively create an additional 175,000 jobs in energy production and service industries by 2010 compared with continuing with today's energy mix. A 1994 follow-up study found that implementing the Clinton administration's Climate Change Action Plan would lead to 157,000 more jobs by the year 2000 than a "business-as-usual" plan would, and 260,000 more jobs by 2010. Much of this job creation would come from energy efficiency improvements that would free up funds for investment in activities that would require more jobs than energy production, but shifting to renewable sources of energy is also important.[17]

The jobs in industries that create clean supplies of energy will be high-quality ones. Many of them involve design, whether it is new solar technologies or windmills, or efficient buildings, and hence earn large salaries and provide creative work. And those jobs in clean energy industries that are less creative are nevertheless safer than equivalent jobs in the fossil-fuel industries. Illnesses such as black lung disease, for example, common among coal miners, do not affect people who work with renewable technologies.

More significant than the direct job creation aspect, however, is the fact that shifting to sustainable energy industries is important for strengthening economies overall. A more efficient and cleaner energy economy makes all industries that consume energy more efficient and cleaner, which improves their prospects and creates jobs making all sorts of other products. That is where the most fundamental job creation occurs.[18]

Photovoltaic cells and wind turbines are not the only forms of solar or renewable energy available, and it is unlikely that any single renewable technology will dominate. Regional variations in economics and the availability of sunlight will favor some approaches over others. Solar-powered heat engines, dams, fuel cells that turn hydrogen into electricity, and biological processes involving enzymes driven by sunlight are among other valuable technologies. They will make important additions to future renewable energy schemes.[19]

As regulations tighten on pollution, it is renewable energy that will benefit at the expense of fossil fuels. Whether through domestic regulations on urban air pollution or international treaties for carbon emissions, the world is moving toward doing more to protect public health. This paints a bright picture for renewables.

RISE OF THE STEEL MINIMILL

For industry to be sustainable, it will have to derive far more of its materials from recycling than it does today. Recycled material requires less energy to process than virgin stock, depends less on new mining activities, and reduces the discard of materials. Industries equipped to use scrap materials as their stock are not only sustainable over the years, they also have a competitive advantage in the marketplace because they save money by not purchasing costlier unprocessed materials.[20]

Each ton of recycled steel saves 2,500 pounds of iron ore, 1,000 pounds of coal, and 40 pounds of limestone. Only one third as much energy is needed to produce steel from scrap as from virgin materials. Materials savings, in turn, mean a reduced environmental toll: more than a half-ton of earthen material is left undisturbed, for instance, for each ton of iron ore not mined.[21]

Steel producers that work from scrap are growing quickly, and facilities called minimills have come to symbolize that growth by pushing older, more polluting companies out of large parts of the steel market and dominating U.S. steel production. From about 5 percent of the U.S. steel market at the end of the sixties, minimills now supply 35 percent. The Development Centre of the Organisation for Economic Co-operation and Development projects that electric arc furnaces, the kind used by minimills, will account for half of world steel output by the end of this decade.[22]

Minimills are small, highly efficient factories that use scrap instead of iron ore, processing it in electric arc furnaces instead of traditional ones. During the eighties, they drove traditional steelmakers virtually out of the business of making construction bars and beams. Until recently, minimill products were limited to certain grades and shapes of steel, but that is now changing. Minimills recently became able to produce sheet steel— one of the last bastions of traditional steelmaking. In 1989, a minimill first succeeded in making sheet steel; now that mill is the fourth largest steel producer in the United States.[23]

A flurry of firms are pursuing this success with sheet steel, and some minimills are experimenting with steelmaking processes that could further revolutionize the $30-billion U.S. industry. One attempt is under way, for example, to convert iron carbide directly into steel, saving large amounts of energy and bypassing intermediate steps. This would also cut costs by $30–50 a ton, down from about $270 a ton. Another goal is to cast directly from liquid steel into thin strips, eliminating the need for huge rolling machines that squeeze and stretch cables into coils.[24]

Because steel recycling is so profitable, it has become a crowded industry, and these additions to the market are going to increase competition. (See Figure 9–3.) The world has the capacity to produce far more steel than is needed, and European firms laid off hundreds of thousands of steelworkers in the early nineties as their capacity was too large. Even China, with its strong demand for new buildings and machines, has recently laid off steelworkers. Minimills will have to survive, if they can, under this state of heavy competition. What is likely to emerge are companies that survive by producing with unprecedented efficiency, bypassing any unnecessary procedures and capitalizing on available sources of scrap or easily accessible ores.[25]

Minimills also have been able to improve their efficiency by taking on new types of materials and using new processes. For example, between 1989 and 1992 the number of North American markets for scrap from steel cans tripled, as flexible mills were increasingly able to use cans for their scrap.[26]

Minimills are ideal for many developing countries that have small, dispersed markets and need modest amounts of steel at low capital costs. Worldwide, though, most countries have a long way to go toward improving the efficiency of their steel production. The former Soviet Union, one of the big five steel producers (along with the United States, Japan, China, and Germany), recycles little steel and relies heavily on virgin iron ores and inefficient open hearth furnaces, which cannot use more than 45 percent scrap. Steel production there requires 31 gigajoules of energy per ton—some 70 percent more than in Italy or Spain, the most efficient producers. Italy and Spain use only 18 gigajoules of energy to produce a ton of steel, a rate they accomplish by using scrap metal almost entirely.[27]

In Eastern Europe, by contrast, the electric arc furnace has been providing less than 13 percent of steel production. China and India also still rely heavily on the open hearth furnace, using more than twice as much energy per ton of steel produced as in Italy and Spain.[28]

Worldwide, the growth of steel recycling may be slowed by impurities in scrap metal that make recycled metals brittle. Copper, especially, is frequently mixed in with scrap metals, such as recycled automobile parts. Metals produced with it and other extraneous elements can only be made into a limited group of products, such as reinforcing bars. As a result, minimills and other recycling technologies sometimes do not compete directly with more traditional basic oxygen furnaces because they cannot make the same products, though this is gradu-

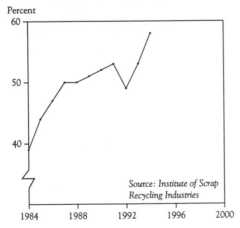

Percent

Source: Institute of Scrap Recycling Industries

Figure 9-3. Recycled Content of U.S. Steel, 1984-94

ally changing with improving electric arc technology.[29]

Such barriers to the growth of recycling can be overcome if industry focuses on the entire flow of materials through the economy. By planning during the design and production stages for the dismantlement of motor vehicles, household appliances, and other sources of scrap, as some manufacturers are now doing, limitations on the reclamation of steel and other valuable substances can be overcome. Automobiles, for instance, can be built without copper and other elements that hinder recycling, or processes can be designed in advance that allow products to be taken apart easily after disposal. That is where the fullest potential for recycling lies.

In Highland Park, Michigan, technicians at the Vehicle Recycling Development Center, a joint effort of the Big Three automakers that went into full operation in summer 1994, are doing exactly that. They dissect subassemblies, weigh each component, and videotape and time the procedures. Their aim is to design cars for easier dismantling—DFD (design for disassembly), as it has been dubbed. This closes the production loop by making products whose components can be refurbished and reused or disposed of safely at the end of the product's life. The ease of destruction is now as important as the ease of construction. And the same idea is being applied to everything from coffeepots to Caterpillar tractors, from photocopiers to cameras.[30]

Deconstruction has long been the key to the success of minimills. The United States already reuses a remarkable 75 percent by weight of nearly every American automobile. Cars are first stripped of valuable parts such as engines, generators, alternators, and other components that can be refurbished and resold by some 12,000 auto parts recyclers. Next,

the metal carcasses wind up in 200 shredders that make steel fragments and new car bodies. In Europe, an estimated 20 million cars a year will be dismantled by the end of the decade. Several companies, including BMW, are building cars that come apart. BMW has pushed the recycled portion of a car to 80 percent by weight and is aiming for 95 percent.[31]

This deconstruction and reprocessing process means large increases in employment. The first link in this work chain is the dismantler, who sells parts from vehicles. After the parts have been removed, the dismantler sells the hulk to a shredder. Metallic materials like iron, aluminum, and copper are separated by magnetic and other methods, leaving behind plastics, glass, rubber, and dirt. Jobs are also created for designers, who need to select materials and make design schemes to facilitate reuse, recycling, or reclamation.[32]

On the other hand, minimills have become efficient by cutting out some of the stages of the older production process. From the mining of virgin ores and their transport to the ability to skip steps like the rolling of rods into flat products, many phases have been eliminated. Fewer workers are needed at mills for each ton of steel produced. The net effect is an industry that shifts jobs toward work that is less harmful to the environment. And much work is eliminated that previously took place in dark mines or with metals heated to high temperatures in noisy, hot factories. Although the new jobs created in processing scrap are not entirely safe, they are a major improvement over some of the most hazardous industries of the past.[33]

A mature industrial society with a stable population could live largely on recycled steel, with air and water pollution only a small fraction of what they are when primary minerals were used. Except for losses due to impurities, rusting, and the unavoidable destruction of some steel from recycling, metal can be used over and over again, indefinitely.

A REVOLUTION IN PAPER RECYCLING

Since early 1994, big changes have come to recycling in North America, and in particular they have come to paper recycling. As recently as 1993, North American markets for many recovered materials were unreliable, prices were low, and many communities were unsure about their long-term ability to sell the materials they collected. But now prices have taken off, these markets provide a reliable source of valuable material, and in some cases the supply of scrap cannot even keep up with demand. Between January 1994 and March 1995, for example, the average U.S. price of old newsprint—which had hovered near or below zero since mid-1991—rose twenty-twofold, despite growing collection capacities.[34]

Suddenly, wastepaper that once seemed a burden has become a major asset, and communities that had the foresight to set up solid recycling programs a few years ago are beginning to reap real rewards. New York City, which two years ago paid $6 million a year to get rid of its newsprint, now expects to earn tens of millions of dollars from selling the same material. The amount of paper recovered from U.S. municipal waste doubled between 1985 and 1993, to 26 million tons, and recovered paper consumption is growing more than twice as fast as total fiber consumption.[35]

This welcome turn of events has several sources: Rising demand for paper in economies that rebounded from recession in the early nineties boosted prices. The rise of government and private procurement programs that give preference to recycled fibers is also responsible for recycling's new value. And as people's experience with recycling has grown, many people trust recycled products that they were once apprehensive of. Finally, large capital investments have been made in firms to process scrap, a necessary change from the past, when most effort went into the collection of scrap but not to its remanufacture.

The boom in paper recycling is vital to the world's forests and the species that live there as well as to the sustainability of industry. Globally, the pulp and paper industry may consume as many as 4 billion trees annually, some of them stripped from old-growth forests that cannot be replaced. In making pulp, the industry each year dumps 950,000 tons of organochlorine effluents, including highly toxic and carcinogenic dioxins, into rivers. It pumps roughly 100,000 tons of acid rain-producing sulfur dioxide into the air. It emits another 20,000 tons of chloroform, which causes liver disease and is a suspected carcinogen. And it is a major user of fossil-fuel-generated electric power. Recycling firms will reduce all these burdens, though not eliminate them.[36]

Yet it is profitability that really drives the desire to invest in recycling. The American Forest & Paper Association, the main industry trade group, estimates that its members will invest a total of $10 billion in recycling by the end of the nineties, and they have a goal of recycling or reusing half of the paper produced in the United States by 2000. New plants added several million tons of paper-recycling capacity in 1995, and they need more supplies of scrap. This will cause prices to rise further. In 1992, companies had to pay to have newspaper scrap hauled away. But by early 1994 they could sell it, and after a continuous rise since, newspaper scrap now sells for more than $40 a ton. Cardboard scrap now sells for more than $70 a ton, a complete reversal of the past situation.[37]

Government is also behind the rise in paper recycling. The U.S. government is the world's largest buyer of paper—at 300,000 tons per year of paper. In 1993, President Clinton issued an executive order requiring that all paper purchased by the federal government contain 20 percent post-consumer recycled content by the end of 1994, increasing to 30 percent by 1998.[38]

Thirteen states also now have standards for minimum recycled content of newsprint; 15 more have negotiated voluntary agreements with newspaper publishers to increase their purchasing of recycled content. California has become the laboratory for the most extensive effort in North America to develop recycling industries. The state has created 40 Recycling Market Development Zones— enterprise zones targeted toward recycling-based businesses.[39]

Some other countries are following suit. Belgium, for instance, has mandated an "ecotax" on paperboard used for food packaging, but the tax is waived if the board is made from recycled material. And other countries have a large appetite for paper scrap. Asia is a big importer of scrap, much of it originating in the United States and Germany. By 1992, Taiwan was the world's largest importer, and used 98 percent scrap in its paper production. Denmark had reached 97 percent, Mexico 81 percent, and Thailand 80 percent.[40]

As with steel recycling and sources of steel scrap, paper manufacturers are now setting up shop near the best sources of their raw materials: cities and industries that produce wastepaper. These companies are signing long-term contracts with cities and private firms to purchase paper scrap the way they used to buy up forests. Instead of land rights,

they now buy wastepaper rights. The challenge for a company is to get as many contracts as it can for cheap scrap in order to keep prices down and the scrap out of the hands of competitors. This is causing many firms to relocate.[41]

Communities that had the foresight to set up solid recycling programs a few years ago are beginning to reap real rewards.

The scale of the material is large. In most industrial countries, about 60 percent of landfilled material is paper or paperboard. Thus scrap paper can rival timber from tree farms as the dominant source, and timber from old-growth forests will not be needed at all. Currently, however, de-inking mills use about 15–50 cubic meters of water per ton of recycled paper. This amount will have to be reduced if recycling is to take place in water-scarce regions. Fortunately, technology is being designed that is likely to improve the efficiency of such water use.[42]

Yet another boost to recycling has come with improved paper-making technologies. Until recently, industry did not have the technology to make recycled paper appear uniformly smooth, clean, and white. Also, industry was concerned that recycled fibers could not meet high quality standards because they are shorter and weaker than virgin fibers. Over the past two or three years, however, the technologies for making high-grade paper with recycled stock have improved greatly. New methods of deinking, of crisscrossing and layering the fibers for maximum strength, and of pulping have improved quality to the point where recycled grades are virtually indistinguishable from their virgin counterparts.[43]

And in the past, the paper industry only accepted high-grade, carefully sorted papers as stock for recycled writing paper. Some new mills, however, can make high-grade paper out of a much wider mix of office paper discards. This should increase the post-consumer content of high-grade paper.[44]

In terms of jobs, this switch away from primary timber to scrap paper is perfectly natural and mirrors a switch from primary timber to tree farms. In Australia, for instance, employment in the timber industry has been falling since the fifties, while production has increased—more wood has been produced by fewer people. Between 1963 and 1988, more than 20,000 jobs were lost in sawmilling, a 60-percent reduction, and almost 10,000 were lost in timberfelling and removal, a 40-percent reduction. Only 5 percent of the value that the wood products industry adds to the Australian economy comes from wood-chipping of native forests. The rest comes from the manufacuture of veneers, panels, and pulp and paper, and from sawmilling. Although the industry as a whole employs 59,300 people, only 600 work directly in wood-chipping.[45]

Processing is much more job-intensive than extraction: logging 1 million board-feet of American timber generates only 3 jobs, for example, while milling it into lumber creates 20 and turning it into furniture generates 80. And reprocessing jobs can be sustained indefinitely, because they do not rely on finite supplies of minerals or harvestable timber. This means that shifting from pulp made out of virgin materials to pulp from recycling moves production toward the more job-intensive parts of the manufacturing process, and away from the parts where jobs had already been lost.[46]

Paper recycling has become a vital tool for restoring the natural balances of the world's forests. Not only are trees left standing, but the myriad species who live in them, below them, and among them will be left living. The forest's ability to moderate local climates by absorbing and releasing water will be maintained, its ability to anchor soils and reduce erosion will continue, and its aesthetic value will be preserved.

RENAISSANCE OF THE BICYCLE AND TRAIN

Even though cars run on fossil fuels put unsustainable amounts of carbon into the atmosphere, it may not be carbon emissions that ultimately limit automobile use. They could be avoided, after all, by such technologies as electric vehicles with batteries that store solar power. And eventually, solar power might be stored in hydrogen, which could run cars whose pollution would be only the water created when the hydrogen combines with oxygen.

A more severe limit on automobile use is the large amount of land required by each car for roads and parking spaces. This constraint is most pronounced in Asia, which has well over half the world's people but only about a third of its cropland. Putting a car in every garage of China and India would use up land that is needed for other uses, particularly for cropland. In China, each person has less than 0.8 hectares of grainland on average. Adding an amount of concrete sufficient for one parking space and a small stretch of road for each family could reduce that by enough to make the difference between a full diet and an inadequate one.[47]

Not only does an auto-centered transport system eat up land in the countryside, it also leads to overcongestion and pollution in the cities. Bangkok, Thailand, has paved over most of its famous canals with roads in an attempt to reduce its severe traffic congestion. But the city presently adds about 600 new cars every day to the traffic stream, equivalent to an extra 3 kilometers of bumper-to-bumper traffic. At that rate, in less than four years enough cars are added to fill the entire road system with one lane of traffic—a rate that is unsustainable in physical terms that any tourist can see.[48]

Instead of excessive dependence on automobiles, future personal transport needs in crowded countries are more likely to be met successfully by a combination of rail and bicycle transport. For people in countries like the United States, who are accustomed to thinking about automobiles as the only serious form of transportation, this blend at first sounds inadequate. In fact, bicycles already dominate Asian transportation, and some of the most exciting technological advances have recently come with such railroads as Japan's bullet trains and France's Train à Grande Vitesse (TGV).

The world builds more than three times as many bicycles every year as cars. (See Figure 1-5 in Chapter 1.) Bicycles in Asia alone transport more people than do all the world's autos. Moreover, automobile production is not growing, and fewer cars are made today than in 1989, whereas bicycle production is growing quickly. The world produced twice as many bikes last year as it did at the start of the eighties, and production is up more than 20 percent since the start of the nineties.[49]

In some European countries, bicycles are a significant part of the personal transport system. In Denmark, one in five journeys is made by cycle. In the Netherlands, two out of three children cycle to school, and in one Dutch city, cycling accounts for more than 40 percent of journeys to work. Moreover, these high cycling rates occur in two countries that can easily afford automobiles but have chosen bikes. In other European countries that rely less on bicycles, the potential for cycling is enormous. In Britain, for example, three quarters of all journeys are of less than nine kilometers, perfect for bicycling, yet only 3 percent of journeys are made by bike. One British group has calculated that if the rate of cycling there reached the levels found in countries like the Netherlands and Denmark, carbon monoxide, nitrogen oxide, and carbon dioxide pollution would decrease by 10 percent.[50]

Future personal transport needs in crowded countries are more likely to be met successfully by a combination of rail and bicycle transport.

Super-fast trains like the bullet trains of Japan and the TGV of France have not yet reached most regions. When they do, it will signal the renaissance of rail. The greatest improvements in rail technology, however, will come with trains that do not even touch rails. A family of technologies that suspend a train in the air and guide it by magnetic forces has the potential to propel trains at remarkable speeds. A speed of 517 kilometers (321 miles) per hour was achieved in a test back in 1979, for example.[51]

The combination of rail and bicycles takes advantage of the bicycles' ability to travel in any direction at any time and trains' ability to move people at high speed. People who cannot afford cars can afford bikes and trains, and both require little land. Japan and the Netherlands are particularly advanced in their bicycle/rail commuter systems, and Germany is following.[52]

Many countries are not backing the bicycle and rail combination, however. This is a particular surprise in China, the most bicycle-centered country in the world and one where most people can only afford rail transport. Until recently, China had accomplished something that few other countries can claim. By building an estimated 43 million bicycles in 1994, it emitted little or no carbon into the atmosphere from the additions to its personal-transport choices, an accomplishment that no country in Europe or North America and few in East Asia can boast. And one that is becoming increasingly important.[53]

If many of China's 1.2 billion people purchase cars, the roads will come to a standstill of gridlock.

Yet today, official policy in China favors the automobile. The nation currently has only 1.8 million automobiles, less than 5 percent of which are privately owned. But seeing cars as an essential part of "development," the government has limited the number of bicycles allowed on certain streets, to make room for more cars. Guangzhou, in South China, banned bicycles from 11 main streets during rush hours, for instance, and bicycles are now prohibited on the Bund in Shanghai. Unfortunately, this is a shift away from sustainability.[54]

Funded by rapid economic growth, cars have taken to the roads in China, and many families aspire to own one. Cities have become congested with traffic, and along with pollution from coal-burning factories and from cigarettes, car exhausts have made respiratory disease the leading cause of death in China. This increase in automobile dependence cannot go on forever. If many of the country's 1.2 billion people purchase cars, the roads will come to a standstill of gridlock, and the costs of pollution and traffic fatalities will be prohibitive.[55]

More important, though, the Chinese government is seeking to protect grainland, not wishing to import large amounts of grain or cotton or other crops. The country has been losing more than 1 percent a year of its grainland since the late eighties.[56]

Another important policy is that of conserving or creating jobs, especially in countries like China that have many people to find work for. Currently, no studies are available on the employment differences between automobile and bicycle production. It seems certain, however, that manufacturing larger, more complex cars would involve many more jobs than producing bicycles would. Yet this does not necessarily mean that a bicycle-based economy would lack jobs. Savings to consumers from money not spent on cars and not invested in the automobile industry would go instead to other industries, creating jobs in those fields. This would cause expansion in economic sectors in countries that today are desperate for investment.

And rather than purchase cars from abroad, many developing countries could use bicycles and invest the money they save in industries that export their own products, or that produce goods for local consumption. Moreover, their reduced reliance on gasoline, which many developing countries import, frees up further funds for investment. Space not devoted to parking for cars can be used instead in urban areas for businesses or homes. Large expenditures from governments and industries go to maintaining an automobile infrastructure, and freeing up those funds could contribute a large part of the investment that countries around the world need.

The gains that come from efficiency of transportation and from reducing expenditures on transportation are similar to those that come from improved energy efficiency. Countries like Japan and Germany have done well in the last two decades by spending less on energy than most of their competitors. Now countries that spend less on both energy and personal transport can benefit from the other opportunities for their money.

This is a particularly important time for Asian countries such as China and India. They are on the threshold of developing large-scale personal transport systems, but they are not yet too far down the wrong road to change direction. North America and Europe have locked themselves into automobile dependence and will struggle to escape it even if they do attempt such a transition. But Asia is still mostly oriented toward more sustainable transport, and could further develop its bicycles and trains with great success.

By starting now with impressive rail technologies from Japan, France, or other countries, for example, India could put itself in a few years where people in many wealthier countries will wish they were. By keeping its bicycle network, China can conserve its cropland, cut its air pollution, and calm its cities. These would be steps toward sustainability.

THE ZERO-EMISSION FACTORY

A masterpiece of sustainable industry would be the zero-emissions factory. These facilities belong mostly to the future, as only a handful of attempts have

been made to operate them today. They are an enticing topic of research, though, as they would reduce the costs of production even as they eliminated pollution and the costs of cleaning it up. From a public relations point of view, a zero-emissions factory would be a stroke of genius at a time when many consumers are willing to choose products based not only on quality but also on methods of production. As William McDonnough, Dean of Architecture at the University of Virginia, has said, "It's not cradle to grave, it's cradle to cradle."[57]

The concept of cradle-to-cradle responsibility for products can cause some problems elsewhere in the life cycle of a product. Substituting steel for plastic on cars improves recyclability, for example, but also increases weight and so means more fuel is consumed as the vehicle is driven. As a result, thinking through and planning for such sustainable industry requires cooperation among various disciplines and industries. But it is through this interaction that the greatest successes will be achieved.[58]

Research into these facilities has recently begun at the United Nations University in Tokyo, with a new Zero Emissions Research Initiative. The focus is how production can use all input factors, somewhat the way that traditional societies have long used all parts of any animals they consume or all of their crops. The Chinese Academy of Sciences has submitted a study on a zero-emissions fermentation industry. Projects are being done on new ways to produce paints and dyes and other materials needed by industry.[59]

Other research has found solutions to many of the pieces of the puzzle that as a whole could become a zero-emissions factory. The search for dyes that would not result in chemical pollution, for example, has progressed, and some dyes have been found that color wool and ramie fabric and later decompose back into the soil with no harm.[60]

Paints are being created that use fewer solvents and produce fewer emissions. Paint is still responsible for an estimated 8 percent of the volatile organic compunds emitted into the atmosphere, despite reductions during recent years. The Paint Research Association in England and Southampton University are trying to synthesize a new type of paint based on the way insects form their tough, protective exoskeletons from water-soluble precursors. The goal is to devise polymers with water-attracting and water-repelling components, together with chains that behave as adhesive clasps. This would allow factories and products with reduced emissions.[61]

Zero-emissions factories are far pleasanter places to work, and their staffs value the high-quality work that they do.

Recovering heavy metals is particularly important because of their potential harm to human health and ecosystems. In the case of cadmium, some 1,300 out of a possible 16,000 tons were recovered in 1986 (the latest year for which data are available), with the rest escaping into the environment. With lead, 106,000 out of 189,000 tons of industrial wastes were recovered. Automotive storage batteries constituted much of this, as 95 percent of them were collected and reprocessed. But some of the most important recoveries of all will take place within factories that never let lead and other heavy metals out. They will design products that do not need those metals either for their own materials or in their production, or they will use closed-cycle processes that reuse or trap all the heavy metals.[62]

Beer brewing provides an example of a closed-cycle manufacturing process. Spent grain from beer has no value for a brewer, but it is an excellent feed for the cultivation of earthworms that are high-quality chicken feed. Likewise, leftovers from the brewing process can be used to make other liquors, soya sauce, or vinegar, allowing complete recovery of leftovers without needing substantial additional energy. Investments must be made, of course, before such a process can be completed. But once it is, it generates additional revenues from other products to make up for the money spent. This method is currently being used by brewers in Namibia, Tanzania, and Fiji, among other places.[63]

It is unclear whether zero-emissions factories would create more jobs or fewer than today's factories. What is clear, though, is that they are far pleasanter places to work, and that their staffs value the high-quality work that they do. In Reno, Nevada, the post office began making improvements along these same lines when it bought more-efficient lights and lowered a ceiling to heat and cool the building and improve acoustics. Postal workers responded to these improvements with a 6-percent rise in productivity and a reduction in mail-sorting errors—benefits that were completely unexpected by the investors, whose original goal was energy efficiency. More pleasant lighting and a quieter workplace, it turned out, were important to people's work.[64]

Even larger gains in productivity and improvements in morale have been enjoyed by aerospace companies and in many other industries. Yet these changes fall far short of the comprehensive improvements needed by a zero-emissions factory. Future experiments, research, and investments will tell whether productivity and morale rise even higher as the development of these factories proceeds.[65]

The zero-emissions or closed-cycle factory has an analogy in the earth's climate. As it developed, the climate was not always in the balance it has achieved today. The earliest living cells on earth produced carbon dioxide the same way today's cells do. But other organisms did not exist to convert the CO_2 back to other gases like oxygen. They would have choked eventually on the carbon dioxide buildup if not for the development of a closed cycle. The system stabilized eventually with the appearance of new organisms, such as blue-green algae capable of recycling CO_2 into sugars and cellulose, thus closing the carbon cycle.[66]

Environmental scientist Robert Ayres points out that the system was still not stable at that point. It was only with the evolution of two more biological processes—aerobic respiration and aerobic photosynthesis—that the oxygen cycle was closed, with oxygen converted into carbon dioxide and vice versa. And other biological processes, such as nitrification and denitrification, had to appear to close the nitrogen and other cycles.[67]

Evolution responded to unstable situations—open cycles—by inventing new organisms to stabilize the system by closing the cycles. But it took several billion years before the biosphere reached its present degree of stability. In the case of today's industrial system, the time scales have been drastically shortened. Human activity already dominates natural processes in many respects. The world will now quickly have to find ways to close the cycles of its production, whether in an individual factory, in the market for a particular product or material, or in the economy as a whole.

10

Harnessing the Market for the Environment

David Malin Roodman

Evidence continues to accumulate that it is in the very nature of industrial economic systems to degrade the environment on which they depend and hurt the people they serve. Some signs have been alarmingly graphic; others, dangerously subtle. In the city of Teplice, in the Czech Republic, children wear filter masks to school to protect their growing lungs from the soot and sulfur pouring out of nearby coal plants. In parts of India, China, the Middle East, and the western United States, farmers pump water from the aquifers beneath their feet as rapidly as if they were aboard a sinking ship—and ironically, they are, for water tables are falling steadily. Meanwhile, in Fiji, Grenada, and other small island nations, residents fear that a global warming–induced sea level rise could literally wipe their homelands off the map.[1]

If present trends continue, such prob-lems will only grow worse. Global economic growth is now accelerating as Latin America, Asia, and the former Eastern bloc nations scramble to emulate the western economic model. The millions of victims of air pollution to date could be joined by many millions more. Emissions of the greenhouse gas carbon dioxide (CO_2) could double by 2050, mostly from increasing fossil fuel use; yet the consensus among climatologists is that this would be 5–10 times higher than the maximum level that would avoid climate change. Today's environmental policies often alleviate the symptoms of environmental unsustainability by prescribing end-of-the-pipe solutions, but the disease is still spreading. This suggests that the real problems run much deeper, and will require deeper solutions.[2]

One of the most fundamental flaws of market-based economies is that the prices they use to guide buying decisions and allocate resources rarely reflect the full costs of environmental damage. When coal plant operators in Teplice

We are grateful to the Wallace Genetic Foundation for their support for this chapter and related work on this topic.

pump untreated emissions into the air, and when Texas farmers pump groundwater onto their fields, the costs they impose on this and future generations do not appear in their general ledgers. As a result, nothing signals them that the societal costs of pollution and depletion can outweigh the benefits. Worse, nothing tells them that unilateral decisions to pollute—even when the economic benefits exceed the costs—can violate basic societal values about the sanctity of human health and property.

To make the market system reflect rather than obscure ecological realities, societies need to enforce a principle that is at once radical and obvious: that people and businesses should pay the full costs of the harm they do others. To "make polluters pay," governments need to sell limited numbers of permits for pollution and resource depletion, or to tax these activities directly, in the way many already tax cigarettes to discourage smoking.

By increasing the cost of environmental degradation, governments will provide a powerful incentive for business to operate in more environmentally sound ways. If businesses also pass the higher costs on to their customers, sticker prices will come to reflect true environmental prices, encouraging consumers to spend money on less damaging products and services. In the long run, taxes and permit systems will stimulate cleaner and more resource-efficient technologies and life-styles.

As revenues from environmental taxes and charges rise, governments can cut other taxes to hold the overall tax burden constant. For example, a government that levies a charge on carbon emissions can recycle the revenues back into the economy by cutting general taxes on wages or corporate profits. Overall, industries that emitted little carbon would receive more in tax cuts than they paid in environmental charges,

which would stimulate employment and investment in cleaner industries while discouraging it in dirtier ones. And if properly targeted, such tax cuts can actually ameliorate problems such as unemployment, falling wages, or stagnant investment, even as they guide industrial economies toward ecological sustainability.

In fact, just such a shift appears to be under way worldwide. At the moment, many environmental charges are too low to reflect the full costs of environmental destruction. And many governments still heavily subsidize such activity. Nevertheless, like the gradual emergence of modern taxes on income, wage, and sales about a century ago, a great wave in the history of taxation is on the horizon. If it rises to its full potential—the elimination of environmentally destructive subsidies and the imposition of taxes and permit charges that reflect full environmental costs—it will create a trillion-dollar swing in the global tax burden in favor of environmental protection.

THE STATE OF THE WORLD'S TAXES

As long as there have been city-based civilizations there have been ruling classes who have raised funds from the general population to support themselves, their military ventures, and other projects. Written into past and present tax codes are the stories of changing technologies, social and political cultures, economic circumstances, and social values that are the substance of history.

In ancient Babylon, China, and India, and in Incan and Aztec civilizations, there were two major forms of mobile wealth: food and manual labor. Dictatorial priest-kings taxed them both, extracting a tithing or more from peasants' grain harvests and conscripting their labor for soldiering or building irrigation canals or pyramids. As trade and commerce flourished in the increasingly sophisticated societies of ancient Greece and Rome, taxes on the wealth of the growing upper class and on traded commodities such as salt and textiles became lucrative and easier to administer because of the small number of taxpayers involved.[3]

Taxes on constructive activities such as work, investment, and commerce discourage the very things they tax.

Many of the taxes from the ancients survive in various forms but have become less important sources of revenue. For example, the modern property tax is the direct descendant of the in-kind grain tax. And taxes on the trade and sale of specific products live on in the form of cigarette and gasoline taxes. Altogether, however, these taxes account for less than 20 percent of government revenue today.[4]

After the Industrial Revolution, public budgets expanded rapidly in western nations—faster than economies as a whole—reflecting the climbing cost of weapons and war, the rise of social welfare programs, and the introduction of subsidies for industries such as agriculture and energy. To fund this growth, public officials haltingly adopted broad-based taxes on income, profits, and wages—levies with little historical precedent—and extended the sales (or value added) tax to most goods and services.

For example, Austria, the Nether-lands, and Great Britain made early use of the income tax in 1799–1815 to fund the wars against Napoleon. In Britain, the tax reappeared in 1842, again as a supposedly temporary measure, but rising demands on the treasury assured its continuance, despite political resistance. In the United States, the income tax was first pressed into service during the Civil War, later struck down by the Supreme Court, and finally backed by constitutional amendment in 1913. In the western world as a whole, taxes on sales, profits, wages, and income became the norm by the end of World War II. Revenues from these new taxes continued to balloon and now account for the majority of government receipts.[5]

The tax codes of most developing countries look more like those of classical times because now, as then, the majority of families and businesses there earn too little to justify the administrative effort of computing personal incomes and corporate profits. In India, 75 percent of revenue comes from taxes on imports, exports, and domestic sales. Tax rates are relatively low in poorer countries, however, typically equal to 5–20 percent of gross domestic product (GDP), compared with 30–40 percent in industrial countries. As formal economic activity in developing countries increases, their tax codes will probably come to look more like those in the West. Today the German government raises 52 times as much revenue per citizen as the Indian government does; only 28 percent of that money flows in from sales and trade. (See Table 10–1.)[6]

In addition to generating large revenues, broad-based taxes have other advantages. For example, almost all income tax systems in use today are at least modestly progressive, taking proportionally more from higher-income people than from poor, on the assumption that the rich can afford to give up larger

Table 10-1. Tax Revenue, Total and by Source, Selected Countries, 1993

Country	Total Revenue		Sources[1]			
	Per Person	Share of GDP	Profits and Income	Wages[2]	Sales and Trade[3]	Property
	(1994 dollars[4])	(percent)	(percent share of total tax revenue)			
Germany	7,443	39	31	39	28	3
United States	7,315	30	42	29	17	11
Japan	6,155	29	41	34	14	11
Russia	1,938	36	29	28	31	12[5]
Thailand[6]	1,098	16	31	1	64	3
Iran[6]	416	7	28	26	41	4
India[6]	144	11	25	0	75	0.3

[1]Some rows do not total 100 due to rounding, and because small taxes on other sources are not shown. [2]Includes employee and employer contributions to social security funds. [3]Includes general taxes on turnover, sales, and value added; taxes on specific products such as gasoline and cigarettes; and taxes on imports and exports. [4]Converted from domestic currencies on the basis of purchasing power parities. [5]Includes nonproperty and nontax sources. [6]Central governments only.
SOURCE: Worldwatch estimates, based on Organisation for Economic Co-operation and Development, *Revenue Statistics of OECD Member Countries 1960–1994* (Paris: 1995), on World Bank, *World Data 1995: World Bank Indicators on CD-ROM* (electronic database) (Washington, D.C.: 1995), on U.N. Development Programme, *Human Development Report 1995* (New York: Oxford University Press, 1995), and on International Monetary Fund, *World Economic Outlook May 1995* (Washington, D.C.: 1995).

shares of their income without endangering their health or their lives. In addition, broad-based taxes tend to dampen boom-bust economic cycles. During recessions, as incomes and profits fall, so do tax revenues, temporarily reducing the burden of government on the economy.

In the process of solving some problems, however, modern taxes created others. In ancient times, there was little to tax besides necessities, and farmers would not have sown fewer seeds even when they knew the king would usurp a share of their crop, since they still needed to feed their families. But today, in countries where most people live comfortably above subsistence, consumers and businesses are more able to adapt buying and investment decisions to avoid taxes. As a result, taxes on constructive activities such as work, investment, and commerce discourage the

very things they tax. Though governments return to the economy whatever revenues they raise, this does not compensate for distortions created by perverse tax incentives. Since global tax revenues equal more than $7.5 trillion annually, or at least one third of measured economic output, and since about 90 percent of that flows from levies on constructive activities, it is clear that taxes are now a major force shaping modern economies.[7]

In the United States, according to one model, the $535 billion of payroll taxes raised in 1993 to fund social security programs cost the economy $157 billion (2.6 percent of GDP), as, for example, some employers found that high labor costs made expansion prohibitively expensive. Similarly, the $132 billion raised in corporate income taxes cut GDP by $81 billion (1.3 percent), as companies found that the expected after-tax profits on some investments such as new factories fell too low to justify the risks. Like Shylock in Shakespeare's *The Merchant of Venice*, who would have exacted a pound of his enemy's flesh from "nearest his heart," taxes exact a toll both through how much they take and what they take it from.[8]

The payroll taxes and the reduction in new investment also can put upward pressure on unemployment when it is already rising and downward pressure on wages when they are falling. In the United States, for instance, for every dollar a worker earned in 1991, an average of 20 percent went to payroll taxes, pushing many working families toward poverty. In Japan, the ratio was 30 percent, and in Western Europe, 40 percent. To the extent that wage taxes come out of employer's pockets, this raises the cost of labor and encourages automation. This appears to be one reason that the ranks of the jobless in Western Europe grew from 2.6 percent of the labor force in 1973 to 11.3 percent in 1994. (See Figure 10-1.) In 1993, the European Commission proposed that member governments begin to use envi-

ronmental taxes, such as levies on energy use and carbon emissions, to fund cuts in payroll taxes. This, economic studies suggest, would reduce unemployment in the short term—and, if adopted internationally, in the long term as well.[9]

Employers in the United States appear to have a stronger bargaining position in the job market, so they can force employees to absorb most of the wage taxes. This is one reason that people can still get jobs there but also that wages have stagnated overall and even declined at the bottom end of the job market. As a result, the percentage of families with children living below the poverty line despite having full-time workers climbed from 8.3 percent in 1975 to 11.1 in 1994. (See Figure 10–1.)[10]

UNDERTAXATION OF ENVIRONMENTAL DESTRUCTION

An appreciation of the powerful incentive effects of modern taxes leads to a simple conclusion, but one that governments have only recently begun to understand. Since taxes in industrial economies inevitably tend to discourage what they tax, society should decide what sorts of economic activity it wants less of, and then tax them first. The failure to do this is at the heart of today's environmental crises.

To people accustomed to thinking of taxes as a necessary evil, it can be surprising that they can be a force for economic improvement, regardless of what they fund. Yet the idea is well established in neoclassical economics, dating

Figure 10-1. Unemployment and Poverty Trends, European Union and United States, 1973-94

back to 1920. In *The Economics of Welfare*, British economist Arthur C. Pigou pointed out that many people and businesses make decisions that impose costs on others. The sulfur and smoke he no doubt witnessed pouring from coal-burning factories and fireplaces was a prime example: to those living nearby, the damages to property values and health were significant and tangible. Yet coal users felt little disincentive to pollute beyond the point where the costs to society outweighed the benefits. London smogs between 1873 and 1892 are thought to have taken at least 2,000 lives.[11]

The solution, Pigou argued, was for governments to use taxes to make polluters pay the full costs of the harm they did. Then when they tallied up the costs and benefits of pollution for themselves, they would also take society's interests into account. This would force steelmakers to find cleaner ways to make steel or to raise their prices to cover the tax bills, which would encourage their customers to use the metal more efficiently or search for alternatives. The lack of environmental taxes made the economy less efficient at meeting people's needs and wants. The problem, as it has been put more recently by Ernst von Weizsäcker, president of the Wuppertal Institute in Germany, is that "prices do not tell the ecological truth."[12]

For example, the hidden costs of driving in the United States—including the value of time wasted in traffic jams, the decline in property values near roads because of noise, the cost of financing a formidable military presence in the Middle East, the deaths and injuries from accidents, lung disease, and global warming—total roughly $300–350 billion per year, according to two recent U.S studies. These hidden costs are equivalent to a substantial 5 percent or more of U.S. GDP and 63–74¢ per liter of gasoline or diesel ($2.40–2.80 per gal-

lon), compared with the 32¢ per liter ($1.20 per gallon) that Americans pay at the pump. Partly as a result, Americans drive far beyond the point where the costs to society outweigh the benefits.[13]

Resource depletion, like pollution, also carries a hidden cost: that of depriving future generations of access to limited natural resources, such as oil and old-growth timber. If future generations were alive now, they could bid in the market for the resources, forcing prices up and encouraging people today to use less. Instead, resource prices stay myopically low, creating an additional incentive to consume them as if there were no tomorrow. Including the hidden cost of oil depletion, for instance, would push the price tag for driving even higher.

Though the exact dollar values reached in these studies are clearly open to debate, the conclusions that prices often hide true costs is inescapable. If the market cost of gasoline doubled in the United States and the price of pollution rose tenfold in Germany, environmental destruction—and its societal costs—would drop dramatically, and overall economic performance would improve.

Yet worldwide, governments actually subsidize environmental destruction. Some, though not all, of these subsidies appear to be on their way out. The U.S. government, under the antiquated 1872 Mining Law, sells land laden with billion-dollar deposits of gold, platinum, and other metals at the 1872 prices of $6 or $12 per hectare and foots the bill—now estimated at $32–72 billion—for cleaning up pollution from abandoned mines. In California, landowners can buy water that costs the federal government $49 per thousand cubic meters to deliver and that can be worth as much as $325 on the open market sometimes for as little as $2.80. Germany provides $4.6 billion in subsidies to the domestic coal industry, though this may be phased out after 2000.[14]

Centrally planned economies have long provided heavy subsidies for environmental destruction. Of the estimated $230 billion in global fossil subsidies in 1991, fully $172 billion occurred in the Soviet Union, $14 billion in China, and $9.5 billion in Poland. The subsidies propped up state-run energy monopolies, letting them keep their prices low, encouraging wasteful energy use, and leading to serious environmental problems ranging from acid rain to water pollution. Nevertheless, as former Eastern bloc countries reduce government involvement in the economy, most are now lowering or eliminating subsidies for fossil fuels, agriculture, and other activities—which is one reason that coal use fell 33 percent in the former Soviet Union between 1989 and 1994, oil use declined 44 percent, and fertilizer use, 55 percent.[15]

Many developing countries have also heavily subsidized pesticide, fertilizer, electricity, and water use. And they have financed logging, drilling, and mining, particularly in "underdeveloped" rural areas where natural resources are accessible, where residents are generally poor and powerless, and where the temptation to ignore the environmental impact of resource extraction is greatest. Well-drilling is still subsidized in the Indian state of Tamil Nadu, for instance, though water tables there are falling. In 1985, Egypt, Senegal, and Indonesia all covered more than 80 percent of the cost of pesticides for farmers; since then, however, Indonesia has joined other countries in working to scale back these subsidies. Brazil once cut income taxes by up to 50 percent for investors who plowed the credits into developing the Amazon region, but Brazilian officials believe that the termination of the credits in 1988 contributed to the deforestation slowdown that began at that time.[16]

One estimate put the global total for subsidies for activities with environmental side effects at roughly $800 billion a year in the early nineties, though this number has probably fallen since the collapse of the Eastern bloc. Eliminating the hundreds of billions of dollars of subsidies that remain, however, would allow governments to cut the tax burden on the global economy instantly by perhaps 5 percent or more. In many countries, that would do more than any tax or permit charge yet to protect the environment.[17]

THE RISE OF MARKET MECHANISMS

Like the nineteenth-century income tax innovators, policymakers in many parts of the world are once again tinkering with the tax code. From water pollution taxes in the Netherlands to air pollution levies in China, hundreds of environmental taxes are now in use, most less than 15 years old. And a few countries have used these levies to fund cuts in income and payroll taxes. These forays into environmental taxation have generally been cautious, and some have run into serious problems. But the learning process has begun. Policymakers are participating in a process as old as civilization: adapting the tax code to the times. Like the millennia-old levies on trade and land, the mainstays of today's tax codes are unlikely to disappear, although they may decline in importance.

This development is also a major change for those charged with protecting the environment. During the last 30 years, governments have generally preferred legal codes over tax codes in addressing environmental problems—writing prescriptive rules and standards on everything from sewage treatment to pesticide production. Regulatory and fiscal approaches to environmental policy each have their own strengths and weaknesses. Yet it seems clear that governments have not exploited market approaches to their full potential, while they have sometimes overstretched regulation. The challenge that many countries are now taking up is to find a better balance between the two.

Environmental regulators have scored some important successes in the last several decades. In Western Europe, for example, they can point to a 35-percent reduction in emissions of sulfur dioxide (SO_2), a major acid rain ingredient, between 1970 and 1990, due substantially to rules requiring flue gas scrubbers in coal plants. In the United States, tightening tailpipe emissions standards for new cars has cut automobile emissions of nitrogen oxides (a smog and acid rain precursor) by 46 percent and carbon monoxide by 60 percent, despite a 65-percent increase in kilometers driven.[18]

More generally, direct government involvement is often important for protecting the public interest. If waste incinerators continue to be built, for instance, they are likely to be disproportionately located in poor and minority neighborhoods unless these communities have the legal means to protect themselves. Likewise, laws—not market forces—are what protect endangered species, manage nuclear waste, and ban pollutants that may be deemed unacceptable in any amount, such as DDT or dioxins. Finally, neither rigid laws nor taxes will suffice to manage complex ecosystems such as forests and fisheries; that will take more dynamic institutions.

Most studies of environmental regulation have found that it does businesses surprisingly little harm. For example, between 1970 and 1990, the U.S. industries that spent the most on pollution control fared significantly better than average in global competition, according to Robert Repetto, an economist at the World Resources Institute in Washington, D.C. The prod of new pollution rules often stimulates companies to change and innovate, making them more, not less, competitive, argues Michael Porter of the Harvard Business School. When they work to cut resource waste, companies often discover ways to reduce financial waste and create better products.[19]

Governments have not exploited market approaches to their full potential, while they have sometimes overstretched regulation.

Engineers at ICI Americas, based in Wilmington, Delaware, discovered just such a connection when they redesigned supermarket refrigeration equipment to run on a substitute for ozone-depleting chemicals due to be phased out in industrial countries at the end of 1995: the new equipment is up to 10 percent more energy-efficient.[20]

Nevertheless, regulations are increasingly being pushed beyond their limits. Because they focus on means rather than ends, they tend to discourage innovation. And though they may work well when there is a front-runner solution to a problem (such as putting catalytic converters on cars), they tend to break down in the face of complexity. A joint study by the U.S. Environmental Protection Agency (EPA) and the Amoco Corporation documented an example of this at the company's Yorktown, Virginia, refinery. Regulations required Amoco to build a $31-million wastewater treatment plant to stop emissions of cancer-causing benzene into the air. Meanwhile, because of a quirk in the law, benzene emissions from the nearby loading dock, where oil was transferred from tankers to the refinery, went unregulated. Had it been allowed to, Amoco could have cut emissions by the same amount at the loading dock for just $6 million. As one exasperated refinery official put it, "Give us a goal to meet rather than all the regulations. . . . That worked in the 1970's, when the pollution problems were much more visible and simpler. It's not working now."[21]

The growing use of environmental taxes and permit systems is one response to this plea. Policymakers in many parts of the world are realizing that whenever they can express their environmental goals in a single number—how many tons of benzene should be permitted into an airshed each year, for example, or how much water pumped from an aquifer—and whenever pollution or depletion rates can be estimated, market-oriented approaches can efficiently replace many regulations. Such quantifiable problems include urban smog, acid rain, overfishing, depletion and pollution of ground and surface waters, and emissions of airborne toxics, ozone-depleting chemicals, and greenhouse gases.

In the Netherlands, a tax system has reduced industrial pollution of rivers and lakes since the mid-seventies. Gradually rising charges for heavy metal emissions have spurred companies to cut emissions while letting them figure out the cheapest ways to do so. Between 1976 and 1991, total emissions of lead, mercury, and other heavy metals fell by 83–97 percent, primarily because of the charges, according to statistical analysis. (See Figure 10–2.) Generally the companies for whom cleaning up was cheapest did it the most. The enterprises may also have passed part of the taxes on to their consumers through higher prices, causing them to lose business—another way to reduce emissions from the factories.

And heightened demand for pollution control equipment has spurred Dutch manufacturers to develop better and cheaper models, bringing down the costs of pollution control and making the Netherlands a global leader in this market. The taxes have in effect sought the path of least economic resistance in cleaning up the country's waters.[22]

Instead of taxing pollution or resource depletion, some governments are auctioning off permits for the right to pollute or deplete resources. To phase out the use of chlorofluorocarbons, Singapore has been auctioning off limited and declining numbers of permits for producing or importing the chemicals on a quarterly basis. It does the same for new cars, to control the crowded city-state's automobile fleet. (In 1992, the cost of a permit represented about a quarter of the price of a new Honda Civic.)[23]

Through a permit system, society can impose a ceiling on the amount of pollution or resource use that will take place each year, and then allow the market to settle on a price for it. In contrast, with ecological taxes, governments set the price and let the market decide the

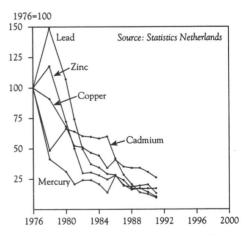

Figure 10-2. Industrial Discharges of Selected Heavy Metals into Surface Waters, The Netherlands, 1976-91

amount. But these "market mechanisms" are more alike than different: they can both raise money for the government, and they both use the market to discourage ecological destruction.

Most governments that have used permits, however, have given them away to companies rather than sell them, and then have let the firms trade the permits among themselves, creating a market for pollution or resource use. In 1992, EPA created the world's largest such trading system, designed to cut utilities' and other plants' total SO_2 emissions to roughly half the 1980 level by 2000. It preallocated almost all the permits to companies, based on their past emissions. A company that wants to pollute above its initial allocation has to buy permits from one that has cut back (by investing in energy efficiency, installing scrubbers, or switching to low-sulfur coal or natural gas). This flexibility will save industry an estimated $1.9–3.1 billion a year by 2002 compared with the traditional regulatory approach. But by giving away valuable permits, the government in effect subsidizes industry for past emissions even as it taxes it for current ones, making pollution-intensive products such as electricity seem cheaper to consumers than they really are.[24]

Surprisingly, some of the countries with the least experience with market economics—former and current centrally planned economies—levy what are the world's most sophisticated ecological taxes. Pollution tax codes in China, Estonia, Poland, and Russia now cover hundreds of air and water pollutants, toxic and radioactive waste, and even noise. In Poland, these revenues are relatively high, at 1 percent of total tax receipts. These systems have developed over the last 20 years out of a communist tradition of using fines to enforce environmental standards (at least in the breach), and in response to the particu-

larly ruinous environmental toll of central planning. They are used mostly for funding environmental protection agencies, as well as for grants and subsidized loans to industry for pollution control investments.[25]

Some governments are auctioning off permits for the right to pollute or deplete resources.

These pollution levy systems are, however, often less impressive in practice than on paper. Emissions below officially permitted levels are usually exempted from taxation. Corruption and inflation in the nineties have softened the bite of most of the taxes, so that paying the tax is often cheaper than pollution control. In addition, many companies are still state-run and pass their costs on to customers or the central government, making them less responsive to market signals. Nevertheless, the tax systems are a foundation for what could eventually become a set of robust environmental taxes.[26]

Many developing countries use environmental market mechanisms, but rarely with the same sophistication. As part of its effort to get the lead out of gasoline, Malaysia has adjusted its gas taxes to make leaded fuel 2.8 percent more expensive than unleaded. Partly as a result, the market share of unleaded gas has shot from 0 to 60 percent since 1991. Since lead has been linked both to emphysema and to lower intelligence test scores among children, there seems little doubt that the modest charge has easily paid for itself. Thailand and Turkey also favor unleaded fuel with lower taxes.[27]

Several developing countries use tradable permits to allocate renewable resources. Chile has auctioned off tradable fishing permits for a few fisheries, and farmers in parts of Algeria, Brazil, Chile, India, Mexico, Morocco, Pakistan, Peru, and Tunisia trade water rights in this way. Many of these systems developed without formal government involvement and are quite old. In the southern part of the Brazilian state of Ceará, farmers have traded water rights for at least a century.[28]

Among industrial countries, Japan has made perhaps the least use of market mechanisms, though it does use revenues from an SO_2 tax to compensate air pollution victims. Its tradition of close cooperation between industry and government is apparently antithetical to the arm's-length relationship implicit in taxation.[29]

In contrast, there are now hundreds of ecological taxes in other western industrial countries, on everything from plastic shopping bags and motor oil to carbon emissions. Many of the charges are too modest to affect behavior much, and are used more to fund environmental programs. But increasingly they are being seen as environmental tools in their own right—and ones that replenish rather than drain government treasuries. For example, the city of Victoria, British Columbia, instituted a trash tax of $1.20–2.10 per bag in 1992, along with a strong recycling program. Household waste generation fell by 18 percent within 12 months. The United States, Denmark, and Australia have combined regulations and taxes to phase out production of ozone-depleting chemicals. Since it started in 1990, the U.S. tax raised $3 billion by late 1994.[30]

One group of environmental taxes easily brings in the most money in industrial countries, however: taxes on motor fuels, which raise more than $170 billion a year, or 2.6 percent of total tax revenues, mostly from gasoline sales. The United States has by far the lowest gasoline tax, averaging 9¢ per liter (34¢ per gallon) in 1994, with taxes in Australia, Canada, Japan, and New Zealand in the range of 20–30¢ per liter (75¢–$1.14 per gallon). In the European Union, though, taxes of 40–85¢ per liter ($1.51–3.22 per gallon) push gasoline prices two to four times higher than in the United States. Many factors, including population density, city planning, and the convenience of public transit and bike path networks, shape people's decisions about driving. But where gasoline is cheaper, it is clearly used more. (See Table 10–2.)[31]

One of the most innovative tax initiatives to date appeared in the heavily polluted state of Louisiana in 1991. The state government began grading petrochemical and other companies on a scale from 50 to 100, based on their history of compliance with environmental laws, the number of people they employed for the amount of pollution they generated, and related factors. Companies with low scores lost up to half the standard tax deduction for new investment. In the first year, 12 firms agreed to cut toxic emissions enough to lower the state's total by 8.2 percent. Many of the pollution reduction plans cost the companies more than they earned in tax credits, showing that the fear of a tarnished public image was giving the tax system added kick. In another testament to the system's power, businesses disliked it so much that they fought successfully for its repeal in 1992.[32]

Tradable permits are also catching on in industrial countries. Following the lead EPA set with its sulfur trading system, authorities in Massachusetts and Southern California are instituting trading systems to reduce smog-causing chemicals from factories and power plants. New Zealand governs almost all its fisheries with tradable permits, and Australia, the United States, and Canada are doing so increasingly.[33]

Table 10-2. Gasoline Tax, Price, and Use, Selected Industrial Countries, 1993

Country	Tax	Total Price[1]	Use
	(dollars per liter[2])		(liters per person)
United States	0.09	0.34	1,600
Canada	0.21	0.46	1,124
Australia	0.24	0.53	936
Japan	0.30	0.65	364
Germany	0.48	0.66	497
Sweden	0.55	0.78	627
Italy	0.72	1.00	400
Portugal	0.85	1.21	235

[1]Prices are for premium unleaded, except for Japan, where only regular unleaded is sold.   [2]Converted from domestic currencies on the basis of purchasing power parities.
SOURCES: Organisation for Economic Co-operation and Development, *Energy Prices and Taxes* (Paris: various editions), United Nations, *Energy Statistics Yearbook* (New York: 1995).

But it is in Northern Europe that the use of market mechanisms is flourishing most. In 1991, Sweden enacted the world's first environmental tax shift. It reduced total income taxes by $1.65 billion—1.4 percent of all tax revenues—while initiating a tax on SO_2 of $3,050 per ton, a tax on CO_2 worth $120 per ton of carbon by 1995, and other environmental charges. After one year of the SO_2 tax, sulfur emissions dropped by 16 percent. In 1993 and 1995, Denmark followed suit, introducing a 3-percent shift in the government funding burden from income taxes to an array of new ecological levies, including ones on water use, pesticides, CO_2, and batteries.[34]

As of late 1995, the ruling coalition in the Netherlands planned to shift 0.7 percent of total tax revenue from labor to energy, and policymakers in Austria were considering a small 0.3–0.5 percent shift from labor or income to energy. Norway, which already has a carbon tax larger than Sweden's, will also consider a tax shift in 1996. And in a surprise reversal that could signal the waking of a sleeping giant, German Minister of Economics Günter Rexrodt also endorsed a tax shift in 1995. If Germany joins the bandwagon, much of Western Europe could soon follow. The burgeoning support for tax shifting in Europe may mark the beginning of a truly global movement.[35]

MAKING THE MOST OF THE MARKET

Like many powerful tools, market mechanisms need to be handled with care. Applied in their purest forms they can, for example, impose impossible pollution measurement burdens on businesses, cost the poor disproportionately, or create economic upheaval if adopted too quickly. Just as governments modify the workings of the market to advance societal goals besides efficiency, such as the right to a safe work environment, and to correct market imperfections, such as the tendency to form monopolies, they will need to do the same to make the most of environmental market mechanisms.

Some of the greatest practical and philosophical challenges to market mechanisms relate to measurement. Calculating pollution and the harm it causes is often difficult or expensive, so governments that want to use taxes or permits have to measure what they can, and estimate what they cannot. For example, many industrial countries already test cars periodically to measure engine emissions; these tests could be combined with odometer readings to provide a practical, if rough, basis for a tax. Similarly, the Scandinavian countries tax fertilizer sales rather than the actual amount of fertilizers that drain off of farmlands and into surface waters, since that would be impractical to gauge.[36]

Even after the effects of pollution or resource use are estimated, translating them into money terms is also difficult—but again, this should not necessarily prevent the use of market mechanisms. It seems almost meaningless to ask what the cost—in cash terms—is to the community of Nikel, Russia, of living downwind from the world's largest nickel processing plant and suffering the world's highest birth defect rate. Assessing the oil needs of future generations and the weight to give their needs seems equally difficult.[37]

A tax or permit trading system for global problems such as greenhouse gas emissions will work best if instituted uniformly around the world.

The paradox is that policymakers already make such choices routinely. Whenever they regulate, and even when they decide not to, they make implicit trade-offs between jobs and health, profits and nature. Market mechanisms

force them to make the judgments more explicitly, but in the end, the important thing is that they do their best to choose fair trade-offs.[38]

As with any revenue-raising measure, enforcement is crucial, as is the accountability of the enforcers. In New Zealand, the government has often issued too many fishing permits, under pressure from large fishing companies, resulting in overfishing. Fortunately, environmentalists and small fishers do have a voice in the public process that determines total catch levels, and have fought successfully to lower quotas totals in a growing number of fisheries. Yet in 1992, it was estimated that up to 80 percent of the fish sold domestically in New Zealand passed through the black market, evading permit limits. Monitoring actual catches by fleets of boats that operate over thousands of square kilometers, often at night, has proved difficult and expensive.[39]

Interestingly, environmental taxes are sometimes easier to enforce than other taxes, especially in the developing world. Systemic corruption among tax collectors there often turns income taxes—even when they appear progressive—into ways to draw money from lower-income taxpayers up through the bureaucracy and into the pockets of rich elites at the top. In contrast, those who pay environmental taxes are often members of a small, well-defined group (such as utilities or oil refiners), so efforts to enforce the taxes and audit the enforcers can be more concentrated and therefore more effective.[40]

To work most effectively, taxes and trading systems also need to match the geographic scope of the problems they are trying to solve. Tax levels or permit allocations aimed at smog prevention, for example, can vary from city to city. In contrast, a tax or permit trading system for global problems such as greenhouse gas emissions will work best if instituted uniformly around the world. Violating this principle of geographic appropriateness, the U.S. SO_2 trading system is nationwide, though it is intended to solve a set of regional acid rain problems. One New York utility found itself embroiled in controversy when it decided to cut emissions and sell its extra permits upwind to several midwestern utilities, provoking a lawsuit from the state government because the plan would actually increase acid rain in New York.[41]

Market mechanisms need to respect the legal and cultural landscape as well. Unlike pollution and large-scale extraction of nonrenewable resources, the use of renewable resources is traditional almost everywhere. Without special provisions, market mechanisms can disrupt traditional and sustainable ways of life. In Chilean water auctions, begun in 1981, most of the permits ended up in the hands of a few well monied bidders such as major fruit growers; fortunately for traditional farmers, the government had preallocated water rights to them based on their historical use levels.[42]

Allocations based on "historical use," of course, will only be as just as the history they are based on. The indigenous Maori had been fishing the coastal waters of New Zealand for centuries before westerners began joining them in large numbers in the thirties. After World War II, larger fishing boats became more common and total catch exploded. By the seventies, many fisheries were being overfished. When the New Zealand government put most of the country's coastal fisheries under permit trading systems in 1986, it allocated the permits on the basis of how much each fisher had caught in the early eighties. Since total catch had to be scaled back—up to 80 percent for some species—many Maori received shares too small to live on, despite their ancestral claims. Meanwhile, the relative newcomers ended up ahead of where they had started a few decades

earlier. The Maori turned to the courts, where they fought successfully to increase their permanent allocations in 1989 and 1992.[43]

Another subtle but important consideration in designing permit systems is whether the permits should be good for a certain amount of pollution or resource use, or for a certain amount per year for many years or even forever. Buying a long-term permit, like purchasing a house instead of renting, requires much more cash up front, which can handicap many small resource users without deep pockets or easy credit access. In addition, since most tradable fishing and water rights created so far have been permanent ones, they have often become private property in their new owners' eyes. If authorities decide in the future that it is in the public interest to revoke or reallocate some of these rights—for instance, by shifting water from agriculture to wetlands or cities—they may face legal challenges that they are confiscating private property. Such a challenge, if successful, would make these permit systems a policy approach of no return. In contrast, permits in most pollution trading systems are each worth a certain amount and are allocated on an ongoing basis, which makes it much easier for the systems to evolve over time.[44]

One of the greatest public concerns about environmental market mechanisms in industrial countries is that they tend to be regressive, taking proportionally more money from the poor than from the rich. A $100-per-ton carbon tax in the United States would use up on average 3.7 percent of the spending budget of the poorest 10 percent of households, for instance, but only 2.3 percent among the richest 10 percent. This is because poorer people spend more of their money on tangible necessities such as housing, food, and forms of transport that are made and moved by machine, and thus entail more pollution and resource use than do intangible luxuries such as theater tickets or restaurant meals. (In developing countries, however, the poor depend much less on manufactured goods, so environmental taxes there primarily impinge on the middle and upper classes.)[45]

To ensure that instituting environmental market mechanisms does not exacerbate inequities, it is therefore critical that policymakers simultaneously address the overall progressivity of the tax code. For example, if governments cut wage or sales taxes, which are also regressive, or make income taxes more progressive, they can minimize the impact of environmental taxes on the poor. They can also increase funding for programs that help the poor pay their heating bills or that put insulation and efficient heaters into their homes. Each measure will reach distinct but overlapping populations, so they need to be combined carefully for greatest benefit.[46]

Distributional issues also arise from the effects of environmental policy on industry. The trade-offs can be especially difficult to justify in terms of policy and politics when companies' environmental costs rise while those of their foreign competitors—who may operate beyond the reach of a tax or permit system—do not. This is why Denmark, Norway, and Sweden, all small nations that depend heavily on trade, provide a variety of exemptions for industry from carbon taxes, and why the energy tax increases contemplated in Austria and the Netherlands in late 1995 would also fall primarily on consumers. To provide similar protection, the United States backs up its ozone depleter tax with import duties on products made with or containing the taxed chemicals.[47]

The biggest potential obstacles to such border corrections come from international free trade agreements such as the Maastricht Treaty, which created the European Union (E.U.), and the revised General Agreement on Tariffs and Trade, which created the World Trade Organization (WTO). Both treaties work to prohibit the use of taxes and subsidies that protect domestic industries. Yet the European Commission set an important precedent in 1995 by upholding Danish CO_2 tax rebates for energy-intensive industries as environmental policies, even as it acknowledged that they apparently contravened E.U. trade laws. Similarly, in 1994, the WTO's predecessor court upheld the U.S. "gas guzzler" tax even though it mostly affected inefficient Japanese- and European-made luxury cars, arguing that the tax was not intended to restrain trade. Whether the WTO will permit environmental tax rebates on exports, though, is still unclear.[48]

In the long run, the best solution is for countries to harmonize environmental taxes and to integrate permit trading systems as much as possible, especially when they address international problems such as acid rain, ozone depletion, and global warming. Until economic superpowers such as Germany, Japan, and the United States join the movement toward the use of market mechanisms, though, the freedom of small, pioneering countries to tax imported products and provide rebates for exported ones will be crucial to the continued development of the approach worldwide.

Underlying the international competitiveness issues is an unavoidable tension between the need to make major changes in how economies operate and the desire to minimize the pain of adjustment. If humanity is to create an industrial society in which people do not injure each other and their descendants simply by getting up and going to work each day, the global economy will have to change radically. Many industries will have to reinvent themselves. Some may have to disappear altogether. It will be nearly impossible, for example, to get carbon emissions down to the level needed for climate stability without phasing out the coal industry.[49]

The decline of unsustainable industries will inevitably lead to economic hardship. The operations of resource-based industries often dot the landscapes of rural regions endowed with oil or iron, and company towns sprout up around them. As these industries go, so go many of the regional—or, as in the case of Saudi Arabia, national—economies they support. The collapse of an entire regional economy can force workers to choose between long-term joblessness and moving away. It is important, therefore, that governments phase major tax changes in as slowly as environmental circumstances permit, to give people time to adjust. In the face of long-term problems such as reducing carbon emissions, businesses can slowly shift from resource- and pollution-intensive ways of operating—for example, from paper production to paper recycling. Workers in dying industries would have time to retrain, perhaps with government assistance, and move to more sustainable industries such as solar energy and recycling, or even to retire and let their children move on. (See Chapter 9.)

GOING THE DISTANCE

Taken together, environmental market mechanisms today have the distinct look of a revolutionary policy approach about to explode out of its early experimental phase and into the mainstream. The limited experience so far has been valuable in showing how market mechanisms work, and how they work best. Now the challenge for policymakers is not so much the intellectual one of understanding the theory and practice of market mechanisms. It is, rather, the political one of articulating a vision of fiscal policy reform that addresses the major economic problems of our age, and of building effective coalitions to make that vision a reality.

In the face of urgent environmental problems, governments can phase in many of the charges in just a few years— as, for example, the U.S. government did with its ozone depleter tax. Market mechanisms aimed at problems that will require longer-term change, such as tax or permit systems for greenhouse gas emissions, could be implemented more gradually. But even in these cases, the quicker humanity begins to engineer change, the more predictable and gradual—and thus less costly—the process can be.

It is important that governments phase major tax changes in as slowly as environmental circumstances permit, to give people time to adjust.

Over time, as taxes (or permit charges) on solid waste production, water use, air and water pollution, greenhouse gas emissions, fishing, and logging were phased in to reflect the societal costs of these activities, governments would garner revenues running into the hundreds of billions of dollars annually. Eliminating environmentally destructive subsidies would swell the fund even more. Once the taxes reached their full rates, or the quota allocations shrank to sustainable levels, however— in some cases, this would be well into the next century—falling pollution and resource depletion rates would bring revenues down too. In counterpoint, other taxes could shrink at first, but would eventually need to climb again. Yet these changes would not be rapid by historical standards: most of today's taxes were minor or nonexistent a century ago.

In terms of fiscal and environmental impacts, market mechanisms that effectively addressed carbon emissions would loom over all others.

In response to the price signals, a sustainable industrial economy would gradually take shape. In the ideal, people and businesses would increasingly conserve resources and recycle wastes, making the concept of pollution nearly obsolete. They would draw renewable energy from the sun or the earth's hot interior, wood from sustainably managed forests, and only as much food and water as global nutrient and hydrologic cycles could sustainably provide. Like an ecosystem, the global economy would gradually evolve in ways too complicated to envision, reaching for the day when it could function healthily within its natural limits.

In terms of fiscal and environmental impacts, market mechanisms that effectively addressed one environmental problem—carbon emissions—would loom over all others. A global tax collected by each country would likely work better than a tradable permit system, because it would provide businesses and consumers with a stable, predictable charge for emissions, with the acceptable loss of some year-to-year certainty about total global emissions. The Framework Convention on Climate Change signed in 1992 at the Rio Earth Summit provides much of the international legal and political machinery to design and implement such a tax. To be equitable, the revenue would have to be redistributed globally on a per capita basis. This would result in a large cash transfer from rich countries to poorer ones that are responsible for much less of the CO_2 buildup in the global atmosphere but that would suffer at least equally from the consequences. As the U.N. Development Programme has noted: "Such flows would be neither aid nor charity. They would be the outcome of a free market mechanism that penalizes the richer nations' overconsumption of the global commons." Such a huge transfer of wealth, however, seems unlikely.[50]

Since global climate change requires long-term solutions, a carbon tax could start low and then gradually climb over the next century. A tax of $22.50 a ton in 1996 that then rose by 5 percent a year for 50 years or more, for instance, would roughly suffice to stabilize global carbon emissions through 2040 and nearly eliminate them by 2100, according to a recent survey of five economic models by the Energy Modeling Forum at Stanford University. Revenues would peak in 2040–60 at $700 billion to $1.8 trillion. Meanwhile, economic growth would be only 0.04 percent lower each year on average. (Some models project more growth; others less.) Since climate models predict that some warming would still occur unless emissions fell even faster, starting the carbon tax at a higher level—perhaps $50 a ton—could be worth the trade-off of somewhat lower economic growth for significantly more climate risk protection.[51]

To date, an imbalance that has limited the scope of most market mechanisms is that the people who stand to lose from them—typically, environmentally destructive businesses—are usually much better organized and financed than the those who stand to gain—usually the general public. For politicians, charging for pollution or resource use has often meant going out on a limb: on one side they have faced adamant industry opposition; on the other, a poorly informed public. The politically convenient thing to do has been to return the tax revenues to industry in some other form, or, equivalently, to give away permits for free, in effect subsidizing companies for past destructive behavior.[52]

Sometimes politicians have been able to designate the funds for environmental protection programs rather than return them to industry. Such earmarking can be important in developing countries where environmental agencies are often underfunded, and can be popular with voters who mistrust governments to spend the money wisely on their own. But in the long run, this approach tends to limit market mechanisms to a minor role in addressing many environmental problems.[53]

Governments would only be able to absorb the revenues from carbon taxes and other large market mechanisms if they applied them to funding general government activities, cutting budget deficits, or cutting other taxes. Environmental charge proposals would then enter a broader realm of economic, fiscal, and political issues. Economic modeling has shown that the way these large revenue flows are used can substantially determine the effects of market mechanisms on employment, economic growth, and development. It can also determine their political fate.[54]

When President Bill Clinton proposed an energy tax in 1993, its costs were clear to those who would pay it, but since it was to be used to cut the deficit, its benefits were much fuzzier, even to the sharpest economists. Political support for the tax was thus weak. Major manufacturers and energy producers launched a multimillion-dollar lobbying campaign against the tax—the largest such effort ever mounted to stop a bill in

U.S. history—and discovered a President quick to compromise. Many voters also disliked the Clinton bill. Tellingly, though, the only scrap of it that survived the congressional battle was a 1.1¢ per liter (4.3¢ per gallon) gasoline and diesel tax, a levy that came largely out of the pockets of consumers, not businesses. Even when budget deficits are large, it may be more pragmatic, therefore, to shift the burden of taxation rather than increase it.[55]

An energy tax proposal by Greenpeace Germany in 1994 exemplifies the powerful mix of ideas that has given impetus to revenue-neutral ecological tax shifting in Western Europe. It envisions a tax that would push energy prices up by roughly 7 percent a year over at least 15 years. The government would pool the tax receipts taken directly from consumers and then mail "eco bonus" checks worth a flat amount per person to every home in the country. Poorer households, which spend less than average on energy, would gain from the system, while rich households would lose—though very slightly compared with their high incomes. Likewise, industry would get its money back in the form of across-the-board payroll tax cuts. Meanwhile, total energy use would fall by 2010 to 14 percent below what it would be without tax reform, according to the German Institute for Economic Research, a major economic think tank in Berlin.[56]

In contrast to the Clinton tax, the Greenpeace proposal has exploited divisions within industry, and has garnered popular support. Under it, industries that use the most energy and the least labor, such as chemical manufacturers, steelmakers, and coal miners, would see their costs rise. They were responsible for 46 percent of value added in private industry in 1988, but only 42 percent of employment. Cleaner, more labor-intensive, industries—from education to telecommunications—represented 50 percent of output and 54 of employment; they would save money. The automobile industry, with 4 percent of output and employment, would break even. Thus a comfortable majority of the electorate in private industry would work for companies that would break even or gain. (See Table 10–3.) In addition, the tax is projected to create 600,000 jobs within 10 years.[57]

Not surprisingly, the proposal has won support from many businesses and labor groups, tipping the political balance toward tax shifting in Germany. The appliance maker AEG, the Tupperware company, and a dozen other big businesses have signed on with environmentalists to fight for tax reform. Even the head of BMW has endorsed the idea, perhaps because he believes, like U.S. automakers, that energy taxes will encourage consumers to invest a little extra in more energy-efficient cars. The German metal workers' union IG-Metall, the largest union in Europe, has also voiced strong support. With employment already falling steadily in the German iron and steel industries, it is clear that the status quo offers little security for union members. Payroll tax cuts and an accelerated transition to a sustainable, more labor-intensive steel recycling industry would do them more good. It would create more jobs—and jobs that would last.[58]

In other parts of the world, the tax cuts in tax shift proposals could address different nonenvironmental goals. In the United States, tax shifts away from labor would help fight the stagnating and declining wages that now worry much of the electorate. In developing countries—especially India and China, which burn large amounts of coal—carbon

Table 10-3. Selected Losers and Winners Under Greenpeace Germany Tax Shift Proposal

Industry	Share of Value Added[1]	Share of Employment[1]	Price Change[2]
	(percent)	(percent)	(percent)
Industries That Lose	45.7	42.1	—
Coal[3]	0.6	0.8	+50.7
Chemicals	3.7	2.3	+12.5
Iron and Steel	0.8	0.7	+ 5.0
Automobile Industry	4.1	4.1	0.0
Industries That Gain	50.1	53.8	—
Construction	3.9	4.8	− 0.5
Electrical Equipment	4.5	4.8	− 1.4
Postal and Telecommunications	2.6	2.2	− 5.7

[1]Percentages are of private-sector output and employment only, for 1988. Columns may not add to 100 due to rounding.   [2]After 15 years of tax shift phase-in, assuming industry costs and savings are fully passed on to customers.   [3]Coal production subsidies, unless phased out, would still exceed taxes.
SOURCES: Statistisches Bundesamt, *Volkswirtschaftliche Gesamtrechnungen* (Stuttgart: Metzler-Poeschel, 1990); Michael Kohlhaas, German Institute for Economic Research (DIW), Berlin, private communication and printout, July 6, 1995; Hans Wessels, DIW, Berlin, private communication and printout, August 10, 1995; Worldwatch estimates based on these sources.

taxes and other environmental market mechanisms could become major sources of revenue, allowing governments there to reduce their dependence on trade, sales, and corporate profits taxes, which discriminate against the poor and hamper investment.[59]

Market-based tools enjoy a unique double aspect: they simultaneously shape behavior and raise revenues that can be put to other uses. This allows them to serve both environmental sustainability and shorter-term goals. Tools, though, do no good in themselves. Forcing economic development onto an ecologically sound path will also take leadership at every level of government. It is critical that policymakers at the national level—especially those of economic superpowers, such as the United States, Germany, and Japan—marshal domestic as well as international support for action. It will be politically difficult for countries with smaller economies to go far on their own if the international competitiveness of major domestic industries is at risk.

History's most effective political leaders have been those who found ways to work within the context of their times, yet toward a vision of what had to follow. Market mechanisms offer one powerful way to strike the political bargains and make the major policy changes needed to meet the great economic challenge of our time: reconciling the power of industrialism with the protection of human health and the environment. To use these tools well, today's leaders will have to combine pragmatism and vision in ways worthy of the billions of people whose health and livelihoods hang in the balance. With stakes so high, we should demand no less from our leaders.

Notes

Chapter 1. The Acceleration of History

1. The concept of the acceleration of history was first introduced with a brief discussion in the overview chapter of Lester R. Brown, Nicholas Lenssen, and Hal Kane, *Vital Signs 1995* (New York: W.W. Norton & Company, 1995).

2. Joel E. Cohen, "How Many People Can Earth Hold?" *Discover*, November 1992.

3. Current and historical world economic information in 1987 dollars from Lester R. Brown, "World Economy Expanding Faster," in Brown, Lenssen, and Kane, op. cit. note 1, with data derived from World Bank and International Monetary Fund tables; information on East Asia and China from International Monetary Fund, *World Economic Outlook May 1995* (Washington, D.C.: 1995).

4. U.N. Development Programme, *Human Development Report 1994* (New York: Oxford University Press, 1994).

5. These trends are all documented in Brown, Lenssen, and Kane, op. cit. note 1.

6. Information on fisheries decline based on statistical data in the U.N. Food and Agriculture Organization (FAO) fisheries database, FISHSTAT-PC, FAO Fisheries Statistics Division, Rome, 1994. Estimate of 100 million tons sustainable catch from FAO-sponsored publication, J.A. Gulland, ed., *The Fish Resources of the Ocean* (Surrey, U.K.: Fishing News Ltd., 1971). This estimate is meant to include traditional bony fish ranging from commonly eaten species such as cod and had-dock to the small shoaling species such as the Peruvian anchovy. Estimate also based on FAO, *Fishery Statistics: Catches and Landings* (Rome: various years). The 1989 fish harvest of 100 million tons includes both the marine catch and aquaculture production. Annual population increase from Population Reference Bureau (PRB), *1995 World Population Data Sheet* (Washington, D.C.: 1995).

7. Greenpeace quote from William Branigin, "Global Accord Puts Curbs on Fishing," *Washington Post*, August 4, 1995.

8. Sandra Postel, *Last Oasis: Facing Water Scarcity* (New York: W.W. Norton & Company, 1992).

9. Sandra Postel, "Where Have All the Rivers Gone?" *World Watch*, May/June 1995.

10. See Chapter 3 for a discussion of growing conflicts over shared river systems.

11. Kenton Miller and Laura Tangley, *Trees of Life: Saving Tropical Forests and Their Biological Wealth* (Boston, Mass.: Beacon Press, 1991).

12. Figure of 1,000 tons from FAO, *Yield Response to Water* (Rome: 1979).

13. Norman Myers, *Ultimate Security: The Environmental Basis of Political Stability* (New York: W.W. Norton & Company, 1993).

14. U.S. Bureau of the Census projections, published in Francis Urban and Ray Nightingale, *World Population by Country and Region, 1950–90, with Projections to 2050* (Washington, D.C.: U.S. Department of Agriculture (USDA), Economic Research Service (ERS),

1993); seafood prices from FAO, *Fishery Statistics: Trade and Commerce* (Rome: various years), with updates from Adele Crispoldi, Fishery Statistician, Fishery Information, Data and Statistics Service, Fisheries Department, FAO, Rome, unpublished printout, September 12, 1994.

15. Figure 1–1 from USDA, *World Agricultural Production* (Washington, D.C., various issues); USDA, ERS, "Production, Supply, and Demand View" (electronic database), Washington, D.C., August 1995; Foreign Agricultural Service, *Grain: World Markets and Trade*, USDA, Washington, D.C., August 1995; grain price information from International Monetary Fund, *International Financial Statistics*, various years.

16. China's grain exports from USDA, *Grain: World Markets and Trade*, op. cit. note 15; grain prices from "Futures Prices," *Wall Street Journal*, various editions.

17. Figure 1–2 from USDA, "World Agricultural Supply and Demand Estimates," Washington, D.C., September 12, 1995.

18. Grain-to-fish conversion ratio from Ross Garnaut and Guonan Ma, East Asian Analytical Unit, Department of Foreign Affairs and Trade, *Grain in China* (Canberra: Australian Government Publishing Service, 1992); grain-to-poultry ratio derived from Robert V. Bishop et al., *The World Poultry Market—Government Intervention and Multilateral Policy Reform* (Washington, D.C.: USDA, 1990); grain-to-pork ratio from Leland Southard, Livestock and Poultry Situation and Outlook Staff, ERS, USDA, Washington, D.C., private communication, April 27, 1992; population of Belgium from PRB, op. cit. note 6; annual growth in seafood catch from Brown, Lenssen, and Kane, op. cit. note 1.

19. USDA, "Production, Supply, and Demand View," op. cit. note 15.

20. Irrigated area from FAO, *Production Yearbooks* (Rome: various years); per capita figures derived from United Nations, Department of International Economic and Social Affairs, *World Population Prospects, 1990* (New York: 1991).

21. Postel, op. cit. note 8.

22. Fertilizer trends from FAO, op. cit. note 20, from FAO, *Fertilizer Yearbooks* (Rome: various years), and from International Fertilizer Industry Association (IFA), *Fertilizer Consumption Report* (Paris: 1992); world grain harvest data from Brown, Lenssen, and Kane, op. cit. note 1.

23. IFA, op. cit. note 22.

24. Figure 1–3 from FAO, op. cit. note 20, from FAO, op. cit. note 22, and from IFA, op. cit. note 22; for declining response to fertilizer, see Duane Chapman and Randy Barker, *Resource Depletion, Agricultural Research, and Development* (Ithaca, N.Y.: Cornell University, 1987).

25. Author's calculations based on USDA, "Production, Supply, and Demand View," op. cit. note 15, and on Bureau of the Census, op. cit. note 14.

26. "Futures Prices," op. cit. note 16; FAO, op. cit. note 14.

27. Consultative Group on International Agricultural Research (CGIAR), "Renewal of the CGIAR: Draft Documents on Major Issues," Ministerial-level meeting documents, CGIAR Secretariat, Washington, D.C., February 9–10, 1995; John Madeley, "Rice—The Next Generation," *Financial Times*, February 18, 1994.

28. Grain prices in China from Martin Wolf, "Zooming in on the Threat of Inflation," *Financial Times*, November 7, 1994; "Vietnam to Limit Exports of Rice for Four Months," *Journal of Commerce*, May 19, 1995.

29. World population electronic database from Ray Nightingale, USDA, ERS, Washington, D.C., July 1995.

30. PRB, op. cit. note 6; Bureau of the Census, op. cit. note 14.

31. Figure 1–4 from Bureau of the Census, op. cit. note 14, from USDA, "Production, Supply, and Demand View", op. cit. note 15, and from USDA, "World Grain Database" (unpublished printout), Washington, D.C., April 1989.

32. Carl Haub, "Population Change in the Former Soviet Republics," *Population Bulletin*, December 1994; Michael Specter, "Plunging Life Expectancy Puzzles Russia," *New York Times*, August 2, 1995; Russia's natural rate of decrease from PRB, op. cit. note 6.

33. FAO, *Food Outlook*, August/September 1995.

34. "Iran: Fewer Means Better," *The Economist*, August 5, 1995; "Peru's Chief Pushes Birth Control, Stirring Dispute," *New York Times*, August 12, 1995.

35. Joseph C. Farman et al., "Large Losses of Total Ozone in Antarctica Reveal Seasonal ClO(x)/NO(x) Interaction," *Nature*, May 16, 1985; Montreal Protocol information from William K. Stevens, "Peril to Ozone Hastens a Ban on Chemicals," *New York Times*, November 26, 1992; "Ministers Approve Stepped Up Timetable to Phase Out Ozone Depleting Substances," *International Environment Reporter*, January 13, 1993; chlorofluorocarbon production estimates from DuPont, Wilmington, Del., private communication.

36. Michael Grubb, "Viewpoint: The Berlin Climate Conference; Shifting Alliances Break Political Deadlock," *EC Energy Monthly*, April 21, 1995; Carol Werner and Jennifer Morgan, "Cities Endorse AOSIS Protocol," *ECO* (NGO Newsletter, Berlin), March 30, 1995.

37. Christopher Flavin, "Storm Warnings: Climate Change Hits the Insurance Industry," *World Watch*, November/December 1994.

38. USDA, op. cit. note 17.

39. Christopher Flavin and Nicholas Lenssen, *Power Surge: Guide to the Coming Energy Revolution* (New York: W.W. Norton & Company, 1994).

40. California wind farm potential from Paul Gipe, Gipe and Associates, Tehachapi, Calif., private communication and printout, April 7, 1994; 1994 wind generator installation estimates (Germany and India) from Birger Madsen, BTM Consult, Ringkobing, Denmark, private communication, Febrary 23, 1995, and from Paul Gipe, Paul Gipe and Associates, Tehachapi, Calif., private communication, February 22, 1995.

41. Madsen, op. cit. note 40; Gipe, February 22, 1995, op. cit, note 40; potential in the three U.S. states from D.L. Elliott, L.L. Windell, and G.L. Gower, *An Assessment of the Available Windy Land Area and Wind Energy Potential in the Contiguous United States* (Richland, Wash.: Pacific Northwest Laboratory, 1991); wind potential in Europe from Andrew Garrad, *Wind Energy in Europe: Time for Action* (Rome: European Wind Energy Association, 1991); hydropower estimate from United Nations, *1990 Energy Statistics Yearbook* (New York: 1992).

42. Joseph Kahn, "China's Next Great Leap: The Family Car," *Wall Street Journal*, June 24, 1994; Sun Shangwu, "Building Eats Up Farmland as More Mouths Need Food," *China Daily*, July 18, 1994; John Griffiths, "Car Production Set to Double by Year 2000," *Financial Times*, July 3, 1995.

43. Figure 1–5 from *Interbike Directory 1995* (Newport Beach, Calif.: Primedia, Inc. 1995), from American Automobile Manufacturers Association (AAMA), *World Motor Vehicle Data*, 1994 ed. (Detroit, Mich.: 1994), from AAMA, *AAMA Motor Vehicle Facts & Figures '94* (Detroit, Mich: 1994), and from John Lawson, Director, DRI/McGraw-Hill, London, private communication, November 23, 1994.

44. Donald O. Mitchell and Merlinda D. Ingco, International Economics Department, *The World Food Outlook* (Washington. D.C.: World Bank, 1993).

45. Ibid.

46. USDA, "Production, Supply, and Demand View," op. cit. note 15.

47. Mario Molina and F. Sherwood Rowland, "Stratospheric Sink for Chlorofluoromethanes: Chlorine Atom Catalysed Destruction of Ozone," *Nature*, June 28, 1974; Farman et al., op. cit. note 35.

48. Lyme's disease from Marc Lappé, *Evolutionary Medicine: Rethinking the Origins of Disease* (San Francisco: Sierra Club Book, 1994); "No One Can Say Why Virus Striking Zaire is So Deadly," *New York Times*, May 13, 1995; "Ebola Outbreak Profoundly Changes Life in Zairian City," *Washington Post*, May 22, 1995; Global Programme on AIDS, "Current and Future Dimensions of the HIV/AIDS Pandemic: A Capsule Summary," World Health Organization, Geneva, 1992.

49. Richard Elliot Benedick, *Ozone Diplomacy: New Directions in Safeguarding the Planet* (Cambridge, Mass.: Harvard University Press, 1991).

50. Fishing fleet subsidy information from FAO, *Marine Fisheries and the Law of the Sea: A Decade of Change*, Fisheries Circular No. 853 (Rome: 1993); coal subsidies in Germany from Organisation for Economic Co-operation and Development, International Energy Agency, *Energy Policies of IEA Countries: 1992 Review* (Paris: 1993).

Chapter 2. Facing Up to the Risks of Climate Change

1. Intergovernmental Panel on Climate Change (IPCC), *The IPCC Assessment of Knowledge Relevant to the Interpretation of Article 2 of the UN Framework Convention on Climate Change: A Synthesis Report* (draft), Geneva, July 31, 1995; Tom M.L. Wigley, "A Successful Prediction?" *Nature*, August 10, 1995.

2. *United Nations Framework Convention on Climate Change, Text* (Geneva: U.N. Environment Programme/World Meteorological Organization Information Unit on Climate Change, 1992); for details on carbon emission trends, see section entitled "Greenhouse Gas Escalator."

3. C.C. Keeling and T.P. Whorf, "Atmospheric CO_2 Records from Sites in the SIO Air Sampling Network," in Thomas A. Boden et al., eds., *Trends '93: A Compendium of Data on Global Change* (Oak Ridge, Tenn.: Oak Ridge National Laboratory, 1994); Timothy Whorf, Scripps Institution of Oceanography, La Jolla, Calif., private communication, February 2, 1995; Thomas E. Graedel and Paul J. Crutzen, *Atmosphere, Climate, and Change* (New York: Scientific American Libraries, 1992); V. Ramanathan et al., "Trace Gas Trends and Their Potential Role in Climate Change," *Journal of Geophysical Research*, June 20, 1985.

4. Heat trapping gas estimate is based on radiative forcing figures for various greenhouse gases contained in IPCC, *Climate Change: The IPCC Scientific Assessment* (New York: Cambridge University Press, 1990); H. Wilson and J. Hansen, "Global and Hemispheric Temperature Anomalies from Instrumental Surface Air Temperature Records," in Boden et al., op. cit. note 3; James Hansen, NASA Goddard Institute for Space Studies, New York, private communication, January 30, 1995; William K. Stevens, "A Global Warming Resumed in 1994, Climate Data Show," *New York Times*, January 27, 1995.

5. Richard A. Kerr, "Greenhouse Skeptic Out in the Cold," *Science*, December 1, 1989; Richard A. Kerr, "Greenhouse Science Survives Skeptics," *Science*, May 22, 1992; Patrick Michaels, *Sound and Fury: Science and Politics of Global Warming* (Washington, D.C.: Cato Institute, 1992); Richard Lindzen, "Absence of Scientific Basis," *Research & Exploration*, Spring 1993.

6. For funding by coal industry, see masthead of *World Climate Report*, edited by Patrick J. Michaels, Ivy, Va.; J.F.B. Mitchell et al., "Climate Response to Increasing Levels of

Greenhouse Gases and Sulphate Aerosols," *Nature*, August 10, 1995.

7. Stephen H. Schneider, "Detecting Climatic Change Signals: Are There Any 'Fingerprints'?" *Science*, January 21, 1994.

8. J.C. King, "Recent Climate Variability in the Vicinity of the Antarctic Peninsula," *International Journal of Climatology*, May 1994; *The Australian*, March 1, 1995; Keith R. Briffa et al., "Unusual Twentieth-Century Summer Warmth in a 1,000-year Temperature Record from Siberia," *Nature*, July 13, 1995; Molly Moore, "New Delhi Cools Off—At 98 Degrees," *Washington Post*, June 14, 1994.

9. Malcolm W. Browne, "Most Precise Gauge Yet Points to Global Warming," *New York Times*, December 12, 1994; David J. Thomson, "The Seasons, Global Temperature, and Precession," *Science*, April 7, 1995.

10. IPCC, op cit. note 1; Karl quoted in "Reading the Patterns," *The Economist*, April 1, 1995; Hasselmann cited in Richard Monastery, "Dusting the Climate for Fingerprints," *Science News*, June 10, 1995.

11. IPCC, op. cit. note 1.

12. Ibid.

13. M. Patrick McCormick, Larry W. Thomason, and Charles R. Trepte, "Atmospheric Effects of the Mt Pinatubo Eruption," *Nature*, February 2, 1995; IPCC, op. cit. note 1; Figure 2–1 from Mitchell et al., op. cit. note 6 and from data supplied by Bob Davis, Hadley Centre for Climate Prediction and Research, Bracknell, U.K., October 5, 1995.

14. IPCC, *Climate Change 1992: The Supplementary Report to the IPCC Assessment* (Cambridge University Press: 1992).

15. A. Scott Denning, Inez Y. Fung, and David Randall, "Latitudinal Gradient of Atmospheric CO_2 Exchange with Land Biota," *Nature*, July 20, 1995; P. Ciais et al., "A Large Northern Hemisphere Terrestrial CO_2 Sink Indicated by the 13C/12C Ratio of Atmospheric CO_2," *Science*, August 25, 1995.

16. George M. Woodwell and Fred T. Mackenzie, eds., *Biotic Feedbacks in the Global Climatic System* (New York: Oxford University Press, 1995); Deborah MacKenzie, "Where Has All the Carbon Gone?" *New Scientist*, January 8, 1994.

17. Raja S. Ganeshram et al., "Large Changes in Oceanic Nutrient Inventories from Glacial to Interglacial Periods," *Nature*, August 31, 1995; Louis A. Codispoti, "Is the Ocean Losing Nitrate?" *Nature*, August 31, 1995.

18. IPCC, op. cit. note 1.

19. World Bank, "Earth Faces Water Crisis," press release, Washington, D.C., August 6, 1995.

20. IPCC, op. cit. note 1.

21. Ibid.; Hamburg cited in William K. Stevens, "Scientists Say Earth's Warming Could Set Off Wide Disruptions," *New York Times*, September 18, 1995.

22. Northern Finland and Hopkins Institute information from Charles Petit, "New Hints of Global Warming," *San Francisco Chronicle*, April 17, 1995.

23. James P. Bruce, "Challenges of the Decade: Natural Disasters and Global Change," address at Symposium on the World at Risk: Natural Hazards and Climate Change, Massachusetts Institute of Technology, Cambridge, Mass., January 14–16, 1992; G.A. Berz, "Greenhouse Effects on Natural Catastrophes and Insurance," The Geneva Papers on Risk Insurance, July 17, 1992; National Oceanic and Atmospheric Administration (NOAA) quote from Thomas R. Karl et al., "Trends in U.S. Climate During the Twentieth Century," *Consequences*, Spring 1995; Paul Simons, "Why Global Warming Could Take Britain by Storm," *New Scientist*, November 7, 1992; Craig R. Whitney, "Rhine Floods Worst in Century; 50,000 Homeless," *New York Times*, December 25, 1994.

24. Emanual estimate and Friedman calculation included in Doug Cogan, "Bracing for Bigger Storms," *Investor's Environmental Report*, Vol. 3, No. 1, 1993; see also Munich Re, *Windstorm*, Munich Re special publication, Munich, Germany, 1990.

25. Robert C. Sheets, "Catastrophic Hurricanes May Become Frequent Events Along the United States East and Gulf Coasts," Testimony before Government Affairs Committee, U.S. Senate, Washington, D.C., April 29, 1993; Greenpeace International, *The Climate Time Bomb: Signs of Climate Change from the Greenpeace Database* (Amsterdam: 1994), supplemented by "Update," March 1995.

26. Greg Steinmetz, "Andrew's Toll: As Insurance Costs Soar, Higher Rates Loom," *Wall Street Journal*, January 6, 1993; E.N. Rappaport and R.B. Sheets, "A Meteorological Analysis of Hurricane Andrew," *Lessons of Hurricane Andrew*, Special Publication of the Annual National Hurricane Conference, April 13–16, 1995.

27. Dork L. Sahagian, Frank W. Schwartz, and David K. Jacobs, "Direct Anthropogenic Contributions to Sea Level Rise in the Twentieth Century," *Nature*, January 6, 1994; Browne, op. cit. note 9; IPCC, op. cit. note 1.

28. Asian Development Bank, *Climate Change in Asia: Thematic Overview* (Manila: 1994).

29. Rene Bowser et al., *Southern Exposure: Global Climate Change and Developing Countries* (Washington, D.C.: Center for Global Change, 1992); Cynthia Rosenzweig and Martin L. Parry, "Potential Impact of Climate Change on World Food Supply," *Nature*, January 13, 1994; David E. Pitt, "Computer Vision of Global Warming: Hardest on Have-Nots," *New York Times*, January 18, 1994; A.J. Michael, *Planetary Overload: Global Environmental Change and the Health of the Human Species* (Cambridge: Cambridge University Press, 1993); C.E. Ewan et al., eds., *Health in the Greenhouse: The Medical and Environmental Health Effects of Global Climate Change* (Can-

berra: Australian Government Publishing Service, 1993); IPCC, op. cit. note 1.

30. G. Marland, R.J. Andres, and T.A. Boden, "Global, Regional, and National CO_2 Emission Estimates From Fossil Fuel Burning, Cement Production, and Gas Flaring: 1950–1992" (electronic database) (Oak Ridge, Tenn.: Carbon Dioxide Information Analysis Center, Oak Ridge National Laboratory, 1995); Keeling and Whorf, op. cit. note 3; IPCC, *Radiative Forcing of Climate Change: The 1994 Report of the Scientific Assessment Working Group of IPCC* (Bracknell, U.K.: IPCC Working Group I Technical Support Unit, 1994).

31. Figure 2–2 from Marland, Andres, and Boden, op. cit. note 30, and from Worldwatch estimates based on ibid. and on British Petroleum (BP), *BP Statistical Review of World Energy* (London: Group Media & Publications, 1995).

32. Gross national product data for 1993 adjusted for purchasing power parity from *The World Bank Atlas 1995* (Washington, D.C.: World Bank, 1995).

33. *United Nations Framework Convention on Climate Change*, op. cit. note 2; Worldwatch estimates from Marland, Andres, and Boden, op. cit. note 30, and from BP, op. cit. note 31.

34. Worldwatch estimates from Marland, Andres, and Boden, op. cit. note 30, and from BP, op. cit. note 31.

35. Ibid.; Population Reference Bureau, *1994 World Population Data Sheet* (Washington, D.C.: 1994).

36. Worldwatch estimates from Marland, Andres, and Boden, op. cit. note 30, and from BP, op. cit. note 31.

37. Ibid.; Jessica Hamburger, *China's Energy and Environment in the Roaring Nineties: A Policy Primer* (Washington, D.C.: Pacific Northwest Laboratory, 1995).

38. Chancellor Helmut Kohl, speech to the First Conference of the Parties to the

United Nations Framework Convention on Climate Change, Berlin, April 5, 1995; U.S. Climate Action Network and Climate Network Europe, *Independent NGO Evaluations of National Plans for Climate Change Mitigation: OECD Countries, Third Review, January 1995* (Washington, D.C.: U.S. Climate Action Network, 1995); International Energy Agency (IEA), *Climate Change Policy Initiatives, Volume 1: OECD Countries* (Paris: Organisation for Economic Co-operation and Development (OECD), 1994); Christopher Flavin, "Wind Power Soars," in Lester R. Brown, Nicholas Lenssen, and Hal Kane, *Vital Signs 1995* (New York: W.W. Norton & Company, 1995); gasoline tax from IEA, *Energy Prices and Taxes, First Quarter, 1995* (Paris: OECD, 1995); carbon equivalent estimate by Worldwatch.

39. Nathaniel Nash, "German High Court Bans Energy Subsidy on Utility Bills," *New York Times*, December 8, 1994; reverse carbon tax estimate by Worldwatch based on Ibid. and on BP, op. cit. note 31; "Accord on German Coal Subsidies Highlights Bonn Coalition Rift," *European Energy Report*, March 17, 1995.

40. President William J. Clinton and Vice President Albert Gore, Jr., *The Climate Change Action Plan* (Washington, D.C.: The White House, 1993); William K. Stevens, "U.S. Prepares to Unveil Blueprint for Reducing Heat-Trapping Gases," *New York Times*, October 12, 1993; Gary Lee, "Sorting Out the Sources of Greenhouse Gases," *Washington Post*, October 26, 1993; Joel Darmstadter, "The U.S. Climate Change Action Plan: Challenges and Prospects," *Resources*, Winter 1995.

41. Natural Resources Defense Council from U.S. Climate Action Network and Climate Network Europe, op. cit. note 38.

42. U.S. Climate Action Network and Climate Network Europe, op. cit. note 38; Dwight Van Winkle, "Japan's CO_2 Emissions Rise Post-2000," *Climate Forum* (electronic conference on Econet), June 12, 1995.

43. U.S. Climate Action Network and Climate Network Europe, op. cit. note 38; IEA, *Climate Change Policy Initiatives*, op. cit. note 38; Ministry of the Environment, *Climate Protection in Denmark* (Copenhagen: Danish Environmental Protection Agency, 1994).

44. Author's observations, based on discussions with delegations in Berlin.

45. Stephen Kinzer, "U.N. Parley Delegates Back Talks on Global Warming," *New York Times*, April 8, 1995; Timothy Noah, "Rio Summit Group Sets Date for Limits on Some Emissions," *Wall Street Journal*, April 10, 1995; Michael Grubb, "Viewpoint: The Berlin Climate Conference; Shifting Alliances Break Political Deadlock," *EC Energy Monthly*, April 21, 1995.

46. "Smoke," *The Economist*, April 8, 1995; Carol Werner and Jennifer Morgan, "Cities Endorse AOSIS Protocol," *ECO* (NGO Newsletter, Berlin), March 30, 1995.

47. Berlin insurance meeting description from author's observations, Berlin, March 26, 1995; H.R. Kaufmann, "Storm Damage Insurance—Quo Vadis?" paper produced by Swiss Re, Zurich, Switzerland, November 1990.

48. Allstate representative quoted in Doug Cogan, "Bracing for Bigger Storms: Hurricane Andrew May Be a Harbinger of Trouble for the Insurance Industry if the Globe Warms," *Investor's Environmental Report*, Vol. 3, No. 1, 1993.

49. Data in Figure 2–3 from Gerhard A. Berz, Munich Reinsurance Company, Munich, Germany, private communication, September 1, 1995; Gerhard A. Berz, "Global Warming and the Insurance Industry," *Interdisciplinary Science Reviews*, Vol. 18, No. 2, 1993; Franklin W. Nutter, Reinsurance Association of America, testimony before Subcommittee on Clean Air and Nuclear Regulation, Committee on Environment and Public Works, U.S. Senate, Washington, D.C., April 14, 1994.

50. Franklin W. Nutter, speech at Conference on Financing Strategies for Renewable Energy & Efficiency, New York, N.Y., May 11, 1994.

51. Lloyds representative quoted in Jeremy Leggett, "A Looming Capital Crisis for Oil? Taking Bearings in the Greenhouse in a Post Brent-Spar World," presented to the Aspen Environmental Roundtable, Aspen, Colo., September 18, 1995.

52. Colin D. Woodroffe, "Preliminary Assessment of the Vulnerability of Kiribati to Accelerated Sea Level Rise," in Joan O'Callahan, ed., *Global Climate Change and The Rising Challenge of the Sea*, Proceedings of the IPCC Workshop Held at Margarita Island, Venezuela, March 9–13, 1992 (Silver Spring, Md.: NOAA, 1994).

53. "South Takes Tentative First Steps at Climate Conference," *Third World Economics*, April 1–15, 1995; Heherson T. Alvarez, "From the Peoples of Asia and the Pacific: A Plea," speech at the First Conference of the Parties to the United Nations Framework Convention on Climate Change, Berlin, April 3, 1995.

54. "Proposed Elements of a Mandate for Consultations on Commitments in Articles 4.2(a) and 4.2(b)," draft proposal, Berlin, April 1995; "South Takes Tentative First Steps," op. cit. note 53; "High Priest of the Carbon Club," *Der Spiegel*, April 3, 1995; Liz Barratt-Brown, Alden Meyer, and Annie Petsonk, "U.S.: No Place to Hide," *ECO* (NGO Newsletter, Berlin), April 3, 1995; Kirsty Hamilton, "Aussie NZ Sell Out?" *ECO*, April 7, 1995; Fred Pearce, "Don't Stop Talking About Tomorrow . . .," *New Scientist*, April 15, 1995.

55. "Conclusion of Outstanding Issues and Adoption of Decisions," United Nations Framework Convention on Climate Change, Berlin, April 7, 1995; Karan Capoor and Annie Petsonk, "The Climate Summit: From Rio to Berlin and Beyond," *Hotline*, June 1995.

56. Capoor and Petsonk, op. cit. note 55; Grubb, op. cit. note 45.

57. Tim Jackson, "Joint Implementation and Cost-Effectiveness Under the Framework Convention on Climate Change," *Energy Policy*, February 1995; "Conflicts of Interest on the Greenhouse," *Nature*, April 6, 1995; Sierra Club, "Risky Business: Why Joint Implementation is the Wrong Approach to Global Warming Policy," Washington, D.C., April 1995; Jyoti K. Parikh, "Joint Implementation and North-South Cooperation for Climate Change," *International Environmental Affairs*, Winter 1995; U.S. Initiative on Joint Implementation, press release, U.S. Environmental Protection Agency and U.S. Department of Energy, Washington, D.C., April 20, 1995.

58. "Conclusion of Outstanding Issues and Adoption of Decisions," op. cit. note 55.

59. *United Nations Framework Convention on Climate Change*, op. cit. note 2.

60. IEA, *World Energy Outlook* (Paris: OECD, 1995.)

61. William R. Cline, *The Economics of Global Warming* (Washington, D.C.: Institute for International Economics, 1992); J. Sathaye and J. Christensen, "Methods for the Economic Evaluation of Greenhouse Gas Mitigation Options," *Energy Policy*, Special Issue, November 1994; R. Richels and J. Edmonds, "The Economics of Stabilizing Atmospheric CO_2 Concentrations," *Energy Policy*, April/May 1995.

62. Christopher Flavin and Nicholas Lenssen, *Power Surge: Guide to the Coming Energy Revolution* (New York: W.W. Norton & Company, 1994); J.H. Ausubel, "Technical Progress and Climatic Change," *Energy Policy*, April/May 1995.

63. Cline, op cit, note 61; Sylvia M. Rothen, "The Greenhouse Effect in Economic Modeling" (draft), Human Ecology Group, Swiss Federal Institute for Environmental

Science and Technology, Dubendorf, Switzerland, October 1994.

64. Flavin and Lenssen, op. cit. note 62.

65. Global Climate Coalition, *What the Experts Say About Global Climate Change* (Washington, D.C.: 1994); John Shlaes, "Statement of Global Climate Coalition," U.S. State Department Global Climate Change Consultation, Washington, D.C., August 3, 1994.

66. Mark Mansley, *Long Term Financial Risks to the Carbon Fuel Industry from Climate Change* (London: The Delphi Group, 1994).

67. Jeremy Leggett, *Climate Change and the Insurance Industry* (London: Greenpeace International, 1994).

68. Richard Elliot Benedick, *Ozone Diplomacy: New Directions in Safeguarding the Planet* (Cambridge, Mass.: Harvard University Press, 1991).

Chapter 3. Forging a Sustainable Water Strategy

1. Tod Robberson, "Mexico in Mid-Crisis," *Washington Post*, May 29, 1995; Robert Bryce, "Water Wars Erupt Along Rio Grande," *Christian Science Monitor*, May 19, 1995; "US-Mexico: State Dept. Turns Down Water-Loan Request," *Greenwire*, May 22, 1995, based on Enrique Rangel, *Dallas Morning News*, May 19, 1995.

2. Population projection from Population Reference Bureau (PRB), *1995 World Population Data Sheet* (Washington, D.C.: 1995).

3. World water use rounded from I. A. Shiklomanov, "World Fresh Water Resources," in Peter H. Gleick, ed., *Water in Crisis: A Guide to the World's Fresh Water Resources* (New York: Oxford University Press, 1993); 1,000 ton figure from U.N. Food and Agriculture Organization (FAO), *Yield Response to Water* (Rome: 1979).

4. Irrigated area from FAO, *1990 Production Yearbook* (Rome: 1991), adjusted for the United States and Taiwan with irrigated area data from, respectively, U.S. Department of Agriculture (USDA), Economic Research Service (ERS), *Agricultural Resources, Cropland, Water and Conservation*, Washington, D.C., September 1991, and Sophia Hung, USDA, ERS, private communication, June 21, 1991; harvest estimate of 40 percent is approximate, and is based on a 36-percent estimate in W. Robert Rangeley, "Irrigation and Drainage in the World," in Wayne R. Jordan, ed., *Water and Water Policy in World Food Supplies* (College Station, Tex.: Texas A&M University Press, 1987), on a 47-percent estimate (just for grain) in Montague Yudelman, "The Future Role of Irrigation in Meeting the World's Food Supply," in Soil Science Society of America, *Soil and Water Science: Key to Understanding Our Global Environment* (Madison, Wisc.: 1994), and on a general statement that 40 percent of world's food supply comes from irrigated land from Ismail Serageldin, *Toward Sustainable Management of Water Resources* (Washington, D.C.: World Bank, 1995).

5. Worldwatch Institute estimate based on USDA, ERS, "Production, Supply, and Demand View" (electronic database), Washington, D.C., August 1995, and on U.S. Bureau of the Census projections, published in Francis Urban and Ray Nightingale, *World Population by Country and Region, 1950–1990, with Projections to 2050* (Washington, D.C.: USDA, ERS, 1993); annual flow of Colorado from U.S. Bureau of Reclamation, "Managing the Lower Colorado River to Meet Contemporary Needs," Lower Colorado Region, Boulder City, Nev., undated; annual flow of Huang He from Gleick, op. cit. note 3; annual flow of Nile from John Waterbury, *Hydropolitics of the Nile Valley* (Syracuse, N.Y.: Syracuse University Press, 1979); population projections from PRB, op. cit. note 2.

6. Grainland area trend from Lester R. Brown, "Grain Area Unchanged," in Lester R. Brown, Hal Kane, and Ed Ayres, *Vital Signs 1993* (New York: W.W. Norton & Company, 1993).

7. Table 3–1 based on the following sources: High Plains from Edwin D. Gutentag et al., *Geohydrology of the High Plains Aquifer in Parts of Colorado, Kansas, Nebraska, New Mexico, Oklahoma, South Dakota, Texas, and Wyoming* (Washington, D.C.: U.S. Government Printing Office, 1984); based on net extraction rates in Dork L. Sahagian, Frank W. Schwartz, and David K. Jacobs, "Direct Anthropogenic Contributions to Sea Level Rise in the Twentieth Century," *Nature*, January 6, 1994, this assumes an annual average depletion rate of 12 billion cubic meters from 1980–90 and adds it to the depletion estimate in Gutentag et al., op. cit. this note; irrigated area decline from Darrell S. Peckham and John B. Ashworth, *The High Plains Aquifer System of Texas, 1980 to 1990: Overview and Projections* (Austin, Tex.: Texas Water Development Board, 1993); California from California Department of Water Resources, *California Water Plan Update*, Vol. 1 (Sacramento: 1994); Southwest U.S. from T.W. Anderson et al., "Central Alluvial Basins," in W. Back, J.S. Rosenshein, and P.R. Seaber, eds., *Hydrogeology* (Boulder, Colo.: Geological Society of America, 1988); Albuquerque projection from "City's Conservation Plan on Target," *The Groundwater Newsletter* (Water Information Center, Inc., Denver, Colo.), February 28, 1995; Mexico from Juan Manuel Martinez Garcia, Director General of Hydraulic Construction and Operation, Mexico City, private communication, October 21, 1991; Arabian Peninsula from Jamil Al Alawi and Mohammed Abdulrazzak, "Water in the Arabian Peninsula: Problems and Perspectives," in Peter Rogers and Peter Lydon, eds., *Water in the Arab World* (Cambridge, Mass.: Harvard University, 1994); Abdulla Ali Al-Ibrahim, "Excessive Use of Groundwater Resources in Saudi Arabia: Impacts and Policy Options," *Ambio*, February 1991; African Sahara from Sahagian, Schwartz, and Jacobs, op. cit. this note; India from "Alarming Ground Water Depletion in Haryana and Punjab," *IARI News* (Indian Agricultural Research Institute, New Delhi), October-December 1993; A. Vaidyanathan, "Second India Series Revisited: Food and Agriculture," prepared for World Resources Institute, Washington, D.C.; Harald Frederiksen, Jeremy Berkoff, and William Barber, *Water Resources Management in Asia* (Washington, D.C.: World Bank, 1993); China from Xu Zhifang, unpublished paper prepared for World Water Council—Interim Founding Committee, March 1995; Southeast Asia from Frederiksen, Berkoff, and Barber, op. cit. this note.

8. Raj Chengappa, "India's Water Crisis," *India Today*, May 31, 1986, excerpted in *World Press Review*, August 1986; Daniel Zaslavsky, Israeli Water Commissioner, Tel Aviv, private communcation, March 5, 1992; "Pollution, Salinity Affecting Domestic Water Sources," *Jerusalem Post*, June 20, 1991, as reprinted in *JPRS Report: Environmental Issues*, July 9, 1991; Israel Ministry of the Environment, "State Comptroller Report: The Water Quantity Crisis," *Israel Environment Bulletin*, Spring 1991.

9. Peter H. Gleick et al., *California Water 2020: A Sustainable Vision* (Oakland, Calif.: Pacific Institute for Studies in Development, Environment, and Security, 1995).

10. Frederiksen, Berkoff, and Barber, op. cit. note 7.

11. Sandra Postel, "Irrigation Expansion Slowing," in Lester R. Brown, Hal Kane, and David Malin Roodman, *Vital Signs 1994* (New York: W.W. Norton & Company, 1994).

12. Sandra Postel, *Last Oasis: Facing Water Scarcity* (New York: W.W. Norton & Company, 1992); Dina L. Umali, in *Irrigation-Induced Salinity* (Washington, D.C.: World Bank, 1993), cites sources suggesting that 2–3 million hectares a year may be coming out of production due to salinization, which, if accurate, would counteract the 2 million hectares of average annual irrigation expansion in recent years.

13. Figures for 1957 from Gleick et al., op. cit. note 9; California Department of Water Resources, op. cit. note 7.

14. Urbanization in 2025 from Gershon Feder and Andrew Keck, "Increasing Competition for Land and Water Resources: A Global Perspective," World Bank, Washington, D.C., March 1995; Frederiksen, Berkoff, and Barber, op. cit. note 7; 300 cities from Xu, op. cit. note 7; Patrick E. Tyler, "China Lacks Water to Meet Its Mighty Thirst," *New York Times*, November 7, 1993.

15. International Boundary and Water Commission, El Paso, Tex., private communication, October 4, 1995.

16. Klaus Lampe, "' . . . Our Daily Bread,'" *Swiss Review of World Affairs*, September 1994.

17. Sandra Postel, "Where Have All the Rivers Gone?" *World Watch*, May/June 1995; in Figure 3–1, 1905–49 is flow at Yuma, Arizona, from U.S. Geological Survey, and 1950–92 is flow at southerly international boundary from International Boundary and Water Commission.

18. Global demand from Postel, op. cit. note 12; Jan A. Veltrop, "Importance of Dams for Water Supply and Hydropower," in Asit K. Biswas, Mohammed Jellali, and Glenn Stout, *Water for Sustainable Development in the 21st Century* (Oxford: Oxford University Press, 1993); current number of dams from Patrick McCully, International Rivers Network, Berkeley, Calif., private communication, February 1995.

19. Gleick et al., op. cit. note 9.

20. Alejandro Robles, executive director, Mexico program, Conservation International, Washington, D.C., private communication, February 1995; Jim Carrier, "The Colorado: A River Drained Dry," *National Geographic*, June 1991.

21. Frederiksen, Berkoff, and Barber, op. cit. note 7; threatening of Bengal tiger from M. Roushanuzzaman, "Water Straining Relations Between India-Bangladesh," *Depthnews Asia* (Manila), June 1995.

22. Khalil H. Mancy, "The Environmental and Ecological Impacts of the Aswan High Dam," in H. Shuval, ed., *Developments in Arid Zone Ecology and Environmental Quality* (Philadelphia, Pa.: Balaban ISS, 1981); Gilbert White, "The Environmental Effects of the High Dam at Aswan," *Environment*, September 1988.

23. Fred Pearce, "High and Dry in Aswan," *New Scientist*, May 7, 1994; John D. Milliman, James M. Broadus, and Frank Gable, "Environmental and Economic Implications of Rising Sea Level," *Ambio*, Vol. 18, No. 6, 1989.

24. Philip Micklin, "The Aral Crisis: Introduction to the Special Issue," *Post-Soviet Geography*, May 1992; Figure 3–2 from Philip Micklin, as published in Gleick, op. cit. note 3.

25. Micklin, "The Aral Crisis," op. cit. note 24.

26. Loss of fish species from Judith Perera, "A Sea Turns to Dust," *New Scientist*, October 23, 1993; Philip Micklin, "Touring the Aral: Visit to an Ecological Disaster Zone," *Soviet Geography*, February 1991.

27. Thomas F. Homer-Dixon, "Environmental Scarcities and Violent Conflict," *International Security*, Summer 1994.

28. Ibid.; Miriam R. Lowi, "West Bank Water Resources and the Resolution of Conflict in the Middle East," Occasional Paper Series, Project on Environmental Change and Acute Conflict, University of Toronto and American Academy of Arts and Sciences, September 1992; swimming pools from David A. Schwarzbach, "Promised Land. (But What About the Water?)," *The Amicus Journal*, Summer 1995; Information Division, "Israeli-Palestinian Interim Agreement, Annex III—Protocol Concerning Civil Affairs," Israeli Foreign Ministry, Jerusalem, September 1995.

29. Homer-Dixon, op. cit. note 27.

30. Michael Goldman, "Tragedy of the Commons or the Commoners' Tragedy: The

State and Ecological Crisis in India," *CNS*, December 1993.

31. Homer-Dixon, op. cit. note 27.

32. Thomas Naff, "Conflict and Water Use in the Middle East," in Rogers and Lydon, op. cit. note 7; perspective on Six Day War from Daniel Hillel, *Rivers of Eden: The Struggle for Water and the Quest for Peace in the Middle East* (New York: Oxford University Press, 1994).

33. Naff, op. cit. note 32; Egypt irrigated area from FAO, op. cit. note 4.

34. Z. Abate, "The Integrated Development of Nile Basin Waters," in P.P. Howell and J.A. Allan, eds., *The Nile: Sharing a Scarce Resource* (Cambridge: Cambridge University Press, 1994).

35. Author's visit to the region; examples of local-regional conflict from David R. Smith, "Climate Change, Water Supply, and Conflict in the Aral Sea Basin," presented at the PriAral Workshop 1994, San Diego State University, San Diego, Calif., March 1–4, 1994; "Central Asia: The Silk Road Catches Fire," *The Economist*, December 26, 1992–January 8, 1993.

36. Postel, op. cit. note 12.

37. Sandra Postel, "The Politics of Water," *World Watch*, July/August 1993.

38. Quote reported in John Murray Brown, "Turkey, Syria Set Talks on Euphrates," *Washington Post*, January 22, 1993; Manuel Schiffler, report on the Interdisciplinary Academic Conference on Water in the Middle East, German Development Institute, Berlin, June 17–18, 1995.

39. Shared rivers from Asit K. Biswas, "Management of International Water Resources: Some Recent Developments," in Asit K. Biswas, ed., *International Waters of the Middle East* (Oxford, UK: Oxford University Press, 1994), who points out that the actual number of international rivers must be higher than the 214 estimated by a now-defunct United Nations agency.

40. For discussion of the work of the ILA and ILC, see Stephen C. McCaffrey, "Water, Politics, and International Law," in Gleick, op. cit. note 3.

41. John Battersby, "Dispute Over Precious Water on West Bank Slows Talks," *Christian Science Monitor*, August 3, 1995; Schwarzbach, op. cit. note 28.

42. American Society of Civil Engineers from "Study Seeks Standards for Global Water-Sharing," *U.S. Water News*, December 1994.

43. McCaffrey, op. cit. note 40.

44. "Extracts from the Minutes of the 3rd Meeting of the Ministers of Water Affairs in the Nile Basin on Tecconile," and Annex 2, "Project on the Nile Basin Cooperative Framework, Draft Terms of Reference for a Panel of Experts Constituted by the Tecconile Council of Ministers," Arusha, Tanzania, February 9–11, 1995.

45. Peter Rogers, "The Value of Cooperation in Resolving International River Basin Disputes," *Natural Resources Forum*, May 1993; refugee movement from Sheila Jones, "When the Ganges Runs Dry," *Financial Times*, May 9, 1994.

46. Janusz Kindler, "Regional Integrated Perspective on Future Water Needs and Demands with an Example from the Aral Sea Basin" (draft), prepared for Comprehensive Freshwater Assessment Programme Workshop on Scenarios and Water Futures, Stockholm Environment Institute, Boston, September 1995.

47. D.J. Blackmore, "Integrated Catchment Management—The Murray-Darling Basin Experience," presented at Water Down Under '94, Adelaide, Australia, November 21–25, 1994.

48. International Conference on Water and the Environment: Development Issues for the 21st Century, "The Dublin Statement and Report of the Conference," Dublin, Ireland, January 26–31, 1992; United Nations, *Agenda 21: The United Nations Program of Action From Rio* (New York: U.N. publications, 1992); World Bank, *Water Resources Management: A World Bank Policy Paper* (Washington, D.C.: 1993).

49. Brian Gray, "The Modern Era in California Water Law," *Hastings Law Journal*, January 1994.

50. John H. Cushman, Jr., "U.S. and California Sign Water Accord," *New York Times*, December 16, 1994.

51. Aral Sea Program Unit, "Aral Sea Program—Phase 1," World Bank, Washington, D.C., May 1994; N.F. Glazovskiy, "Ideas on an Escape from the 'Aral Crisis,' " *Soviet Geography*, February 1991.

52. Bureau of Reclamation study by Richard W. Wahl, *Markets for Federal Water: Subsidies, Property Rights, and the Bureau of Reclamation* (Washington, D.C.: Resources for the Future, 1989); municipal costs from Harald D. Frederiksen, "The Water Crisis in the Developing World: Misconceptions about Solutions," *Journal of Water Resources Planning and Management*, January/February 1996.

53. Vaidyanathan, op. cit. note 7; B. Vadhanaphuti et al., "Water Resource Planning and Management of the Chao Phraya River Basin, Thailand," prepared for World Bank Workshop on Water Resources Management Policies, June 25–28, 1991.

54. Postel, op. cit. note 12.

55. Willem Van Tuijl, *Improving Water Use in Agriculture: Experiences in the Middle East and North Africa* (Washington, D.C.: World Bank, 1993); Paul Polak, "Progress Report on IDE Low Cost Drip Irrigation System," International Development Enterprises, Lakewood, Colo., April 9, 1995; Paul Polak, President, International Development Enterprises, Lakewood, Colo., private communication, June 12, 1995. The low cost is attributable to simple materials and a movable dripper line (one for every seven rows of crops).

56. Worldwide irrigation efficiency from Postel, op. cit. note 12; Andrew A. Keller and Jack Keller, "Effective Efficiency: A Water Use Efficiency Concept for Allocating Freshwater Resources," Center for Economic Policy Studies, Winrock International, Arlington, Va., 1995.

57. Aral Sea basin situation from Jeremy Berkoff, World Bank, "The Relevance of Water Market Concepts in Central Asia," date unknown.

58. Renato Gazmuri Schleyer and Mark W. Rosegrant, "Chilean Water Policy: The Role of Water Rights, Institutions, and Markets," in Mark W. Rosegrant and Renato Gazmuri Schleyer, *Tradable Water Rights: Experiences in Reforming Water Allocation Policy* (Arlington, Va.: Irrigation Support Project for Asia and the Near East, 1994).

59. Mateen Thobani, "Tradable Property Rights to Water," FPD Note No. 34, World Bank, Washington, D.C., February 1995; Tushaar Shah, *Groundwater Markets and Irrigation Development* (Bombay: Oxford University Press, 1993).

60. Kuppannan Palanisami, "Evolution of Agricultural and Urban Water Markets in Tamil Nadu, India," in Rosegrant and Schleyer, op. cit. note 58.

61. Robert Wigington, "Market Strategies for the Protection of Western Instream Flows and Wetlands," Natural Resources Law Center, University of Colorado School of Law, Boulder, Colo., August 1990; Peter Steinhart, "The Water Profiteers," *Audubon*, March 1990.

62. High Plains Underground Water Conservation District No. 1, "Water District Receives Additional Ag Loan Funding from

TWDB," *The Cross Section*, November 1994; program savings from Ken Carver, High Plains Underground Water Conservation District, Lubbock, Tex., private communication, October 3, 1995.

63. Amy Vickers, "The Energy Policy Act: Assessing Its Impact on Utilities," *Journal AWWA* (Journal of the American Water Works Association), August 1993.

64. Ibid.; see also Janice A. Beecher, "Integrated Resource Planning," *Journal AWWA* (Journal of the American Water Works Association), June 1995.

65. Serageldin, op. cit. note 4.

Chapter 4. Sustaining Freshwater Ecosystems

1. Historic data from U.S. Fish and Wildlife Service, *Pacific Salmon Management*, Briefing Document in Region 1 Fisheries (Portland, Oreg.: 1991), as cited in James B. Petit, "Solid Faith in Small Acts," *ilahee*, Winter 1994; additional data on historic populations and harvest from Carolyn Alkire, *The Living Landscape, Vol. 1: Wild Salmon as Natural Capital* (Washington, D.C.: The Wilderness Society, 1993); 1992 returns from John C. Ryan, *State of the Northwest*, Northwest Environment Watch Report No. 1 (Seattle, Wash.: Northwest Environment Watch, 1994); hatchery-born fish from Jack K. Sterne, Jr., "Supplementation of Wild Salmon Stocks: A Cure for the Hatchery Problem or More Problem Hatcheries," *Coastal Management*, Vol. 23, 1995, pp. 123–52; 1994 returns to Redfish lake from Tom Kenworthy, "Agency Outlines Salmon Protection Plan," *Washington Post*, March 21, 1995.

2. Water resource estimates from Alan P. Covich, "Water and Ecosystems," in Peter H. Gleick, ed., *Water in Crisis: A Guide to the World's Fresh Water Resources* (New York: Oxford University Press, 1993); extinction estimates from Peter B. Moyle and Robert A. Leidy, "Loss of Biodiversity in Aquatic Ecosystems: Evidence from Fish Faunas," in P.L. Fiedler and S.K. Jain, eds., *Conservation Biology: The Theory and Practice of Nature Conservation, Preservation, and Management* (New York: Chapman and Hall, 1992).

3. Figure 4–1 from The Nature Conservancy and the Network of Natural Heritage Programs and Conservation Data Centres, Arlington, Va., unpublished data, 1995; historic fish estimates from Robert R. Miller, James D. Williams, and Jack E. Williams, "Extinctions of North American Fishes During the Past Century," *Fisheries*, November/December 1989, and from Jack E. Williams et al., "Fishes of North America Endangered, Threatened or of Special Concern: 1989," *Fisheries*, November/December 1989.

4. Stuart L. Pimm et al., "The Future of Biodiversity," *Science*, July 21, 1995; Jonathan Coddington, speech at The Living Planet in Crisis: Biodiversity Science and Policy Conference, American Museum of Natural History, New York, March 9–10, 1995.

5. Table 4–1 is based on the following: global, Europe, and South Africa from Moyle and Leidy, op. cit. note 2; Amazon River from Michael Goulding, "Flooded Forests of the Amazon," *Scientific American*, March 1993; Asia from Brian Groombridge, ed., *Global Biodiversity: Status of the Earth's Living Resources* (New York: Chapman and Hall, 1992); North America from Moyle and Leidy, op. cit. note 2, and from The Nature Conservancy and the Network of Natural Heritage Programs and Conservation Data Centres, op. cit. note 3; Mexico from Salvador Contreras-B. and M. Lourdes Lozano-V., "Water, Endangered Fishes, and Development Perspectives in Arid Lands of Mexico," *Conservation Biology*, June 1994; Lake Victoria from Les Kaufman, "Catastrophic Change in Species-Rich Freshwater Ecosystems: The Lessons of Lake Victoria," *BioScience*, December 1992, and from Rosemary Lowe-McConnell, "Fish Faunas of the African Great Lakes: Origins, Diversity and Vulnerability," *Conservation Biology*, September 1993.

6. American Fisheries Society (AFS) study from Miller, Williams, and Williams, op. cit note 3; percent of U.S. rivers free-flowing from A.C. Benke, "A Perspective on America's Vanishing Streams," *Journal of the North American Benthological Society*, 1990, as cited in David S. Wilcove and Michael J. Bean, eds., *The Big Kill: Declining Biodiversity in America's Lakes and Rivers* (Washington, D.C.: Environmental Defense Fund, 1994); percent of inland waters artificially controlled from U.S. Bureau of the Census, *Statistical Abstract of the United States, 1990: The National Data Book* (Washington, D.C.: U.S. Government Printing Office, 1990), as cited in National Research Council, *Restoration of Aquatic Ecosystems: Science, Technology, and Public Policy* (Washington, D.C.: National Academy Press, 1992); U.S. wetlands lost from T.E. Dahl, *Wetland Losses in the United States 1780's to 1980's* (Washington, D.C.: Fish and Wildlife Service, U.S. Department of the Interior, 1990).

7. AFS study in Miller, Williams, and Williams, op. cit. note 3; number of exotics in North America from Charles Boydstun, Pam Fuller, and James D. Williams, "Nonindigenous Fish," in E. T. LaRoe et al., eds., *Our Living Resources: A Report to the Nation on the Distribution, Abundance, and Health of U.S. Plants, Animals, and Ecosystems* (Washington, D.C.: National Biological Service, U.S. Department of the Interior, 1995); exotic species as a percent of states' fisheries from Billy Goodman, "Keeping Anglers Happy Has a Price," *BioScience*, May 1991.

8. Amazon River length and discharge from Igor A. Shiklomanov, "World Fresh Water Resources," in Gleick, op. cit. note 2.

9. Species numbers and forest ecology from Goulding, op. cit. note 5; fish catch and consumption from Peter B. Bayley and Miguel Petrere, Jr., "Amazon Fisheries: Assessment Methods, Current Status, and Management Options," in Douglas P. Dodge, ed., *Proceedings of the International Large River Symposium (LARS)*, Canadian Special Publication of Fisheries and Aquatic Sciences 106 (Ottawa, Ont., Canada: Department of Fisheries and Oceans, 1989).

10. Flooded forest remaining in lower Amazon and quote from Goulding, op. cit. note 5; Tambaqui decline from Eliot Marshall, "Homely Fish Draws Attention," *Science*, February 10, 1995.

11. Number of dams from International Commission on Large Dams (ICOLD), as cited in World Resources Institute, *World Resources 1992–93* (New York: Oxford University Press, 1992); dam starts from ICOLD, "Status of Dam Construction in 1993," as cited in Gary Gardner and Jim Perry, "Dam Starts Up," in Lester R. Brown, Nicholas Lenssen, and Hal Kane, *Vital Signs 1995* (New York: W.W. Norton & Company, 1995).

12. Mary F. Wilson and Karl C. Halupka, "Anadromous Fish as Keystone Species in Vertebrate Communities," *Conservation Biology*, June 1995.

13. Extent of original habitat from Joseph Cone, "Solo Coho," *The New Pacific*, Winter 1993/1994; watershed size from Adam Diamant and Zach Wiley, *Water for Salmon: An Economic Analysis of Salmon Recovery Alternatives in the Lower Snake and Columbia Rivers*, prepared for the Northwest Power Planning Council (New York: Environmental Defense Fund, April 1995).

14. Dams in basin from Diamant and Wiley, op. cit. note 13; salmon migration time and mortality from Ryan, op. cit. note 1; extent of river impoundments from Wilcove and Bean, op. cit. note 6.

15. Forest lost from Douglas E. Booth, "Estimating Prelogging Old-Growth in the Pacific Northwest," *Journal of Forestry*, October 1991; impact of logging from Christopher A. Frissell, *A New Strategy for Watershed Restoration and Recovery of Pacific Salmon in the Pacific Northwest*, (Corvallis, Oreg.: Pacific Rivers Council, no date); coho listing from "Coho Salmon Proposed as 'Threatened Species'," *New York Times*, July 21, 1995; Ca-

nadian salmon data from T.G. Northcote and
D.Y. Atagi, "Pacific Salmon Abundance
Trends in the Fraser River Watershed Com-
pared with Other British Columbia Sys-
tems," in Deanna J. Stouder, Peter A. Bisson,
and Robert J. Naiman, eds., *Pacific Salmon and
Their Ecosystems: Status and Future Options* (New
York: Chapman & Hall, Inc., in press).

16. Resident species status from M.G.
Henjum et al., *Interim Protection for Late-succes-
sional Forests, Fisheries, and Watersheds: National
Forests East of the Cascade Crest, Oregon and
Washington* (Bethesda, Md.: The Wildlife So-
ciety, 1994).

17. AFS study reported in Willa Nehlsen,
Jack E. Williams, and James A. Lichatowich,
"Pacific Salmon at the Crossroads: Stocks at
Risk from California, Oregon, Idaho and
Washington," *Fisheries*, March/April 1991;
range extinction data from The Wilderness
Society, *The Living Landscape, Vol. 2: Pacific
Salmon and Federal Lands* (Washington, D.C.:
1993); healthy stocks from Charles W. Hunt-
ington, Clearwater BioStudies, Inc., Canby,
Oreg., and from Charles W. Huntington,
Willa Nehlsen, and Jon Bowers, "Healthy
Native Stocks of Anadromous Salmonids in
the Pacific Northwest and California," pre-
pared for Oregon Trout, Portland, Oreg.,
December 31, 1994.

18. Hatchery impacts from Jessica Max-
well, "Swimming with Salmon," *Natural History*, September 1995, from National Fish
and Wildlife Foundation/The Conservation
Fund, "Report of the National Fish Hatchery
Review Panel," Washington, D.C., December
30, 1994, from Pacific Rivers Council, *Coastal
Salmon and Communities at Risk: The Principles of
Coastal Salmon Recovery* (Eugene, Oreg.:
1995), from Ray Ring, "The West's Fisheries
Spin out of Control," *High Country News*, September 18, 1995, and from Sterne, op. cit.
note 1; interbreeding from Nehlsen, Williams, and Lichatowich, op. cit. note 17; National Marine Fisheries Service listing decision from Wilcove and Bean, op. cit. note 6.

19. Natural variations from James A. Lichatowich and Lars E. Mobrand, "Analysis of
Chinook Salmon in the Columbia River from
an Ecosystem Perspective," Prepared for
U.S. Department of Energy, Mobrand Bio-
metrics, Vashon Island, Wash., January 1995;
conflicts from Pacific Rivers Council, op. cit.
note 18, from Alkire, op. cit. note 1, from
Paul Koberstein, "The Decline and Fall of
Salmon," *High Country News*, November 15,
1993, from Mark Clayton, "Latest Fish Fight:
'Captain Canada' Takes on Alaska," *Christian
Science Monitor*, July 12, 1995, from Bernard
Simon, "Canada Closes Sockeye Salmon
Fishery," *Financial Times*, August 12, 1995,
from William DiBenedetto, "US, Canada
Seek Salmon Mediator as Talks go Belly Up,"
Journal of Commerce, August 3, 1995, from Bob
Holmes, "Fishermen and Loggers Square Up
Over Salmon," *New Scientist*, April 29, 1995,
from Bob Holmes, "Saving Snake River's
Wild Salmon," *New Scientist*, April 22, 1995,
and from Charles McCoy, "Regulators Slash
Salmon Talk in West, Highlighting Threat to
Fish's Survival," *Wall Street Journal*, April 13,
1992; tribal issues from Sterne, op. cit. note
1, from Timothy Egan, "Indians of Puget
Sound Get Rights to Shellfish," *New York
Times*, January 27, 1995, and from Alkire, op.
cit note 1.

20. Economic analyses from Diamant and
Wiley, op. cit. note 13, and from Karen Garri-
son and David Marcus, *Changing the Current:
Affordable Strategies for Salmon Restoration in the
Columbia River Basin* (San Francisco: Natural
Resources Defense Council, 1994); strategies
from Frissell, op. cit. note 15, from Alkire,
op. cit. note 1, from The Wilderness Society,
op. cit. note 17, from Lichatowich and Mo-
brand, op. cit. note 19, from Huntington,
Nehlsen, and Bowers, op. cit. note 17, from
Henjum et al., op. cit. note 16, from Pacific
Rivers Council, op. cit. note 18, and from
Sterne, op. cit. note 1.

21. Post-dam wild salmon information
from U.S. Fish and Wildlife Service, op. cit.
note 1; engineer's quote from M.C. James,

"Report of the Division of Commerical Fishing," *Transactions of the American Fisheries Society* (Washington, D.C.: AFS, 1938), quoted in Nehlsen, Williams, and Lichatowich, op. cit. note 17; Beard quoted in N. Tangwisutijit, "Reclaiming Respect for Rivers: A Conversation with Dan Beard," *World Rivers Review*, Fourth Quarter 1994.

22. William Barnes, "Dash to Dam the Mekong Raises Ecology Fears," *Financial Times*, December 14, 1994.

23. Monsoon season volume from Yuan Shu, "Nations Find Unity in Taming the Mekong," *The World Paper*, November 1994; spawning fish estimate from Barnes, op. cit. note 22; population data from "New Mekong River Basin Development Will Spur Hydro Development, Groups Charge," *International Environmental Reporter*, April 19, 1995.

24. "New Mekong River Basin Development," op. cit. note 23.

25. Barnes, op. cit. note 22.

26. Indonesian battlefield quote from Richard J. Grant, "Go With the Flow," *Worldlink*, July/August 1995; electricity demands from Shu, op. cit. note 23; see, for example, the Statement on Cooperation for the Sustainable Development of the Mekong River Basin by Thai nongovernmental groups dated April 4, 1995, posted on the ECONET.

27. "Mekong Politics: 'New Era', Same Old Plans," *Watershed: People's Forum on Ecology*, June 1995; Grainne Ryder, "Overview of Regional Plans," *World Rivers Review*, Fourth Quarter 1994.

28. Fish species lost from Dave Hubbel, "Thailand's Pak Mun Dam: A Case Study," *World Rivers Review*, Fourth Quarter 1994; compensation information from "Community Voices: Speaking Out on the Pak Mun Dam," *Watershed: People's Forum on Ecology*, June 1995.

29. Barry L. Johnson, William B. Richardson, and Teresa J. Naimo, "Past, Present and Future Concepts in Large River Ecology," *BioScience*, March 1995; J.V. Ward and J.A. Stanford, "Riverine Ecosystems: The Influence of Man on Catchment Dynamics and Fish Ecology," in Dodge, op. cit. note 9.

30. Peter B. Bayley, "Understanding Large River-Floodplain Ecosystems," *BioScience*, March 1995; Ward and Stanford, op. cit. note 29.

31. James A. Gore and F. Douglas Shields, Jr., "Can Large Rivers Be Restored?" *BioScience*, March 1995; Ward and Stanford, op. cit. note 29.

32. Antonin Lelek, "The Rhine River and Some of its Tributaries Under Human Impact in the Last Two Centuries," in Dodge, op. cit. note 9; drinking water information from Marlise Simons, "Salmon Does Not Mean the Rhine's Water is Safe to Drink," *New York Times*, May 25, 1995.

33. Flood data for 1995 from Haig Simonian, "Flood of Tears on the Rhine," *Financial Times*, February 8, 1995; historic flood data from "Dyke Disaster," *Down to Earth*, March 15, 1995.

34. Rhine ecology data from Lelek, op. cit. note 32; dams from Simonian, op. cit. note 33.

35. Floodplain loss from Fred Pearce, "Greenprint for Rescuing the Rhine," *New Scientist*, June 26, 1995; effects of flood control devices from E. Goldsmith and N. Hildyard, *The Social and Environmental Effects of Large Dams, Vol. One: Overview* (Cornwall, U.K.: Wadebridge Ecological Centre, 1984).

36. Lelek, op. cit. note 32; salmon catch from Pearce, op. cit. note 35.

37. Simonian, op. cit. note 33; Pearce, op. cit. note 35.

38. Information on levees from Mary Fran Myers and Gilbert F. White, "The Challenge of the Mississippi Flood," *Environment*, December 1993; wetland loss from U.S. Fish

and Wildlife Service, *Figures on Wetlands Lost in Mississippi Basin Prepared for Post Flood Recovery and the Restoration of Mississippi Basin Floodplains Including Riparian Habitat and Wetlands* (St. Louis, Mo.: Association of State Wetland Managers, 1993), as cited in Wilcove and Bean, op. cit. note 6.

39. Flood records for 1993 from J.D. Wilson, "Midwest's Great Flood of '93 Spawns New Floodplain Management Actions," *Earth Observation Magazine*, April 1995; levee damage from Myers and White, op. cit. note 38.

40. Evolution of Mississippi River management and early estimates of 1993 flood costs from Myers and White, op. cit. note 38; flow through artificial channels from Jeff Hecht, "The Incredible Shrinking Mississippi Delta," *New Scientist*, April 14, 1990; post-modification flood increases from L.B. Leopold, "Flood Hydrology and the Floodplain," in G.F. White and M.F. Myers, eds., *Water Resources Update—Coping with the Flood: The Next Phase* (Carbondale, Ill.: The University Council on Water Resources, 1994), as cited in Richard E. Sparks, "Need for Ecosystem Management of Large Rivers and Their Floodplains," *BioScience*, March 1995; flood loss estimates from William Stevens, "The High Costs of Denying Rivers Their Floodplains," *New York Times*, July 20, 1993, as cited in Deborah Moore, "What Can We Learn From The Experience of The Mississippi?" Environmental Defense Fund, San Francisco, September 7, 1994; estimates for historic floods and $12 billion for 1993 from ibid.; estimate of $16 billion for 1993 from Wilson, op. cit. note 39.

41. Moore, op. cit. note 40.

42. Myers and White, op. cit. note 38; General Accounting Office estimate reported in Robert S. Devine, "The Trouble with Dams," *Atlantic Monthly*, August 1995.

43. Task Force recommendations from Myers and White, op. cit. note 38; National Research Council, op. cit. note 6.

44. J.R. Whitley and R.S. Campbell, "Some Aspects of Water Quality and Biology of the Missouri River," *Trans. Missouri Acad. Sci.*, 1974, as cited in Ward and Stanford, op. cit. note 29; Ted Williams, "The River Always Wins," *Audubon*, July/August 1994.

45. R.L. Welcomme, *River Fisheries*, Fisheries Technical Paper 262 (Rome: Food and Agriculture Organization, 1985), as cited in Sparks, op. cit. note 40; Louisiana fish and wetlands from J.M. Hefner et al., *Southeast Wetlands: Status and Trends, Mid-1970's to Mid-1980's* (Atlanta, Ga.: Fish and Wildlife Service, U.S. Department of the Interior, 1994).

46. North American mussel fauna from Frank Kuznik, "America's Aching Mussels," *National Wildlife*, October/November 1993; extinctions since 1900 from Larry Master, "Aquatic Animals: Endangerment Alert," *Nature Conservancy*, March/April 1991; current mussel status from James D. Williams et al., "Conservation Status of Freshwater Mussels of the United Sates and Canada," *Fisheries*, September 1993; current mussel listings under Endangered Species Act from John H. Cushman, Jr., "Freshwater Mussels Facing Mass Extinction," *New York Times*, October 3, 1995.

47. Mussels functions from Kuznik, op. cit. note 46; herring example from S.L.H. Fuller, "Historical and Current Distributions of Freshwater Mussels (Mollusca: Bivalvia: Uniondae) in the Upper Mississippi River," in J. Rasmussen, ed., *Proceedings of the UMRCC Symposium on Upper Mississippi River Bivalve Mollusks* (Rock Island, Ill.: Upper Mississippi River Conservation Committee, 1980), as cited in Sparks, op. cit. note 40.

48. Mississippi River Basin declines from James Wiener et al., "Biota of the Upper Mississippi River Ecosystem," in LaRoe et al., op. cit. note 7; Mississippi river fauna and ecology from Sparks, op. cit. note 40; Yangtze River from Audrey Topping, "Ecological Roulette: Damming the Yangtze," *Foreign Affairs*, September/October 1995.

49. Basin size data and ecological communities from The Nature Conservancy, Great Lakes Program, *The Conservation of Biological Diversity in the Great Lakes Ecosystem: Issues and Opportunities* (Chicago: 1994); population data from James L. Tyson, "Delicate Ecosystem, Great Lakes Weighs the Economic Demands of Heavy Industry Manufacturing with the Environment's Needs," *Christian Science Monitor*, March 14, 1994; industrial and agricultural activity from Steve Thorp and David R. Allardice, "A Changing Great Lakes Economy: Economic and Environmental Linkages," State of the Lakes Ecosystem Conference, Working Paper, Great Lakes Commission, Ann Arbor, Mich., October 1994; wetlands loss from Ronald E. Erickson, "The National Wetlands Inventory in the Great Lakes Basin of the United States," in *Wetlands of the Great Lakes: Protection and Restoration Policies; Status of the Science*, Proceedings of an International Symposium (New York: The Association of State Wetland Managers, Inc., 1994); water quality from U.S. Environmental Protection Agency (EPA), *The Quality of Our Nation's Water: 1992* (Washington, D.C.: 1994).

50. Historical overview of pollution from George R. Francis and Henry A. Reiger, "Barriers and Bridges to the Restoration of the Great Lakes Basin Ecosystem," in Lance H. Gunderson et al., eds., *Barriers & Bridges to the Renewal of Ecosystems and Institutions* (New York: Columbia University Press, 1995); basin outflow estimate from U.S. General Accounting Office, *Pesticides: Issues Concerning Pesticides Used in the Great Lakes Watershed* (Washington, D.C.: 1993); airborne pollutant load from Michigan Department of Natural Resources, *State of the Great Lakes: 1993 Annual Report* (Lansing, Mich.: Office of the Great Lakes, 1993); distant origins of some airborne pollutants from Barry Commoner, as reported in "Inventory of Emission Sources, Deposition to Great Lakes Basin Released by Researcher," *International Environmental Reporter*, May 31, 1995.

51. Fish consumption advisories from EPA, op. cit. note 49; for complete database, see EPA, Office of Water, "National Listing of Fish Consumption Advisories Database," Washington, D.C., July 1995; estimates of chemicals entering system from Tyson, op. cit. note 49; chemicals monitored from Francis and Reiger, op. cit. note 50.

52. Bioaccumulation from Theo Colborn, "Global Implications of Great Lakes Wildlife Research," *International Environmental Affairs*, Winter 1991, from Theo Colborn and Coralie Clement. eds., *Chemically-Induced Alterations in Sexual and Functional Development: The Wildlife/Human Connection* (Princeton, N.J.: Princeton Scientific Publishing Co., Inc, 1992), and from Sheila Myers, Jack Manno, and Kimberly McDade, "Human Health Effects Research: Priorities and Issues," *Great Lakes Research Review*, February 1995; water/fish consumption estimates from International Joint Commission 1993 report, as cited in Tyson, op. cit. note 49.

53. Endocrine disruptor action from Colborn, op. cit. note 52, from Colborn and Clement, op. cit. note 52, and from Robert J. Hesselberg and John E. Gannon, "Contaminant Trends in Great Lakes Fish," in LaRoe et al., op. cit. note 7; sperm counts from E. Carlsen et al., "Evidence for Decreasing Quality of Semen During Past 50 Years," *British Medical Journal*, Vol. 305, 1992, as cited in Sue Dibb, "Swimming in a Sea of Oestrogens: Chemical Hormone Disrupters," *The Ecologist*, January/February 1995.

54. Historic fish catches from Robert M. Hughes and Reed F. Noss, "Biological Diversity and Biological Integrity: Current Concerns for Lakes and Streams," *Fisheries*, May/June 1992; surviving natives from Theodora E. Colborn et al., *Great Lakes Great Legacy?* (Washington, D.C.: The Conservation Foundation, 1990).

55. Sport and commercial fishery economics from Colborn et al., op. cit. note 54; number of exotics from EPA, *A Phase I Inventory of Current EPA Efforts to Protect Ecosystems* (Wash-

ington, D.C.: 1995); post-seaway estimates from Great Lakes Commission, "Great Lakes Panel on Aquatic Nuisance Species: Annual Report," Ann Arbor, Mich., March 1995; lamprey impact on lake trout catch data and initiation of Great Lakes Fishery Commission from Colborn et al., op. cit. note 54; lamprey control information from Michigan Department of Natural Resources, op. cit. note 50.

56. Tom Kenworthy, "Zebra Mussels May Threaten California Irrigation System," *Washington Post*, August 22, 1995; reproduction and ecology from Great Lakes Commission, op. cit. note 55; Detroit example from O'Neill and MacNeill, 1991, as cited in Michael L. Ludyanskiy, Derek McDonald, and David MacNeill, "Impact of the Zebra Mussel, A Bivalve Invader," *BioScience*, September 1993; economic cost estimate and expected spread from ibid.

57. Progress under Great Lakes Water Quality Agreement from Francis and Reiger, op. cit. note 50; pollution reductions from Robert J. Hesselberg and John E. Gannon, "Contaminant Trends in Great Lakes Fish," in LaRoe et al., op. cit. note 7.

58. EPA, op. cit. note 55.

59. Rift Valley lake ecology from Lowe-McConnell, op. cit. note 5, and from E. Barton Worthington and Rosemary Lowe-McConnell, "African Lakes Reviewed: Creation and Destruction of Biodiversity," *Environmental Conservation*, Autumn 1994; lake size from Shiklomanov, op. cit. note 8.

60. Endemic fish loss estimates from Lowe-McConnell, op. cit. note 5; Kaufman, op. cit. note 5.

61. Journalists Environmental Association of Tanzania and Panos Institute, *Current State of the Lake Report* (London: Panos Institute, 1994).

62. Perch adaptability from Lowe-McConnell, op. cit. note 5; eutrophication and perch population explosion from Kaufman, op. cit. note 5; commercial catch data from "Fishing

Industry Devouring Itself," *Panoscope*, July 1994; Figure 4–2 from Kenyan Marine and Fisheries Research Institute, as cited in Kaufman, op. cit. note 5.

63. Kaufman, op. cit. note 5.

64. Pollution and land use pressure from "Lake Victoria's Sea of Troubles," *Panoscope*, July 1994, and from Journalists Environmental Association of Tanzania and Panos Institute, op. cit. note 61; war casualties from "Tide of Horror from Rwandan War," *Panoscope*, July 1994; water hyacinth from "Battling the Killer Weed," *Panoscope*, July 1994.

65. Les Kaufman, Boston University, Boston, Mass., private communication, October 11, 1995.

66. John B. Loomis, " Measuring the Economic Benefits of Removing Dams and Restoring the Elwha River: Results of a Contingent Valuation Survey," *Water Resources Research* (in press); National Research Council, op. cit. note 6.

67. Paul L. Angermeier and James R. Karr, "Biological Integrity versus Biological Diversity as Policy Directives," *BioScience*, November 1994.

Chapter 5. Preserving Agricultural Resources

1. Hunger figures from Margaret Biswas, "Agriculture and Environment: A Review, 1972–1992," *Ambio*, May 1994.

2. Lester R. Brown, "Grain Production Rebounds," in Lester R. Brown, Nicholas Lenssen, and Hal Kane, *Vital Signs 1995* (New York: W.W. Norton & Company, 1995); Figure 5–1 from U.S. Department of Agriculture (USDA), Economic Research Service (ERS), "Production, Supply, and Demand View" (electronic database), Washington, D.C., November 1994, with updates from Foreign Agricultural Service, *Grain: World Markets and Trade*, USDA, Washington, D.C., July 1995; population data from U.S. Bureau of the

Census, as published in Francis Urban and Ray Nightingale, *World Population by Country and Region, 1950–90, with Projections to 2050* (Washington, D.C.: USDA, ERS, 1993); food demand increases from Jonathan Harris, *World Agriculture: Regional Sustainability and Ecological Limits* (Medford, Mass.: Center for Agriculture, Food and Environment, School of Nutrition, Tufts University, 1995).

3. Food demand increases from Harris, op. cit. note 2.

4. Harvested grain area calculated from data in Foreign Agricultural Service, op. cit. note 2; Lester R. Brown, "Grain Area Unchanged," in Brown, Lenssen, and Kane, op. cit. note 2; rice production in nineties from U.N. Food and Agriculture Organization (FAO), *FAO Production Yearbook 1992* (Rome: 1994).

5. Figure 5–2 and world grain stocks from USDA, ERS, "Production, Supply, and Demand View" (electronic database), Washington, D.C., August 1995.

6. Gershon Feder and Andrew Keck, "Increasing Competition for Land and Water Resources: A Global Perspective," World Bank, Washington, D.C., 1995; Gerhard K. Heilig, "Lifestyles and Global Land-use Change: Data and Theses," International Institute for Applied Systems Analysis, Laxenburg, Austria, September 1995.

7. Pierre Crosson and Jock Anderson, "Resources and Global Food Prospects: Supply and Demand for Cereals to 2030," World Bank Technical Paper Number 184, World Bank, Washington, D.C., 1992; harvested grain area from USDA, op. cit. note 5.

8. Patrick E. Tyler, "On the Farms, China Could be Sowing Disaster," *New York Times*, April 10, 1995; late eighties' land loss from Heilig, op. cit. note 6; Chinese fed from lost land is a Worldwatch calculation based on Chinese rice yields in FAO, op. cit. note 4; Zhao Liang, "Crops vs Concrete Crisis Raises Voices of Concern," *China Daily Business Weekly*, March 20, 1995; "Farmland De-

creases Drastically," *China Daily*, February 10, 1995.

9. Jakarta, Dhaka, and Bangkok data and 1990 World Bank study from Dipasis Bhadra and Antonio Salazar P. Brandao, "Urbanization, Agricultural Development, and Land Allocation," World Bank Discussion Paper 201, Washington, D.C., 1993; Java data from Scott Thompson, "The Evolving Grain Markets in Southeast Asia," in *Grain: World Markets and Trade*, USDA, Foreign Agricultural Service, Washington, D.C., June 1995; rice loss is a Worldwatch calculation based on FAO, op. cit. note 4.

10. Bhadra and Brandao, op. cit. note 9; Robert L. Kellogg et al., "Highlights from the 1992 National Resources Inventory," *Journal of Soil and Water Conservation*, November/December 1994.

11. USDA, op. cit note 5; USDA, Soil Conservation Service, *Summary Report: 1992 National Resources Inventory* (Washington, D.C.: 1994).

12. Sea level rise from Intergovernmental Panel on Climate Change, *The IPCC Assessment of Knowledge Relevant to the Interpretation of Article 2 of the UN Framework Convention on Climate Change: A Synthesis Report* (draft), Geneva, July 31, 1995; World Bank, "Issues and Options in Greenhouse Gas Emissions Control: Summary Report," Washington, D.C., December 1994; Kurt Kleiner, "Climate Change Threatens Southern Asia," *New Scientist*, August 27, 1994.

13. L.R. Oldeman et al., *World Map of the Status of Human-Induced Soil Degradation: An Explanatory Note*, 2nd ed. (Wageningen, Netherlands, and Nairobi: International Soil Reference and Information Centre and U.N. Environment Programme, 1991); Worldwatch calculation assumes a modest grain yield of 3 tons per hectare, and that a ton of grain feeds 6 people for a year; current losses to degradation from David Pimentel et al., "Environmental and Economic Costs of Soil Erosion and Conservation Benefits," *Science*,

February 24, 1995, and from Sara J. Scherr et al., "Land Degradation in the Developing World: Implications for Food, Agriculture, and Environment to the Year 2020," International Food Policy Research Institute (IFPRI), Washington, D.C., June 1995; African and Asian degradation from World Resources Institute, *World Resources 1992–93* (New York: Oxford University Press, 1992).

14. General Accounting Office (GAO), *Conservation Reserve Program: Alternatives Are Available for Managing Environmentally Sensitive Cropland* (Washington, D.C.: 1995).

15. FAO quoted in Pierre Crosson, "Future Supplies of Land and Water for World Agriculture," revised version of a paper presented to February 1994 conference at IFPRI, August 1995; Virginia H. Dale et al. "Emissions of Greenhouse Gases from Tropical Deforestation and Subsequent Uses of the Land," in National Research Council, *Sustainable Agriculture and the Environment in the Humid Tropics* (Washington, D.C.: National Academy of Sciences, 1993).

16. Amount of degradation calculated using land degraded by agricultural mismanagement, overgrazing, and half of the extent of deforested land; Oldeman et al., op. cit. note 13.

17. Oldeman et al., op. cit. note 13; erosion rates from S.A. El-Swaify, "State of the Art for Assessing Soil and Water Conservation Needs and Technologies," in Ted L. Napier et al., eds., *Adopting Conservation on the Farm: An International Perspective on the Socioeconomics of Soil and Water Conservation* (Ankeny, Iowa: Soil and Water Conservation Society, 1994).

18. Soil and Water Conservation Society, *Farming for a Better Environment* (Ankeny, Iowa: 1995); Paul Harrison, *The Third Revolution: Population, Environment, and a Sustainable World* (London: Penguin Books, 1992).

19. Definitions from Oldeman et al., op. cit. note 13; agricultural land degradation data from L.R. Oldeman, International Soil

Reference and Information Centre, Wageningen, Netherlands, private communication, September 21, 1995.

20. Productivity loss calculation suggested by Pierre Crosson, "Soil Erosion Estimates and Costs," *Science*, July 28, 1995; food demand increase from Harris, op. cit. note 2.

21. USDA, op. cit. note 5.

22. Lester R. Brown, "Fertilizer Use Continues Dropping," in Brown, Lenssen, and Kane, op. cit. note 2; importance of nonnutrient soil elements, and the effects of erosion on them, from Soil and Water Conservation Society, op. cit. note 18.

23. Ann P. Kinzig and Robert H. Socolow, "Human Impacts on the Nitrogen Cycle," *Physics Today*, November 1994; Ann P. Kinzig, Princeton University, Princeton, N.J., private communication, October 31, 1995.

24. Scientific Committee on Problems of the Environment, "Phosphorus Cycles and Transfers in the Global Environment," SCOPE Newsletter 47, Paris, December 1994–January 1995; phosphorus fertilizer consumption data from FAO, "Fertilizer," Statistics Series No. 106, Rome, 1991; phosphorus supply from Larry D. King, "Soil Nutrient Management in the United States," in Clive A. Edwards et al., *Sustainable Agricultural Systems* (Ankeny, Iowa: Soil and Water Conservation Society, 1990).

25. Jonathan Tolman, "Poisonous Runoff From Farm Subsidies," *Wall Street Journal*, September 8, 1995.

26. Conservation Technology Information Center, "1994 National Crop Residue Management Survey: Executive Summary," West Lafayette, Ind., 1994; Soil Conservation Service, "1992 National Resources Inventory: Highlights," USDA, Washington, D.C., 1992.

27. Center for Semiarid Agroforestry, Rocky Mountain Research Station, U.S. Forest Service, "Agroforestry: Working Trees for Agriculture," Lincoln, Nebr., USDA, un-

dated; Peter R. Schaefer, "Trees and Sustainable Agriculture," *American Journal of Alternative Agriculture*, Vol. 4, Nos. 3 and 4, 1989.

28. Water use by agriculture from World Resources Institute, *World Resources 1994–95* (New York: Oxford University Press, 1994); irrigated area from FAO, *1990 Production Yearbook* (Rome: 1991), adjusted for the United States and Taiwan with irrigated area data from, respectively, USDA, ERS, *Agricultural Resources, Cropland, Water and Conservation*, Washington, D.C., September 1991, and Sophia Hung, USDA, ERS, private communication, June 21, 1991; harvest estimate of 40 percent is approximate, and is based on a 36-percent estimate in W. Robert Rangeley, "Irrigation and Drainage in the World," in Wayne R. Jordan, ed., *Water and Water Policy in World Food Supplies* (College Station, Tex.: Texas A&M University Press, 1987), on a 47-percent estimate (just for grain) in Montague Yudelman, "The Future Role of Irrigation in Meeting the World's Food Supply," in Soil Science Society of America, *Soil and Water Science: Key to Understanding Our Global Environment* (Madison, Wisc.: 1994), and on a general statement that 40 percent of world's food supply comes from irrigated land from Ismail Serageldin, *Toward Sustainable Management of Water Resources* (Washington, D.C.: World Bank, 1995).

29. Sandra Postel, *Last Oasis: Facing Water Scarcity* (New York: W.W. Norton & Company, 1992). These 26 countries have renewable water resources of less than 1,000 cubic meters per person per year; IFPRI, "A 2020 Vision for Food, Agriculture, and the Environment," Washington, D.C., June 13, 1995.

30. China from You Wen-Rui, "Environmental Issues in Water Development in China," *Environmental Issues in Land and Water Development* (Bangkok: FAO Regional Office for Asia and the Pacific, 1992); Iran from Anthony Young et al., *Land Degradation in South Asia: Its Severity, Causes, and Effects upon the People* (Rome: FAO, 1994); Arabian Peninsula figure is a Worldwatch calculation based on

data in Jamil al Alawi and Mohammed Abdulrazzak, "Water in the Arabian Peninsula: Problems and Perspectives," in Peter Rogers and Peter Lydon, eds., *Water in the Arab World: Perspectives and Prognoses* (Cambridge, Mass.: Division of Applied Sciences, Harvard University, 1994); Maharashtra from Raj Chengappa, "India's Water Crisis," *World Press Review*, August 1986; Gujarat from A. Vaidyanathan, "Second India Series Revisited: Food and Agriculture," Madras Institute of Development Studies, Madras, India, 1994; Haryana from Marcus Moench, "Approaches to Groundwater Management: To Control or Enable," *Economic and Political Weekly*, September 24, 1994; Southern Great Plains from Wendell Holmes and Mindy Petrulis, "Declining Water Levels in the Texas High Plains Translate to Declining Economic Performance," USDA, ERS, Washington, D.C., 1988; Jacob W. Kijne and Marcel Kuper, "Salinity and Sodicity in Pakistan's Punjab: A Threat to Sustainability of Irrigated Agriculture?" *Water Resources Development*, Vol. 11, No. 1, 1995.

31. Dork L. Sahagian, Frank W. Schwartz, and David K. Jacobs, "Direct Anthropogenic Contributions to Sea Level Rise in the Twentieth Century," *Nature*, January 6, 1994.

32. FAO, *State of Food and Agriculture 1993* (Rome: 1993); Mark Rosegrant and Mark Svendsen, "Asian Food Production in the 1990s: Irrigation Investment and Management Policy," IFPRI, Washington, D.C., 1993; FAO, "Water Development for Food Security," Rome, March 1995.

33. Projection for 2025 and data for India, Indonesia, and Malaysia from Ramesh Bhatia, Upali Amerasinghe, and K.A.U.S. Imbulana, "Productivity and Profitability of Paddy Production in the Muda Scheme, Malaysia," *Water Resources Development*, Vol. 11, No. 1, 1995; "Water Shortage Could Derail China's Development," *Depthnews*, June 12–17, 1995.

34. Thomas S. Maddock and Walter G. Hines, "Meeting Future Public Water Supply

Needs: A Southwest Perspective," *Water Resources Bulletin*, April 1995.

35. Ian Anderson, "Australia's Growing Disaster," *New Scientist*, July 29, 1995; California data from World Bank, "Earth Faces Water Crisis," press release, Washington, D.C., August 6, 1995.

36. Cynthia Rozensweig et al., *Climate Change and World Food Supply*, Research Report No. 3 (Oxford: Environmental Change Unit, 1993).

37. Willem Van Tuijl, *Improving Water Use in Agriculture: Experiences in the Middle East and North Africa*, Technical Paper Number 201 (Washington, D.C.: World Bank, 1993); Government of Israel, *The Environment in Israel* (Jerusalem: Ministry of the Environment, 1992).

38. Vaclav Smil, "How Many People Can the Earth Feed?" *Population and Development Review*, June 1994; Prabhu Pingali and Mark W. Rosegrant, "Confronting the Environmental Consequences of the Green Revolution in Asia," IFPRI, Washington, D.C., August 1994; Peter H. Gleick et al., *California Water 2020: A Sustainable Vision* (Oakland, Calif.: Pacific Institute for Studies in Development, Environment, and Security, 1995); Stefan Klotzli, "The Water and Soil Crisis in Central Asia: A Source for Future Conflicts?" Center for Security Studies and Conflict Research, Swiss Federal Institute of Technology, Zurich, May 1994.

39. Kristin Helmore and Annu Ratta, "The Surprising Yields of Urban Agriculture," *Choices*, April 1995; Asit K. Biswas, "Environmental Sustainability of Egyptian Agriculture: Problems and Perspective," *Ambio*, February 1995.

40. Sales data from Pesticide Action Network North America Updates Service, "Growth in 1994 World Agrochemical Market," Pesticide Action Network, San Francisco, April 28, 1995; Barbara Dinham, ed., *The Pesticide Trail: The Impact of Trade Controls*

on Reducing Pesticide Hazards in Developing Countries (London: The Pesticides Trust, 1995).

41. Figure for 1965 from Biswas, op. cit. note 1; current data from David Pimentel, "Pest Management, Food Security and the Environment," Cornell University, Ithaca, N.Y., unpublished, March 1995; Figure 5–3 from Peter Weber, "Resistance to Pesticides Growing," in Lester R. Brown, Hal Kane, and David Malin Roodman, *Vital Signs 1994* (New York: W.W. Norton & Company, 1994); U.S. increase 1945–89 from David Pimentel et al., "Environmental and Economic Costs of Pesticide Use," *BioScience*, November 1992; resistance's role in crop losses from Michael Hansen, *Escape from the Pesticide Treadmill: Alternatives to Pesticides in Developing Countries* (Mount Vernon, N.Y.: Institute for Consumer Policy Research, 1987); Asian pesticide usage from Jumanah Farah, *Pesticide Policies in Developing Countries: Do They Encourage Excessive Use?* Discussion Paper No. 238 (Washington, D.C.: World Bank, 1994).

42. Farah, op. cit. note 41; malaria in India from Pimentel et al., op. cit. note 41; development time from Barbara Dinham, *The Pesticide Hazard* (London: Zed Books, 1993); development costs from Farah, op. cit. note 41.

43. Farah, op. cit. note 41.

44. Dirk Johnson, "Weed Killers in Tap Water in Corn Belt," *New York Times*, August 18, 1995; "Herbicides in Drinking Water Cause EPA Concern in Midwest," *Washington Post*, August 18, 1995; World Health Organization estimate from Pimentel et al., op. cit. note 41; other estimates from Dinham, op. cit. note 42; Farah, op. cit. note 41; 1993 report on Indonesia from Dinham, op. cit. note 40; "10,000 Pesticide Deaths in China," *Pesticide News*, March 1994.

45. Pimentel, op. cit. note 41.

46. Ibid.; timing of application from Jules N. Pretty, *Regenerating Agriculture* (London: Earthscan, 1995).

47. V. Bernson and G. Ekstrom, "Swedish Policy to Reduce Pesticide Use," *Pesticide Outlook*, Vol. 2, No. 3, 1991; "Dutch Pesticide Use Continues to Decline," and "WWF Canada Considers Pesticide Reduction Proposals," *Pesticide News*, December 1994; Texas from Pimentel, op. cit. note 41.

48. Michael Hansen, "Alternatives to Pesticides in Developing Countries, Preliminary Report," Institute for Consumer Policy Research, Mount Vernon, N.Y., May 1986.

49. Role of agroecosystem diversity from Pretty, op. cit. note 46; role of crop rotations from Pimentel, op. cit. note 41.

50. FAO, "Intercountry Programme for the Development and Application of Integrated Pest Control in Rice in South and Southeast Asia, Phase I and II," Rome, 1994; "Global IPM Facility Announced," *Global Pesticide Campaigner* (Pesticide Action Network, San Francisco), June 1995.

51. Organisation for Economic Co-operation and Development (OECD), "Agricultural Policies, Markets, and Trade in OECD Countries: Monitoring and Outlook, 1995," Paris, 1995.

52. FAO, op. cit. note 50.

53. Ibid.; GAO, op. cit. note 14.

54. American Farmland Trust, "A Guide to Agricultural Conservation Easements" (pamphlet), Washington, D.C., August 1995.

55. Robert L. Paarlberg, *Countrysides at Risk* (Washington, D.C.: Overseas Development Council, 1994); number of research institutes from Consultative Group on International Agricultural Research (CGIAR), "Renewal of the CGIAR: Draft Documents on Major Issues," Ministerial-level meeting documents, CGIAR Secretariat, Washington, D.C., February 9–10, 1995.

56. Worldwatch estimate based on United Nations, *World Energy Supplies, 1950–1974* (New York: 1976), on OECD, International Energy Agency, *Energy Balances of OECD Countries* (Paris: various years), on U.S. Department of Energy, Energy Information Administration, *Annual Energy Review 1992* (Washington, D.C.: U.S. Government Printing Office, 1993), on British Petroleum, *BP Statistical Review of World Energy* (London: Group Media & Publications, 1993), on Robert Summers and Alan Heston, "The Penn World Table (Mark 5): An Expanded Set of International Comparisons, 1950–88," *Quarterly Journal of Economics*, May 1991, and electronic database, and on International Monetary Fund, *World Economic Outlook*, October 1993.

57. Waste rate from Biswas, op. cit. note 1; grain bag from Joseph Axelrod, GrainPro, Boston, Mass., private communication, July 31, 1995.

58. Lester R. Brown, "World Feedgrain Use Up Slightly," in Brown, Lenssen, and Kane, op. cit. note 2; grain for beef, pork, and poultry from Lester R. Brown and Hal Kane, *Full House: Reassessing the Earth's Population Carrying Capacity* (New York: W.W. Norton & Company, 1994); grain savings are Worldwatch calculation.

59. Poultry consumption from USDA, op. cit. note 5; Smil, op. cit. note 38.

60. Mario Giampietro, "Sustainability and Technological Development in Agriculture," *BioScience*, November 1994.

Chapter 6. Understanding the Threat of Bioinvasions

1. Jonathan Weiner, *The Beak of the Finch: A Story of Evolution in Our Time* (New York: Alfred A. Knopf, 1994).

2. Ibid.; Bruce E. Coblentz, "Exotic Organisms: A Dilemma for Conservation Biology," *Conservation Biology*, September 1990.

3. Ian A.W. Macdonald et al., "Wildlife Conservation and the Invasion of Nature Re-

serves by Introduced Species: A Global Perspective" in J.A. Drake et al., eds., *Biological Invasions: A Global Perspective* (Chichester, U.K.: John Wiley and Sons, 1989); Paul A. Stone, Howard L. Snell, and Heidi M. Snell, "Behavioral Diversity as Biological Diversity: Introduced Cats and Lava Lizard Wariness," *Conservation Biology*, June 1994; Coblentz, op. cit. note 2.

4. These cases are documented throughout this chapter.

5. Edward O. Wilson, *The Diversity of Life* (New York: W.W. Norton & Company, 1992); Vernon H. Heywood, "Patterns, Extents and Modes of Invasions by Terrestrial Plants," in Drake et al., op. cit. note 3; Coblentz, op. cit. note 2.

6. Unsuccessful and apparently harmless invasions from Daniel S. Simberloff, "Community Effects of Introduced Species," in Matthew H. Nitecki, ed., *Biotic Crises in Ecological and Evolutionary Time* (New York: Academic Press, 1981); Dennis J. Russell and George H. Balazs, "Colonization by the Alien Marine Alga *Hypnea musciformis* (Wulfen) J. Ag. (Rhodophyta: Gigartinales) in the Hawaiian Islands and Its Utilization by the Green Turtle, *Chelonia mydas* L.," *Aquatic Botany*, Vol. 47, 1994. Table 6–1 is drawn from the following: rats from C.W. Previté-Orton, *The Shorter Cambridge Medieval History* (Cambridge: Cambridge University Press, 1952, rpt. 1978), from Christopher Lever, *Naturalized Mammals of the World* (London: Longman, 1985), and from Macdonald et al., op. cit. note 3; smallpox from Gordon G. Whitney, *From Coastal Wilderness to Fruited Plain: A History of Environmental Change in Temperate North America From 1500 to the Present* (Cambridge: Cambridge University Press, 1994), from Roger G. Kennedy, *Hidden Cities: The Discovery and Loss of Ancient North American Civilization* (New York: Free Press, 1994), and from Laurie Garrett, *The Coming Plague: Newly Emerging Diseases in a World Out of Balance* (New York: Farrar, Straus, Giroux, 1994);

rinderpest from Andy Dobson, "The Ecology and Epidemiology of Rinderpest Virus in Serengeti and Ngorongoro Conservation Area," in A.R.E. Sinclair and P. Arcese, eds., *Serengeti II: Research, Management and Conservation of an Ecosystem* (Chicago: University of Chicago Press, 1995); English sparrow from Christopher Lever, *Naturalized Birds of the World* (New York: John Wiley, 1987); wild oats from H.A. Mooney and J.A. Drake, "The Ecology of Biological Invasions," *Environment*, June 1987. Table 6–2 is drawn from the following: zebra mussel from Amy J. Benson and Charles P. Boydstun, "Invasion of the Zebra Mussel in the United States," in Edward T. LaRoe et al., eds., *Our Living Resources: A Report to the Nation on the Distribution, Abundance, and Health of U.S. Plants, Animals, and Ecosystems* (Washington, D.C.: National Biological Service, U.S. Department of the Interior, 1995), from Robin M. Taylor, ed., *Sea Grant Zebra Mussel Report: An Update of Research and Outreach* (Columbus, Ohio: Ohio Sea Grant College Program, 1995), and from Michael L. Ludyanskiy, Derek McDonald, and David MacNeill, "Impact of the Zebra Mussel, a Bivalve Invader," *BioScience*, September 1993; Asian tiger mosquito from George B. Craig, Jr., "The Diaspora of the Asian Tiger Mosquito," in Bill N. McKnight, ed., *Biological Pollution: The Control and Impact of Invasive Exotic Species* (Indianapolis: Indiana Academy of Science, 1993); grasses from Quentin C.B. Cronk and Janice L. Fuller, *Plant Invaders: The Threat to Natural Ecosystems*, WWF and UNESCO "People and Plants" Conservation Manual 2 (London: Chapman and Hall, 1995), from Clifford W. Smith, "The Alien Plant Problem in Hawaii," in Ted D. Center et al., eds., *Proceedings of the Symposium on Exotic Pest Plants* (Washington, D.C.: National Park Service, 1991), and from Robert Devine, "The Cheatgrass Problem," *Atlantic*, May 1993; tilapia from Geoffrey Fryer, "Biological Invasions in the Tropics: Hypothesis Versus Reality," in P.S. Ramakrishnan, ed., *Ecology of Biological Invasions in the Tropics*, Proceedings of an International

Workshop Held at Nainital, India (New Delhi: International Scientific Publications, 1989), and from Walter R. Courtenay, Jr., "Biological Pollution Through Fish Introductions," in McKnight, op. cit. this note; sweet pittosporum from Cronk and Fuller, op. cit. this note. Estimate of 10 percent from Elizabeth Culotta, "Biological Immigrants Under Fire," *Science*, December 6, 1991.

7. Islands' vulnerability to invasion from Peter M. Vitousek, "Diversity and Biological Invasions of Oceanic Islands," in E.O. Wilson and Frances M. Peter, eds., *Biodiversity* (Washington, D.C.: National Academy Press, 1988), and from Coblentz, op. cit. note 2; house cats from Lever, *Naturalized Mammals*, op. cit. note 6; rats from ibid., and from Macdonald et al., op. cit. note 3; brown tree snake from T.H. Fritts and G.H. Rodda, "Invasions of the Brown Tree Snake," in LaRoe et al., op. cit. note 6, and from Julie A. Savidge, "Extinction of an Island Forest Avifauna by an Introduced Snake," *Ecology*, June 1987.

8. Goats from Lever, *Naturalized Mammals*, op. cit. note 6, and from Bruce E. Coblentz, "Effects of Feral Goats (*Capra hircus*) on Island Ecosystems," *Biological Conservation*, Vol. 13, 1978; Gough Island tree example from Macdonald et al., op. cit. note 3; Dai Hayward, "Poisonous Jam Prescribed for Possum Power," *Financial Times*, July 31, 1991; Helen Goss, "The Mysterious Case of the Wobbly Possum," *New Scientist*, August 5, 1995.

9. George Laycock, *The Alien Animals* (Garden City, N.Y.: Natural History Press, 1966); Michael B. Usher, Terence J. Crawford, and Jean L. Banwell, "An American Invasion of Great Britain: The Case of the Native and Alien Squirrel (*Sciurus*) Species," *Conservation Biology*, March 1992.

10. L. James Lester, "Marine Species Introductions and Native Species Vitality: Genetic Consequences of Marine Introductions" in M. Richard DeVoe, ed., *Introductions and Transfers of Marine Species: Achieving a Balance Between Economic Development and Resource Protection*, proceedings of a conference and workshop, October 30–November 2, 1991, Hilton Head, S.C. (n.p.: South Carolina Sea Grant Consortium, 1992).

11. Grasses from Cronk and Fuller, op. cit. note 6, from Smith, op. cit. note 6, and from Devine, op. cit. note 6; *Chromolaena odorata* from Macdonald et al., op. cit. note 3, and from Cronk and Fuller, op. cit. note 6.

12. Iceplant example from Macdonald et al., op. cit. note 3, and from Cronk and Fuller, op. cit. note 6; Hawaiian example from Smith, op. cit. note 6.

13. Salmon example from U.S. Congress, Office of Technology Assessment (OTA), *Harmful Non-Indigenous Species in the United States* (Washington, D.C.: U.S. Government Printing Office, 1993); cats from Macdonald et al., op. cit. note 3.

14. *Spartina anglica* example from John D. Thompson, "The Biology of an Invasive Plant," *BioScience*, June 1991; Bolivian weed potato from OTA, op. cit. note 13.

15. Dobson, op. cit. note 6; Hamish McCallum and Andy Dobson, "Detecting Disease and Parasite Threats to Endangered Species and Ecosystems," *TREE* (Trends in Ecology and Evolution), May 1995.

16. Garrett, op. cit. note 6.

17. Craig, op. cit. note 6; G. Smith and A.P. Dobson, "Sexually Transmitted Diseases in Animals," *Parasitology Today*, Vol. 8, No. 5, 1992.

18. John M. Randall, "Exotic Weeds in North American and Hawaiian Natural Areas: The Nature Conservancy's Plan of Attack," in McKnight, op. cit. note 6; Macdonald et al., op. cit. note 3.

19. Ludyanskiy, McDonald, and MacNeill, op. cit. note 6.

20. Tammy Keniry and J. Ellen Marsden, "Zebra Mussels in Southwestern Lake Michigan," in LaRoe et al., op. cit. note 6; Benson

and Boydstun, op. cit. note 6; Taylor, op. cit. note 6; Ludyanskiy, McDonald, and Mac-Neill, op. cit. note 6; Courtenay, op. cit. note 6.

21. Opposum shrimp example from Jeff Fox and Ed Bruggemann, *Native Fish, Introduced Fish: Genetic Implications*, Report of a Workshop for Aquaculture and Park Managers, Policymakers, Environmentalists, and University Scientists, Convened in 1992 by the National Audubon Society (Washington, D.C.: National Audubon Society, 1992); Madagascar grebes from Macdonald et al., op. cit. note 3.

22. There is an extensive literature on the relationship between disturbance and invasion (which is not an absolute correlation). See, for instance, A.E. Newsome and I.R. Noble, "Ecological and Physiological Characters of Invading Species," in R.H. Groves and J.J. Burdon, eds., *Ecology of Biological Invasions* (Cambridge: Cambridge University Press, 1986); Michael J. Crawley, "What Makes a Community Invasible?" in A.J. Gray, M.J. Crawley, and P.J. Edwards, eds., *Colonization, Succession and Stability* (Oxford: Blackwell, 1987); and Francesco di Castri, "On Invading Species and Invaded Ecosystems: The Interplay of Historical Chance and Biological Necessity," in F. di Castri, A.J. Hansen, and M. Debussche, eds., *Biological Invasions in Europe and the Mediterranean Basin* (Boston: Kluwer Academic Publishers, 1990).

23. Walter R. Tschinkel, "The Fire Ant (*Solenopsis invicta*): Still Unvanquished," in McKnight, op. cit. note 6; Julie Grisham, "Attack of the Fire Ant," *BioScience*, October 1994; Craig R. Allen, R. Scott Lutz, and Stephen Demarais, "Red Imported Fire Ant Impacts on Northern Bobwhite Populations," *Ecological Applications*, Vol. 5, No. 3, 1995.

24. Spread of Mediterranean weeds from Marilyn D. Fox, "Mediterranean Weeds: Exchanges of Invasive Plants Between the Five Mediterranean Regions of the World," in di Castri, Hansen, and Debussche, op. cit. note 22, and from R.H. Groves, "The Biogeogra-

phy of Mediterranean Plant Invasions," in R.H. Groves and F. di Castri, eds., *Biogeography of Mediterranean Invasions* (Cambridge: Cambridge University Press, 1991); exotic percentages of floras from Heywood, op. cit. note 5; rates of invasion into Hawaii from Randall, op. cit. note 18, and from OTA, op. cit. note 13.

25. OTA, op. cit. note 13.

26. Comb jelly from John Travis, "Invader Threatens Black, Azov Seas," *Science*, November 26, 1993; *Mimosa pigra* from Cronk and Fuller, op. cit. note 6; reports of post-invasion stability are available in, for instance, Fox, op. cit. note 24, and in C.H. Fernando and Juraj Holcik, "Some Impacts of Fish Introductions into Tropical Freshwaters," in Ramakrishnan, op. cit. note 6; for arguments that invasion tends to create instability, see, for instance, Warren Herb Wagner, Jr., "Problems with Biotic Invasives: A Biologist's Viewpoint," in McKnight, op. cit. note 6, Coblentz, op. cit. note 2, and Macdonald et al., op. cit. note 3.

27. United Nations Conference on Trade and Development (UNCTAD), *Review of Maritime Transport 1993* (New York: United Nations, 1994); Craig, op. cit. note 6; OTA, op. cit. note 13.

28. Organisms found in containers from OTA, op. cit. note 13; Asian tiger mosquito from Craig, op. cit. note 6; New Zealand inspections from Faith Thompson Campbell and Scott E. Schlarbaum, *Fading Forests: North American Trees and the Threat of Exotic Pests* (New York: Natural Resources Defense Council, 1994).

29. Merchant ships (the total for the 35 most important maritime countries) from UNCTAD, op. cit. note 27; ballast water as a pathway from James T. Carlton, "Marine Species Introductions by Ships' Ballast Water: An Overview," in DeVoe, op. cit. note 10; Courtenay, op. cit. note 6.

30. Results of the Oregon study are in James T. Carlton and Jonathan B. Geller,

"Ecological Roulette: The Global Transport of Nonindigenous Marine Organisms," *Science*, July 2, 1993; red tide from Gustaaf M. Hallegraeff and Christopher J. Bolch, "Transport of Toxic Dinoflagellate Cysts via Ships' Ballast Water," *Marine Pollution Bulletin*, January 1991, and from James T. Carlton, "Dispersal of Living Organisms Into Aquatic Ecosystems as Mediated by Aquaculture and Fisheries Activities," in Aaron Rosenfield and Roger Mann, eds., *Dispersal of Living Organisms Into Aquatic Ecosystems* (College Park, Md.: Maryland Sea Grant, 1992).

31. Air traffic statistics from Garrett, op. cit. note 6, and from the *1991* and *1995 Information Please Almanac* (Boston: Houghton Mifflin); Duane J. Gubler, "Emergent and Resurgent Arboviral Diseases as Public Health Problems," in B.W.J. Mahy and D.K. Lvov, eds., *Concepts in Virology, From Ivanovsky to the Present* (Chur, Switzerland: Harwood Academic Publishers, 1993); African mosquitoes reported in Britain in Susan Litherland, "Health–Britain; Tropical Diseases Creep Towards Cold Countries," IGC Networks Headlines Digest, Interpress News Service, September 22, 1994; brown tree snake at Hawaiian airports in Alan Burdick, "It's Not the Only Alien Invader," *New York Times Magazine*, November 13, 1994; Fritts and Rodda, op. cit. note 7.

32. Olive from L.D. Pryor, "Forest Plantations and Invasions in the Mediterranean Zones of Australia and South Africa," in Groves and di Castri, op. cit. note 24; avocado from Bruce Coblentz, Oregon State University, Corvallis, Oreg., personal communication, September 11, 1995; cardamom from Heywood, op. cit. note 5; black pepper from T.C. Whitmore, "Invasive Woody Plants in Perhumid Tropical Climates," in Ramakrishnan, op. cit. note 6; *Chromolaena odorata* from Joan Baxter, "*Chromolaena odorata*: Weed for the Killing or Shrub for the Tilling?" *Agroforestry Today*, April–June 1995, and from Michael B. Usher, "Biological Invasions Into Tropical Nature Reserves," in Ramakrishnan, op. cit. note 6.

33. Thomas L. Fleischner, "Ecological Costs of Livestock Grazing in Western North America," *Conservation Biology*, September 1994; Dennis Morgan, "Cows and Forest Health," *Wild Forest Review*, July/August 1995; Alan B. Durning and Holly B. Brough, *Taking Stock: Animal Farming and the Environment*, Worldwatch Paper 103 (Washington, D.C.: Worldwatch Institute, July 1991); prairie dogs from Dean Biggins and Jerry Godbey, "Black-Footed Ferrets," in LaRoe et al., op. cit. note 6; Reed F. Noss, "Cows and Conservation Biology," *Conservation Biology*, September 1994.

34. Monterey pine from Cronk and Fuller, op. cit. note 6; invasiveness of eucalyptus from Pryor, op. cit. note 32; eucalyptus in Brazil from "Judge Rules Steel Firms in Minas Gerais Must Use Their Own Eucalyptus Trees for Fuel," *International Environment Reporter*, July 26, 1995; "Eucalyptus Threatens Biodiversity," Preservation of Natural Diversity, Topic 321, January 24, 1994 (online extract and translation of an article in *O Estado de Sao Paulo*, January 2, 1994); eucalyptus planting in Africa from C. Dustin Becker, Abwoli Y. Banana, and William Gombya-Ssembajjwe, "Early Detection of Tropical Forest Degradation: An IFRI Pilot Study in Uganda," *Environmental Conservation*, Spring 1995.

35. North American wood imports, U.S. Forest Service inventory, and woodwasp invasion from Campbell and Schlarbaum, op. cit. note 28; nematode and yellow jacket invasion from OTA, op. cit. note 13.

36. Aquaculture statistics from U.N. Food and Agriculture Organization, Fisheries Information, Data and Statistics Service, *FAO Fisheries Circular 815*, Revision 6 (Rome: 1994), and from Nick C. Parker, "Economic Pressures Driving Genetic Changes in Fish," in Rosenfield and Mann, op. cit. note 30; for promotion of aquaculture in developing countries, see, for instance, Rodolfo Fernandez, "Better Fish Species Developed to Meet Growing Demand," Depthnews, Ma-

nila, November 1994, and Fernando and Holcik, op. cit. note 26; lack of containment facilities in developing countries from Walter R. Courtenay, Jr., and James D. Williams, "Dispersal of Exotic Species From Aquaculture Sources, With Emphasis on Freshwater Fishes," in Rosenfield and Mann, op. cit. note 30; Mozambique tilapia from Fryer, op. cit. note 6; exotic domination of Central and South American fisheries from Fernando and Holcik, op. cit. note 26.

37. Inadequate containment in industrial countries and blue tilapia from Courtenay and Williams, op. cit. note 36; seaweed planting from Michael Neushul et al., "Introduction of Marine Plants for Aquaculture Purposes," in Rosenfield and Mann, op. cit. note 30; contaminated aquaculture shipments from Carlton, op. cit. note 30.

38. Lori Ann Thrupp, Gilles Bergeron, and William F. Waters, *Bittersweet Harvests for Global Supermarkets: Challenges in Latin America's Agricultural Export Boom* (Washington, D.C.: World Resources Institute, 1995); Gary Cohen, "Aquaculture Floods Indian Villages," *Multinational Monitor*, July/August 1995; Beena Pandey and Sachin Chaturvedi, "Prospects for Aquaculture in India," *Biotechnology and Development Monitor*, December 1994; Sam Howe Verhovek, "Virus Imperils Texas Shrimp Farms," *New York Times*, June 14, 1995; Donald V. Lightner et al., "Geographic Dispersion of the Viruses IHHN, MBV and HPV as a Consequence of Transfers and Introductions of Penaeid Shrimp to New Regions for Aquaculture Purposes," in Rosenfield and Mann, op. cit. note 30.

39. Jane Rissler and Margaret Mellon, *Perils Amidst the Promise: Ecological Risks of Transgenic Crops in a Global Market* (Cambridge, Mass.: Union of Concerned Scientists, 1993); transgenic crop statistics from "Traits Most Commonly Tested in Transgenic Crop Field Trials," *Gene Exchange*, July 1995.

40. Thomas T. Chen et al., "Fish Genetic Engineering: A Novel Approach in Aquaculture," in Rosenfield and Mann, op. cit. note 30; Parker, op. cit. note 36; "Fast-Growing Transgenic Fish," *Gene Exchange*, July 1995; "Genetic Planners Hope for Ideal Tree," *Financial Times*, June 14, 1995.

41. "Experimental Releases of Genetically Engineered Organisms," *Gene Exchange*, July 1995; "China Conducts the World's Largest Tests of Transgenic Organisms," *Gene Exchange*, December 1994.

42. David Pimentel, "Pest Management, Food Security, and the Environment," Cornell University, Ithaca, N.Y., unpublished, March 1995; Mooney and Drake, op. cit. note 6; rats and sparrows from "No Respite from Rodents," *Far Eastern Agriculture*, July/August 1994, from Lever, *Naturalized Mammals*, op. cit. note 6, and from Lever, *Naturalized Birds*, op. cit. note 6.

43. Pimentel, op. cit. note 42; wild oats from Mooney and Drake, op. cit. note 6.

44. Black sigatoka from Matthew H. Royer, "Global Pest Information Systems— Can We Make Them Work?" in Robert P. Kahn, ed., *Plant Protection and Quarantine, Vol. 3: Special Topics* (Boca Raton, Fla.: CRC Press, 1989); Russian wheat aphid from Fred Powledge, "The Food Supply's Safety Net," *BioScience*, April 1995; fruit fly and U.S. statistics from OTA, op. cit. note 13.

45. Thrupp, Bergeron, and Waters, op cit. note 38.

46. Robert Steiner, "Insect Swarms Threaten Asia Cotton Crop," *Wall Street Journal*, July 18, 1994; Farhan Bokhari, "Pakistan Reeling After Third Cotton Failure," *Financial Times*, January 27, 1995; James Dao, "Worst Blight Since Ireland's Is Chilling Potato Farmers," *New York Times*, July 30, 1995; pesticide resistance statistics from David Pimentel et al., "Environmental and Economic Costs of Pesticide Use," *BioScience*, November 1992.

47. Campbell and Schlarbaum, op. cit. note 28; OTA, op. cit. note 13.

48. Sven Wunder, "Conservation Status of Native Forests in Chile," Topic 118, *Forest Programme Newsletter* 19 (IUCN Regional Office for South America), August 9, 1994; Eduardo Silva, "Environmental Policy in Chile: The Politics of the Comprehensive Law," in Frank Fischer and Michael Black, eds., *Greening Environmental Policy: The Politics of a Sustainable Future* (New York: St. Martin's, 1995).

49. Verhovek, op. cit. note 38; Travis, op. cit. note 26; Keniry and Marsden, op. cit. note 20.

50. H.A. Mooney and J.A. Drake, "Biological Invasions: A SCOPE Program Overview," in Drake et al., op. cit. note 3; Fryer, op. cit. note 6; Les Kaufman, "Catastrophic Change in Species-Rich Freshwater Ecosystems: The Lessons of Lake Victoria," *BioScience*, December 1992; Yvonne Baskin, "Losing a Lake," *Discover*, March 1994; "Fishing Industry Devouring Itself," *Panoscope*, July 1994.

51. Kaufman, op. cit. note 50; Baskin, op. cit. note 50; Fryer, op. cit. note 6.

52. Craig, op. cit. note 6; Gubler, op. cit. note 31; D.J. Gubler and E.W. Trent, "Emergence of Epidemic Dengue/Dengue Hemorrhagic Fever as a Public Health Problem in the Americas," *Infectious Agents and Diseases*, Vol. 2, No. 6, 1993.

53. Don C. Schmitz et al., "The Ecological Impact and Management History of Three Invasive Alien Aquatic Plant Species in Florida," in McKnight, op. cit. note 6; Cronk and Fuller, op. cit. note 6; "Southern African Environmental Issues No. 11: Water Hyacinth," CEP Factsheet, Communicating the Environment Programme, Harare, Zimbabwe, 1995; "Ants Get a Transforming Charge," *Science News*, December 1989; Michael D. Lemonick, "Ants in Our Pants," *Time*, June 5, 1995.

54. OTA, op. cit. note 13; Keniry and Marsden, op. cit. note 20; Ludyanskiy, McDonald, and MacNeill, op. cit. note 6.

55. Stanley A. Temple, "The Nasty Necessity: Eradicating Exotics," *Conservation Biology*, June 1990; for lack of attention to exotics, see, for instance, Coblentz, op. cit. note 2, and Faith Thompson Campbell, "Legal Avenues for Controlling Exotics," in McKnight, op. cit. note 6.

56. See, for instance, OTA, op. cit. note 13, and Richard J. Hobbs and Stella E. Humphries, "An Integrated Approach to the Ecology and Management of Plant Invasions," *Conservation Biology*, August 1995.

57. OTA, op. cit. note 13; Campbell and Schlarbaum, op. cit. note 28; Jane E. Brody, "Invader From Asia Increases Gypsy Moth Threat," *New York Times*, May 30, 1995.

58. Figure 6–1 from Victoria Nuzzo, "Distribution and Spread of the Invasive Biennial *Alliaria petiolata* (Garlic Mustard) in North America," in McKnight, op. cit. note 6.

59. For the unpopularity of control programs, see Temple, op. cit. note 55; use of Bt against the Asian gypsy moth from Campbell and Schlarbaum, op. cit. note 28.

60. Manfred Mackauer, Lester E. Ehler, and Jens Roland, eds., *Critical Issues in Biological Control* (Andover, U.K.: Intercept Press, 1990); John J. Drea, "Classical Biological Control—An Endangered Discipline?" in McKnight, op. cit. note 6; OTA, op. cit. note 13; M. Miller and G. Aplet, "Biological Control: A Little Knowledge Is a Dangerous Thing," *Rutgers Law Review*, Winter 1993; Courtenay, op. cit. note 6; invasion of the prickly pear moth from H. Kass, "Once a Savior, Moth Is Now a Scourge," *Plant Conservation*, Vol. 5, No. 2, 1990.

61. Temple, op. cit. note 55; Lisa Jones, "Sexy Weapon Thwarts Bugs," *High Country News*, November 14, 1994; Malcolm W. Browne, "New Animal Vaccines Spread Like Diseases," *New York Times*, November 26, 1991.

62. Randy G. Westbrooks, "Exclusion and Eradication of Foreign Weeds from the

United States by USDA APHIS," in McKnight, op. cit. note 6; David O. Kelch and Maran Brainard Hilgendorf, "Slow the Spread of Zebra Mussels and Protect Your Boat and Motor, Too," fact sheet, Ohio Sea Grant College Program, Columbus, Ohio, 1994.

63. Cargo ship lighting from Brody, op. cit. note 57; ballast water systems from Carlton, op. cit. note 29.

64. OTA, op. cit. note 13; Campbell, op. cit. note 55; Cronk and Fuller, op. cit. note 6.

65. Francis M. Harty, "How Illinois Kicked the Exotic Habit," in McKnight, op. cit. note 6; S. Puri, S. Singh, and B. Bhushan, "Evaluation of Fuelwood Quality of Indigenous and Exotic Tree Species of India's Semi-Arid Region," *Agroforestry Systems*, Vol. 26, 1994; Régine Debrabandere and Jeanette Clarke, "Participatory Extension Tools for Planning Village-Based Tree Nurseries: A Case Study From Mutoko District, Zimbabwe," *Forests, Trees and People*, April 1995.

Chapter 7. Confronting Infectious Diseases

1. Director-General, "WHO Report on the Tuberculosis Epidemic, 1995: Stop TB at the Source," World Health Organization (WHO), Geneva, March 1995; Special issue, *World Health*, July/August 1993; 30 million figure from Paul John Dolin, Mario C. Raviglione, and Arata Kochi, *A Review of Current Epidemiological Data and Estimation of Future Tuberculosis Incidence and Mortality* (Geneva: WHO, 1993); TB Program, *Tuberculosis Notification Update*, WHO, Geneva, December 1993; Dr. Richard Bumgarner, TB Program, WHO, Geneva, private communication, February 15, 1994.

2. Figure of $13 from Director-General, op. cit. note 1; Christopher Murray, Karel Styblo, and Annik Rouillon, "Tuberculosis," in Dean T. Jamison et al., eds., *Disease Control Priorities in Developing Countries*, (Washington, D.C.: World Bank, 1993); Director-General, op. cit. note 1; World Bank, *World Development Report 1993: Investing in Health* (New York: Oxford University Press, 1993).

3. The Harvard Working Group on New and Resurgent Diseases, "New and Resurgent Diseases: The Failure of Attempted Eradication," *The Ecologist*, January/February 1995.

4. Report of the Director-General, *The World Health Report 1995: Bridging the Gaps* (Geneva: WHO, 1995).

5. Mortality data from ibid.; antibiotic-resistant strains from Dr. Stuart B. Levy, Director, Center for Adaptation Genetics and Drug Resistance, Tufts University School of Medicine, Boston, Mass., private communication, June 8, 1995.

6. Report of the Director-General, op. cit. note 4; Susan Okie, "500 Million Infected With Tropical Ills," *Washington Post*, March 28, 1990; more than 100 infectious diseases from Andrew A. Arata, Vector Biology and Control Project (now the Environmental Health Project), U.S. Agency for International Development, "Impact of Environmental Changes on Endemic Vector-borne Diseases," presented at Achieving Health for All: Economic and Social Policy, Seattle, Wash., September 10–13, 1989; Duane J. Gubler, "Vector-Borne Diseases," in Ruth A. Eblen and William R. Eblen, eds., *The Encyclopedia of the Environment* (Boston, Mass.: Houghton Mifflin Company, 1994); Council for Agricultural Science and Technology, "Foodborne Pathogens: Risks and Consequences," Task Force Report No. 122, Ames, Iowa, September 1994.

7. Nigeria from J.M. Meegan, "Yellow Fever Vaccine," *WHO/EPI/General*, Vol. 91, No. 6, 1991, and from T.P. Monath, "Yellow Fever: Victor, Victoria? Conqueror, Conquest? Epidemics and Research in the Last Forty Years and Prospects for the Future,"

American Journal of Tropical Medicine and Hygiene, Vol. 45, 1991, as cited in Duane J. Gubler, "Emergent and Resurgent Arboviral Diseases As Public Health Problems," in B.W.J. Mahy and D.K. Lvov, eds., *Concepts in Virology: From Ivanovsky to the Present* (Chur, Switzerland: Harwood Academic Publishers, 1993); Vietnam from "World Malaria Situation in 1992: Middle South Asia, Eastern Asia and Oceania," *Weekly Epidemiological Record*, November 4, 1994.

8. Drug-resistant pneumonia from Levy, op. cit. note 5; malaria from David Brown, "When Disease Resists," *Washington Post*, February 14, 1994; HIV data from Report of the Director-General, op. cit. note 4; HIV in Asia from John Ward Anderson, "India Seen as Ground Zero in Spread of AIDS to Asia," *Washington Post*, August 17, 1995.

9. Smallpox from Laurie Garrett, *The Coming Plague: Newly Emerging Diseases in a World Out of Balance* (New York: Farrar, Straus, and Giroux, 1994); measles from Stanley O. Foster, Deborah A. McFarland, and A. Meredith John, "Measles," in Jamison et al., op. cit. note 2; "Number of Cases of Measles Reported Globally, 1974–1989," *World Health Statistics Quarterly*, Vol. 45, 1992; polio from Dean T. Jamison et al., "Poliomyelitis," in Jamison et al., op. cit. note 2; "Special Issue: Towards a World Without Polio," *World Health*, January/February 1995; Frances Williams, "End to Polio by 2000," *Financial Times*, April 7, 1995; "China Plans Anti-Polio Sweep," *Wall Street Journal*, December 2, 1993; World Bank, op. cit. note 2.

10. Hal Kane, "Immunization Rates Soar," in Lester R. Brown, Hal Kane, and David Malin Roodman, *Vital Signs 1994* (New York: W.W. Norton & Company, 1994).

11. Ruth L. Berkelman et al., "Infectious Disease Surveillance: A Crumbling Foundation," *Science*, April 15, 1994; National Center for Infectious Diseases, *Addressing Emerging Infectious Disease Threats: A Prevention Strategy for the United States* (Atlanta, Ga.: Centers for Diseases Control and Prevention (CDC), 1994); most significant health achievement from Sir MacFarlane Burnet and David O. White, *Natural History of Infectious Disease*, 4th ed. (Cambridge: Cambridge University Press, 1972), as cited in Christopher H. Foreman, Jr., *Plagues, Products and Politics: Emergent Public Health Hazards and National Policymaking* (Washington, D.C.: Brookings Institution, 1994).

12. Harvard Working Group on New and Resurgent Diseases, op. cit. note 3; Richard M. Krause, "Foreword," in Stephen S. Morse, ed., *Emerging Viruses* (New York: Oxford University Press, 1993). Dr. Krause originally made this comment at the 1982 House Appropriations hearings for the National Institute of Allergy and Infectious Diseases.

13. Beverly E. Griffin, "Live and Let Live," *Nature*, March 3, 1994; John Maynard Smith, "Bacteria Break the Antibiotic Bank," *Natural History*, June 1994.

14. Robin Marantz Henig, *A Dancing Matrix: Voyages Along the Viral Frontier* (New York: Alfred A. Knopf, 1993); 1,000 copies from Dr. Stephen Morse, Rockefeller University, New York, private communication, October 17, 1995.

15. Common biological pattern from Edward O. Wilson, *The Diversity of Life* (Cambridge, Mass.: Harvard University Press, 1992), from Garrett, op. cit. note 9; from Marc Lappé, *Evolutionary Medicine: Rethinking the Origins of Disease* (San Francisco: Sierra Club Books, 1994), and from Dr. Paul Epstein, Harvard School of Public Health, Cambridge, Mass., private communication, March 2, 1995; ecological disruptions from Paul Epstein and Ross Gelbspan, "Climate and Health: Should We Fear a Global Plague? Yes—Disease is the Deadliest Threat of Rising Temperatures," *Washington Post*, March 19, 1995; influence of social behavior from Bennett Lorber, "Rattlesnake Powder, Lawn Darts, Hot Tubs, Sushi, and Sex, or Changing Patterns of Infectious Diseases Revis-

ited," *American Journal of Pharmacology*, Vol. 163, 1991.

16. Disruptions from Garrett, op. cit. note 9; Lappé, op. cit. note 15; tuberculosis from Director-General, op. cit. note 1.

17. Japanese encephalitis and general discussion of disruptions from Stephen S. Morse, "Factors in the Emergence of Infectious Diseases," *Emerging Infectious Diseases* (CDC), January/March 1995.

18. Karl Johnson, "Emerging Viruses in Context: An Overview of Viral Hemorrhagic Fevers," in Morse, op. cit. note 12; 20,000 Argentineans from WHO, "Viral Hemorrhagic Fevers: Report of a WHO Expert Committee," *Technical Report Series*, No. 712, 1985, as cited in Garrett, op. cit. note 9.

19. *Cryptosporidium* from Joan B. Rose, Charles N. Haas, and Charles P. Gerba, "Waterborne Pathogens: Assessing Health Risks," *Health and Environment Digest*, June 1993; influenza from Christoph Scholtissek, "Cultivating a Killer Virus," *Natural History*, January 1992; Robert G. Webster, "Influenza," in Morse, op. cit. note 12.

20. Lyme disease from Lappé, op. cit. note 15; Richard S. Ostfeld et al., "Ecology of Lyme Disease: Habitat Associations of Ticks (*Ixodes scapularis*) in a Rural Landscape," *Ecological Applications* (Ecological Society of America), May 1995; spread of Lyme disease throughout the United States from Lawrence K. Altman, "U.S. Agency Reports Lyme Disease Cases Up by 58% in '94," *New York Times*, June 23, 1995; James E. Herrington, "An Update on Lyme Disease," *Health and Environment Digest*, August 1995; 13,000 cases from Daniel B. Fishbein and David T. Dennis, "Tick-borne Diseases: A Growing Risk," *New England Journal of Medicine*, August 17, 1995.

21. "Manmade malaria" from N. L. Karla, *Status Report on Malaria and Other Health-Related Aspects of the Sardar Sarovar Projects, and Recommendations Regarding Short-Term and Long-Term Remedial Measures*, January 1992, as cited in Bradford F. Morse and Thomas R. Berger, *Sardar Sarovar: The Report of the Independent Review* (Ottawa: Resource Futures International Inc., 1992).

22. Rimjhim Jain, "Mosquitoes Storm the Desert," *Down to Earth*, November 30, 1994; Max Martin and Ambika Sharma, "The Microbes Strike Back" *Down to Earth*, January 15, 1995; quote from Karla, op. cit. note 21.

23. M.J. Bouma, H.E. Sondorp, and H.J. van der Kaay, "Climate Change and Periodic Malaria," *The Lancet*, June 4, 1994; Colombian outbreak from Dr. Paul Epstein, Harvard School of Public Health, Cambridge, Mass., private communication, September 29, 1995.

24. Lack of built-in immunity from Fred Pearce, "Global Alert Over Malaria," *New Scientist*, May 13, 1995; Michael E. Loevinsohn, "Climatic Warming and Increased Malaria Incidence in Rwanda," *The Lancet*, March 19, 1994.

25. Encephalitis from Andrew Dobson and Robin Carper, "Biodiversity: Health and Climate Change," *The Lancet*, October 30, 1993; "The Heat Is On," *Down to Earth*, April 30, 1994.

26. Willem J.M. Martens, Jan Rotmans, and Louis W. Niessen, "Climate Change and Malaria Risk: An Integrated Modelling Approach," Global Dynamics and Sustainable Development Program, Research for Man and the Environment (RIVM), National Institute of Public Health and Environmental Protection, Bilthoven, Netherlands, March 1994; Willem J.M. Martens et al., "Potential Risk of Global Climate Change on Malaria Risk," *Environmental Health Perspectives*, May 1995.

27. Dr. Paul Ewald, Biologist, Amherst College, Amherst, Mass., private communication, April 22, 1995; see also Paul W. Ewald, *Evolution of Infectious Disease* (New York: Oxford University Press, 1994).

28. Human migration from George A. Gellert, "International Migration and Con-

trol of Communicable Diseases," *Social Science Medicine*, Vol. 37, No. 2, 1993; "viral traffic" coinage from Stephen S. Morse, "Regulating Viral Traffic," *Issues in Science and Technology*, Fall 1990.

29. Morse, op. cit note 17.

30. Mexico from William H. McNeill, *Plagues and People* (Garden City, N.Y.: Anchor Press/Doubleday, 1976).

31. Air travel from International Air Transport Association (IATA), "Review of Air Transport Development in 1994," in IATA, *World Air Transport Statistics* (Montreal, Que., Canada: 1995); Robert E. Shope and Alfred S. Evans, "Assessing Geographic and Transport Factors, and Recognition of New Viruses," in Morse, op. cit. note 12.

32. Kinshasa highway from Richard Preston, *The Hot Zone* (New York: Anchor Books Doubleday, 1994); AIDS data for Kinshasa, Zaire, from W. Henry Mosley and Peter Cowley, "The Challenge of World Health," *Population Bulletin*, December 1991; global AIDS data from Aaron Sachs, "HIV/AIDS Cases Rise at Record Rates," in Lester R. Brown, Nicholas Lenssen, and Hal Kane, *Vital Signs 1995* (New York: W.W. Norton & Company, 1995).

33. D.J. Gubler and D.W. Trent, "Emergence of Epidemic Dengue/Dengue Hemorrhagic Fever as a Public Health Problem in the Americas," *Infectious Agents and Disease*, Vol. 2, No. 6, 1993.

34. Ibid.; D.J. Gubler, "Dengue and Dengue Hemorrhagic Fever in the Americas," in Southeast Asia Regional Office of WHO, *Dengue/Dengue Hemorrhagic Fever*, Monograph No. 22, New Delhi, 1993; Puerto Rico from Jane Stevens, "Dengue Cases on the Rise," *Washington Post* (Health Section), June 6, 1995.

35. Discussion of different mosquito vectors for dengue from Gubler, op. cit. note 34; tire shipment from Joshua Lederberg, Robert E. Shope, and Stanley C. Oaks, Jr., eds., *Emerging Infections: Microbial Threats to Health in the United States* (Washington, D.C.: Institute of Medicine, National Academy Press, 1992); U.S. cities from Robin Marantz Henig, "The New Mosquito Menace," *New York Times*, September 13, 1995; Rajiv Chandrasekaran, "Bold and Bloodthirsty," *Washington Post*, August 17, 1995.

36. Gubler and Trent, op. cit. note 33.

37. Rahul Shrivastava, "A Plague on This Country," *Down to Earth*, October 31, 1994; Meghan Kinney, "Plague and Aid," in "Special Edition: Fighting World Health Crises," *Emergency Preparedness News* (Business Publishers, Inc.), October 1994; Paul Epstein, "Climate Change Played a Role in India's Plague," *New York Times*, November 13, 1994.

38. Mahish McDonald, "Surat's Revenge: India Counts the Mounting Costs of Poverty," *Far Eastern Economic Review*, October 13, 1994; Stefan Wagstyl, "A Shock to the System," *Financial Times*, October 5, 1994; John F. Burns, "India's City of Plague: Cesspool of Urban Ills," *New York Times*, October 3, 1994.

39. Disease surveillance and medical community from Shrivastava, op. cit. note 37; Declan Butler, "India Ponders the Flaws Exposed by Plague," and K. S. Jayaraman and Declan Butler, " . . . As Doubts Over Outbreak Rumble On," both in *Nature*, November 10, 1994; Lawrence K. Altman, "Lesson of Plague: Beware of 'Vanquished' Diseases," *New York Times*, September 27, 1994; "Plague: India," *Weekly Epidemiological Record*, February 3, 1995.

40. McNeill, op. cit. note 30; annual costs of influenza from Working Group on Emerging and Re-emerging Infectious Diseases, Committee on International Science, Engineering, and Technology, *Global Microbial Threats in the 1990s* (Washington, D.C.: National Science and Technology Council, 1995); "Flu Shots for Working-Age People Cut Winter Sick Days, Report Says," *Washington Post*, October 5, 1995.

41. Murray Feshbach, *Ecological Disaster: Cleaning Up the Hidden Legacy of the Soviet Regime* (New York: Twentieth Century Fund Press, 1995); diphtheria data from "Expanded Program on Immunization: Diphtheria Epidemic in the Newly Independent States of the Former USSR, 1990–1994," *Weekly Epidemiological Record*, May 19, 1995; Black Sea from Michael Specter, "Russia Moves on Cholera Epidemic in South," *New York Times*, August 20, 1994; Andrei Ivanov and Judith Perera, "Another Cholera Outbreak in Ukraine; Russia on Alert," Inter-Press Service, July 4, 1995; plankton detection from Epstein, op. cit. note 15.

42. Donatus de Silva, "Vaccinating Against War," *Our Planet*, Vol. 7, No. 3, 1995.

43. Relative illness figure from Stig Regli, "Risk vs. Risk: Proposed Decision Tree for Drinking Water Management," *Health and Environment Digest*, June 1993; 25 million figure from Water Solidarity Network, *Water and Health in Underprivileged Urban Areas* (Paris: 1994); diarrhea from José Martines, Margaret Phillips, and Richard G. A. Feachem, "Diarrheal Diseases," in Jamison et al., op. cit. note 2; Report of the Director-General, op. cit. note 4.

44. Waldman from "WHO Steps up Fight Against Cholera and Dysentery in Southern Africa," press release, WHO, Geneva, December 2, 1993; ORT data from UNICEF, *The State of the World's Children 1995* (New York: Oxford University Press, 1995); Report of the Director-General, op. cit. note 4.

45. "Human Parasites Related to an Aquatic Environment," in James A. Lee, "Health Considerations for Economic Development," *The Environment, Public Health and Human Ecology: Considerations for Economic Development* (Baltimore, Md.: Johns Hopkins University Press, 1985).

46. U.N. Development Programme, *Human Development Report 1994* (New York: Oxford University Press, 1994); UNICEF,

op. cit. note 44; urban developing areas from The Joint Academies Committee on the Mexico City Water Supply of the National Research Council and Academia Nacional de la Investigacíon Científica, A.C., Academia Nacional de Ingeniería, A.C., *Mexico City's Water Supply: Improving the Outlook for Sustainability* (Washington, D.C.: National Academy Press, 1995).

47. Environmental Protection Agency estimate from "The Health Costs of Drinking Water Contamination: Waterborne Infectious Disease," *Environmental and Energy Study Institute Weekly Bulletin*, Washington, D.C., August 15, 1994; North American cases from Pierre Payment et al., "A Randomized Trial to Evaluate the Risk of Gastrointestinal Disease due to Consumption of Drinking Water Meeting Current Microbiological Standards," *American Journal of Public Health*, June 1991, as cited in Rose, Haas, and Gerba, op. cit. note 19.

48. U.S. data and cryptosporidiosis at low dose from Gunther F. Craun, "Waterborne Disease Outbreaks in the United States of America: Causes and Prevention," *World Health Statistics Quarterly*, Vol. 45, 1992; Erik D. Olson, "You Are What You Drink . . . Cryptosporidium and Other Contaminants Found in the Water Served to Millions of Americans," Natural Resources Defense Council Briefing Paper, Washington, D.C. June 1995; Morris data from "Health Costs of Drinking Water Contamination," op. cit. note 47.

49. Feshbach, op. cit. note 41; Movchanok from Michael Specter, "Russia Fights a Rising Tide of Infection: Epidemics Straining Health Care System," *New York Times*, October 2, 1994.

50. "Cholera in 1993, Part I," *Weekly Epidemiological Record*, July 15, 1994; James Brooke, "Cholera Kills 1,100 in Peru and Marches On, Reaching the Brazilian Border," *New York Times*, April 19, 1991; Luis Loyola and Patricio Hevia, "Keeping Cholera

at Bay," *World Health*, May/June 1993; $750 million from Epstein, op. cit. note 23; $200 billion from "The Centers for Disease Control and Prevention Strategy of Emerging Infectious Disease Threats," *Population and Development Review*, September 1994.

51. Joint Academies Committee, op. cit. note 46; Craun, op. cit. note 48.

52. Water Solidarity Network, op. cit. note 43.

53. Paul R. Epstein, Timothy E. Ford, and Rita R. Colwell, "Marine Ecosystems," *The Lancet*, November 13, 1993; Paul R. Epstein, "Algal Blooms in the Spread and Persistence of Cholera," *BioSystems*, Vol. 31, 1993.

54. Fred Pearce, "Dead in the Water," *New Scientist*, February 4, 1995; Marlise Simons, "Dead Mediterranean Dolphins Give Nations Pause," *New York Times*, February 2, 1992.

55. Stuart B. Levy, *The Antibiotic Paradox: How Miracle Drugs Are Destroying the Miracle* (New York: Plenum Press, 1992).

56. Smith, op. cit. note 13.

57. Levy, op. cit. note 55.

58. Naso quote from Gene Bylinsky, "The New Fight Against Killer Microbes," *Fortune*, September 5, 1994; Levy, op. cit. note 5; $4 billion from American Society for Microbiology (ASM), *Report of the ASM Task Force on Antibiotic Resistance* (Washington, D.C.: 1995).

59. Brown, op. cit. note 8.

60. Malawi and Zaire from "World Malaria Situation in 1992, Part I: Africa and the Americas," *Weekly Epidemiological Record*, October 21, 1994; $1.8 billion from Report of the Director-General, op. cit. note 4; Vietnam from "World Malaria Situation in 1992, Part III: Middle South Asia, Eastern Asia and Oceania," *Weekly Epidemiological Record*, November 4, 1994.

61. New Guinea from ASM, op. cit. note 58; Sharon Kingman, "Resistance a European Problem, Too," *Science*, April 15, 1994; Atlanta from Jo Hofmann et al., "The Prevalence of Drug-Resistant *Streptococcus pneumoniae* in Atlanta," *New England Journal of Medicine*, August 24, 1995.

62. Levy, op. cit. note 55; Levy, op. cit. note 5.

63. ASM, op. cit. note 58.

64. Lederberg, Shope, and Oaks, op. cit. note 35; "Disease Fights Back," *The Economist*, May 20, 1994; costs of drug-resistant TB from "Directly Observed Therapy Effective Against TB," *Washington Post*, April 28, 1994; Melinda Henneberger, "Study Sees a New Threat in Tuberculosis Infections," *New York Times*, June 16, 1994; Working Group on Emerging and Re-emerging Infectious Diseases, op. cit. note 40; Director-General, op. cit. note 1.

65. Hungary from Rachel Nowak, "Hungary Sees an Improvement in Penicillin Resistance," *Science*, April 15, 1994; David Brown, " 'Wonder Drugs' Losing Healing Aura," *Washington Post*, June 26, 1995; "CDC Backs More Sparing Use of Antibiotics," *Washington Post*, September 29, 1995.

66. Melinda S. Meade, John W. Florin, and Wilbert M. Gesler, *Medical Geography* (New York: Guilford Press, 1988); McNeill, op. cit. note 30.

67. Emmanuel Mwero, "Tsetse Control: Something Old, Something New," *Ceres*, March/April 1995; David Baron, "The Pros and Cons of the Tsetse Fly's Existence Opined," *All Things Considered*, National Public Radio, August 29, 1995; Paul R. Epstein, David J. Rogers, and Rudi Slooff, "Satellite Imaging and Vector-borne Disease," *The Lancet*, May 29, 1993.

68. Tim Beardsley, "Better Than a Cure," *Scientific American*, January 1995.

69. Working Group on Emerging and Re-emerging Infectious Diseases, op. cit. note 40, citing WHO data; World Bank, op. cit. note 2; Beardsley, op. cit. note 68; Helen Saxenian, "Optimizing Health Care in Developing Countries," *Issues in Science and Technology*, Winter 1994–95; Peter Cowley and Dean T. Jamison, "The Cost-Effectiveness of Immunization," *World Health*, March/April 1993.

70. John Mugabe, "Africa Must Raise its Budgets for Human Health Research," *Biotechnology and Development Monitor*, December 1993; D.A. Henderson, "Strategies for the Twenty-First Century: Control or Eradication?" *Archives of Virology* (Special Issue of the Journal of the Virology Division of the International Union of Microbiological Societies), 1992.

71. Dr. Oyewale Tomori, College of Medicine, Ibadan, Nigeria, private communication to Dr. Stephen S. Morse, Rockefeller University, October 30, 1993.

72. Cited in Ann Gibbons, "Where Are 'New' Diseases Born?" *Science*, August 6, 1993.

73. Forty-Eighth World Health Assembly, "Communicable Diseases Prevention and Control: New, Emerging, and Re-emerging Infectious Diseases," WHO, Geneva, May 12, 1995.

74. Dorothy Preslar, Washington ProMED Officer, Federation of American Scientists, private communication, July 14, 1995; Ebola from John Schwartz, "Computers Used to Fight A Much Deadlier Virus," *Washington Post*, May 20, 1995; tracking Ebola in Kikwit from John Woodall, ProMED List Moderator, "Moderator's Account: The Ebola Outbreak," New York State Department of Health, Albany, N.Y., May 8, 1995.

75. T. Demetri Vacalis, Christopher L.R. Bartlett, and Cheryl G. Shapiro, "Electronic Communication and the Future of International Public Health Surveillance," *Emerging Infectious Diseases* (CDC), January/March 1995.

Chapter 8. Upholding Human Rights and Environmental Justice

1. Marlise Simons, "Brazilian Who Fought to Protect Amazon is Killed," *New York Times*, December 24, 1988; Andrew Revkin, *The Burning Season: The Murder of Chico Mendes and the Fight for the Amazon Rain Forest* (New York: Plume, 1990); Susanna Hecht and Alexander Cockburn, *The Fate of the Forest: Developers, Destroyers, and Defenders of the Amazon* (New York: HarperCollins, 1990).

2. Hecht and Cockburn, op. cit. note 1; I. Foster Brown et al., "Empowering Local Communities in Land-Use Management: The Chico Mendes Extractive Reserve, Acre, Brazil," *Cultural Survival Quarterly*, Winter 1995; Stephan Schwartzman, "Extractive Reserves: The Rubber Tappers' Strategy for Sustainable Use of the Amazon Rainforest," in John O. Browder, ed., *Fragile Lands of Latin America: Strategies for Sustainable Development* (Boulder, Colo.: Westview Press, 1989); Philip M. Fearnside, "Extractive Reserves in Brazilian Amazonia: An Opportunity to Maintain Tropical Rain Forest under Sustainable Use," *BioScience*, June 1989; John O. Browder, "The Limits of Extractivism: Tropical Forest Strategies Beyond Extractive Reserves," *BioScience*, March 1992.

3. Revkin, op. cit. note 1.

4. James K. Boyce, "Inequality as a Cause of Environmental Degradation," *Ecological Economics*, Vol. 11, 1994, pp. 169–78; Robert D. Bullard, ed., *Unequal Protection: Environmental Justice and Communities of Color* (San Francisco: Sierra Club Books, 1994); Barbara Rose Johnston, ed., *Who Pays the Price? The Sociocultural Context of Environmental Crisis* (Washington, D.C.: Island Press, 1994).

5. Acre land distribution from Revkin, op. cit. note 1, and from Stephan Schwartzman, "Land Distribution and the Social Costs of

Frontier Development in Brazil: Social and Historical Context of Extractive Reserves," in Daniel C. Nepstad and Stephan Schwartzman, eds., *Non-Timber Products from Tropical Forests: Evaluation of a Conservation and Development Strategy—Advances in Economic Botany, Vol. 9* (New York: The New York Botanical Garden, 1992). Similar trends are documented in Hecht and Cockburn, op. cit. note 1, in Marianne Schmink and Charles H. Wood, *Contested Frontiers in Amazonia* (New York: Columbia University Press, 1992), and in Erick G. Highum and Karen Parker, "Development, Rights, and the Rainforests," *Peace Review*, Fall 1994.

6. Bunyan Bryant, ed., *Environmental Justice: Issues, Policies, Solutions* (Washington, D.C.: Island Press, 1995); Richard Hofrichter, ed., *Toxic Struggles: The Theory and Practice of Environmental Justice* (Philadelphia: New Society Publishers, 1993); James K. Boyce, "Equity and the Environment: Social Justice Today as a Prerequisite for Sustainability in the Future," *Alternatives*, Vol. 21, No. 1, 1995; North Carolina from Robert D. Bullard, *Dumping in Dixie: Race, Class, and Environmental Quality* (Boulder, Colo.: Westview Press, 1990); Narmada from Human Rights Watch/Asia, "Before the Deluge: Human Rights Abuses at India's Narmada Dam," *News from Asia Watch*, June 17, 1992, and from "Sardar Sarovar Project: Review of Resettlement and Rehabilitation in Maharashtra," *Economic and Political Weekly*, August 21, 1993; South Africa from Alan B. Durning, *Apartheid's Environmental Toll*, Worldwatch Paper 95 (Washington, D.C.: Worldwatch Institute, May 1990).

7. Michael J. Kane, "Promoting Political Rights to Protect the Environment," *The Yale Journal of International Law*, Winter 1993; Amartya Sen, "Freedoms and Needs: An Argument for the Primacy of Political Rights," *The New Republic*, January 10 and 17, 1994; Human Rights Watch, *Indivisible Human Rights: The Relationship of Political and Civil Rights to Survival, Subsistence and Poverty* (New York: 1992).

8. Nigeria letter from Stephen Mills, Associate Representative, International Program, Sierra Club, Washington, D.C., private communication, October 13, 1995; Kothari quote from Ashish Kothari, Lecturer in Environmental Studies, Indian Institute of Public Administration, New Delhi, private communication, July 25, 1995.

9. Audrey R. Chapman, "Earth Rights and Responsibilities: Human Rights and Environmental Protection—Symposium Overview," *The Yale Journal of International Law*, Winter 1993.

10. Ibid.

11. Missing human component in wilderness preservation from Arturo Gomez-Pompa and Andrea Kaus, "Taming the Wilderness Myth," *BioScience*, April 1992, from Margaret E. Keck, "Parks, People and Power: The Shifting Terrain of Environmentalism," *NACLA Report on the Americas*, March/April 1995, from "When Conservation is Not Enough: Bringing the Community Back into View," *Surviving Together*, Spring 1995, and from Michael Wells and Katrina Brandon with Lee Hannah, *People and Parks: Linking Protected Area Management with Local Communities* (Washington, D.C.: World Bank, 1992); India's protected areas from Ashish Kothari, Saloni Suri, and Neena Singh, "Protected Areas in India: A New Beginning," *Economic and Political Weekly*, forthcoming, from Sarbani Sarkar et al., *Joint Management of Protected Areas in India: Report of a Workshop* (New Delhi: Indian Institute of Public Administration, 1995), and from Neena Singh and Ashish Kothari, "Balancing Act: The Interim Report on Rajaji National Park," *Frontline*, June 30, 1995; Madhya Pradesh example from Jules N. Pretty and Michael P. Pimbert, "Beyond Conservation Ideology and the Wilderness Myth," *Natural Resources Forum*, Vol. 19, No. 1, 1995.

12. Kerry Kennedy Cuomo, "Human Rights and the Environment: Common Ground," *The Yale Journal of International Law*, Winter 1993; Sangita Wilk-Sanatani, "Les-

sons Learned at the World Conference on Human Rights," *Environmental Conservation*, Autumn 1993.

13. Holmes Rolston, III, "Rights and Responsibilities on the Home Planet," *The Yale Journal of International Law*, Winter 1993.

14. Bruce Stutz, "The Sea Cucumber War," *Audubon*, May/June 1995; Macarena Green, "Crisis in the Galápagos Islands," *Wild Lands Advocate*, April 1995.

15. Richard Stone, "Fishermen Threaten Galápagos," *Science*, February 3, 1995; James Brooke, "Ban on Harvesting Sea Cucumber Pits Scientists Against Fishermen," *New York Times*, November 2, 1993; Valle quote from Stutz, op. cit. note 14.

16. Robert K. Hitchcock, "International Human Rights, the Environment, and Indigenous Peoples," *Colorado Journal of International Environmental Law and Policy*, Winter 1994; Alan Thein Durning, *Guardians of the Land: Indigenous Peoples and the Health of the Earth*, Worldwatch Paper 112 (Washington, D.C.: Worldwatch Institute, December 1992); Brown et al., op. cit. note 2.

17. Michael Posner, "Rally Round Human Rights," *Foreign Policy*, Winter 1994–95; Fali S. Nariman, "The Universality of Human Rights," *International Commission of Jurists—The Review*, No. 50, 1993; Jack Donnelly, "Human Rights in the New World Order," *World Policy Journal*, Spring 1992; Center for the Study of Human Rights, *Twenty-Five Human Rights Documents* (New York: Columbia University, 1994).

18. Margaret Keck and Kathryn Sikkink, "International Issue Networks in the Environment and Human Rights," prepared for the XVII International Congress of the Latin American Studies Association, Los Angeles, September 24–27, 1992; Human Rights Watch (HRW) and Natural Resources Defense Council (NRDC), *Defending the Earth: Abuses of Human Rights and the Environment* (Washington, D.C.: 1992); Cuomo, op. cit.

note 12; Wilk-Sanatani, op. cit. note 12; Kane, op. cit. note 7.

19. Paul G. Harris, "Global Equity and Sustainable Development," *Peace Review*, Fall 1994; Adriana Fabra Aguilar and Neil A. F. Popovic, "Lawmaking in the United Nations: The UN Study on Human Rights and the Environment," *Reciel*, Vol. 3, No. 4, 1994.

20. HRW and NRDC, op. cit. note 18.

21. Fernandez and Dara from "Activists at Risk in US and Abroad," *Earth Island Journal*, Summer 1995; additional information on Dara from Amnesty International, "Kingdom of Cambodia: Human Rights and the New Government," New York, March 14, 1995. Table 8–1 is drawn from the following: Kozhevnikov from HRW and NRDC, op. cit. note 18; D'Achille from Kane, op. cit. note 7; Domoldol from Rainforest Action Network, "Philippine Rainforest Leader Murdered," Action Alert #64, San Francisco, September 1991; Maathai from Cuomo, op. cit. note 12, and from Mary Ann French, "The Woman and Mother Earth," *Washington Post*, June 2, 1992; Pence from Jim Robbins, "Target Green: Federal Land Managers under Attack," *Audubon*, July/August 1995, and from "Forest Ranger Becomes Target of 2 Bombings," *New York Times*, August 6, 1995.

22. David Helvarg, *The War Against the Greens: The "Wise Use" Movement, the New Right, and Anti-Environmental Violence* (San Francisco: Sierra Club Books, 1994); David Helvarg, "Property Rights and Militias: The Anti-Enviro Connection," *The Nation*, May 22, 1995.

23. "The Goldman Environmental Prize Winners for 1995," *Earth Island Journal*, Summer 1995; Charles McCoy, "Goldman Environmental Prizes Likely to Go to California Woman, Nigerian," *Wall Street Journal*, April 17, 1995; Raymond Bonner, "Trying to Document Rights Abuses," *New York Times*, July 26, 1995.

24. Johnston, op. cit. note 4.

25. Robert D. Bullard, *Dumping in Dixie: Race, Class, and Environmental Quality* (Boulder, Colo.: Westview Press, 1990); Robert M. Frye, "Environmental Injustice: The Failure of American Civil Rights and Environmental Law to Provide Equal Protection from Pollution," *Dickinson Journal of Environmental Law and Policy*, Fall 1993; Benjamin A. Goldman, *Not Just Prosperity: Achieving Sustainability with Environmental Justice* (Washington, D.C.: National Wildlife Federation, 1993).

26. Johnston, op. cit. note 4.

27. Ken Saro-Wiwa, "Stand by Me and the Ogoni People," *Earth Island Journal*, Summer 1995; Human Rights Watch/Africa, "Nigeria: The Dawn of a New Dark Age," New York, October 1994; "Government in Nigeria Accused of Repression," *Financial Times*, November 11, 1994; "Nigerian Oil Activist on Trial," *The Ecologist*, January/February 1995; "Persecution of Ken Saro-Wiwa," *New African*, May 1995; Environmental Defense Fund, "Environment, Human Rights Groups Demand Niger Delta Cleanup," Washington, D.C., May 26, 1995; Stephen Buckley, "Nigeria Hangs Playwright, Eight Activists," *Washington Post*, November 11, 1995.

28. Steve Kretzmann, "Nigeria's 'Drilling Fields'," *Multinational Monitor*, January/February 1995; Geraldine Brooks, "Slick Alliance: Shell's Nigerian Fields Produce Few Benefits for Region's Villagers," *Wall Street Journal*, May 6, 1994.

29. Kretzmann, op. cit. note 28; Brooks, op. cit. note 28.

30. Three Gorges from Audrey R. Topping, "Ecological Roulette: Damming the Yangtze," *Foreign Affairs*, September/October 1995; Lena H. Sun, "Dam Could Alter Face of China," *Washington Post*, December 31, 1991. Table 8–2 is drawn from the following: Udege from Anjali Acharya, "The Fate of the Boreal Forests," *World Watch*, May/June 1995, and from Kevin Schafer and Martha Hill, "The Logger and the Tiger," *Wildlife Conservation*, May/June 1993; Wales from "Opencast Miners Plunder Wales," *The Ecologist*, January/February 1995; Yami from Global Response, "GRAction #6/95, Nuclear Waste Dumping—Environmental Racism/Taiwan," Boulder, Colo., September 8, 1995, and from "The Stink on Orchid Island," *The Economist*, August 26, 1995; Ecuador from Thomas S. O'Connor, "'We Are Part of Nature': Indigenous Peoples' Rights as a Basis for Environmental Protection in the Amazon Basin," *Colorado Journal of International Environmental Law and Policy*, Winter 1994, and from David Holmstrom, "Texaco Has Left Ecuador, But Its Impact Remains," *Christian Science Monitor*, March 25, 1994; Malawi from Bill Derman and Anne Ferguson, "Human Rights, Environment, and Development: Dispossession of Fishing Communities on Lake Malawi," in Johnston, op. cit. note 4.

31. Fred Pearce, "The Biggest Dam in the World," *New Scientist*, January 25, 1995; Human Rights Watch/Asia, "The Three Gorges Dam in China: Forced Resettlement, Suppression of Dissent, and Labor Rights Concerns," New York, February 1995; Dai Qing, *Yangtze! Yangtze!* (London: Earthscan, 1994).

32. Sandra Burton, "Taming the River Wild," *Time*, December 19, 1994; Population Reference Bureau (PRB), *1995 World Population Data Sheet* (Washington, D.C.: 1995); study by Chinese Academy of Sciences from Pearce, op. cit. note 31.

33. Environment Department, *Resettlement and Development: The Bankwide Review of Projects Involving Involuntary Resettlement, 1986–1993* (Washington, D.C.: World Bank, 1994).

34. David Western and R. Michael Wright, eds., *Natural Connections: Perspectives in Community-based Conservation* (Washington, D.C.: Island Press, 1994); John Friedmann and Haripriya Rangan, eds., *In Defense of Livelihood: Comparative Studies on Environmental Action* (West Hartford, Conn.: Kumarian Press, 1993); Charlie Pye-Smith and Grazia Borrini Feyerabend with Richard Sandbrook, *The*

Wealth of Communities: Stories of Success in Local Environmental Management (West Hartford, Conn.: Kumarian Press, 1994); Christine Meyer and Faith Moosang, eds., *Living with the Land: Communities Restoring the Earth* (Philadelphia: New Society Publishers, 1992). Table 8–3 is drawn from the following: India from Vithal Rajan, "Power of the Poor," *Resurgence*, September/October 1994; Yanesha from Manuel Lázaro, Mario Pariona, and Robert Simeone, "A Natural Harvest," *Cultural Survival Quarterly*, Spring 1993; Egypt from Laila Kamel, "Learning from the Poor," *Earth Island Journal*, Summer 1994; California from Michael Corbett, "California Tribe Wins Control of Native Lands and Plans Nature Park," *Christian Science Monitor*, April 5, 1995; Nepal from Vijayalakshmi Balakrishnan, "Trekking to Balanced Development," *Down to Earth*, August 15, 1992, and from Michael P. Wells, "A Profile and Interim Assessment of the Annapurna Conservation Area Project, Nepal," in Western and Wright, op. cit. in this note; Kakadu from M.A. Hill and A.J. Press, "Kakadu National Park: An Australian Experience in Comanagement," in Western and Wright, op. cit. in this note.

35. Pye-Smith and Feyerabend with Sandbrook, op. cit. note 34.

36. Ibid.

37. Muhammad Yunus, "New Development Options Towards the 21st Century," Grameen Bank, Dhaka, Bangladesh, undated; Manfred A. Max-Neef, *Human Scale Development: Conception, Application, and Further Reflections* (New York: The Apex Press, 1991); Bruce Rich, *Mortgaging the Earth: The World Bank, Environmental Impoverishment, and the Crisis of Development* (Boston: Beacon Press, 1994); Mahbub ul Haq, *Reflections on Human Development* (New York: Oxford University Press, 1995).

38. The Ecologist, *Whose Common Future? Reclaiming the Commons* (Philadelphia: New Society Publishers, 1993); Wolfgang Sachs, *Global Ecology: A New Arena of Political Conflict* (London: Zed Books, 1993).

39. Hilary F. French, *Partnership for the Planet: An Environmental Agenda for the United Nations*, Worldwatch Paper 126 (Washington, D.C.: Worldwatch Institute, July 1995).

40. World Resources Institute (WRI), *World Resources 1994–95* (New York: Oxford University Press, 1994); Jyoti Parikh et al., "Consumption Patterns: The Driving Force of Environmental Stress," Indira Gandhi Institute of Development Research Discussion Paper No. 59, Bombay, 1991.

41. PRB, op. cit. note 32; Alan Durning, *How Much Is Enough? The Consumer Society and the Future of the Earth* (New York: W.W. Norton & Company, 1992).

42. WRI, op. cit. note 40; John E. Young, *Mining the Earth*, Worldwatch Paper 109 (Washington, D.C.: Worldwatch Institute, July 1992).

43. Jennifer R. Kitt, "Waste Exports to the Developing World: A Global Response," *The Georgetown International Environmental Law Review*, Vol. 7, 1995; Jennifer Clapp, *Dumping on the Poor: The Toxic Waste Trade with Developing Countries*, Occasional Paper No. 5 (Cambridge, U.K.: University of Cambridge, Global Security Programme, 1994); Greenpeace, "Database of Known Hazardous Waste Exports from OECD to non-OECD Countries, 1989–March 1994," Washington, D.C., March 1994, prepared for the Second Conference of Parties to the Basel Convention, March 21–25, 1994, Geneva.

44. Clapp, op. cit. note 43; Third World Network, *Toxic Terror: Dumping of Hazardous Wastes in the Third World* (Penang, Malaysia: 1989).

45. Gary Lee, "Proposal to Log Suriname's Rain Forest Splits the Needy Nation," *Washington Post*, May 13, 1995; Anthony DePalma, "In Suriname's Rain Forests, A

Fight Over Trees vs. Jobs," *New York Times*, September 4, 1995.

46. Lee, op. cit. note 45; Russell A. Mittermeier, "Economic Crisis in Suriname Threatens Ecological Eden," *Christian Science Monitor*, April 19, 1995.

47. The Human Rights Council of Australia Inc., *The Rights Way to Development: A Human Rights Approach to Development Assistance* (Sydney: 1995); Iglesias's letter from Lee, op. cit. note 45, and from Nigel Sizer, "Suriname's Fire Sale," *New York Times*, May 14, 1995.

48. Mittermeier, op. cit. note 46; Russell A. Mittermeier, "What Costa Rica Can Teach Suriname," *Wall Street Journal*, September 1, 1995.

49. For per capita carbon emissions, see Table 2–2 in Chapter 2; Atiq Rahman, Nick Robins, and Annie Roncerel, eds., *Exploding the Population Myth: Consumption versus Population—Which is the Climate Bomb?* (Brussels: Climate Action Network, 1993).

50. Hilary F. French, *After the Earth Summit: The Future of Environmental Governance*, Worldwatch Paper 107 (Washington, D.C.: Worldwatch Institute, March 1992); Richard Elliot Benedick, *Ozone Diplomacy: New Directions in Safeguarding the Planet* (Cambridge, Mass.: Harvard University Press, 1991).

51. Aguilar and Popovic, op. cit. note 19.

52. Human Rights Council of Australia, op. cit. note 47.

53. Aguilar and Popovic, op. cit. note 19; "The 1994 Draft Declaration of Principles on Human Rights and the Environment," Geneva, 1994; Commission on Human Rights, Sub-Commission on Prevention of Discrimination and Protection of Minorities, *Human Rights and the Environment: Final Report*, prepared by Fatma Zohra Ksentini, Special Rapporteur, Forty-sixth session, Item 4 of the provisional agenda, July 6, 1994; "Resolution on Human Rights and the Environ-

ment," *Environmental Law Network International Newsletter*, February 1995; Allan McChesney, "Linking Human Rights, Environment, and Sustainability," *ECODECISION*, Winter 1995.

54. Center for the Study of Human Rights, op. cit. note 17; Aguilar and Popovic, op. cit. note 19; French, op. cit. note 50; Commission on Human Rights, op. cit. note 53; Gunter Hoog and Angela Steinmetz, eds., *International Conventions on Protection of Humanity and Environment* (New York: Walter de Gruyter Publishers, 1993); Ferdinando Albanese, "Towards a New Human Right?" *Naturopa*, No. 70, 1992; Kristi N. Rea, "Linking Human Rights and Environmental Quality," in Lawrence E. Susskind, William R. Moomaw, and Adil Najam, eds., *Papers on International Environmental Negotiation, Vol. IV* (Cambridge, Mass.: The Program on Negotiation at Harvard Law School, 1994).

55. Aguilar and Popovic, op. cit. note 19; Rea, op. cit. note 54; Amnesty International, *Summary of Selected International Procedures and Bodies Dealing with Human Rights Matters* (New York: 1989); Hurst Hannum, ed., *Guide to International Human Rights Practice* (Philadelphia: University of Pennsylvania Press, 1984); Susan E. Brice, "Convention on the Rights of the Child: Using a Human Rights Instrument to Protect Against Environmental Threats," *The Georgetown International Environmental Law Review*, Vol. 7, 1995.

56. Aguilar and Popovic, op. cit. note 19; Commission on Human Rights, Sub-Commission on Prevention of Discrimination and Protection of Minorities, *Human Rights and the Environment: Progress Report*, prepared by Fatma Zohra Ksentini, Special Rapporteur, Forty-fourth session, Item 4 of the provisional agenda, July 2, 1992; Neil Popovic, Attorney, International Program, Sierra Club Legal Defense Fund, San Francisco, private communication, October 12, 1995.

57. Center for the Study of Human Rights, op. cit. note 17; Nici Nelson and Susan

Wright, *Power and Participatory Development: Theory and Practice* (London: Intermediate Technology Publications, 1995); Judith Plant and Christopher Plant, *Putting Power in its Place: Create Community Control!* (Philadelphia: New Society Publishers, 1992); Camilla Toulmin, "Empowering the People," *Our Planet*, Vol. 6, No. 5, 1994; Anisur Rahman, *People's Self-Development: Perspectives on Participatory Action Research—A Journey Through Experience* (London: Zed Books, 1994); Burkina Faso from Fiona Hinchcliffe et al., *New Horizons: The Economic, Social, and Environmental Impacts of Participatory Watershed Development*, Gatekeeper Series No. 50 (London: International Institute for Environment and Development, 1995).

58. The Environmental Law Reporter, *Community Right-to-Know Deskbook* (Washington, D.C.: Environmental Law Institute, 1988); Mexico from Mark J. Spalding, "Resolving International Environmental Disputes: Public Participation and the Right-to-Know," *Journal of Environment and Development*, Winter 1995.

59. David Sarokin, "A Proposal to Create a Corporate Social Environmental Impact Statement," *New Solutions*, Spring 1995; World Bank from Nancy C. Alexander, Bread for the World Institute, Testimony on the World Bank, Poverty, and Popular Participation to the Banking Subcommittee on Domestic and International Monetary Affairs, U.S. House of Representatives, Washington, D.C., March 27, 1995.

60. Environmental Law Reporter, op. cit. note 58; U.S. Environmental Protection Agency, Office of Pollution Prevention and Toxics, *1993 Toxics Release Inventory: Public Data Release* (Washington, D.C.: 1995).

61. Sanford Lewis, "Moving Forward Toward Environmental Excellence: Corporate Environmental Audits, Disclosure, and Stakeholder Empowerment," *New Solutions*, Spring 1995.

62. Chico Mendes Extractive Reserve from Brown et al., op. cit. note 2; Nunavik Inuit Indians from William B. Kemp and Lorraine F. Brooke, "Towards Information Self-Sufficiency: The Nunavik Inuit Gather Information on Ecology and Land Use," *Cultural Survival Quarterly*, Winter 1995; Geographic Information Systems from Michael E. Marchand and Richard Winchell, "Tribal Implementation of GIS: A Case Study of Planning Applications with the Colville Confederated Tribes," *Cultural Survival Quarterly*, Winter 1994, and from Theodore S. Glickman, "Measuring Environmental Equity with Geographical Information Systems," *Renewable Resources Journal*, Autumn 1994.

63. International Development Research Centre, "Northern Manitoba Band Teaches Water-Testing Skills to Chileans," *Leads*, April 1995.

64. Operations Policy Department, *The World Bank and Participation* (Washington, D.C.: World Bank, 1994); Alexander, op. cit. note 59; The Honorable J. Brian Atwood, Administrator, U.S. Agency for International Development, "Statement of Principles on Participatory Development," Washington, D.C., November 16, 1993.

65. Figure of 25 million from Water Solidarity Network, *Water and Health in Underprivileged Urban Areas* (Paris: 1994).

Chapter 9. Shifting to Sustainable Industries

1. For details of these developments, see various chapters in Lester R. Brown, Nicholas Lenssen, and Hal Kane, *Vital Signs 1995* (New York: W.W. Norton & Company, 1995).

2. For details of Aral Sea shrinkage, see Chapter 3; John Pomfret, "Black Sea, Strangled by Pollution, Is Near Ecological Death," *Washington Post*, June 20, 1994; Tom Horton and William M. Eichbaum, *Turning the Tide:*

Saving the Chesapeake Bay (Washington, D.C.: Island Press, 1991); John Jacobs, Maryland Department of Natural Resources, "Eastern Oyster, Fishery Statistics of the United States" (unpublished printout), April 1994, and Virginia Marine Resource Committee, "Oyster Ground Production" (unpublished printout), Newport News, Va., April 1994.

3. Timothy Egan, "Oregon Thrives As It Protects Owls," *In Business*, November/December 1994, reprinted from the *New York Times*; Daniel Glick, "Having Owls and Jobs Too," *National Wildlife*, August/September 1995.

4. Megan Ryan, "CFC Production Plummeting," in Brown, Lenssen, and Kane, op. cit. note 1; Paul Gipe, Paul Gipe & Associates, Tehachapi, Calif., private communication, September 8, 1995; Nicholas Lenssen, "Nuclear Power Flat," in Brown, Lenssen, and Kane, op. cit. note 1.

5. *Interbike Directory 1995* (Newport Beach, Calif.: Primedia, Inc. 1995).; American Automobile Manufacturers Association (AAMA), *World Motor Vehicle Data*, 1994 ed. (Detroit, Mich.: 1994).

6. Hardin B. C. Tibbs, "Industrial Ecology: An Environmental Agenda for Industry," *Annals of Earth*, Vol. 11, No. 1, 1993.

7. Paul D. Maycock, "1995 World PV Module Survey," *PV News*, February 1995; Neelam Matthews, "Dynamic Market Rapidly Unfolds," *Windpower Monthly*, September 1994.

8. Figure 9–1 from Maycock, op. cit. note 7; Figure 9–2 from Christopher Flavin, "Wind Power Soars," in Brown, Lenssen, and Kane, op. cit. note 1.

9. British Petroleum, *BP Statistical Review of World Energy* (London: Group Media & Publications, 1995); United Nations, *World Energy Supplies* (New York: various years).

10. Christopher Flavin and Nicholas Lenssen, *Power Surge: Guide to the Coming Energy Revolution* (New York: W.W. Norton & Company, 1994).

11. Ibid.

12. Ibid.

13. Paul Lewis, "World Bank Cancels Nepal Project Loan," *New York Times*, August 16, 1995.

14. Nicholas Lenssen, "Solar Cell Shipments Expand Repidly," in Brown, Lenssen, and Kane, op. cit. note 1; Christopher Flavin, "Wind Power Soars," in ibid.

15. South African homes figure from "Solar Power: Night and Day," *The Economist*, September 9, 1995; Lynne Duke, "U.S. to Help S. Africa Boost Energy, Create Jobs," *Washington Post*, August 26, 1995.

16. The Editors, "The Simple Act of Breathing: A Worldwide Problem," *International Wildlife*, September/October 1995; Curtis A. Moore, "Poisons In The Air," *International Wildlife*, September/October 1995.

17. Frank Muller, Skip Laitner, and Lyuba Zarsky, "Jobs Benefits of Expanding Investment in Solar Energy," *Solar Industry Journal*, Fourth Quarter 1992; Skip Laitner, consultant, Arlington, Va., private communication, October 2, 1995.

18. Laitner, op. cit. note 17.

19. William Hoagland, "Solar Energy," *Scientific American*, September 1995.

20. Steel Recycling Institute, "A Few Facts About Steel," Factsheet, Pittsburgh, Pa., 1994.

21. Ibid.; Nicholas Lenssen and David Malin Roodman, "Making Better Buildings," in Lester R. Brown et al., *State of the World 1995* (New York: W.W. Norton & Company, 1995); Gary Gardner, "Steel Recycling Rising," in Brown, Lenssen, and Kane, op. cit. note 1.

22. Donald F. Barnett and Robert W. Crandall, *Up From the Ashes: The Rise of the Steel Minimill in the United States* (Washington,

D.C.: The Brookings Institution, 1986); current figure from Greg Crawford, Steel Recycling Institute, Pittsburgh, Pa., private communication, October 12, 1995; Martin Brown and Bruce McKern, *Aluminum, Copper And Steel in Developing Countries* (Paris: Development Centre, Organisation for Economic Co-operation and Development, 1987).

23. John Holusha, "Steel Mini-Mills Could Bring Boon or Blood Bath," *New York Times*, May 30, 1995.

24. Ibid.

25. Figure 9–3 is Worldwatch calculations, based on Institute of Scrap and Recycling Industries, Washington, D.C., private communication, January 25, 1995; Anthony Robinson, "Europe's Other Steel Industry Reels: Output Has Halved as Markets Collapse to East and West," *Financial Times*, February 19, 1993; Gao Anming, "Steel Giant to Cut 80,-000 from Force," *China Daily*, March 22, 1993.

26. Steve Apotheker, "Looking for Steel Cans," *Resource Recycling*, February 1992.

27. Andrew Baxter, "Future Seen for Steel Mini-mills in Developing Countries," *Financial Times*, October 28, 1993; Andrea N. Ketoff, "Facts and Prospects of the Italian End-Use Energy Structure," presented at the Global Workshop on End-Use Energy Strategies, São Paulo, Brazil, June 4–15, 1984; Spain's efficiency from World Bank, *Energy Efficiency in the Steel Industry with Emphasis on the Developing Countries* (Washington, D.C.: 1984).

28. William U. Chandler, *Energy Productivity: Key to Environmental Protection and Economic Progress*, Worldwatch Paper 63 (Washington, D.C.: Worldwatch Institute, January 1985). During the last decade, factories in these regions have not been modernized very much.

29. Marc Ross, University of Michigan, Ann Arbor, Mich., private communication, March 24, 1992.

30. Gene Bylinsky, "Manufacturing for Reuse," *Fortune*, February 6, 1995.

31. Richard L. Klimisch, "Designing the Modern Automobile for Recycling," in Branden R. Allenby and Deanna J. Richards, eds., *The Greening of Industrial Ecosystems* (Washington, D.C.: National Academy Press, 1994).

32. Ibid.

33. Holusha, op. cit. note 23.

34. John E. Young, "The Sudden New Strength of Recycling," *World Watch*, July/August 1995.

35. Ibid.

36. Ed Ayres, "Whitewash: Pursuing the Truth About Paper," *World Watch*, September/October 1992.

37. Young, op. cit. note 34.

38. Bureau of National Affairs, "Executive Order on Federal Procurement, Recycling, Waste Prevention Signed By President Clinton October 20, 1993," Washington, D.C.

39. Young, op. cit. note 34.

40. "Belgian Greens Exact Promise for Measure to Impose Eco-Tax on Wide Range of Products," *International Environment Reporter*, February 10, 1993; *Pulp and Paper* (Pulp and Paper International, Miller Freeman, Inc., Brussels), October 1993.

41. Bernard Simon, "Sky May be the Limit for Prices in Paper Business," *Financial Times*, February 2, 1995.

42. Gunter Pauli and Eng-Leong Foo, "The Application of the ZERI-Methodology to the Recycling of Paper," Proposal for Funding, Zero Emissions Research Initiative, United Nations University, Tokyo, July 1995.

43. "More Mixing, Better Paper Diversion," *BioCycle*, August 1993; Robert Steuteville, "Capital Intensive Pulping," *Biocycle*, November 1993.

44. "More Mixing, Better Paper Diversion," op. cit. note 43; Steuteville, op. cit. note 43.

45. Peter Wright and Gini Stanley, "Creating Jobs, Saving Forests," *Habitat Australia*, August 1995.

46. Nancy Chege, "Roundwood Production Unabated," in Lester R. Brown, Hal Kane, and David Malin Roodman, *Vital Signs 1994* (New York: W.W. Norton & Company, 1994).

47. Population Reference Bureau (PRB), *World Population Data Sheet 1995* (Washington, D.C.: 1995); World Resources Institute, *World Resources Report 1994–95* (New York: Oxford University Press, 1994); Lester R. Brown and Hal Kane, *Full House: Reassessing the Earth's Population Carrying Capacity* (New York: W.W. Norton & Company, 1994).

48. Jeff Kenworthy, "Automobile Dependence in Bangkok: An International Comparison with Implications for Planning Policies," *World Transport Policy & Practice*, Vol. 1, No. 3, 1995.

49. *Interbike Directory 1995*, op. cit. note 5; AAMA, op. cit. note 5.

50. "Cycling: More Puff, Less Smoke," *The Economist*, September 2, 1995.

51. Toni R. Eastham, "High-Speed Rail: Another Golden Age?" *Scientific American*, September 1995.

52. Ibid.

53. *Interbike Directory*, op. cit. note 5.

54. Susan Lawrence, "Driving on China's Road to Riches," *U.S. News & World Report*, November 29, 1994; Wu Weinong, "Will Cars Push Bikes Off Chinese Roads?" *China Daily*, December 5, 1994.

55. Lawrence, op. cit. note 54; PRB, op. cit. note 47.

56. Lester R. Brown, *Who Will Feed China? Wake-up Call for a Small Planet* (New York: W.W. Norton & Company, 1995).

57. McDonnough quoted in Robert Frenay, "Bioregionalism: Reading Nature's Blueprints," *Audubon*, September/October 1995.

58. Klimisch, op. cit. note 31.

59. United Nations University, "Zero Emissions Research Initiative: Status Report," United Nations University, Tokyo, June 1995.

60. Frenay, op. cit. note 57.

61. Jenny Luesby, "Palette of New Pigments," *Financial Times*, August 29, 1995; Vanessa Houlder, "The Elusive Colour Green," *Financial Times*, August 29, 1995.

62. David T. Allen and Nasrin Behmanesh, "Wastes as Raw Materials," in Allenby and Richards, op. cit. note 31.

63. Gunter Pauli, President, Zero-Emissions Research Initiative, United Nations University, Tokyo, private communication, September 19, 1995; Gunter Pauli and Eng-Leong Foo, "The Application of the ZERI-Methodology to Wastes from Beer Breweries," Proposal for Funding, Zero Emissions Research Initiative, United Nations University, Tokyo, July 1995.

64. Joseph J. Romm, *Lean and Clean: How To Boost Profits and Productivity by Reducing Pollution* (New York: Kodansha International, 1994).

65. Ibid.

66. Robert U. Ayres, "Industrial Metabolism: Theory and Policy," in Allenby and Richards, op. cit. note 31.

67. Ibid.

Chapter 10. Harnessing the Market for the Environment

1. Curtis A. Moore, "Poisons in the Air," *International Wildlife*, September/October 1995; Sandra Postel, *Last Oasis: Facing Water Scarcity* (New York: W.W. Norton & Company, 1992); Anjali Acharya, "Small Islands: Awash in a Sea of Troubles," *World Watch*, November/December 1995.

2. Moore, op. cit. note 1; William Pepper et al., "Emission Scenarios for the IPCC: An Update," prepared for the IPCC Working Group I, May 1992; R.T. Watson et al., "Greenhouse Gases and Aerosols," in Intergovernmental Panel on Climate Change (IPCC), *Climate Change: The IPCC Scientific Assessment* (Cambridge: Cambridge University Press, 1990).

3. Carolyn Webber and Aaron Wildavsky, *A History of Taxation and Expenditure in the Western World* (New York: Simon and Schuster, 1986).

4. Worldwatch estimate, based on International Monetary Fund (IMF), *Government Finance Statistics Yearbook 1994* (Washington, D.C.: 1994), on IMF, *World Economic Outlook October 1994* (Washington, D.C.: 1994), on Organisation for Economic Co-operation and Development (OECD), *Revenue Statistics of OECD Member Countries 1960–1994* (Paris: 1995), on World Bank, *World Data 1994: World Bank Indicators on CD-ROM* (electronic database) (Washington, D.C.: 1994), and on Thomas Sterner, "Environmental Tax Reform: Theory, Industrialized Country Experience, and Relevance in LDCs," Unit for Environmental Economics, Department of Economics, Göteborg University, Göteborg, Sweden, 1994.

5. Webber and Wildavsky, op. cit. note 3.

6. Worldwatch estimates of tax burdens are converted to U.S. dollars on the basis of purchasing power parities, and are based on OECD, op. cit. note 4, on World Bank, op. cit. note 4, and on IMF, *World Economic Outlook May 1995* (Washington, D.C.: 1995).

7. Edgar K. Browning, "On the Marginal Welfare Cost of Taxation," *The American Economic Review*, March 1987; figures are Worldwatch estimates, based on IMF, *Government Finance Statistics Yearbook*, op. cit. note 4, on IMF, *World Economic Outlook*, op. cit. note 4, on OECD, op. cit. note 4, on World Bank, op. cit. note 4, and on Sterner, op. cit. note 4. Estimates exclude local and regional govern-ment revenue in developing countries, but include non-tax revenue there. "Constructive activities" excludes land taxes, which are estimated at roughly half of total property taxes worldwide, and environmental taxes, which have been tabulated for OECD countries and are estimated at half of excise taxes in non-OECD countries.

8. Worldwatch estimates, based on average deadweight burden rates from Dale W. Jorgenson and Yun Kun-Young, "The Excess Burden of Taxation in the U.S.," HIER Discussion Paper No. 1528, Harvard University, Cambridge, Mass., 1990, as cited in Roger C. Dower and Mary Beth Zimmerman, "The Right Climate for Carbon Taxes: Creating Economic Incentives to Protect the Atmosphere," World Resources Institute (WRI), Washington, D.C., 1992, and on OECD, op. cit. note 4; *The Riverside Shakespeare* (Boston: Houghton Mifflin Company, 1974).

9. Commission of the European Communities (CEC), *European Economy* (Luxembourg: Office for Official Publications of the European Communities (OOP), 1994); CEC, *Growth, Competitiveness, Employment: The Challenges and Ways Forward Into the 21st Century*, White Paper (Luxembourg: OOP, 1993); Figure 10–1 is based on CEC, *European Economy*, op. cit. this note, on Isaac Shapiro and Sharon Parrott, "An Unraveling Consensus: An Analysis of the Effect of the New Congressional Agenda on the Working Poor," Center on Budget and Policy Priorities (CBPP), Washington, D.C., 1995, and on David Booth, CBPP, Washington, D.C., private communication, October 12, 1995; G. de Wit, "The Effects in Employment of a Shift in Taxation from Labour to the Environment," Centre for Energy Conservation and Environmental Technology (CEST), Delft, Netherlands, April 1994; Giorgio Brunello, "Is the Double Dividend Hypothesis a Cure for European Unemployment?" *Feem Newsletter* (Fondazione Eni Enrico Mattei, Milan), No. 1, 1995.

10. "The Unemployment Crisis: Diagnosis and Remedies," *World of Work*, December 1994; parallels between U.S. and West European situations from Paul Krugman, "Europe Jobless, America Penniless?" *Foreign Policy*, Summer 1994.

11. A.C. Pigou, *The Economics of Welfare* (New York: AMS Press, 1978); Peter Brimblecombe, *The Big Smoke: A History of Pollution in London Since Medieval Times* (London: Methuen & Co., 1987).

12. Pigou, op. cit. note 11; Ernst Ulrich von Weizsäcker, "Let Prices Tell the Ecological Truth," *Our Planet*, Vol. 7, No. 1, 1995.

13. Charles Komanoff, "Pollution Taxes for Roadway Transportation," *Pace Environmental Law Review*, Fall 1994; James J. MacKenzie, Roger C. Dower, and Donald D.T. Chen, "The Going Rate: What it Really Costs to Drive," WRI, Washington, D.C., 1992 (the Komanoff and MacKenzie estimates are not directly comparable because each includes some costs that the other ignores, such as the hidden cost of free parking included in the MacKenzie study and the costs of traffic congestion in the Komanoff study); equivalent fuel prices are Worldwatch estimates, based on OECD, *Energy Balances of OECD Countries 1991–1992* (Paris: 1994).

14. Courtney Cuff, Ralph de Gennaro, and Gawain Kripke, "The Green Scissors Report," Friends of the Earth, Washington, D.C., 1995; Mason Gaffney, "The Taxable Surplus in Water Resources," *Contemporary Policy Issues*, October 1992; "EU Subsidies Declined In Germany Last Year," *Journal of Commerce*, April 6, 1995; "Controversial Bavarian Plan For Coal Aid Cuts Would Slash German Output To 20mt By 2005," *European Energy Report*, May 12, 1995.

15. Bjorn Larsen and Anwar Shah, "World Fossil Fuel Subsidies and Global Carbon Emissions," Background Paper for *World Development Report 1992*, World Bank, Washington, D.C., October 1992; subsidy decline from Bjorn Larsen, World Bank, Public Economics Division, Washington, D.C., private communication, August 3, 1995; British Petroleum (BP), *BP Statistical Review of World Energy* (London: Group Media & Publications, 1995); Lester R. Brown, "Fertilizer Use Continues Dropping," in Lester R. Brown, Nicholas Lenssen, and Hal Kane, *Vital Signs 1995* (New York: W.W. Norton & Company, 1995).

16. Ronald T. McMorran and David C.L. Nellor, "Tax Policy and the Environment: Theory and Practice," IMF Working Paper, IMF, Washington, D.C., 1994; Barbara Crossette, "Severe Water Crisis Ahead for Poorest Nations in Next 2 Decades," *New York Times*, August 10, 1995; Lester R. Brown, Christopher Flavin, and Sandra Postel, *Saving the Planet: How To Shape An Environmentally Sustainable Global Economy* (New York: W.W. Norton & Company, 1991).

17. Norman Myers, Headington, U.K., private communication, July 6, 1995; figure of 5 percent is a Worldwatch estimate, based on ibid., on IMF, *Government Finance Statistics Yearbook*, op. cit. note 4, on IMF, *World Economic Outlook*, op. cit. note 4, on OECD, op. cit. note 4, on World Bank, op. cit. note 4, and on Sterner, op. cit. note 4.

18. WRI, *World Resources Database* (electronic database) (Washington, D.C.: 1994); U.S. Environmental Protection Agency (EPA), Office of Air Quality and Planning Standards, *National Air Pollutant Emission Estimates: 1900–1991* (Research Triangle Park, N.C.: 1992); Hilary F. French, "Clearing the Air," in Lester R. Brown et al., *State of the World 1990* (New York: W.W. Norton & Company, 1990); Oak Ridge National Laboratory, *Transportation Energy Data Book: Edition 12* (Oak Ridge, Tenn.: 1992); U.S. Department of Transportation, Federal Highway Administration, *Highway Statistics 1991* (Washington, D.C.: 1991).

19. Robert Repetto, "Jobs, Competitiveness, and Environmental Regulation: What Are the Real Issues?" WRI, Washington, D.C., 1995; Michael E. Porter, "The Compet-

itive Advantage of Nations," *Harvard Business Review*, March/April 1990.

20. Randy Wellman, ICI Americas, Wilmington, Del., private communication, October 10, 1995.

21. Amoco details and official's quote from Keith Schneider, "Unbending Regulations Incite Move to Alter Pollution Laws," *New York Times*, November 29, 1993.

22. Hans Th. A. Bressers and Jeannette Schuddeboom, "A Survey of Effluent Charges and Other Economic Instruments in Dutch Environmental Policy," in OECD, *Applying Economic Instruments to Environmental Policies in OECD and Dynamic Non-member Economies* (Paris: 1994); Jan Paul van Soest, CEST, Delft, Netherlands, private communication, October 11, 1995; Figure 10–2 is based on Kees Baas, Central Bureau of Statistics, The Hague, Netherlands, private communication and printout, September 19, 1995.

23. David O'Connor, "The Use of Economic Instruments in Environmental Management: The East Asian Experience," in OECD, op. cit. note 22.

24. Claire Schary, EPA, Acid Rain Division, Washington, D.C., private communication, October 10, 1995; Jeffrey Taylor, "Auction of Rights To Pollute Fetches About $21 Million," *Wall Street Journal*, March 31, 1993; figure of $1.9–3.1 billion from "Air Pollution: Allowance Trading Offers an Opportunity to Reduce Emissions at Less Cost," U.S. General Accounting Office, Washington, D.C., December 1994.

25. Victoria P. Summers, "Tax Treatment of Pollution Control in the European and Central Asian Economies in Transition and Other Selected Countries," in Charles E. Walker, Mark A. Bloomfield, and Margot Thorning, eds., *Strategies for Improving Environmental Quality and Increasing Economic Growth* (Washington, D.C.: Center for Policy Research, 1995); Michel Porter, "China Charges for Pollution," *The OECD Observer*, February/March 1995; figure of 1 percent is based on Summers, op. cit. this note, and on IMF, *World Economic Outlook*, op. cit. note 4.

26. Summers, op. cit. note 25; Porter, op. cit. note 25.

27. Earth Summit Watch, "Four in '94. Two Years After Rio: Assessing National Actions to Implement Agenda 21," Natural Resources Defense Council and Campaign for Action to Protect the Earth, New York, December 1994.

28. Rögnvaldur Hannesson, Norwegian School of Economics and Business Administration, Bergen-Sandviken, Norway, "The Political Economy of ITQs," prepared for Symposium on Fisheries Management, University of Washington, Seattle, June 14–16, 1994; Larry D. Simpson, "Are Water Markets a Viable Option?" *Finance & Development*, June 1994.

29. OECD, *Environmental Taxes in OECD Countries* (Paris: 1995); "Environmental Agency Report Favors Introduction of Environmental Taxes, Levies," *International Environment Report*, June 14, 1995; "Agency Panel To Study Introduction of Environmental Tax," *Environmental Issues*, August 5, 1994.

30. John Moffet and François Bregham, "The User Pay Waste Management Initiative for Recycling Household Waste," in Robert J.P. Gale and Stephan R. Barg, eds., *Green Budget Reform: An International Casebook of Leading Practices* (London: Earthscan, 1995); J. Andrew Hoerner, "Tax Tools for Climate Protection: The U.S. Ozone-depleting Chemicals Tax," in ibid.; Australian and Danish taxes from OECD, op. cit. note 29; U.S. Office of Management and Budget, *Budget of the United States Government, Fiscal Year 1996* (Washington, D.C.: U.S. Government Printing Office, 1995). The U.S. tax was instituted primarily to absorb windfall profits created by new regulations that restricted the supply of ozone-depleting chemicals; it appears to have been set high enough, however, to actually accelerate their phaseout.

31. Figure of $170 billion is a Worldwatch estimate, using market exchange rates and based on OECD, op. cit. note 29; OECD, *Energy Prices and Taxes* (Paris: various years); Marcia Lowe, "Shaping Cities," in Lester R. Brown et al., *State of the World 1992* (New York: W.W. Norton & Company, 1992); T. Sterner, "The Price of Petroleum Products," in Thomas Sterner, ed., *Economic Policies for Sustainable Development* (Dordrecht, Netherlands: Kluwer Academic Publishers, 1994).

32. J. Andrew Hoerner, "The Louisiana Environmental Tax Scorecard," in Gale and Barg, op. cit. note 30.

33. California and Massachusetts from David P. Novello, "Capturing the Market's Power," *The Environmental Forum*, September/October 1994; use of fishing permit systems from Rögnvaldur Hannesson, Norwegian School of Economics and Business Administration, Bergen-Sandviken, Norway, private communication, June 7, 1995.

34. Ministry of the Environment and Natural Resources, "The Swedish Experience: Taxes and Charges in Environmental Policy," Stockholm, 1994; Anders Nørskou, Ministry of Finance, Copenhagen, private communications, September 29 and October 3, 1995.

35. Koos van der Vaart, Ministry of Finance, The Hague, Netherlands, private communication, October 4, 1995; Martina Schuster, Federal Ministry of the Environment, Vienna, private communication, October 2, 1995; Norway's carbon tax is from OECD, op. cit. note 29; Odd Froean, Ministry of the Environment, Oslo, private communication, October 12, 1995; "Economics Minster Says He Supports National CO_2 Tax If Wider Accord Fails," *International Environment Reporter*, June 14, 1995.

36. Scandinavia from OECD, op. cit. note 29.

37. Michael Specter, "Far North in Russia, the Mines' Fatal Blight," *New York Times*, March 28, 1994.

38. Laurence Tribe, "Ways Not to Think About Plastic Trees: New Foundations for Environmental Law," *Yale Law Journal*, Vol. 83, 1974, p. 1315.

39. Nikki Scarancke, Greenpeace, Auckland, and Maori former fisher, private communication, October 8, 1995; Leith Duncan, "Closed Competition: Fish Quotas in New Zealand," *The Ecologist*, March/April and May/June 1995.

40. Anwar Shah and Bjorn Larsen, "Carbon Taxes, the Greenhouse Effect, and Developing Countries," Background Paper for *World Development Report 1992*, World Bank, Washington, D.C., 1992.

41. Matthew L. Wald, "Lilco's Emissions Sale Spurs Acid Rain Concerns," *New York Times*, March 18, 1993; Matthew L. Wald, "Suit Attacks Swap Plan on Pollution," *New York Times*, March 14, 1993.

42. Mateen Thobani, "Tradable Property Rights to Water," *Viewpoint*, Private Sector Development Department, World Bank, Washington, D.C., February 1995.

43. Scarancke, op. cit note 39; Duncan, op. cit. note 39.

44. Hannesson, op. cit. note 28; Simpson, op. cit. note 28; Scarancke, op. cit. note 39.

45. James Poterba, "Tax Policy to Combat Global Warming: On Designing a Carbon Tax," in Rudiger Dornbusch and James Poterba, eds., *Global Warming: Economic Policy Responses* (Cambridge, Mass.: The MIT Press, 1991); World Bank, *Monitoring Environmental Progress: A Report on Work in Progress* (Washington, D.C.: March 1995 draft).

46. Robert Greenstein and Frederick C. Hutchinson, "Offsetting the Effects of Regressive Tax Increases on Low- and Moderate-Income Households," CBPP, Washington, D.C., 1990.

47. Ministry of the Environment and Natural Resources, op. cit. note 34; "Danish Government Proposes New Taxes on Car-

bon Dioxide, Sulfur Emissions," *International Environment Reporter*, April 19, 1995; Tom Radahl, Ministry of Finance, Oslo, private communication, October 10, 1995; Hoerner, op. cit. note 30; Schuster, op. cit. note 35; van der Vaart, op. cit. note 35.

48. Hilary Barnes, "Danish Emissions Tax Gets Go-Ahead," *Financial Times*, July 15–16, 1995; Peter Behr, "Trade Panel Upholds U.S. Auto Fuel Law," *Washington Post*, October 1, 1994; WTO view of export rebates from J. Andrew Hoerner, Center for Global Change, University of Maryland, College Park, Md., private communication, August 9, 1995.

49. Paul Hawken, *The Ecology of Commerce: A Declaration of Sustainability* (New York: Harper Collins, 1993).

50. Ernst U. von Weizsäcker and Jochen Jesinghaus, *Ecological Tax Reform* (London: Zed Books, 1992); Shah and Larsen, op. cit. note 40; U.N. Development Programme, *Human Development Report 1994* (New York: Oxford University Press, 1994).

51. John P. Weyant, Energy Modeling Forum, Stanford University, Stanford, Calif., unpublished manuscript, June 1995, and private communication and printout, October 10, 1995; IPCC, op. cit. note 2.

52. Hannesson, op. cit. note 28. Taxes, like permits that are given away, can be refunded according to historical pollution or resource use patterns, an approach that has been called "incremental tax"; see J. Andrew Hoerner and Frank Muller, "The Impact of a Broad-Based Energy Tax on the Competitiveness of U.S. Industry," *Natural Resources Tax Review*, July/August 1993.

53. Porter, op. cit. note 25; Sergio Margulis, "The Use of Economic Instruments in Environmental Policies: The Experiences of Brazil, Mexico, Chile and Argentina," in OECD, op. cit. note 22.

54. One study that explores the effects of different revenue "recycling" options is Bruce Schillo et al., "The Distributional Impacts of a Carbon Tax," Energy Policy Branch, EPA, Washington, D.C., unpublished, August 4, 1992.

55. Dawn Erlandson, "The Btu Tax Experience: What Happened and Why It Happened," *Pace Environmental Law Review*, Fall 1994; Dawn Erlandson, Friends of the Earth, Washington, D.C., private communication, May 11, 1995.

56. Stefan Bach, Michael Kohlhaas, and Barbara Praetorius, "Ecological Tax Reform Even If Germany Has to Go it Alone," *Economic Bulletin* (German Institute for Economic Research (DIW), Berlin), July 1994.

57. Worldwatch estimates, based on Statistisches Bundesamt, *Volkswirtschaftliche Gesamtrechnungen* (Stuttgart: Metzler-Poeschel, 1990), on Michael Kohlhaas, DIW, Berlin, private communication and printout, June 20, 1995, and on Hans Wessels, DIW, Berlin, private communication and printout, August 10, 1995; jobs figure is from Bach, Kohlhaas, and Praetorius, op. cit. note 56.

58. Kristina Steenbock, Consultant to Greenpeace Germany, New York, private communication, June 16, 1995; "Group Gets Support for CO_2 Tax from 16 German Producers, Service Industries," *International Environment Reporter*, September 21, 1994; Big 3 Carmakers Back Higher Gasoline Taxes," *Journal of Commerce*, December 21, 1992.

59. Coal use from BP, op. cit. note 15.

Index

Afghanistan, 50, 53
agriculture, 78–94
  bioinvasion, 104–10
  Consultative Group on International
    Agricultural Research, 11, 92
  cropland loss, 6, 9, 43–44, 79–83, 108
  crop loss, 15, 81
  farm subsidies, 91–92
  fertilizer use, 9–10, 84–85
  land degradation, 83–86
  management strategies, 91–94
  pest management, 88–91
  water scarcity, 40–44, 86–88
AIDS, 19, 115–16, 119, 123
air pollution, 14, 21–26, 153, 156, 167
Alliance of Small Island States, 35
Alliance to Save Energy (U.S.), 156
Allstate company, 34
Alvarez, Heherson, 35
American Fisheries Society, 61, 62, 65
American Forest & Paper Association, 160–61
American Gas Association, 156
American Society of Civil Engineers, 52
Amnesty International, 135
Amoco Corporation, 175–76
Andrus, Cecil, 60
Animal and Plant Health Inspection Service
    (U.S.), 111–12
aquaculture, 8–9, 105
aquifer depletion
  conservation technologies to combat, 56, 58
  economic effects, 86–87
  through accelerated use, 5, 9, 10, 25, 41–43,
    81–82
Aral Sea basin, 46–47
Argentina, 120
Army Corps of Engineers, 70
Arnold, Ron, 138
Asian Development Bank, 28
Australia
  bioinvasion, 102, 112
  carbon emissions, 31

employment, 162
  water management, 53, 87
automobiles
  economic impact, 15–16, 164–65, 173
  emissions, 31
  energy tax effects, 185
  fuel economy standards, 32
  pollution permits, 175–76
  recycling, 159, 165, 166
  safety standards, 34
  use limits, 162–63
Ayres, Robert, 167

Bangladesh
  cropland loss, 81
  flood damage, 27, 28
  infectious disease, 128
  water conflicts, 5–6, 50, 52–53
Bayley, Peter, 68
Beard, Dan, 66
Belgium, 9, 161
bicycles, 15–16, 33, 153, 162–65
biodiversity, 96
bioinvasion, 95–113
  agricultural species, 104–10
  ecology, 96–101
  economic effects, 107–10
  ecosystem destruction, 101–03
  fish, 62–63, 72–76, 95–109
  infectious disease, 97, 100–01, 109
  invasion pathways, 103–06
  management strategies, 110–13
  mosquito, 100, 104, 109, 124
  rodents, 96, 97–99, 100
  timber species, 101–03, 105, 108, 110,
    112
  zebra mussel, 101, 103–04, 112
biotechnology, 106–07
Blackmore, Don, 53
Brazil, 29–30, 133–35
breakbone fever, 121, 123–24
Britain, 99, 163, 166

Bureau of Indian Affairs (U.S.), 150
Bureau of Reclamation (U.S.), 66

Cambodia, 66–67
Canada
  bioinvasion, 102, 112
  biotechnology, 106–07
  carbon emissions, 31
  crop loss, 15
  Lubicon Lake Indians, 148–49
  North American Free Trade Agreement,
    149–50
  pesticide use, 90
  recycling program, 178
  salmon endangerment, 60, 64–66
  water management, 58, 74
carbon emissions
  carbon dioxide, 14, 21, 22, 24, 26, 153, 167
  economic impact, 37
  global rise, 29–33
  stabilization, 19, 36–37, 143, 146
  tax, 19, 31–32, 37–38, 181, 184
  Zero Emissions Research Initiative (U.N.), 165
Centers for Disease Control and Prevention
    (U.S.), 104, 128, 129–30
Chico Mendes Extractive Reserve, 133, 136, 150
Chile, 57, 108, 181
China
  Academy of Sciences, 140, 165
  aquifer depletion, 86
  biotechnology, 107
  carbon emissions, 29–31
  climate policy, 33
  economic growth, 3
  grain imports, 8
  grain prices, 11
  industrialization, 81
  Mekong dam projects, 66–67
  ocean level rise, 82
  pesticide use, 90
  population stabilization, 12–13
  steel production, 158
  Three Gorges Dam project, 64, 140
  transportation system, 15, 162, 164
  tropical storm damage, 27–28
  water scarcity, 5, 44, 87
chlorofluorocarbons (CFCs), 14–19, 22, 143,
    175–76
climate, 21–39
  Climate Change Action Plan (U.S.), 156
  extremes, 25–28, 34
  Framework Convention on Climate Change
    (U.N.), 14, 21–22, 32, 33–39, 155, 184
  global circulation models, 22–23

infectious disease rise, 121–22
Intergovernmental Panel on Climate Change
    (U.N.), 21, 23, 24, 25, 26, 28
  policy, 31–33
  rate of change, 23–24
  tropical storms, 26–27
  see also global warming
Clinton, Bill, 32, 161, 185
closed-cycle factories, 165–67
coal, 22, 183
Coblentz, Bruce, 96
Coddington, Jonathan, 61
Colombia, 127
Colorado River, 5, 44–45
Columbia River, 60
Colwell, Rita, 128
conservation
  aquifer management, 56, 58
  Conservation Reserve Program (U.S.), 92
  energy, 37–38
  forests, 141–43, 145–46
  global campaigns, 143–47
  soil management, 85–86
Consultative Group on International Agricultural
    Research, 11, 92
Costa Rica, 141–43
Costner, Pat, 138
cropland loss, 79–83
  industrialization, 6, 9, 81
  salt buildup, 43, 47
  urbanization, 43–44, 80–82
  viral infestations, 108
Cucapá, 45–46

Dai, Qing, 140
dams
  fisheries impact, 44–46, 63–67
  Mekong basin projects, 66–67
  Sardar Sarovar Dam Project (India), 121
  Senegal River basin, 47
  Three Gorges Dam project (China), 64, 140
Dara, Chan, 138
DDT, 73, 90, 125, 175
Delphi Group, 38
Demirel, Suleyman, 51
dengue fever, 121, 123–24
Denmark
  bicycle use, 163
  climate policy, 32–33
  environmental taxes, 182
  wind-generating capacity, 15
developing countries
  agricultural investment, 92
  carbon emissions, 29, 36

climate change effects, 28
environmental activist movement, 139
environmental market mechanisms, 177–78
food demand, 79
natural resource consumption, 144
pesticide use, 90
tax structure, 170
water contamination, 126
water marketing, 57
see also specific countries
Development Programme (U.N.), 91, 184
diarrheal disease, 126
diet, *see* food
disease, *see* infectious disease; *specific diseases*
drought, 25, 44
Duarte, Jose, 125

Earth Summit, 21, 54
Ebola virus, 19, 132
economy
automobile costs, 15–16, 164–65, 173
bioinvasion effects, 107–10
environmental market mechanisms, 168–87
food prices, 10, 18
global tax restructuring, 169–74
global warming effects, 25–26, 31, 37
subsidized environmental destruction, 172–74
sustainable resource management, 11–12, 16, 20, 152–53, 156
ecosystems, *see* environment; freshwater ecosystems
Ecuador, 136
Egypt
fishery, 46
irrigation technology, 56
water conflicts, 49–50, 51, 52
Electricity Generating Authority of Thailand, 67
El Salvador, 125
Emanual, Kerry, 26–27
Emergency Planning and Community Right-to-Know Act (U.S.), 149, 150
encephalitis, 119, 121–22
endangered species
Endangered Species Act (U.S.), 64, 65, 71
freshwater ecosystems, 45–46, 61, 71
Lake Victoria, 75
salmon stock, 60, 64–66, 69, 100
energy conservation, 37–38
Energy Modeling Forum (Stanford University), 184
Energy Policy Act (U.S.), 32
environment
activism awards, 139
climate change effects, *see* climate

damage taxes, 20–21, 161, 169, 172–74, 176
ecological market model, 168–87
economic balance, 152–53
human rights and, 133–51
industrial damage, 168–69
sustainable yield thresholds, 4–7
taxes, 19–20, 161, 169, 172–74, 176
see also bioinvasion; freshwater ecosystems
Environmental Protection Agency (U.S.), 74, 126, 175, 177, 178
Environment Programme (U.N.), 19, 91
Epstein, Paul, 128
erosion, 6, 83
Ethiopia, 7, 49–52
European Commission, 172
European Union, 12, 15, 132, 182
Ewald, Paul, 122
exotic organisms, *see* bioinvasion

family planning, 14, 20
farmland, *see* cropland loss
farm subsidies, 91–92
Federation of American Scientists, 131
Fernandez, Blanca Jeannette Kawas, 137–38
fertilizer use, 9–10, 84–85
fisheries
Africa's Great Lakes, 74–76
aquaculture, 8–9, 105
bioinvasion, 62–63, 72–76, 95–109
dam effects, 44–46, 63–67
decline, 152
flood-pulse effect, 71
freshwater harvest, 60–61
Galápagos Islands, 136
grain conversion, 9
Great Lakes (U.S.), 73–74
regulation, 5, 180, 181
salmon stock, 60, 64–66, 69, 100
sustainable yield thresholds, 5, 17, 19
see also freshwater ecosystems; oceans
floods, 68–72
infectious disease, 121, 124–25
Mississippi River, 69–72
Rhine River, 68–69
tropical storms, 27, 28
food
demand, 79
global scarcity, 7–11, 16–18, 26
meat consumption, 93–94
postharvest, 93
prices, 10, 18
production, 40–44
sustainable yield thresholds, 4–7, 12

Food and Agriculture Organization (U.N.),
    16–17, 82, 87, 88, 91, 130
forestry
    conservation, 141–43, 145–46
    logging practices, 64, 138, 145–46
forests
    agricultural soil management, 85
    bioinvasion, 101–03, 105, 108, 110, 112
    carbon absorption, 24, 29
    climate change effects, 26
    deforestation, 82, 105
fossil fuels, 14, 19, 24, 29–33, 153, 155
Framework Convention on Climate Change
    see under United Nations
France, 69, 163, 165
freshwater ecosystems, 60–77
    Amazon River, 63
    Aral Sea basin, 46–47
    Colorado River, 5, 44–45
    Columbia River, 60
    dam effects, 63–67
    extinction rates, 60–61
    flood damage, 68–72
    Ganges River, 43, 46
    Great Lakes Water Quality Agreement,
        74
    large lakes, 72–76
    management strategy, 76–77
    Nile River, 46
    Rio Grande River, 6, 40
    species interdependency, 71–72
    threat factors, 61–63
    wetlands, 45–47, 55, 61–62
    see also fisheries
Friedman, Donald, 27

Galápagos islands, 95–96, 98, 136
Ganges River, 43, 46
gasoline tax, 31–32, 178
General Agreement on Tariffs and Trade, 11,
    182
Germany
    carbon emissions, 19, 30–32
    climate policy, 33–34
    energy conservation, 38
    energy tax, 185–86
    flood damage, 68–69
    tax structure, 170
    wind-generating capacity, 15
GLASOD study (U.N.), 82, 83
Global Climate Coalition, 38
global warming
    agricultural effects, 88
    conservation campaigns, 146
        economic effects, 14–15, 25–26, 34
        recorded rise, 6, 22–24
Goldman, Michael, 48
Goldman Foundation, 138–39
Goulding, Michael, 63
grain
    animal feed, 9, 93–94
    carryover stocks, 7–8, 11, 79
    production, 6, 8, 9–10, 15, 17–18, 41, 88
Grant, James P., 125
Great Lakes basin, 72–74
Great Lakes Fishery Commission, 74
Great Lakes Water Quality Agreement, 74
greenhouse gases, see carbon emissions; global
    warming
Greenpeace, 38, 138, 185
Group of 77, 35
Guam, 98
Gubler, Duane, 104

Haiti, 6
Hamburg, Steve, 26
Hasselmann, Klaus, 23
health, see infectious disease
Heywood, Vernon, 96
history, acceleration of, 3–20
HIV, see AIDS
Homer-Dixon, Thomas, 48
Hopkins Institute (Monterey), 26
Howard, Jay, 91
Huang He River, 5
human rights
    environmental justice and, 133–51
    international injustice, 143–47
    local injustice, 137–43
    Universal Declaration of Human Rights (U.N.),
        136
Hungary, 130
hurricanes, 26–27
hydroelectric power, 15, 49–50, 69, 155

ICI Americas, 175
Iglesias, Enrique V., 145–46
income tax, 19–20, 170, 174
India
    carbon emissions, 29–31
    climate changes, 23
    dam effects, 46
    infectious disease, 89, 121, 124–25
    international environmental injustice, 146
    irrigation technology, 56
    pesticide use, 89
    steel production, 158
    tax structure, 170

transportation system, 15
water conflicts, 5–6, 48, 50, 52–53
water scarcity, 87
wind-generating capacity, 155–56
Indonesia
cropland loss, 81
international environmental injustice, 145
pesticide use, 89, 90, 92
water scarcity, 87
industry, 152–67
cropland loss, 6, 9, 81
environmental damage, 168–69
recycling, 153
solar technology, 153–55
steel minimills, 157–60
sustainability, 152–67
zero-emission factories, 165–67
infectious disease, 114–32
AIDS, 19, 115–16, 119, 123
bioinvasion, 97, 100–01, 109
biological mixing, 122–25
biology, 118–22
Centers for Disease Control and Prevention
(U.S.), 104, 128, 129–30
control strategies, 130–32
dengue fever, 121, 123–24
diarrheal disease, 126
diphtheria, 125
drug resistance, 115, 116, 118, 128–30
Ebola virus, 19, 132
encephalitis, 119, 121–22
Junín hemorrhagic fever, 120
Lyme disease, 19, 120, 129
malaria, 116, 120–22, 128–29
plague, 124–25
polio, 116–17
sleeping sickness, 130
smallpox, 131
social burden, 115–18, 122–25
syphilis, 129
tuberculosis, 114, 119, 129–30
water contamination, 125–28
yellow fever, 115–16, 130
insurance industry, 26, 34–35
integrated pest management, 90–91, 92
Interagency Floodplain Management Task Force
(U.S.), 70–71
Inter-American Development Bank, 145
Intergovernmental Panel on Climate Change
(U.N.), 21, 23, 24, 25, 26, 28
International Center for Insect Physiology and
Ecology, 130
International Development Enterprises, 56

International Development Research Centre, 121,
150–51
International Drinking Water Supply and
Sanitation Decade, 126
International Energy Agency, 37
International Joint Commission, 74
International Law Association, 51
International Law Commission (U.N.), 51
International Monetary Fund, 147
International Rice Research Institute, 11, 44
Iran, 50, 53, 86
Iraq, 50–51
irrigation
agriculture productivity, 86–88
aquifer depletion, 9, 10, 25, 41–44, 81–82
fisheries impact, 44–46, 63–67
government subsidies, 55–56
technology, 88
water marketing, 57, 87, 181
Israel
aquifer depletion, 43
irrigation technology, 56
water conflicts, 6, 47–48, 49, 51–52
Italy, 158

Japan
carbon emissions, 29–32
climate policy, 32
environmental market mechanisms, 178
fertilizer use, 9
rail transportation, 163–64, 165
Java, 81
Jenkins, Carol, 131
Junín hemorrhagic fever, 120

Karl, Thomas, 23
Kaufman, Les, 75
Kaufmann, H.R., 34
Kazakstan, 29, 50, 53, 88
Kenya, 75–76, 130, 155
Kenya Medical Research Institute, 131
Kohl, Helmut, 31
Kothari, Ashish, 135
Krause, Richard, 118
Ksentini, Fatma Zohra, 148
Kyrgyzstan, 50, 53, 88

Lake Victoria, 75–76
Lampe, Klaus, 44
land, *see* cropland loss
Laos, 66–67
Leggett, Jeremy, 38
Levy, Stuart, 128
Lindzen, Richard, 22

Lloyd's of London, 34, 35
Loevinsohn, Michael, 121
logging, see forestry
Lubicon Lake Indians, 148–49
Lyme disease, 19, 120, 129

Maastricht Treaty, 182
Madagascar, 101
Madras Institute of Development Studies (India),
    56
malaria, 116, 120–22, 128–29
Malaysia, 87, 145
Mansley, Mark, 38
market mechanisms, 168–87
Massachusetts Institute of Technology, 26–27
Mauritania, 48
Max Planck Institute for Meteorology, 23
McDonnough, William, 165
Mekong River Commission, 66–67
Mendes, Chico, 133–35
Merkel, Angela, 35
methane, 22
Mexico
    National Institute of Ecology, 150
    North American Free Trade Agreement,
        149–50
    water conflicts, 6, 40
    water management, 40, 44, 58
Michaels, Patrick, 22
Micklin, Philip, 47
migrants, see refugees
mining, 138
Mississippi River, 69–72
Molina, Mario, 18
Montreal Protocol, 19, 147
Morris, Robert, 127
Morse, Stephen, 122, 131
Movchanok, Vitaly, 127
Movement for the Survival of the Ogoni People,
    139–40
Mungra, Subhaas, 145
Munich Re, 26, 34

Naff, Thomas, 49
Naso, Robert, 128
National Flood Insurance Program (U.S.), 70
National Hurricane Center (U.S.), 28
National Marine Fisheries Service (U.S.), 65
National Oceanic and Atmospheric
    Administration (U.S.), 23, 26
National Research Council (U.S.), 71, 77
Natural Hazards Research Program, 27
natural resources, 4, 11–12, 144
Natural Resources Defense Council (U.S.), 32

Nature Conservancy, The, 57, 61, 72
Nepal, 50, 52–53, 155
Netherlands
    bicycle use, 163–64
    climate policy, 32–33
    flood damage, 68–69, 69
    National Institute of Public Health and
        Environmental Protection, 122
    pesticide use, 90
New Zealand, 98, 99, 181
Nigeria
    environmental injustice, 135
    Health Ministry, 115
    Movement for the Survival of the Ogoni
        People, 139–40
Nile River, 46
nitrous oxide, 22
North American Free Trade Agreement, 149–50
Northwest Power Planning Council, 66
Norway, 36
Noss, Reed, 105
Nutter, Franklin, 34

oceans
    carbon absorption, 24, 29
    global conservation campaigns, 143, 146
    marine life, 26
    rising water levels, 14–15, 28, 35, 46, 82
    see also fisheries
oil production, 154, 173
Ominayak, Bernard, 148
oral rehydration therapy, 126, 131
Organisation for Economic Co-operation and
    Development, 30, 91, 92, 157
Organization of Petroleum Exporting Countries,
    18
ozone depletion
    CFC reduction, 14, 18, 19
    depleter tax, 183
    global conservation campaigns, 143, 146
    substitute refrigerants, 39, 175

Pakistan, 57, 86
Palestine, 6, 47–48, 51–52
Pan American Health Organization, 127
paper recycling, 160–62
Papua New Guinea, 98, 131
payroll tax, 172, 174
PCBs, 73, 128, 144
Peru, 127
pesticide use, 88–91, 92, 108, 130
Pimm, Stuart, 61
plague, 124–25
Poland, 30, 177

polio, 116–17
pollution
    agricultural runoff, 85
    air, 14, 21–26, 153, 156, 167
    benzene, 175, 176
    cropland, 43, 47
    environmental taxes, 169, 172–75, 176
    environment marketing mechanisms, 174
    habitat degradation, 62
    paper production, 160
    permits, 175–76, 178, 181
    Toxics Release Inventory, 150
    water, 68–69, 72–73, 76
    zero-emission factories, 165–67
population growth
    acceleration of, 3
    resource demands, 4
    stabilization, 12–14, 16, 18
    urbanization, 43, 80
Porter, Michael, 175
Program for Monitoring Emerging Diseases
    (ProMED), 131–32
Project on Environmental Change and Acute
    Conflict, 48

rail transportation, 102–03
recycling
    automobiles, 159, 165, 166
    carbon dioxide, 167
    economic impact, 153
    heavy metals, 166
    incentive programs, 178
    paper, 160–62
    steel, 157–60, 186
refugees, 47, 53
Reinsurance Association of America, 34
renewable energy, 156–57
    see also solar energy; wind energy
Repetto, Robert, 175
Rexrodt, Günter, 179
Rhine River, 68–69
Rhône-Poulenc, 150
rice, 11, 44, 80
Rinderpest virus, 97, 100–01
Rio Grande River, 6, 40
river systems, *see* floods; freshwater ecosystems;
    water
Rowland, Sherwood, 18
Russia
    carbon emissions, 29–30
    crop loss, 15
    infectious disease, 125
    population stabilization, 14
Rwanda, 121

Salmnet, 132
San Miguel Association for Conservation and
    Development, 141–43
Sante Fe de Bogotá Foundation, 127
Saro-Wiwa, Ken, 139
Saudi Arabia, 81
Scientific Committee on Problems in the
    Environment, 96–97
Senegal, 48
Sheets, Robert, 28
Shell Petroleum Development Company, 139–40
Sierra Club, 135, 147–48
Singapore, 106–07
sleeping sickness, 130
smallpox, 131
Smithsonian Institution, 61
soil
    conservation, 85–86, 92–93
    degradation, 83–86, 108
    erosion, 6, 83
    salt buildup, 43, 47
solar energy, 15, 153–55, 156, 162
Solar Energy Industry Association (U.S.), 156
South Africa, 29–30, 99, 156
South Korea, 31
Soviet Union (former), 9, 29–30, 150
Spain, 158
Sri Lanka, 93
steel minimills, 157–60
storm damage, 26–27, 68–72
Sudan, 49–50, 52
sulfate aerosols, 24
sulfur dioxide emissions, 175, 177–78, 181
Suriname, 145
sustainable development
    environmental thresholds, 4–7
    fisheries, 5, 17, 19
    food production, 4–7, 12
    industry, 152–67
    resource management, 11–12, 16, 20, 152–53,
        156
    water, 40–59
Sweden, 90, 179
Swiss Re, 34
Switzerland, 32–33
syphilis, 129
Syria, 49, 50–51

Tabai, Ieremia, 35
Tajikistan, 50, 53
Tanzania, 76
taxes
    carbon, 19, 31–32, 37–38, 181, 184
    collection, 180

taxes *(continued)*
    environmental, 19–20, 161, 169, 172–74, 176
    gasoline, 31–32, 178
    global restructuring, 169–72
    income, 19–20, 170, 174
    ozone depleter, 183
    payroll, 172, 174
    subsidized environmental destruction, 172–74
    water depletion, 58
Temple, Stanley, 110
Thailand
    automobile use, 163
    cropland loss, 81
    Mekong dam projects, 66–67
    water scarcity, 44
Thatcher, Margaret, 39
Third World, *see* developing countries
Thomson, David J., 23
Tomori, Oyewale, 131
Toxics Release Inventory, 150
trade, *see* economy
trains, 162–65
transportation, *see specific form*
tropical storms, 26–27
tuberculosis, 114, 119, 129–30
Turkey, 50–51
Turkmenistan, 50, 53

Uganda, 76
Ukraine, 30
United Kingdom, 14, 31
    see also Britain
United Nations
    Children's Fund (UNICEF), 117, 125
    Conference on Environment and Development
        (Rio), 21, 54
    Covenant on Civil and Political Rights, 137,
        148–49
    Covenant on Economic, Social, and Cultural
        Rights, 137
    Development Programme, 91, 184
    Environment Programme, 19, 91
    Food and Agriculture Organization, 16–17, 82,
        87, 88, 91, 130
    Framework Convention on Climate Change,
        14, 21–22, 32, 33–39, 155, 184
    GLASOD study, 82, 83
    global conservation campaigns, 143–47
    Intergovernmental Panel on Climate Change,
        21, 23, 24, 25, 26, 28
    International Law Commission, 51
    Sub-Commission on Prevention of
        Discrimination and Protection of Minorities,
        147–48

Universal Declaration of Human Rights, 136
Zero Emissions Research Initiative, 165
    see also World Health Organization
United States
    Animal and Plant Health Inspection Service,
        111–12
    aquifer depletion, 42–43, 86
    Army Corps of Engineers, 70
    automobile costs, 173
    biotechnology, 106–07
    Bureau of Indian Affairs, 150
    Bureau of Reclamation, 66
    carbon emissions, 29–32, 36
    Centers for Disease Control and Prevention,
        104, 128, 129–30
    Climate Change Action Plan, 156
    climate policy, 32, 33, 35, 156
    Conservation Reserve Program, 92
    cropland loss, 9, 81, 82
    crop loss, 15
    Department of Agriculture, 15, 81, 103
    disease outbreaks, 19
    Emergency Planning and Community
        Right-to-Know Act, 149, 150
    Endangered Species Act, 64, 65, 71
    Energy Policy Act, 32
    Environmental Protection Agency, 74, 126,
        175, 177, 178
    farm productivity, 10
    fertilizer use, 9
    Fish and Wildlife Service, 102, 109
    Forest Service, 105, 108
    freshwater ecosystem loss, 61–62
    gasoline taxes, 32
    General Accounting Office, 70
    infectious disease, 109
    insurance industry, 26, 34–35
    Interagency Floodplain Management Task
        Force, 70–71
    international environmental injustice, 146
    National Flood Insurance Program, 70
    National Hurricane Center, 28
    National Marine Fisheries Service, 65
    National Oceanic and Atmospheric
        Administration, 23, 26
    North American Free Trade Agreement,
        149–50
    ozone policy, 147, 183
    paper use, 161
    pesticide use, 89, 90
    pollution regulation, 74
    population stabilization, 12
    soil management, 85
    steel industry, 157–59

tax structure, 170–72, 178, 185
tropical storm damage, 27–28
water contamination, 126–27
water management, 54–56, 58, 74
water resource conflicts, 6
water scarcity, 87
wind-generating capacity, 15
Universal Declaration of Human Rights (U.N.),
    136
Uzbekistan, 50, 53, 88

Vaidyanathan, A., 56
Vallehas, Carlos A., 136
Vehicle Recycling Development Center (U.S.),
    159
Venetiaan, Ronald, 145–46
Vietnam, 11, 28, 66–67
von Weizsäcker, Ernst, 173

Waldman, Ronald, 126
water
    agriculture productivity, 40–44, 86–88
    competitive entities, 40, 44, 47–51, 53
    contamination, 125–28, 151
    flood control, 68–72
    government subsidies, 55–59
    Great Lakes Water Quality Agreement, 74
    management strategies, 53–59, 74, 76–77,
        87–88
    marketing, 57, 87, 181
    permit systems, 181
    policy, 40–59
    pollution, 68–69, 72–73, 76
    scarcity, 5–6, 25, 40, 46–51, 58–59
    shared water, 51–53
    see also freshwater ecosystems
wetlands
    Aral Sea basin, 46–47
    Great Lakes basin, 72–74

management, 55
threat factors, 61–62
see also freshwater ecosystems
wheat, 84
Wigley, Tom, 21
Wilson, Edward, 96
wind energy, 15, 16, 31, 154–56
Woods Hole Oceanographic Institution, 46
worker productivity, 166
World Bank
    cropland loss projections, 81
    dam construction, 67, 121
    environmental justice, 150, 151
    environmental policy, 147
    food economy predictions, 16–17
    hydroelectric projects, 155
    integrated pest management, 91
    sea level rise predictions, 82
    water scarcity, 25, 43, 54
    wetlands management, 55
World Health Organization (U.N.)
    AIDS control, 19
    global disease control, 131
    Global Task Force on Cholera, 126
    pesticide poisonings, 90
    polio vaccination, 117
    tuberculosis epidemic, 114
    vaccination programs, 128, 130–31
World Resources Institute, 175
World Trade Organization, 182
Wuppertal Institute (Germany), 173

yellow fever, 115–16, 130

Zaire, 19, 132
zero-emission factories, 165–67
Zero Emissions Research Initiative (U.N.),
    165
Zimbabwe, 112

Now you can import
all the tables
and graphs from
State of the World 1996
and all other Worldwatch
publications into your
spreadsheet program,
presentation software,
or word processor
with the...

1996 WORLDWATCH DATABASE DISK

The Worldwatch Database Disk gives you current data from all Worldwatch publications, including the State of the World and Vital Signs annual book series, World Watch magazine, Worldwatch Papers, and Environmental Alert series books.

The disk covers trends from mid-century onward ... much not readily available from other sources. All data are sourced, and are accurate, comprehensive, and up-to-date. Researchers, professors, reporters, and policy analysts use the disk to --

- ■ Design graphs to illustrate newspaper stories and policy reports
- ■ Prepare overhead projections on trends for policy briefings, board meetings, and corporate presentations
- ■ Create specific "what if?" scenarios for energy, population, or grain supply
- ■ Overlay one trend onto another, to see how they relate
- ■ Track long term trends and discern new ones

Order the 1996 Worldwatch Database Disk for just $89 plus $4 shipping and handling. To order by credit card (Mastercard, Visa or American Express), call 1-800-555-2028, or fax to (202) 296-7365. Our e-mail address is wwpub@worldwatch.org. You can also order by sending your check or credit card information to:

Worldwatch Institute
1776 Massachusetts Ave, NW
Washington, DC 20036